Strangers at Home

CENTER BOOKS IN ANABAPTIST STUDIES

Donald B. Kraybill, *Consulting Editor*
George F. Thompson, *Series Founder and Director*

*Published in cooperation with the Center for American Places,
Santa Fe, New Mexico, and Harrisonburg, Virginia*

Strangers at Home

AMISH AND MENNONITE WOMEN IN HISTORY

edited by   *Kimberly D. Schmidt*

Diane Zimmerman Umble

Steven D. Reschly

THE JOHNS HOPKINS UNIVERSITY PRESS
Baltimore & London

© 2002 The Johns Hopkins University Press
All rights reserved. Published 2002
Printed in the United States of America on acid-free paper
9 8 7 6 5 4 3 2 1

The Johns Hopkins University Press
2715 North Charles Street
Baltimore, Maryland 21218-4363
www.press.jhu.edu

Library of Congress Cataloging-in-Publication Data

Strangers at home : Amish and Mennonite women in history / edited by Kimberly D.
Schmidt, Diane Zimmerman Umble, Steven D. Reschly.
    p.   cm. — (Center books in Anabaptist studies)
Includes bibliographical references and index.
    ISBN 0-8018-6786-X (alk. paper)
    1. Anabaptist women—history.   I. Schmidt, Kimberly D., 1961–   II. Umble, Diane
Zimmerman.   III. Reschly, Steven D.   IV. Series.
    BX4931.2 .A48 2001
    289.7′082—dc21

2001000580

A catalog record for this book is available from the British Library.

To our children

Alexander and Bianca Schmidt Navari

Kate and Eric Umble

Leah, Jessica, and Joel Reschly

Contents

Part 2   Creating Gendered Community

Part 3   (Re)creating Gendered Tradition

Acknowledgments

Like so much of what is best about Mennonites, this book was a community project. Three editors, multiple authors, and scores of interested scholars and community historians encouraged its growth from a germ of an idea, first voiced in 1995, through publication. In 1995 the first academic conference on women of Anabaptist traditions took place at Millersville University in Millersville, Pennsylvania. Titled "The Quiet in the Land? Women of Anabaptist Traditions in Historical Perspective," the conference had two main objectives. First, to uncover the quiet and not-so-quiet histories of women from Mennonite, Amish, and related ethnoreligious groups. Second, to foster a dialogue between scholars of Mennonite women and United States and Canadian women's historians. Even before the conference started, conference planners decided to collaborate on editing a collection of articles. We wanted a volume that would capture the essence of the conference and advance the scholarship represented there. Intense weekend meetings in Lancaster County marked growth spurts in the book's development. Other events, such as new babies, illnesses, family crises, and the untimely death of author Margaret Reynolds also left their mark on our collaboration and this collection.

Through the years of editing this book we have enjoyed a close working relationship with authors, editors, archivists, researchers, photographers, and encouraging friends. We would especially like to thank Kristi Bahrenburg, Anne B. W. Effland, Linda Huebert Hecht, Katherine Jellison, Melvin D. Schmidt, Kathryn Kish Sklar, George F. Thompson, and Randall Jones at the Center for American Places and anonymous reviewers for reading and commenting on portions of the manuscript. The book's progress was aided greatly by student research assistants at Millersville University: Christy Rhoades, Becky Newman, and Patricia Haverstick. Chris Loretz furnished artwork.

Joanne Hess Siegrist mined large collections of photographs, and many of the images in the book are a result of her efforts. Edwin P. Huddle identified photographs from the Ruth Hershey Collection, and Dennis L. Hughes generously contributed photographs from his personal collection. John Thiesen of the Mennonite Library and Archives at Bethel College, North Newton, Kansas; Ruth Schrock at the Archives of the Mennonite Church in Goshen, Indiana; Patricia O'Donnell of the Friends Historical Library at Swarthmore College in Swarthmore, Pennsylvania; and Carolyn Wenger of the Lancaster Mennonite Historical Society and Tom Ryan and Virginia Shelley of the Lancaster County Historical Society in Lancaster County, Pennsylvania, were also particularly helpful in the search for photographs.

The Rosenberger Family Foundation generously supported the editing of the book. The School of Humanities and Social Sciences and the Department of Communication and Theater at Millersville University and the Division of Social Science at Truman State University provided financial and office support for conference planning, photocopying, postage, phone consultations, and travel.

Finally, we thank our families, who probably thought this project would never end. Gifts from mothers to authors are so often overlooked that we would especially like to thank Kimberly's mother, Charlotte Graber Schmidt, who provided childcare at critical moments. Without her aid those long working weekends in Lancaster would not have been possible. Ann Zimmerman, Diane's mother, supported our efforts with her presence, her time, and her example. Steven's mother, Verda Christner Reschly, provided financial support and encouragement.

This book is our gift to the future women of Anabaptist traditions. We hope your histories are as interesting and challenging as those found in the pages of this book.

Strangers
at Home

Insiders and Outsiders

*I*nsiders know. Outsiders see. This perceptual duality—knowing intuitively and seeing consciously—unites this collection of essays. Several are written by insiders, members of the religious and ethnic traditions they examine. Insiders feel their own cultures in their bones, willingly or not, and intuit commonsense local knowledge without a second thought. Outsiders, holders of other traditions, have also contributed to this book. Outsiders must exert conscious effort to understand another culture, but they often appreciate what insiders miss because their own communities are too familiar. Studying the experience of women, and the presence of social structures ordered by gender, takes the perspectives of both insiders and outsiders.

Academic women's history as practiced over the past quarter century has produced its own set of insiders and outsiders. There is a mainstream canon of writings and theories as well as marginal stories seeking points of entry. The mainstream body of scholarship means that no one must start from scratch to study neglected corners of women's history. The neglected corners mean that the mainstream canon can never be completely stabilized and made final. A women's history that takes Anabaptist[1] traditions seriously must both relate to mainstream scholars—the insiders—and adopt an outsider's position independent of that scholarship to develop in directions authentic to the unique communities under study.

The chapters in this volume open a conversation among scholars about how mainstream women's history relates to the histories of ethnoreligious groups in North America that are based in the Anabaptist movement. This collection grows in part out of the first conference on women's history among Anabaptist groups, "The Quiet in the Land? Women of Anabaptist Traditions in Historical Perspective," held June 8–11, 1995, at Millersville University in Millersville, Pennsylvania. Several of these essays were presented at that conference, and the editors have solicited others to extend the discourse begun there. The resulting dialogue not only contributes to the fledgling field of Anabaptist women's history but also advances a multilayered discussion among the voices of women's history and those of Anabaptist women's history so that each may be enriched by the insights of the other.

Both a source and an outgrowth of the modern women's movement, women's history as an academic discipline has moved through a number of stages, from collecting biographies to critical analyses of women's social experience to exploring the ways gender orders domestic and public life. Historian Gerda Lerner's 1975 sequential framework of compensatory, contribution, and theoretical women's history has expanded to include the articulation of gender as a category of analysis.[2] Like race, class, and ethnicity, gender is culturally constructed. That is, social and cultural forces that are historically specific to time and place give form to the experiences, relationships, and institutions of sexual difference.[3] Other recent developments in the social sciences, such as attention to postmodern thought and ethnic diversity, have complicated women's history. There is no longer one overarching framework; now there is an overlapping series of complex discourses about women and gender in the human past.[4] One thread of the conversational network includes Anabaptist women and their descendants.

Openings in Anabaptist Women's History

Anabaptist groups are those that trace all or part of their ancestry to the Anabaptist movements of sixteenth-century Europe.[5] Anabaptism originated in widespread resistance and revolt against the church-state synthesis of early modern Europe. The violence and repression of the Reformation and state building imprinted a deep consciousness of mutual hostility between creators of the resulting social order and members of dissident religious movements. When Ulrich Zwingli handed control of his Zurich reformation to the town council, a few disgruntled disciples started a church free from political control, symbolized by adult baptism. When powerful armies crushed the German Peasants' Revolt of 1525, many participants turned to Anabaptism as a religious expression of the same desire for an egalitarian social order. And when the Münster Anabaptist kingdom fell in 1536, Menno Simons and other Dutch leaders picked up the pieces of a peaceful movement and lent Anabaptists a more permanent name— Mennonites. These three failed attempts to impose a radical version of Christianity on the entire social order tainted Anabaptism with the stain of social revolution and religious heresy, and Anabaptists were persecuted and suppressed with the full weight of both state and church, whether in Catholic or Protestant regions. State builders marginalized and excluded those who did not fit their vision of a homogeneous, unified, and disciplined polity, characterized by obedience to centralized authority and by military service and sanctioned by religion. Through martyr literature and hymnody, these religious societies kept alive the memory of persecution and the consciousness of disengagement from civil society. Their *mentalité* of estrangement reflected and was reinforced by symbolic and structural institutions of autonomous community. Anabaptists developed a suspicious and distant relationship with civil society.[6]

This willingness to dissent and begin anew by separating from civil society led to numerous new movements within Anabaptist traditions. Even Anabaptist origins are diverse, with Dutch and North German, Swiss and South German, and Moravian (Hutterite) versions. A Swiss Brethren division in 1693 produced the Amish; the Church of the Brethren grew from radical communitarian Pietism in the early eighteenth century; and Baptist and Quaker movements claimed some affinity with the Anabaptist heritage.[7]

Just as Anabaptists overall were questioning the existing religious framework, Anabaptist women also challenged normative social structures. At times they transformed hierarchical gender relations. But the record is ambiguous. Anabaptist women most often lived within traditional patriarchal social arrangements. Ambivalence about egalitarian communities and assertive women has been a constant companion to the histories of Anabaptism and its descendant groups.[8] In groups such as the Amish and Mennonites that prized their outsider status in early modern and modern history, Anabaptist women often became outsiders in their own communities, excluded from positions of leadership and treated as potentially dangerous disrupters of an ordered hierarchy of gender. Women often renegotiated their place both inside the community and in opposition to it. Women's stories, and analysis of how gender ordered their lives, contribute to the wholeness of the histories of the communities they called home.

Historical study of these groups as religious bodies is well developed, but there is little treatment of women's history.[9] In the late 1970s a scholarly literature of Mennonite and Amish women's history began to emerge. Much of the scholarship was hortatory or filiopietistic—the underlying agenda was to prove how faithfulness to God empowered women.[10] More recently scholars have applied gender to Anabaptist women's history as a category of analysis.[11] In many of these newer histories, including the work presented in this book, there are common threads that will begin to affect the conversations about women's histories in at least four ways.

First, the experience of Anabaptist women illuminates the relationship of individuals to the community and to broader society. Women's historians took the women's movement slogan "the personal is political" and applied it to the everyday lives of common women. Examinations of women's work, reproductive lives, cultural traditions, and social interactions have made important connections between women's private and common experience and political and social institutions.[12] The ways women relate to their local communities serve as an example. Anabaptist women hail from traditions that are steeped in community-oriented belief systems and practices. For example, the Amish *Ordnung*—the unwritten rules of the community—severely limits individual choice in favor of community conformity in many aspects of life, including child rearing, farming, dress, the use of modern technology, and behavioral patterns between men and women, to name a few. Conformity has specific meanings for women, since they often uphold community standards long after men abandon such restrictions and in the face of overwhelming pressure to change.[13] But how has an emphasis on community conformity shaped Amish and other conservative women's lives, and how can these women's historical experiences speak to the broader field of women's history? More generally, how does being a member of an ethnic and religious minority forge women's experience?

Second, Anabaptist women's history advances religion and ethnicity as topics within women's history. Although a number of studies examine the experiences of Puritan women in colonial New England, including the witch trials in Salem, and though scholars have analyzed women's involvement in the First and Second Great Awakenings and nineteenth-century missions, little has been done on women's experience in ethno-religious groups, especially in rural areas.[14] Many studies of rural and urban communities have overlooked religion as a factor shaping identity and community history, but the impact of religion in Amish and Mennonite communities cannot be ignored. Religious beliefs and ethnic folkways inform Amish and Mennonite women's decisions in even the most mundane matters—from what they eat and wear to career and family-related choices. Anabaptist women's history demonstrates that those who overlook religion miscalculate how ideology shapes and transforms people's lives and choices.

Third, Anabaptist women's history raises critical questions about the assumptions implicit in mainstream scholarship. Is it possible that Anabaptist descendants construct gender relations differently than does the dominant American culture? Were relationships between men and women based on different ideas of masculinity and femininity? And if so, how did these understandings uniquely shape Anabaptist women's lives and histories? For example, recent research has suggested that women in traditionally conservative groups such as Old Order Amish and Old Order River Brethren may not experience gendered limitations in the same way as women in theologically conservative groups such as American fundamentalists and evangelicals.[15] Furthermore, women in transitional groups, on the path to assimilation but not yet there, may face the harshest forms of patriarchy as these groups desperately seek ways to maintain social stability.[16] There is no linear progression from conservative to feminist as mainstream scholarship may imply.

Fourth, Anabaptist women's history raises once again the issue of diversity in the historiography of women. Women's historians have not escaped the criticism of scholars who are interested in exploring the intersections of race, ethnicity, and gender. Early women's history retrieved the experiences of white, middle-class women who were engaged in political struggles. A later development in women's history included a broad diversity of women's voices. Racial, ethnic, and class differences have informed and challenged the field.[17] For the most part Anabaptist women in North America hail from European backgrounds and are white and middle class. Including their stories enriches the larger field and leads to a fuller articulation of diversity within women's history. The three sections of this book provide links to these conversations and prepare the way for further research by exploring different aspects of women's experience in Anabaptist communities.

PART 1: PRACTICE MAKES GENDER

The practice of scholarship itself and the rituals of daily life interact to reveal the complex structuring of gender in religious societies. Scholars practice their disciplines in gendered ways even as they explore how culture creates gendered social structures in the communities they study. The distinctions between "insider" and "outsider" often blur as people relate to one another from multiple perspectives.

Hasia R. Diner discusses the strengths and weaknesses of "insider" and "outsider" positions in the practice of historical study. When writing about Jewish history, Diner is an insider scholar. However, she also has experience as an outsider scholar, as when she wrote *Erin's Daughters*, a history of Irish immigration. What pitfalls and opportunities do scholars face when carrying on their trade among the members of their own groups? There are significant advantages to studying a community one knows well, yet "outsiders" also achieve positive results. For example, insider scholars have unique access to their communities that may not be available to outsider scholars. This is especially true when dealing with more conservative or traditionally minded groups such as the Old Order Amish or Orthodox Jews; both groups are suspicious of outsiders. Diner, an American historian, grew up speaking Yiddish and attending synagogue. She has published significant research on both Jewish and Irish immigrants in America. As a Jewish insider and an Irish outsider, she examines how her own research was affected by her insider and outsider status.

Diane Zimmerman Umble's ethnographic study of Old Order Amish examines the questions they "ask back" in response to her inquiries. The Old Order Amish she studied live in rural, primarily farming communities. Umble found that to gain access to these communities she often had to provide "credentials." Her name and her family connections to Old Order Amish, no matter how remote, allowed her access to wary informants. It is interesting that the men in these groups were more likely to ask about her lineage and to determine her place in relation to her father's and father-in-law's family trees. They did not deem matrilineal lineage significant. But Umble also found it was important to establish her identity as a wife and mother in this traditional community where women's highest status is derived from motherhood. Straddling this chasm between the world of the Old Order Amish and the world of the scholar was complicated because identifying oneself primarily as a wife and mother may strain one's scholarly identity. Maternal associations matter little in the academic world.

Beth E. Graybill submits ethnographic reflections about the "plain dress" of Eastern Pennsylvania Mennonite Church women. As with many ethnoreligious groups, prescriptions about women's dress signify alterable gender definitions and variations in women's power and status in their communities. Graybill's feminist ethnography focuses on the multiple meanings of women's dress and gender roles in this religious culture. Although men's dress was not distinguishable from that of their non-Mennonite neighbors, women's traditional clothing—cape dresses and head coverings—set them apart and forced them to bear the principal burden of separation from the world, a traditional Mennonite value. Nonetheless the women Graybill interviewed articulated many positive reasons for wearing the plain dress.

Margaret C. Reynolds conducted a "participant observer" study of an Old Order River Brethren women's ritual, breadmaking. Significantly a silent ceremony, breadmaking is the only ritual that allows women to occupy a central religious position in this traditional community dominated by men. By analyzing the breadmaking ritual, Reynolds shows how women became the primary bearers of tradition for their group and how the kitchen is the fortress from which the battle against modernity and assimilation is fought. Reynolds highlights how, even in a female-centered ritual, women embody submission to a patriarchal social ordering.

Katherine Jellison examines the household production and consumption of Old Order Amish women during the Great Depression. Her chapter centers on how New Deal government researchers idealized Amish women in Lancaster County, Pennsylvania. The key investigator in Jellison's study is an outsider, Bureau of Agricultural Economics researcher Walter Kollmorgan. A strict sexual division of labor (what the New Dealers called "stable" community) and well-defined production and consumer responsibilities seemed a workable recipe to Kollmorgan and other policymakers seeking to stop the deterioration of rural America during the depression.

The chapters in this section highlight how gender considerations have implications for insider-outsider methodological approaches. Women are situated differently from men in Anabaptist communities: they are simultaneously insiders and outsiders. Even though women may have a family history that reaches back generations in their community, as members of patriarchal religious groups their voices are limited. Their community practices, participation, and influence are often exercised through their husbands' place in the community or through female-centered activities such as the breadmaking ritual and kinship networks. Because of their educational background and the limitations placed on the females by traditional groups, women scholars trying to study these communities may also experience difficulties. Their status as scholars can make them suspect in the more traditional communities, which consider academic learning "worldly" and their pursuit of a perceived "male" profession misguided.

PART 2: CREATING GENDERED COMMUNITY

The topics of immigration, settlement, community formation, and schisms monopolize much of the Anabaptist historical literature. Although these studies make the point that immigration and settlement most often took place in church and large family groupings, rarely have the books and monographs mentioned women's participation in these events. Nonetheless women's culture and gender systems operated at the very beginning of every Anabaptist movement. Women negotiated their sense of place as insiders and outsiders—for and against, within and without—in relation to the confines of gendered community development.

Jeni Hiett Umble examines the spread of the Anabaptist movement through women's guild, household, and kinship networks. During the Reformation Anabaptists were considered heretics, perhaps the ultimate outsiders. Earlier research had posited that the Anabaptist movement appealed primarily to the peasant classes. This earlier research neglected to analyze women's place within the movement. Umble's research suggests that within Anabaptist communities of the sixteenth century, class and gender divisions ebbed and flowed. Her work illuminates how factors like kinship ties, marital status, class position, and guild membership influenced women's modes of cooperation and conflict.

Marlene Epp focuses on women creating and building community, sometimes in the absence of men. Epp traces and analyzes the experiences of female-headed families in Paraguayan Mennonite colonies after World War II. Because these families lacked a male head of household, Mennonite relief workers characterized them as "weak" even though, as Epp discovered, the women who headed them had survived warfare in Ukraine, Stalinist purges, immigration to Paraguay, and a new beginning in a tropical jungle known as "the green hell."

Steven D. Reschly examines the establishment of new Amish communities in nineteenth-century Iowa. After migrating from Europe and the eastern United States, the Amish reproduced their communities in western Iowa in part by emphasizing the importance of female subordination. Fighting against the individualism and freedom found in the United States, Amish leaders strengthened their communities by establishing clear lines of male authority. Empowering the male heads of households gave them greater control over family labor resources, inheritance patterns, migration decisions, farming systems, and other aspects of communal coherence. For the Amish, the pattern of establishing male authority in the household transcends time and place.

Cathy Ann Trotta's research focuses on how Mennonite missionary Martha Moser Voth and her family became integral members of the Hopi community of Oraibi just before the turn of the century. Martha's role in reaching out to the Hopi cannot be overstated. She employed her arts as a housewife to provide food, clothing, household supplies, and medical treatment to Hopi women and their families, and she wrote in her diaries of often having a "houseful of Hopi." Her important contributions were not overlooked by the Hopi, whose matrilineal society was based on maternal clan groupings.

Kimberly D. Schmidt analyzes patterns of conflict in a New York Amish Mennonite community during two controversies. She argues that women's changing work responsibilities exacerbated conflicts that occurred during both the Great Depression of the 1930s and the farm crisis of the 1980s. Schmidt found that even when economic pressures were forcing Amish Mennonite male farmers off the farm, community beliefs and controversy about women's working off-farm made it difficult for women to take jobs to supplement declining farm incomes. In both time periods, some women who worked off the farm rejected church-sanctioned dress regulations. By both these actions they challenged traditional beliefs about women's work and place within the community. Unlike the conservative women in Beth Graybill's study who supported dress regulations, the women in New York did not verbalize positive associations with the cape dress and prayer covering.

Taken together, the articles in this section demonstrate that gender is omnipresent in Anabaptist communities. The analysis of gender is a place to begin when studying a community, not an additive, since the organization of societies according to male/female distinctions occurs at the very beginning of the community. In the Anabaptist world gender orders new religious movements, new settlements, schisms, and even the aftermath of catastrophes such as the loss of life among Russian Mennonites. Beginnings are excellent opportunities to examine old patterns.

PART 3: (RE)CREATING GENDERED TRADITION

"Tradition" and "gender" are not fixed or static entities. Even within the most traditional groups, new ways of defining women's place develop over time. Despite this fluid and flexible reality, Anabaptist groups often treat shifting traditions as timeless rather than changeable. In fact the fiction of changeless tradition often proves a convenient way to maintain patriarchal cultural structures in changing social and political situations. Anabaptist groups are consciously unselfconscious about shifting gender systems.

Linda Huebert Hecht questions an ahistorical view of sixteenth-century Anabaptist women's history. One received perspective asserts that women were "emancipated" by the radical movement and reached equality with men in leadership, persecution, and martyrdom. Instead, Hecht argues that scholars of Anabaptism's early days should take seriously the work of Reformation historians who refer to "windows of time" or "interludes of equality." Protestant women may have achieved some equality with men during early stages of various movements, but equality soon evaporated as the onetime radical communities became established. By applying gender as a category of analysis to the women found in Tirolean court records, she reviews women's contributions to the early movement within their family roles as wives, mothers, daughter, sisters, and maids.

Royden K. Loewen also uses the family as a central organizing unit of analysis. However, the Anabaptists he studies are twentieth-century Mennonites who hailed from the conservative Kleine Gemeinde and Bruderthaler groups. Loewen analyzes how these Mennonite women's understanding of gender changed in different socioeconomic contexts from 1935 to 1975. He compares changing concepts of work and leisure and the resulting shifts in gender definitions among three groups of Mennonite women from Meade, Kansas: self-reliant farm women in charge of household and farmyard production, "cheerful homemakers" on commercialized farms who participated in Home Demonstration Unit Coffee Klatches, and off-farm professional working women. His work highlights the transient nature of gender identities. As with other historical categories of analysis, gender definitions are animated by changes in the economy, ideology, and work.

Barbara Bolz explores the lives of eighteenth-century Quaker journal writers. Her study of Quaker women's use of silence as an empowering force offers a vivid contrast to the silence imposed on Mennonite women, often experienced as limiting and degrading. By listening to the "still, small voice within," Quaker women asserted themselves in public arenas such as the ministry and preaching. Their experience of silence as empowering expanded gender systems in Quaker communities, where women, by following the sacred voice from within, participated in public life. Bolz also explores dimensions of carnal knowledge versus spiritual or religious knowledge. For Bolz's Quaker women, the spirit transcended the body and became, in a sense, genderless.

Julia Kasdorf, drawing on illustrations from six Mennonite poets, traces themes of community and family memory to connect the work of feminist literary scholars and historians. Central to her investigation is the invention of traditions that have gender-specific implications, such as plain dress and oral traditions of storytelling. In contrast to the Quaker women Bolz studied, some of Kasdorf's poets sought to rid themselves of the mind/spirit duality that silences women in Mennonite communities.

Jane Marie Pederson makes connections between comprehensive cultural developments in American history and the social position of Mennonite and Amish women. She relates the experiences of Anabaptist communities to the more general friction between traditional communities and the postmodern era. Pederson's work raises fundamental questions about Anabaptist communities' struggles against modernity. The obsession with women's subordination, evident in many Mennonite and Amish communities, reveals a harsh reality: for many traditional groups, gender inequality is all that remains of their antiworldly or antimodern practices and traditions.

The articles in the third section point toward Anabaptist women as actors in historical dramas. Even as changing traditions amounted to similar gender positions, women often acted from within those positions to question and challenge their subordination. Through poetry and silence, by socializing with each other, and by giving traditional roles new meanings, women struggled to overcome their limited power in Anabaptist groups.

The fifteen essays in this collection evince the multiple insider and outsider positions of situated historical knowledge. Of course the insider/outsider conundrum cannot be limited to the position of women in certain specific religious communities or to that of small communities in relation to mainstream Western cultures. People live in multiple positions—one time insiders, next outsiders, negotiating several social positions at once. For example, the scholar herself may be positioned as outsider by dint of her discipline, even though she may also be an insider to the community she studies. Missionary efforts to other races and ethnicities can become dangerous bridges for missionaries and converts to cross in order to become insiders in the community by choice even while remaining outsiders by birth. Rural and urban residents compete for hegemony in cultural leadership, that is, to be defined as insiders in their culture. Persons living in poverty are treated as "other" by the wealthy. It is worthwhile to recognize the complexity of identifying oneself and others as distinctive or similar. These essays reflect this diversity by engaging a variety of approaches, such as women's studies, anthropology, religion, oral history, ethnography, and literature, and also a variety of organizing categories including class, gender, cultural history, economic history, and public policy.

This collection also encourages a rereading of early modern, modern, and postmodern historiography. Examining Anabaptist religions, women's history, and women's history in Anabaptist societies reveals the multiple voices of situated knowledge known in specific class, geographic, gendered, or racially structured locations in a society. Historical knowledge is also situated, and voices of insiders and voices of outsiders, past and present, give access to that knowledge in sometimes contradictory, sometimes complementary ways. All voices ultimately partake of the same knowledge, albeit imperfectly. Sometimes insiders see and outsiders know.

NOTES

1. We are not limiting the term "Anabaptist" to the sixteenth-century socioreligious movement. The groups that claim Anabaptist heritage range widely and include Mennonites, Amish, Hutterites, Church of the Brethren, Quakers, Baptists, and others. Anabaptist groups represented in this book include traditional groups such as Old Order Amish, Old Order River Brethren, Amish Mennonites, Conservative Mennonites, Bruderthaler, Kleine Gemeinde Mennonites, and Eastern Pennsylvania Mennonites. Also included are more culturally assimilated groups such as the Mennonite Church, General Conference Mennonite Church, and Mennonite Brethren. The diversity in group affiliation points to the contingencies of traditions, practices, and conflicts among Anabaptist communities. To relate these histories to one another, and for simple convenience, we are using the term "Anabaptist" both for the specific sixteenth-century movement and for these later groups that identify with Anabaptism.

2. Gerda Lerner, "Placing Women in History: Definitions and Challenges," *Feminist Studies* 3 (fall 1975): 5–14; reprinted in Gerda Lerner, *The Majority Finds Its Past: Placing Women in History* (New York: Oxford University Press, 1979), 145–59.

3. See Joan W. Scott, "Gender: A Useful Category of Historical Analysis," *American Historical Review* 91 (December 1986): 1053–75; reprinted in Joan Wallach Scott, *Gender and the Politics of History* (New York: Columbia University Press, 1988), 28–50. For discussions of gender as a culturally bound construction see Michelle Zimbalist Rosaldo, "The Use and Abuse of Anthropology: Reflections on Feminist and Cross-Cultural Understanding," *Signs* 5 (spring 1980): 389–417, and Sherry B. Ortner and Harriet Whitehead, "Introduction: Accounting for Sexual Meanings," in *Sexual Meanings: The Cultural Construction of Gender and Sexuality,* ed. Sherry B. Ortner and Harriet Whitehead (New York: Cambridge University Press, 1981), 1–27.

4. Helpful discussions about the practice and theory of women's history include Hilda Smith, "A Prize-Winning Book Revisited: Women's Historians and Women's History, a Conflation of Absence," *Journal of Women's History* 4

(spring 1992): 133–41; Nancy Isenberg, "The Personal Is Political: Gender, Feminism, and the Politics of Discourse Theory," *American Quarterly* 44 (September 1992): 449–58; Louise M. Newman, "Critical Theory and the History of Women: What's at Stake in Deconstructing Women's History," *Journal of Women's History* 2 (winter 1991): 58–68; Judith Walkowitz, Myra Jehlen, and Bell Chevigny, "Patrolling the Borders: Feminist Historiography and the New Historicism," *Radical History Review* 43 (1989): 23–43; and Linda Alcoff, "Cultural Feminism versus Post-structuralism: The Identity Crisis in Feminist Theory," *Signs* 13 (spring 1988): 405–36.

There are numerous histories of women's history. See, for example, Linda Gordon, *U.S. Women's History*, rev. ed. (Washington, D.C.: American Historical Association, 1997); Kathleen M. Brown, "Brave New Worlds: Women's and Gender History," *William and Mary Quarterly*, 3d ser., 50 (April 1993): 311–28; Nancy Hewitt, "Beyond the Search for Sisterhood: American Women's History in the 1980s," *Social History* 10 (October 1985): 299–321.

5. For a general overview of Anabaptists and their descendants, see Cornelius J. Dyck, ed., *An Introduction to Mennonite History: A Popular History of the Anabaptists and Mennonites* 3d ed. (Scottdale, Pa.: Herald Press, 1993); George H. Williams, *The Radical Reformation* (Philadelphia: Westminster Press, 1962; 3d ed. Kirksville, Mo.: Sixteenth Century Journal Publishers, 1992); and C. Arnold Snyder, *Anabaptist History and Theology: An Introduction* (Kitchener, Ont.: Pandora Press, 1995).

6. On Anabaptist origins in Zurich, see Fritz Blanke, *Brothers in Christ: The History of the Oldest Anabaptist Congregation, Zollikon, Near Zürich, Switzerland* (Scottdale, Pa.: Herald Press, 1961); Leland Harder, *The Sources of Swiss Anabaptism: The Grebel Letters and Related Documents* (Scottdale, Pa.: Herald Press, 1985); and Harold S. Bender, *Conrad Grebel, c. 1498–1526: The Founder of the Swiss Brethren* (Goshen, Ind.: Mennonite Historical Society, 1950).

On the relation of Anabaptism to the German Peasants' War, see James M. Stayer, *The German Peasants' War and Anabaptist Community of Goods* (Montreal: McGill-Queens University Press, 1991). For an overview of Münster scholarship, see James M. Stayer, "Was Dr. Kuehler's Conception of Early Dutch Anabaptism Historically Sound? The Historical Discussion of Anabaptist Münster 450 Years Later," *Mennonite Quarterly Review* 60 (July 1986): 261–88, and Ralf Klötzer, *Die Täuferherrschaft von Münster: Stadtreformation und Welterneuerung* (Münster, Germany: Aschendorff, 1992).

7. On the diverse origins of Anabaptism, see James M. Stayer, Werner Pack-

ull, and Klaus Deppermann, "From Monogenesis to Polygenesis: The Historical Discussion of Anabaptist Origins," *Mennonite Quarterly Review* 49 (April 1975): 83–121.

For overviews of Amish history, see John A. Hostetler, *Amish Society*, 4th ed. (Baltimore: Johns Hopkins University Press, 1993), and Steven M. Nolt, *A History of the Amish* (Intercourse, Pa.: Good Books, 1992). See also John D. Roth, trans. and ed., *Letters of the Amish Division: A Sourcebook* (Goshen, Ind.: Mennonite Historical Society, 1993).

On the Hutterites in Europe, see John A. Hostetler, *Hutterite Society* (Baltimore: Johns Hopkins University Press, 1974), chaps. 1–4, and Leonard Gross, *The Golden Years of the Hutterites: The Witness and Thought of the Communal Moravian Anabaptists during the Walpot Era, 1565–1578* (Kitchener, Ont.: Pandora Press, 1980; reprint, Scottdale, Pa.: Herald Press, 1988).

8. Perhaps the earliest scholar to argue that Anabaptist women experienced equality with men in the sixteenth-century movement was George H. Williams, in *The Radical Reformation* (Philadelphia: Westminster Press, 1962), esp. 506–7. Other early scholars have also argued that in the early years men and women were equals. See Lois Barrett, "Women in the Anabaptist Movement," in *Women in the Bible and Early Anabaptism*, ed. Herta Funk (Newton, Kans.: Faith and Life Press, 1975), esp. 33; In another early treatment, however, Keith Sprunger concluded that women were not on equal footing with men. See "God's Powerful Army of the Weak: Anabaptist Women of the Radical Reformation," in *Triumph over Silence: Women in Protestant History*, ed. Richard Greaves, 45–74 (Westport, Conn.: Greenwood Press, 1985).

Later scholars have questioned the early scholarship, most notably M. Lucille Marr, who argues that Williams and others have overstated women's status in the Anabaptist movement; see "Anabaptist Women of the North: Peers in the Faith, Subordinates in Marriage," *Mennonite Quarterly Review* 61 (October 1987): 347–54. See also Frieda Shoenberg Rozen, "The Permanent First Floor Tenant: Women and Gemeinschaft," *Mennonite Quarterly Review* 51 (October 1977): 319–28, and Werner O. Packull, "'We Are Born to Work Like the Birds to Fly': The Anabaptist-Hutterite Ideal Woman," *Mennonite Quarterly Review* 73 (January 1999): 75–86.

Much of this debate may have been put to rest with the publication of C. Arnold Snyder and Linda Huebert Hecht, eds., *Profiles of Anabaptist Women: Sixteenth Century Reforming Pioneers* (Waterloo, Ont.: Wilfrid Laurier University Press, 1996), in which they argue that Anabaptist women's contributions to the movement should not be overlooked and cannot be overstated. True, women were often not the prominent leaders, but the Anabaptist movement was made up of "little people," not the upper classes and prominent citizens. Put in this context, women's contributions assume new significance.

On this general point, that although leadership roles may be shared by men and women, females often do not have comparable power and authority, see Catherine Wessinger, ed., *Women's Leadership in Marginal Religions: Explorations outside the Mainstream* (Urbana: University of Illinois Press, 1993).

9. Basic historiographical essays include Kimberly D. Schmidt and Steven D. Reschly, "A Women's History for Anabaptist Traditions: A Framework of Possibilities, Possibly Changing the Framework," *Journal of Mennonite Studies* 18 (2000): 29–46; Al Reimer, "Where Was/Is the Woman's Voice? The Re-membering of the Mennonite Woman," *Mennonite Life* 47 (March 1992): 20–25; Carol Penner, "Mennonite Women's History: A Survey," *Journal of Mennonite Studies* 9 (1991): 122–35; and Marlene Epp, "Women in Canadian Mennonite History: Uncovering the 'Underside,'" *Journal of Mennonite Studies* 5 (1987): 90–107.

10. Early contributions include Mary Lou Cummings, *Full Circle: Stories of Mennonite Women* (Newton, Kans.: Faith and Life Press, 1978); Elaine Sommers Rich, *Mennonite Women: A Story of God's Faithfulness, 1683–1983* (Scottdale, Pa.: Herald Press, 1983); and Ruth Unrau, *Encircled: Stories of Mennonite Women* (Newton, Kans.: Faith and Life Press, 1986). For biographical information on Anabaptist women, see Snyder and Hecht.

11. Recently published books and articles that are primarily historical, respond to developments in women's history, and include gender as a category of analysis are Rachel Waltner Goossen, *Women against the Good War: Conscientious Objection and Gender on the American Home Front, 1941–1947* (Chapel Hill: University of North Carolina Press, 1997); Snyder and Hecht; Royden K. Loewen, *Family, Church and Market: A Mennonite Community in the Old and the New Worlds, 1850–1930* (Urbana: University of Illinois Press, 1993); Marlene Epp, *Women without Men: Mennonite Refugees of the Second World War* (Toronto: University of Toronto Press, 2000); Marc A. Olshan and Kimberly D. Schmidt, "Amish Women and the Feminist Conundrum," in *The Amish Struggle with Modernity*, ed. Donald B. Kraybill and Marc A. Olshan (Hanover, N.H.: University Press of New England, 1994), 215–30; Steven D. Reschly and Katherine Jellison, "Production Patterns, Consumption Strategies, and Gender Relations in

Amish and Non-Amish Farm Households in Lancaster County, Pennsylvania, 1935–1936," *Agricultural History* 67 (spring 1993): 134–62.

Ethnographic work by Beth E. Graybill and anthropological studies by Linda Boynton Arthur and Pamela E. Klassen also add to this discussion. See Graybill, "Mennonite Women and Their Bishops in the Founding of the Eastern Pennsylvania Mennonite Church," *Mennonite Quarterly Review* 72 (April 1998): 251–74; Arthur, "'Clothing Is a Window to the Soul': The Social Control of Women in a Holdeman Mennonite Community," *Journal of Mennonite Studies* 15 (1997): 11–30; Klassen, *Going by the Moon and Stars: Stories of Two Russian Mennonite Women* (Waterloo, Ont.: Wilfrid Laurier University Press, 1994); Klassen, "Practicing Conflict: Weddings as Sites of Contest and Compromise," *Mennonite Quarterly Review* 72 (April 1998): 225–42; and Klassen, "What's Bre(a)d in the Bone: The Bodily Heritage of Mennonite Women," *Mennonite Quarterly Review* 68 (April 1994): 229–47.

12. Classics in women's history that make connections between women's public and private lives include Linda Kerber, *Women of the Republic: Intellect and Ideology in Revolutionary America* (Chapel Hill: University of North Carolina Press, 1980); Mary Beth Norton, *Liberty's Daughters: The Revolutionary Experience of American Women, 1750–1800* (Boston: Little, Brown, 1980); Thomas Dublin, *Women at Work: The Transformation of Work and Community in Lowell, Massachusetts, 1820–1860* (New York: Columbia University Press, 1979); Alice Kessler-Harris, *Out to Work: A History of Wage-Earning Women in the United States* (Oxford: Oxford University Press, 1982); and Kathryn Kish Sklar, *Catharine Beecher: A Study in American Domesticity* (New Haven: Yale University Press, 1973).

13. See Donald B. Kraybill, "Mennonite Women's Veiling: The Rise and Fall of a Sacred Symbol," *Mennonite Quarterly Review* 61 (June 1987): 298–320; Marlene Epp, "Carrying the Banner of Nonconformity: Ontario Mennonite Women and the Dress Question," *Conrad Grebel Review* 8 (fall 1990): 237–57; and Beth E. Graybill, "Gendered Interpretations: Toward a Feminist Reading of Mennonite Traditions," paper presented at the National Women's Studies Association Conference, Washington, D.C., June 17, 1993.

14. Three significant studies that examine the intersections of gender, ethnicity, and religion are Carol Coburn, *Life at Four Corners: Religion, Gender and Education in a German-Lutheran Community, 1868–1945* (Lawrence: University of Kansas Press, 1992); Jane Marie Pederson, *Between Memory and Reality: Fam-*

ily and Community in Rural Wisconsin, 1870–1970 (Madison: University of Wisconsin Press, 1992); and Sonya Salamon, *Prairie Patrimony: Family, Farming and Community in the Midwest* (Chapel Hill: University of North Carolina Press, 1992).

15. Reschly and Jellison, 160–62.

16. Kimberly D. Schmidt, "Transforming Tradition: Women's Work and the Effects of Religion and Economics in Two Rural Mennonite Communities, 1930–1990" (Ph.D. diss., Binghamton University, 1995).

17. See the summary by Gerda Lerner, "Reconceptualizing Differences among Women," *Journal of Women's History* 1 (winter 1990): 106–22.

Part 1

Practice Makes Gender

1

Insights and Blind Spots

WRITING HISTORY FROM INSIDE
AND OUTSIDE

Hasia R. Diner

Who can best study the history and inner lives of ethnoreligious communities? Historian Hasia R. Diner has conducted research within her own Jewish community as well as within the Irish community. She reflects on the pitfalls and opportunities scholars face when charting the history of their own communities and challenges the notion that insiders always have an advantage. She also explores the advantages and struggles of an outsider looking in. Scholarly discourse that includes both perspectives can elevate and enrich our understanding.

istorians, as well as practitioners of other scholarly disciplines, have argued intensely for more than a century about the insider versus the outsider perspective as the ideal of scholarship. Advocates of both positions have seen the two as polar opposites, as if each offers the only way to understand social and cultural patterns. Each group has felt compelled to dismantle, diminish, and dismiss the other. Partisans argued essentially that scholars of the other side have been deluded by the inherent contradictions of either "objectivity," the dominant motif of the outsider school, or "engagement," the position of the insiders.[1]

Since the late nineteenth century, historians have assiduously staked out the position that "objectivity" offers the only avenue for arriving at the truth. From the emergence of professional historical scholarship first in Germany and then in England and the United States, historians almost universally have claimed that the further scholars stood from their subjects, the more likely they were to discern social, political, economic, or intellectual patterns. The historian, this mode of analysis has said, needs to be outside the inner life of the society being scrutinized in order to weigh evidence, balance factors, and establish a true rendition of the past. In this form of justification, objectivity became a kind of idol to be worshiped as the only standard of scholarship. As a result, the gatekeepers of the world of the humanities and social sciences generally scoffed at the idea of studying one's own past, of exploring one's own culture. Such efforts, it was asserted, put scholars too close to the center to see the larger picture.[2]

Since the late 1960s another ideal of scholarship has emerged to challenge the inherited belief in the god of objectivity. Born of the social activism of the era and coincident with the rise of identity politics, a different paradigm has appeared in history, anthropology, literature, and a range of other disciplines. This new truth holds that insiders, engaged with their subjects in myriad ways, bring to the study of human affairs a level of commitment and a degree of knowledge that the aloof "objectivist" can never achieve. The insights of someone born and raised in a particular cultural milieu far outweigh those an outsider can attain. Sensitive to nuances and gestures, privy to information, at ease with informants, the insider has an advantage in both gathering and interpreting data.

This mode of analysis has also severely challenged the idea that those who advocate objectivity actually achieve it. Although some scholars may have persistently laid claim to aloofness and to a cool distance from their subjects, biases, underlying assumptions, and proclivities of all kinds have clearly surfaced. The canard of "objectivity" has been a smoke screen to keep out undesirable scholars and undesirable ideas.

Both ways of viewing the scholarly enterprise contain elements of reason. The dispassionate outsider with little at stake in the outcome of the issues, with no personal share in a particular narrative, does have the pos-

Hungarian-born Jew Bernard Kautz (1895–1978) wore a plain Mennonite suit when he married Laura Lefever (1891–1974) in 1916. Bernard met Laura while working on a Mennonite farm in Pennsylvania and married her after joining the Mennonite church. (From Joanne Hess Siegrist, *Mennonite Women of Lancaster County*, reproduced with permission of the author.)

sibility of seeing a phenomenon in a way that an insider, with a deep investment in it, could not. On the other hand, the insider, nurtured in the intricacies of a way of life, is privy to insights never allowed to the interloper who comes equipped with the tools of the academy.

In this essay on my experiences as both a scholarly insider and a scholarly outsider, I reflect on the value of both approaches and suggest that only by ongoing discussion among all perspectives can historians reconstruct the past and assign meaning to human behavior. Ultimately the polarity of insider and outsider is not the best way to frame the problem; the dynamic tension between different visions of the scholarly ideal and the constant interplay between them may better serve the advancement of knowledge.

The categories "insider" and "outsider" are ultimately just as imprecise and vague as so many other terms we use without thinking. Historians writing about a world they have never lived in are always outsiders, even though they might share a language, religion, or national background with their subjects. The act of scholarship, the framing of analytic questions about context and meaning, instantly transforms all academics into outsiders. We stand outside the "we" when our questions go beyond those that "true" insiders would ever ask.

The attempt to understand how human beings cope with change and the effort to see how they deal with the large and small tragedies and triumphs of dislocation can provide a universal context that transcends differences and vicariously allows us, as scholars, to "be" at one with people with whom on the surface it seems we share nothing. It is possible, through writing, to become part of a world far beyond our own time and place. By virtue of our humanness, we can all be insiders.

Both writing from the "inside" and looking in from the margins have pitfalls and advantages. I explore some of those here. Neither one is without its problems; neither one dooms the scholar to missing what is essential.

HISTORY FROM THE INSIDE

I began my scholarly career writing in the field of American Jewish history. Broadly trained in American social and ethnic history—and with no formal training in Jewish history—I almost automatically turned to the history of the Jews in America as a subject for seminar papers and ultimately my dissertation. A product of an intensely Jewish home, one where Yiddish was the basic language and my first one, I developed, without understanding why, a Jewish "angle" on my larger interests in the history of immigration, labor, women, and religion in America. In retrospect I see that I began my graduate work at a time in my personal life when I was ambivalent and confused about what it meant to "be" Jewish. I did not necessarily want to experience Jewishness as my European-born and -raised parents did—nor could I—but by engaging in the study of

Jewish history, in a sense I charted for myself a personal path of belonging.

Without knowing it, I was replicating a process that had been going on since the late nineteenth century among those westernized Jewish scholars credited with the first scholarly studies of Judaism and Jewish history, the *Wissenschaft des Judentums* school. They manifested being Jewish through the medium of scholarship, which served as a personally meaningful yet authoritative way to experience Jewishness. Scholarship, I see now, offered me an intellectually and culturally acceptable—that is, American, Western—way to embark on a kind of personal journey. Uncomfortable with formal religion, awkward in the face of the spiritually intense, I found that doing Jewish history filled a void in me that I only later understood.

But as a graduate student I did recognize almost instantly that I "knew" something that would never occur to an outsider. It was not just that my parents had given me linguistic competence in both Yiddish and Hebrew, tools essential to the study of Jewish history, since anyone can formally learn a language. I also had more than two decades of enculturation into a particular world. I had been privy to insider patterns of behavior that I am absolutely certain would have eluded the true outsider who might have wanted to study Jewish life. I understood on a visceral level what it meant to be bicultural, to have at my command a set of behaviors for the inside, almost literally, and another for the outside. The tones and modes of expression of Jewish life were my own, and thus to study them amounted to hooking the texts of the past onto those expressions and experiences that had always been part and parcel of myself.

I wrote a seminar paper on American Jewish reactions to anti-Semitism in the 1910s and 1920s. At a time when hostility toward Jews in the United States emerged as a prominent feature of the social and political landscape, the organs of Jewish public opinion, both the Yiddish press, aimed at immigrant readers, and the English-language Jewish magazines, written for better-off, more Americanized ones, discussed the issue in hushed tones. Yet the same publications that by their silence avoided the harsh realities of anti-Semitism in America spoke out eloquently and passionately against the racism endured by African Americans and chided American society for its hypocrisy and evil. I "knew" that these two journalistic approaches, which also surfaced in various forms of pressure group politics, were connected. They did not just happen to happen at the same time.

I understood that by speaking out in support of the advancement of black Americans, Jews expressed a good deal about themselves and who they were and about what they feared in ways they could not do in their own name. I could use my own experiences as a child growing up in the civil rights era in a deeply Jewish home as a jumping-off point for scholarship. I must have gotten it right, or close enough, since the seminar paper became a dissertation that became a book, published in 1977 and reissued in 1995. I do not believe—although as a belief it cannot be verified—that I would have made the connection had I grown up in a different world.[3]

In doing this kind of insider scholarship, I clearly had access to knowledge others—outsiders—would have to study to "know." Scholars more removed from the primary experience struggle to get at the human dimension of the grand themes that provide the leitmotifs of history. I heard the stories (whether they were true is beside the point) at the dinner table and in the many other places where families talk. Immigration, adaptation to America, Jewish education, Zionism, the labor movement, the Holocaust—subjects that other scholars would have had to sift through libraries of material to find and that for them would lack a human face—were for me my parents and relatives and family friends who had endured these events and experiences. And indeed, as the insider, I had access to stories that never found their way onto paper and into archives.

These stories, the unrecorded, undocumented details both of everyday life and of great events from the perspective not of the movers and shakers but of the ordinary—or not so ordinary—average Jew made up the substance of our family and communal discourse. I understood on a graphic, vivid level not only that statistical generalizations constitute an important part of the historical record, but that the exceptions need to be considered.

American Jewish historians have, for example, recently begun to develop a body of scholarship on the experiences of women. The books and articles emerging in the past decade emphasized the liberating impact of America on Jewish women, particularly their access to education. The orthodoxy that is emerging notes that Jews came to America from a world

Laura Lefever Kautz proudly stands with her husband, Bernard Kautz, and their four children. Grace, their firstborn, reversed her father's footsteps when she left the Mennonite community in Lancaster to work in a Jewish-owned textile industry in New York City from 1953 to 1972. (Photograph courtesy of Lancaster Mennonite Historical Society, Joanne Hess Siegrist Collection, Lancaster, Pennsylvania.)

in which women received little or no education. For them the modernizing impact of America offered itself through classes and learning.[4] Perhaps this is true. I happen to "know" that my mother, the youngest daughter of ten children from a poor, highly observant family, persuaded her mother to send her to school once the family moved to a large Russian city in 1912. Despite the family's poverty and piety, and despite the rigors of World War I and the Russian Revolution, she attended the Kharkov Women's Gymnasium and graduated in 1919 having studied Latin, Greek, astronomy, geometry, history, Russian literature, and so on. When she came to America in the early 1920s and went to work as a milliner, she hardly fit the model of the "daughter of the shtetl" (the Jewish small town of eastern Europe) needing to be modernized. She had already seen American movies, talked on telephones, ridden on trolleys. Her modernization began long before the transoceanic migration. Her story may or may not have been typical—probably not—but I know (since on this matter I can consider myself an insider) that the process of migration to America did not fit a single pattern and that generalizations about the experiences of Jewish women coming to America need to be set against, and ultimately modified in light of, her story and those of others like her that do not fit the mold.

As an insider, I had a point of entry to communal experiences, to their "feel" and essence, that could never be inscribed on the pieces of paper that historians must rely on and cite when reconstructing the past. Historians may find formal texts to chart changes in, for example, Jewish ritual practice in the face of American cultural pressure. But studying the differences between various versions of the prayer book, or the Passover Haggadah, or even curricular materials from Hebrew schools cannot provide the smells, tastes, and sensations surrounding community activities and celebrations that only those who live them can know.

Scholars have had at their command the words of leaders who by necessity had a particular stake in communal developments or in maintaining communal structures. Indeed, much of the history of American Judaism uses the writings and published sermons of rabbis as its information source. By concentrating on those sources and taking them to be the expressions of communal will, historians not only narrowed their focus to a small, highly interested group but lost the insights of those who were being preached at or written to. The laity did not necessarily share the concerns or values of those who left the paper trail. The insider has a tremendous advantage over the dispassionate outsider in terms of understanding how little difference the words of the sermons actually made as American Jews constructed for themselves a patchwork world of practice and belief. The outsider must rely on the words that survive; the insider knows that a whole universe of behavior and values existed side by side as complements or alternatives to the surviving proscriptive texts.

Doing history from the inside does carry its own peculiar price tag, and the liabilities of being too close to a subject need to be juxtaposed to its advantages. First, I have no doubt that the greater the proximity between scholar and subject, the greater the possibility of coming to scholarship with a personal agenda. As I prepared the material for *A Time for Gathering: The Second Migration*, a study of nineteenth-century American Jewish life, I went out of my way to find and incorporate material on women. I wanted to identify women who migrated, settled, and carved out lives for themselves as autonomous individuals, who juggled their concern for their own advancement with concern for that of their families and communities. That is, I wanted them to embody my own definitions of an ideal woman, presumably one I like to see in myself. I am uncertain whether in the course of my research and drafting of the text I made more of the scanty historical record because it squared with my personal agenda, my sense of self, particularly as a Jew and a woman. I have a nagging sense that I made greater claims for the shreds of evidence I found because doing so felt right.[5]

Similarly, in *A Time for Gathering* I constructed an argument about the impact of mass behavior on Jewish religious life, on the pivotal role of the laity in shaping practice and the irrelevance of the rabbinate in controlling behavior. I think I got it right, but I have to admit that during most of the time I worked on this book I belonged to a faction in my congregation at odds with the rabbi. As a member of this community I found myself engaged in a series of disputes with him over the basic question of who has the right to make decisions about the life of the congregation. My group believed that the members—the dues payers, representing the will of the people—should prevail. I can never be certain that in the tumultuous accounts of congregational life in the mid-nineteenth century I did not hear the echoes of the discord of the late 1980s at Congregation Tifereth Israel in Washington, D.C. In my book I clearly took the same political position as I did in my own life. I may have been using my scholarship as a vehicle to score points in the contemporary internal community debate I was a party to. The 1980s and the 1860s were not the same. Yet I recognize in retrospect that as I put my argument together I ended up blurring the vast differences in time.

Second, the historian studying her own group and her own experiences ends up confronting demands and dilemmas that do not touch those engaged with issues outside the scope of their own lives and communities. I have on numerous occasions faced whether scholars of Jewish history ought to get involved in defending the Jewish past against false accusations that emanate not from historians but from contemporary demagogues. Should Jewish historians confront those who deny that the Holocaust ever happened? Should they respond to individuals like Louis Farrakhan who assert that Jews controlled the African slave trade and have been the perpetrators of every imaginable abomination against black people? Do Jewish historians have a special responsibility as Jews, as opposed to their responsibility as historians? Do Jewish historians have a role to play in the Jewish community as agents of defense? While it is easy enough to answer no to these questions by virtue of one's scholarly obligations, it is not entirely clear whether it is ethical to enjoy the benefits of doing "insider" scholarship without taking on any of the obligations.

Doing history from the inside, particularly from the inside of a community that cares a great deal about its history—or at least about how its history gets represented—often puts burdens on the scholar, creating diversions from professional responsibilities. The Jewish community has found many ways to "use" historians in films, lectures, scholar-in-residence series at synagogues, and various community programs that not only drain one's time (a minor matter) but often teeter on the boundary between history and celebration. Although I happen to believe scholars have a responsibility to bring the insights and findings of the academy to the public at large, I am aware of the disjunction between what the audience wants and what the scholar prefers. For the audience such events tend to be occasions for communal self-congratulation, while we historians want to ask analytical and often painful questions. The audience may want to believe that their group's accomplishments stand out as unique and special, whereas a broadly trained social historian may be searching for general patterns of similarity between various groups or trying to understand those accomplishments in the context of particular historical conditions.

As a whole, the Jewish community, however we may define it, has a relatively strong belief in the importance of history. By knowing its past, it wants to confirm that Jews have contributed to the places where they lived, that Jews have always carried with them a distinct way of living and functioning in the world, and that the ways the audience defines its Jewishness—and here they become specific to the particular audience, whether Reform, Conservative, Orthodox, or Zionist—make the most sense. Therefore what I have to say to laypeople seems to matter a great deal.

At times the differences between the historian's approach to the material and the audience's interests stand far apart. The historian's words can truly offend the audience and violate its collective perception of contemporary political events as encoded in discussions of the past. I am constantly invited to speak to Jewish audiences about the history of Jewish interactions with African Americans, an issue the community has defined as crucial. One point I make—and it rarely gets accepted happily—is that Jewish involvement with civil rights and other activities on behalf of black people historically meshed with Jewish self-interest. Someone always rises—usually in the middle of my talk, without asking to speak—and condemns me for making it seem that Jews did what they did for selfish purposes. Basically, what I hear is, Don't you know they will use this against us? My interlocutor in the audience is saying to me, You're a Jew doing Jewish history. You must be careful what you say, because some element or another in the communal agenda is at stake.

Cool scholarly talks like this frequently bring forth negative reactions when the story being told seems to leave certain listeners out or excludes the particular contours of their own or their families' experiences. Lectures on patterns of Jewish immigration always end with the response, "But my grandmother . . ." This proves the point that historical patterns have always been variegated, but it also demonstrates the almost narcissistic engagement people have with the past: the search for the self. There will always be some who listen to my talks in a synagogue or some other Jewish communal setting and take offense when they perceive that the story being told does not portray Jews (or their particular segment of the community) in the best light. In my standard lecture on the history of American Jewish women I bring up two very sensitive subjects, the not insignificant involvement of Jewish women in prostitution (and of Jewish men as procurers and businessmen in the white slave trade) and the relatively high rate of desertion by men. Hands wave in the air. Once again the members of the audience get their ire up because they did not "know" this was true, and it clearly presents a disturbing picture of the past.

It is impressive that this is a communal setting where people care about history. They come out to listen to lectures, taking time from work, family, or leisure to engage with the issues of the past. This surely makes me—as a historian—believe that what I do matters and that my efforts have moved beyond the notice of other professional historians. But demands are being placed on me because of who I am and my relationship to the community. As a scholar I am certainly free not to speak to such audiences. I can stay in my study and do my work just as surely as if I had decided to explore medieval coins or Etruscan trade routes. But I have chosen to study precisely those kinds of topics that move contemporary women and men. I have chosen to "do" American Jewish history, and this inner conflict goes along with that decision. This tug seems to inevitably accompany insider history.

Finally, the insider studying the history of her own group can never be utterly free of accusations from the outside that she lacks objectivity and has been pursuing subjects for personal rather than scholarly reasons. As someone who straddles a number of fields and works both in American Jewish history and in American social-ethnic history more broadly defined, I get a great deal of eyebrow raising from my friends who are American social historians. Some are themselves Jewish, but by virtue of their scholarly interests, political persuasions, and even own sense of ambivalence about being Jewish, they have steered far away from this topic. They have asked me, both directly and indirectly, Why are you doing this? I always thought you were an American social historian (I was once asked, Why do you do this Jewish junk?), in essence placing the experiences of Jews outside the parameters of American history. They assume that by doing Jewish history I am engaging in filiopietism, trying to "make Jews look good."

Since this essay involves in part a personal excursion, I must summarize this analysis of doing insider history from a personal perspective. In the end, after evaluating the pluses and minuses of this kind of scholarship, I find myself no less committed to studying the history of the Jewish people in America. I believe that as a well-trained student of American social history who has a broad view of a range of experiences, I am a better scholar than someone trained only in Jewish history. But my lenses as an insider allow me to peek into an inner world a true outsider would never have seen. My mind-set as a scholar complements my sensibilities as an insider. The stock of memories, experiences, and concerns I bear as a member of a community and the product of a particular world enriches my scholarly repertoire. I recognize the liabilities but affirm the assets. Coming to terms with the two polarities has been a source of insight and creativity rather than of narrowness or tension.

HISTORY FROM THE OUTSIDE

I am not just a Jew who has written about American Jewish history. In 1983 I published *Erin's Daughters in America*, a study of the migration and adaptation of Irish women to the United States.[6] I came to this topic as the true outsider, bringing to it no experiences with "things" Irish, no residue of Irish memories or experiences, no lines to an Irish community. Indeed, I came with no agenda of any kind, because I simply stumbled upon the subject. Yet having fallen into the net of Irish American history, I have come to see the tremendous value of having an outsider tackle historical subjects. My excursion into the history of the Irish in America has convinced me that outsiders have a great deal to bring to a subject precisely because they see patterns that insiders do not recognize as noteworthy.

I set out to write a book on immigrant women in general. I expected to frame this study in a comparative perspective and planned to juxtapose the experiences of a number of immigrant groups, to look for patterns of similarity and difference. The Irish, I assumed, would be just one of the several groups under consideration. It happened that I turned to the Irish first because chronologically they were the earliest of my subjects.

I ended up taking a path I had not set out on. I learned very early in my readings of the secondary material on the Irish in America—much of which had been indeed written by insiders—that Irish women outnumbered Irish men in the immigrant flood. Irish women migrated to America in larger numbers than men and in different ways than most immigrant women. In America they created a string of institutions and behaved in distinctive ways by virtue of the femaleness of their migratory experience. Yet none of the historians before me had stopped to explore this. The comparative study never got written. I wrote *Erin's Daughters* instead.

Why did no Irish or Irish American historian, including women historians deem Irish women's migration worthy of study? I know I am no smarter or more insightful than any of them, yet to me the pattern proved so compelling I could not let this story go unwritten. I had to tell it.

I offer the explanation that, to have considered these patterns notable enough to study, a scholar needed to be attuned to issues of gender and to the importance of focusing on women's experiences as a way of getting to the inner life of a community. The questions these historians asked— before *Erin's Daughters*—focused primarily on men's activity. Earlier historians had been interested in the success of the Irish in politics, both urban and ecclesiastical. In those sectors they found only men. By concentrating so thoroughly on Irish men, they missed the defining characteristic of Irish life that shaped my work. They failed to see, or to see as important, a female-dominated migration and a tradition of work, family, and community shaped by women.

More to the point, though, these other historians did not "see" the pattern. Obviously this statement needs to be clarified. They saw it in that some of them had run across some facts, recorded some data, and quantified some statistics about women in the Irish migration to America. But they failed to "see" it in the sense that they did not isolate the preponderance of women as migrants and as creators of Irish American communities as a significant variable or as a point of social and cultural life that needed to be raised out of its "lived context" and to be scrutinized and analyzed both in its own right and in relation to the full range of social and communal developments around it.

These insider historians did not "see" it in this way because to those who had lived in communities full of lifelong unmarried women, of women marrying "older," of grandmothers, aunts, and neighbors who had been domestic servants, in parishes and neighborhoods where sizable percentages of the women entered religious orders, the pattern was probably so everyday, so mundane, and so usual that it seemed not worthy of historical inquiry. These insiders, it seems, had assumed that the ordinary and obvious do not merit analysis. These women constituted the day-to-day landscape within which these historians had grown up. They were so much a feature of the world that nurtured the historians that they could not see them for what these women they were: major players in a historical drama that made the Irish and Irish immigration to the United States something sui generis and more than worthy of a historian's attention.

To me, the outsider and Jewish historian (I refer to my personal identity, not my academic interest), this female preponderance leaped up from the historical record as remarkable. I found myself amazed as I identified not only the pattern of these women's immigration but also the nature of their work lives, their educational achievements, their assertiveness in their communities, their high level of activism in trade unionism, their specifically female involvement with the church. Each historical episode struck me anew as crying out for full-length, in-depth analysis. The idea of neighborhoods made up of working single women of all ages, of female-centered households and female-headed ones as well, of women leading strikes, of talking back to their employers, jumped off of page and begged for study.

Indeed, the reactions I received in Ireland and among scholars of Irish American history confirmed not only that I was correct in my interpretation, but that as an outsider I was uniquely situated to craft the interpretation. What I was told and continue to be told was, it took an outsider. No Irish person, man or woman, would have thought to do this.

The book has taken on a life of its own. It received extensive and excellent reviews in journals in the United States and Ireland, and almost twenty years later it continues to be assigned in both graduate and undergraduate courses. A dozen or so studies have been published that cite *Erin's Daughters* as their analytic starting point, and an equal number of dissertations are in the works attempting to test the generalizations in my book against the specifics of particular communities or institutions. As a scholar I am pleased with this kind of reaction, but I am more struck by the role this book plays in the Irish community. I am told that Irish American women give each other *Erin's Daughters* as Christmas presents. Book groups in a number of cities have been formed to discuss it, and I frequently get letters from ordinary readers, nonhistorians, who tell me how deeply it has touched them.

I presume I struck a chord in my audience, heavily Irish as it is, and that the statement "it took an outsider" is accurate. I came to this project with no personal agenda. The "story" I wove did not have to come out a particular way. I had no stake in privileging one view of this history over another, and no communal agenda whispered in my ear to push me in one direction or another. I brought to it no experiences, either positive or negative, with an Irish family or an Irish community to steer me toward a particular inclination. I grew up in a city with a minuscule Irish population, and among the non-Jewish classmates and friends I interacted with as a child, I remember none with Irish ancestry.

I set out to write a book, inspired by a scholarly problem that engaged me—the high level of women's participation in the Irish migration to America. I had no background in the study of the Irish other than a good knowledge of the secondary scholarship on the Irish in America and a superficial exposure to the writings of James T. Farrell, Sean O'Casey, William Butler Yeats, and John Millington Synge.

Apart than these, I had to start from scratch. Not only did I have no assumptions about the Irish, I could not operate from a dense base of communal information. In the end this put me in position where I had to construct a picture of the Irish from the ground up, with no baggage to weigh me down. I embarked on writing a history of Irish American women, their migration, adaptation, cultural journey, social options. I could read Irish history from a point of view that heretofore had never been written. I had no guides, and ultimately I profited from a free hand, from a blank slate when it came to matters Irish. I had not grown up with the sights, sounds, smells, and tastes of Irishness resonating within me. I had never been to a Catholic mass or walked the halls of a parochial school in an Irish community. I had never witnessed a Saint Patrick's Day parade, eaten my meals in an Irish American home, drunk beer in a neighborhood bar. I had to go, step by step, through learning what it "felt" like to be Irish. If we add to this that in writing history one is always an outsider—the past is, one writer has told us, "a foreign country"—I moved from the farthest margins to what I hope was the core of understanding.[7]

As a learning experience, the task of understanding a group of people about whom I knew almost nothing posed a tremendous challenge. I faced it with real trepidation. I fretted constantly lest I steer so far from reality that I would not only be dismissed by Irish and Irish American historians but be roundly condemned for having ventured onto turf "off limits" to me. Yet if I can trust the reviews of *Erin's Daughters* here and in Ireland, and if I can measure the outcome by the book's scholarly and public success, I managed to successfully chart for myself a path through unknown territory.

As with my scholarship in Jewish history, I get ample opportunity to speak to community audiences made up heavily, and sometimes exclusively, of Irish women and men. I have to admit I take a different stand than when I speak to Jewish groups. In the latter case my tone is a bit more provocative. As an insider I have the right and obligation to shake people out of the cloak of comfort and self-congratulation that tends to envelop them in such settings. As the outsider addressing a group of Irish people, I am more circumspect about what I say and how I phrase it. I do not avoid such extremely sensitive subjects as alcoholism, domestic violence, spousal desertion (a far greater problem among the Irish than among Jews), crime, mental illness, racism (on the part of the Irish toward blacks and Chinese), anti-Semitism, and indeed almost all the social ills of the nineteenth century. Yet though I do not avoid such issues, I tend to introduce them as more of a minor footnote to the historical narrative than they really were or than the way I would present them as a Jew speaking to Jews. I have to ask myself if I am doing "violence" to historical truth by shying away from speaking more forcefully to community audiences on these subjects. By taking on the persona of the outsider and feeling the need to be respectful of the history they would like to hear, am I engaging in some kind of historical fraud?

I can offer other historians no simple answers to these questions and to others raised by the problems of doing both kinds of history. Being an insider brings with it its particular bag of dilemmas and also its special strengths, and so does writing as an outsider. Neither is better than the other, neither is worse. Each mode of observation enriches our understanding of the past. In the largest sense, a scholarly discourse in which insiders looking out and outsiders looking in meet, talk to each other, and elevate the level of understanding operates to the benefit of all and helps fulfill the goal of scholarship: to further the boundaries of knowledge and understanding. At yet another level, a historian who does both modes learns different yet complementary aspects of being a scholar. And learning is always good.

NOTES

1. The range of issues surrounding the scholarly debate over "objectivity" and insider "knowledge" and the historical development of this problem is most thoroughly discussed in Peter Novick, *That Noble Dream: The "Objectivity Question" and the American Historical Profession* (Cambridge: Cambridge University Press, 1988); see also Clifford Geertz, *Local Knowledge: Further Essays in Interpretive Anthropology* (New York: Basic Books, 1983).

2. See Paul Ritterband and Harold S. Wechsler, *Jewish Learning in American Universities: The First Century* (Bloomington: Indiana University Press, 1994); see also Susanne Klingenstein, *Jews in the American Academy, 1900–1940: The Dynamics of Intellectual Assimilation* (New Haven: Yale University Press, 1991).

3. See Hasia R. Diner, *In the Almost Promised Land: American Jews and Blacks, 1915–1935* (Westport, Conn.: Greenwood Press, 1977; reprint, Baltimore: Johns Hopkins University Press, 1995).

4. See Sydney Weinberg, *The World of Our Mothers: The Lives of Jewish Immigrant Women* (Chapel Hill: University of North Carolina Press, 1988); see also

Susan Glenn, *Daughters of the Shtetl: Life and Labor in the Immigrant Genera-tion* (Ithaca: Cornell University Press, 1990).

5. See Hasia R. Diner, *A Time for Gathering: The Second Migration, 1820–1880,* vol. 2 of *The Jewish People in America,* ed. Henry L. Feingold (Baltimore: Johns Hopkins University Press, 1992).

6. See Hasia R. Diner, *Erin's Daughters in America: Irish Immigrant Women in the Nineteenth Century* (Baltimore: Johns Hopkins University Press, 1983).

7. See David Lowenthal, *The Past Is a Foreign Country* (Cambridge: Cambridge University Press, 1985).

2

Who Are You?

THE IDENTITY OF THE OUTSIDER WITHIN

Diane Zimmerman Umble

How do notions about gender shape the conduct of research within religious communities? Based on ethnographic research among the Old Order Mennonites and Amish, Diane Zimmerman Umble examines the questions Old Order people "ask back" to reveal how those she interviewed constructed her identity as an "outsider within" and how indigenous expectations of gender roles shaped that identity. Accounting for the gendered dimensions of doing research forces scholars to write from multiple and sometimes contradictory perspectives.

*W*ho are you? Old Order Mennonite and Amish persons repeatedly asked me that as I conducted my research among them.[1] I discovered that the question revealed significant interpretative frameworks they employed as they interacted with outsiders, frameworks that became central to my understanding of their history and experience.[2] Popular media portray the Old Order communities as quaint relics of a rural past through images of horse-drawn plows and buggies and fresh-faced children in plain dress walking to one-room schools, lunch pails in hand. What these images fail to show are the members' dynamic struggles to sustain their separateness from the world, maintain their communities, and manage social change. Day after day, season by season, the women, men, and children of the Old Order communities live their lives as a testimony to their religious faith in a postmodern world.

This chapter elaborates on Hasia Diner's concern with the challenge of conducting research across and within ethnic communities and with how it affects women's history (see her chapter in this volume). I focus on the methodological implications for an Anabaptist woman who seeks to tell the stories of Old Order communities and, like Diner, on how ethnic identity shapes the conduct of research. I write from my own place as a woman, an academic, and a Mennonite—or to put it differently, as a feminist Mennonite woman scholar. My Mennonite upbringing, in the heart of Pennsylvania Dutch country, fostered my commitment to peace and social justice, an appreciation for a simple lifestyle, an orientation to religious expression grounded in the context of a faith community, and an identity shaped by an ethos of separation from "the world." Many contemporary Mennonites, particularly those of us who came of age during the Vietnam War, see themselves as marginal with respect to wider American culture. Given this ethnic identity, how does an academic from an Anabaptist tradition, a scholar with a faculty appointment in a state-related university, come to terms with the dissonance created by living in the midst of multiple identities—as our foreparents would say, "being in the world but not of it"? Can that struggle yield insights that enrich our understanding of our own traditions and inform our analyses of the traditions of others?

Patricia Hill Collins uses the phrase "outsiders within" to describe the multiple and contradictory places African American women experience in the academy. Women are, she argues as an African American feminist sociologist, in at least two places at once: outside and within, margin and center.[3] She describes emerging African American feminist thought as a means for bringing to conventional thinking a critical posture that is essential for the creative development of academic disciplines. "Strangers" in academia or "marginal intellectuals" bring to the center aspects of experience that are otherwise obscured.[4]

Much of the historical research on the Amish and Mennonites has been conducted by academics whose appointments are in small Mennon-

Ruth Hershey (1895–1990) was a Lancaster County Mennonite farm wife and mother who took up photography. This photograph of Ruth (left, holding the camera) and her sister Rhoda illustrates her experiments with framing and reflection. Despite her passion for photography, reading, and music, Ruth remained faithful to the disciplines of the Mennonite church and respected its boundaries. (Photograph courtesy of Edwin P. Huddle.)

ite colleges at the margins of the research universities that claim to be the center of scholarly production. Although outside the mainstream, these scholars are integral to the process of articulating Amish and Mennonite historical identity inside the community and beyond. Furthermore, they are preparing undergraduates who go on to academic centers to extend this work as graduate students and future academics. At the same time, the very activity of academic research, with its analytical and critical orientation, often distances academics from the centers of their own communities. The distancing may be even greater for women scholars whose patriarchal cultural heritage often overlooks women's experience and sometimes silences their voices. I do not deny the status I embody as a tenured white, middle-class professor. Nevertheless, the concept of the outsider within resonates with my experience as I conduct research among the Old Order Mennonite and Amish communities, maintain my own ethnic identity as a Mennonite woman, and write as an academic for scholarly audiences within and beyond my community of origin. Here I focus on the dynamics of research and writing in these contexts and ponder the contributions that a Mennonite scholar who is an outsider within can contribute to the wider dialogue about the religious and ethnic aspects of women's history.

I invite you to reflect with me on the dynamics of conducting research while recognizing one's gender, ethnic, and religious identity. Scholars from critical, cultural, and feminist perspectives have criticized the positivist stance of the objective, neutral, impersonal social scientist. Each interview, Charles Briggs has argued, is a "unique, social interaction that involves a negotiation of social roles and frames of reference between strangers."[5] Interviewers and those interviewed are coparticipants in the discourse through which an account is constructed. Feminist scholars have stressed that ethnographers have gendered, racial, and social class identities that enter into the construction of ethnographic accounts.

In an article in *Communication Theory*, Bette Kauffman proposes that the strategies for avoiding, obtaining, and managing research interviews should be considered data. The questions "asked back" to the researcher show how those being researched are active participants in the ethnographic interview. She suggests that "the researcher-researched relationship, as it develops and is expressed in negotiations over the research process, is a map for the analysis more than a qualifier of it."[6]

What follows is an extended description of two interviews—one with an Old Order Mennonite bishop, the other with an Old Order Amish lay historian—that illustrates the dynamics of my own status as an outsider within in relation to Old Order communities and shows the categories of analysis their members used to map my identity. After describing the interviews I will elaborate on the implications of that identity for Anabaptist women researchers.

OLD ORDER MENNONITE AND AMISH ENCOUNTERS

I arrived at the home of an Old Order Mennonite bishop and his wife just after noon on a mild June day.[7] The bishop's wife was clearing away the lunch dishes when I knocked on the door, and the bishop answered. I told him my name, who had sent me, and what I wanted to talk about. He invited me in and offered me a seat on the sofa in the kitchen, then pulled up an office chair on wheels and sat opposite me. His wife sat in a recliner to my right, reading the newspaper and listening to the conversation. A gentle breeze blew through the open window as we discussed the welcome break in a week of temperatures over ninety degrees.

I explained that I had been sent by an Old Order Mennonite historian he knew. I had come to discuss changes in the spring 1995 enforcement of the 1907 "Pennsylvania Ruling," the Old Order Mennonite rules about owing telephones. The bishop launched into a general description of how, to avoid a church split generations before, Bishop Jonas Martin had carefully crafted a compromise that permitted church members to own telephones, though it was discouraged, but prohibited clergy from doing so. He began to recount recent deliberations about telephone ownership among his contemporaries. When I asked him about the roles of specific individuals, he stopped, looked at me, and said, "Wer bischt du?" Who are you?

Several years before, on a blustery, overcast morning in March, I was looking for a retired Old Order Amish farmer I will call Levi. The day before, another Amish man I will call Aaron had suggested that Levi might own a copy of an 1899 Lancaster County atlas. Aaron had also asked me to deliver a letter to Levi. I was exploring the history of an Amish church split in 1909 that occurred after leaders announced that telephones were not permitted in Amish homes. Few written accounts of this split exist, but the Amish keep the story alive in the oral tradition of the community.

Levi was then sixty-five years old, a retired farmer. His son now managed the family farm, and Levi and his wife lived in the *grossdaadi Haus* (grandfather's house), a small house attached to the main farmhouse now occupied by his son's family.[8] Half a dozen dogs and puppies barked and yipped as I drove in. I knocked on the door but no one answered, so I went to the kitchen door of the big house. Inside, a young Amish woman was doing laundry. We spoke through the screen door. She said that if I didn't find Levi in the shop, then he was in the field up the road.

The shop was a rectangular garagelike building on the opposite side of the driveway. The dog pen was attached to the end toward the road. A woodworking shop was in one half, and an Amish buggy occupied the other. I went into the shop and called Levi's name, but no one answered, so I got back in the car and drove up the road to the field the young woman had described. About two hundred feet from the roadside, I saw Levi striding across the field. He wore Amish garb: black broadfall pants, a dark brown jacket without lapels, and a straw hat with a black band. His white hair covered his ears, and he had a long white beard. He was using a hand seeder; the canvas sack slung over his shoulder was fitted at the bottom with a device that spread seed. When he turned a handle like the one on a jack-in-the-box, a wheel attached to the bottom of the sack scattered the seed as he strode evenly across the plowed ground. I scrambled up a four-foot bank into the field and waited until he approached the end of his row.

"Are you Levi?" I called out.

"Yes," he replied. "And who are you?"

Standing in the field, I responded to Levi's question by telling him my name was Diane Umble. "Umble, did you say?" he asked, "What Umble might that be?" I reported the name of my father-in-law and where he lived in Lancaster County. Levi did not know him but asked if I was any relation to "Bishop Christian." Christian Umble was an Old Order Amish bishop at the turn of the century. This question was often asked by Amish people I encountered. I replied that there was some connection several generations back, but I was not sure what it was—perhaps it was through the Fisher family. He asked if I had a copy of *Amish and Amish-Mennonite Genealogies.* I did not.

Then he asked, "Are you from around here?" I had grown up in a town just three miles down the road. "Who are your people?" he asked. I seldom volunteered my father's name, because he has been an insurance and real estate agent in the community for over thirty years. Many Old Order people disapprove of insurance, believing trust should be placed in God. Nevertheless, my father has many Old Order clients who carry liability insurance.

I told Levi who my father was, and Levi knew him. Many years before, my father had helped him buy the land we were standing on. The land had once been owned by my great-grandfather, something I had not known. I asked if I could arrange a "visit" with him, an expression I regularly used for my interviews with Old Order sources. Levi explained that he wanted to finish seeding the field before the rain came. We agreed to meet after lunch, and he told me to go into the shop when I returned.

I returned to Levi's shop in early afternoon. He came out of the house moments after I arrived, carrying his copy of *Amish and Amish-Mennonite Genealogies*. Inside, the shop had a wood-burning stove on one wall. The opposite wall was lined with a long shelf at about chest height, and a workbench with tools occupied the center of the room. Lumber was stacked in one corner and in the loft above. The room was cold; there was no place to sit.

He put the book on the shelf and opened it to the page listing the descendants of Bishop Christian Umble. We tried without success to trace the intervening generations to establish the link to my father-in-law. He explained that all kinds of people stopped to see him for help with genealogical research. Along with woodworking, genealogy was his retirement hobby. He threw some wood on the fire, and we began our visit.

My visit to the kitchen of the Old Order Mennonite bishop followed a similar pattern. He too wanted to know where I lived. "Who are your people?" he asked. He was most interested in my father's family tree. On learning that my father's family name was Zimmerman, the bishop rolled back his chair, walked briskly to another room, and returned with a copy of the Zimmerman genealogy. Beginning with my grandfather, we traced the family back three generations. There he identified "Yockel" (Jacob) Zimmerman, who in 1815 had been ordained bishop in the Groffdale district of the Mennonite Church, the location of contemporary Groffdale Conference of the Old Order Mennonite Church. As I think the bishop suspected, my father's ancestors had "gone liberal." In fact several of my father's uncles had married women whose names did not sound "Mennonite." Once I was placed within the wider Mennonite circle, although in the "liberal" wing, our conversation returned to Old Order Mennonite rules about the telephone.

This emphasis on my family tree continues to be common to my initial encounters with Old Order Mennonite and Amish people, especially men. They actively construct my identity in terms of patrilineal lines. The genealogies of my father-in-law and my father establish my "place" relative to members of the Old Order community. Although my mother's ancestry comes up occasionally in conversation, matrilineal lines have never been traced on these occasions. The effort to "place" me is necessary, in part, because I appear to be "English," the Old Order term for non-Amish people. I drive a car, I speak English, I have short hair, and I dress like an "English" woman. Nevertheless, I was born and raised in Lancaster County, as were my ancestors. I make my home there, and my family names appear in Amish and Mennonite genealogies. My proximity to community boundaries is uncertain and needs to be clarified. One tool used for this clarification is to define me in terms of "heads" of households: my father-in-law and my father and their fathers before them.

My research protocol has been to seek informal sponsorship whenever possible. I usually name the Old Order person who sent me, if I have permission, to signal that another person within the community has been willing to talk to me. In the early stages of my research, most of the interviews were patterned chronologically. I asked descriptive questions about parents, home, and childhood memories of telephone service and practices. I also asked about patterns of communication: how people traveled, where they met and how they exchanged the news, and what occasioned trips to town.

Levi described how neighbors worked together for harvesting and building. I asked about the division of labor. Did women ever take milk to the station or grain to the mill? "That was more of a man's job," he said; "hard work for a woman." I remarked that I had childhood memories from the dairy farm of how heavy milk cans were. He asked my age and said I was a "young springer yet." He then asked if I had a family. At the time I had a kindergarten-age daughter. "You have just one?" he asked. I explained that doctors had thought we would never be able to have children, so having even one child was special. "I bet she is when you have just one," Levi replied.

Once my patrilineal identity was established, Old Order people always asked about my family. When I began this research I had one daughter; my son was born in 1991 when my daughter was seven. The primary role for women in Old Order society is that of mother and homemaker, and children are seen as blessings from God. Although some of the younger generation use birth control, many believe that is tampering with the will of God. By age forty-five the average Amish woman has given birth to 7.1 children.[9] Most Old Order women my age devote their time and energy to caring for children and running a household. My identity was routinely constructed in terms of my role as a mother, and I was asked to account for the small size of my family. I often did so by passing reference to my experience with infertility.

Through the inevitable questions about my family, Old Order participants in this research added another layer to the construction of who I was: mother of "just" two. Motherhood is taken for granted as a significant role in the Old Order social landscape. My gender implies a specific social role, that of mother.

The categories that Old Order people use to construct my identity represent the frames they enlist to shape communication with outsiders. Marking community identity and designating gender roles provide insight into the operative referential frames that help Old Order persons make sense of their world. Their use of these categories provides important clues for interpreting the stories they tell. Gender-inflected notions of community and role performance, especially as they are implicated in maintaining authority within the community, shape my analysis of Old Order responses to the telephone.

Though they asked about my family, Old Order participants seldom asked if I worked outside the home. Nevertheless, I did not conceal the fact that I teach at a nearby university. Furthermore, I told people up front that I was working on a book about the coming of the telephone to Lancaster County and that I was particularly interested in the responses of Old Order communities. For the most part, my academic credentials are of no currency in the Old Order community. Education to the eighth grade in one-room parochial schools is the norm. Members believe that "higher" education does not necessarily make one a better person.

THE CONSTRUCTION OF A RESEARCH IDENTITY

My participation in the construction of a "research identity" with these two Old Order men established common ground on which to begin. It also provided insight into important referential codes among Old Orders that enhanced and guided my later interpretation and analysis. Nevertheless, this particular coconstruction of my identity is one I embrace with ambivalence. As anthropologist Ruth Behar writes, when we become "fictive kin,"[10] the relationship both highlights and formalizes the contradictions and differences among us. After twenty-some years of investment in establishing a professional identity that goes beyond whose daughter, wife, and mother I am, being defined primarily in those terms denies who else I am. Acknowledging the power of the research participant to act as a party in the process does not necessarily make these definitions easier to live with.

I identify with Lana Rakow as she writes about her experiences conducting research in a small midwestern town she called Prospect:

> My feminism was the one aspect of my subjectivity that did not find a home in the identity I had in Prospect. Although I felt accepted into the community as a woman, I felt cautious about discussing my opinions as a feminist. . . . As a woman I developed comfortable relationships with many other women in the community. As a feminist I worried about my responsibility to these woman and about my ability to resolve conflict (of which they were for the most part unaware) between our interpretations of the world. As a woman I was the participant; as a feminist I was the observer. I am aware that the story I am about to tell is one of only many that could be told about Prospect.[11]

Furthermore, accounting for the role of participant in constructing the researcher's identity does not put to rest issues of power. Simply describing that role in the research does not negate the power of the researcher in retelling the story. In the end, those who write continue to create the accounts of the encounters. Behar writes: "It worries me that one does violence to the life history as a story by turning it into the disposable commodity of information. . . . Clearly, any ethnographic representation—and I count my own, of course—inevitably includes a self-representation. Even more subtly, the act of representing 'almost always involves violence of some sort to the subject of the representation,' using as it must some degree of reduction, decontextualization, and miniaturization."[12] Doing violence to the Old Order communities is of particular concern for researchers who write and publish. Members of these communities often feel threatened by external forces beyond their control: zoning ordinances, environmental protection laws, land development pressures that inflate land prices, tourism, and unwanted media attention. Public images of Old Order people contribute to the misrepresentation and oversimplification of their experience. This is heightened for Old Order women, who are dismissed as stereotypically oppressed victims of patriarchy and also viewed as relics of a rural past. To do justice to their history, we must seek to understand the dynamics of patriarchy in their societies, explore the ways they exercise their influence and creativity within perceived conformity, and describe how central they are to the management of cultural identity in the face of ongoing social change. Their identities as wives and mothers, their experiences of sisterhood within the community, and their demonstration of creativity through traditional outlets of gardening, cooking, and sewing must all be seen as expressions of living culture.

Nevertheless, the ethnographer historian finds herself pulled in several competing and compelling directions. For example, how does one balance personal authenticity with research goals? What are the ethics of representing only part of one's self for the sake of creating common ground to communicate from? Does it matter that who I am is constructed in different terms depending on where I am? How does one construct an account that is both outside and within? Can thinking from contradictory positions generate a more nuanced description of the shifting terrains that religion and ethnicity invoke as persons negotiate identities outside and within their own communities?

THE SCHOLARLY IDENTITY

On another level, writing about Old Order Mennonite and Amish communities brings a set of outsider-within dynamics to the academy. Whereas the Old Order communities go to some length to establish my Mennonite identity as a matter of credentialing, academics do just the opposite. In the academy, acknowledging my Mennonite identity elicits responses ranging from disbelief ("But you're not plain," which means, "You don't look like a Mennonite") to outright dismissal ("Then you can't be much of a scholar," implying that members of "quaint" religious sects cannot do serious intellectual work) to suspicion ("If you're religious, then you must not be a feminist"). Though my postmodern feminist sympathies require acknowledging my own particular standpoint, doing so sometimes marginalizes me and my work within the academy. Just as members of the Older Order community deem my academic identity irrelevant, so members of the academic community would prefer to dismiss my religious identity in general and ignore the gender dynamics of the research enterprise in particular.

In the space between the worlds of Old Order communities and the world of the public university exists another place to which I am connected—the world of Mennonite academics, the seedbed for much of the scholarship about the Anabaptist experience. Here too I am an outsider within. I am a Mennonite scholar who forsook the Mennonite center to cast her academic lot with the world of public higher education. Those at the Mennonite center may wonder if I have been so influenced by secular theory that I can no longer value the strengths of my own tradition. Perhaps my intellectual journey away from home frees me to take a more critical stance toward my community by virtue of my perspective from the outside. But the mothers and fathers of Anabaptist historiography may not appreciate a social history that is critical and insists that gender be taken seriously as an organizing category for understanding Mennonite and Amish social experience.

Moving among these various communities has demonstrated to me how formative gender is in organizing and interpreting the meaning of social experience. Overlooking the gendered dimensions of history denies fundamental ways gender shapes social practice. My experience also highlights how any ethnic and religious experience is shaped by the interplay with the "other" or, in the case of the Mennonites and the Amish, with the "world." Historical accounts of religious communities must be embedded in the larger social and cultural dynamics of their times rather than isolated from them. The writing of history also occurs within a context. Contemporary theoretical challenges to account for gender as an organizing category represent the influence of the "other" in current historiography.

My Anabaptist foremothers and forefathers were admonished to live "in the world, but not of it." That perspective remains alive today and shapes the ways Old Order Mennonite and Amish persons interact with an outsider like me. As a writer of historical ethnography, I find the admonition captures my own experience. My academic life makes me a stranger in the Old Order community. My ethnic-religious identity makes me a stranger in the academy. Mennonite women scholars live and work in many worlds but are often outsiders within. This perspective can be a standpoint that enriches interpretations of ethnic and religious identity. The essays in this book, taken together, represent the voices of marginal communities and the women who are marginalized within them. Their experiences can illuminate our developing understanding of the variation in historical experience.

The opportunity to think from multiple and contradictory places makes it possible to articulate once unspoken perspectives that are central to the creative development of Mennonite and Amish women's history. The uncomfortable process can potentially enrich that history and also women's history writ large. The dialogue between Old Order people and those who study them, between academics and their communities of origin, and between the academy and those voices marginalized from the academic centers can provide a forum for uncovering our theoretical blind spots about the roles gender and religion play in historical experience.

NOTES

1. My research focused on the coming of the telephone to Lancaster County and on Old Order Amish and Mennonite responses to a new means of interaction that was disruptive to traditional patterns of communication within their communities. See Diane Zimmerman Umble, *Holding the Line: The Telephone in Old Order Mennonite and Amish Life* (Baltimore: Johns Hopkins University Press, 1996).

2. The Old Order Mennonite (Groffdale Conference) and Old Order Amish communities in Lancaster County, Pennsylvania, represent the most traditional segments of the Mennonite and Amish communities in North America. Both groups use horse and buggy transportation, speak the Low German dialect, educate their children in parochial schools up to the eighth grade, and follow a strict *Ordnung,* or code of conduct, that orders the practices and rituals of community life.

3. See Patricia Hill Collins, "Learning from the Outsider Within: The Sociological Significance of Black Feminist Thought," *Social Problems* 33 (December 1986): 14–32.

4. Ibid.

5. See Charles L. Briggs, *Learning How to Ask: A Sociolinguistic Appraisal of the Role of the Interview in Social Science Research* (New York: Cambridge University Press, 1986), 24.

6. See Bette J. Kauffman, "Feminist Facts: Interview Strategies and Political Subjects in Ethnography," *Communication Theory* 2 (August 1992): 187.

7. I protect the identity of members of the Old Order community, often at their request.

8. When the Amish retire, they move to a smaller part of the "home place," usually an apartment attached to the main house. Their children take over the

day-to-day operation of the farm, but the elders continue to contribute as much as they are able. In this way retired persons remain in the care of their immediate families throughout their lives.

9. See Donald B. Kraybill, *The Riddle of Amish Culture* (Baltimore: Johns Hopkins University Press, 1989), 74.

10. See Ruth Behar, *Translated Woman: Crossing the Border with Esperanza's Story* (Boston: Beacon Press, 1993), 17.

11. See Lana Fay Rakow, *Gender on the Line: Women, the Telephone, and Community Life* (Urbana: University of Illinois Press, 1992), 8.

12. Behar, 271.

3

"To Remind Us of Who We Are"

MULTIPLE MEANINGS OF CONSERVATIVE WOMEN'S DRESS

Beth E. Graybill

What is the meaning of prescriptions for how women and men may dress among traditional Anabaptist groups? Beth E. Graybill conducts a feminist analysis of ethnographic interviews about dress with women of the Eastern Pennsylvania Mennonite Church. She describes how they talk and think about dress and argues that women's adherence to strict dress codes both produces and reflects particular gender roles that constitute the group's primary mark of separation from the wider culture.

I am traveling with a celebrity. As we enter the Texter Mountain Mennonite Church, near Robesonia, Pennsylvania, several women recognize my friend Lois,[1] recently pictured in the local newspaper as coauthor of a Mennonite cookbook. We are welcomed with smiles and warm handshakes.

Here on the female side of the sanctuary, women in long-sleeved pastel print dresses, black stockings, and large white head coverings greet each other with a kiss on the lips.[2] Despite how Lois and I differ from them in appearance (the somber blouse and skirt I chose to wear now seem hopelessly stylish, though no matter what I wore I would have stood out), the women seem pleased that we have joined them for worship at this conservative Mennonite congregation in rural Pennsylvania.

As Lois and I file up front with her married cousin and slide into a third-row pew, I have never been so conscious of my short hair. Later, when we kneel and face the rear to pray, I notice forty-five identical white net coverings hiding long hair primly nestled in buns.

As I glance around the sanctuary at the women's quiet demeanor and their modest, identically styled cape dresses (with an extra layer of fabric over the bodice), I find myself wondering about the relation between conservative Mennonite women's dress and gender roles. To what extent are their gender roles contingent on the clothes they wear? What are the meanings of conservative dress for the women themselves? How does dress both extend and confirm existing gender roles?

DRESS RESEARCH CONSIDERATIONS

Material culture scholar Grant McCracken has written that clothing communicates the properties that inhere in such socially constructed categories as male and female.[3] Specifically, examining women's dress offers revealing insights into the qualities that the wearer and her culture associate with being female. Anthropologists Joanne Eicher and Mary Ellen Roach-Higgins suggest that gendered dress encourages each individual to internalize a complex set of social expectations related to gendered behavior. Moreover, they argue, "dress is both a repository of meanings regarding gender roles and a vehicle for perpetuating or rendering changes in gender roles."[4] That is, dress both produces and reflects particular gender roles.

My research focuses on one particular conservative Mennonite denomination, the Eastern Pennsylvania Mennonite Church. This group numbers about 10,000 people including children. Although rural dwellers, most families no longer make their living through farming; instead, most male breadwinners work in various blue-collar trades.[5] Congregations are centered in Pennsylvania, with smaller numbers in ten other states and one Canadian province as well as the Bahamas, Guate-

Mennonite girls cheer the boys at a softball game at a private Mennonite high school in Lancaster, Pennsylvania, in 1965. Soon after graduation, some of these students or their classmates joined the Conservative Eastern Pennsylvania Mennonites, codifying this dress style in even more severe ways. (Photograph courtesy of Lancaster Mennonite High School.)

mala, and Paraguay. Since the Eastern Church formed in 1968 as a conservative split from a mainstream Mennonite conference, it has grown rapidly, averaging a combined growth rate of 42 percent.[6]

The Eastern Pennsylvania Mennonite Church is governed by a churchwide *Statement of Rules and Discipline,* updated every few years, that forbids (among other things) radio, television, divorce, jewelry (including wedding rings), immodest apparel, and cut hair for women.[7] Members accept modern technology such as electricity, cars, and telephones. Distinctive dress, by far the most visible marker of the group, is much more prescriptive for women than for men, allowing men to "pass" more easily in the outside world. That makes dress, and primarily *women's* dress, the key visible mark of separation from the wider culture, a doctrine known to Mennonites as "nonconformity."[8]

From 1993 to 1996 I explored the multiple meanings of women's dress and gender roles through interviews and participant observation with Eastern Pennsylvania Mennonite women in and around Lancaster County, Pennsylvania. I conducted intensive open-ended interviews with eleven conservative and two formerly conservative Mennonite women aged twenty-four to seventy-nine[9] as well as with two men, both pastors in the denomination. I ate in their homes and went to church with them. We shared recipes and washed dishes together. Although I am not a member of their particular Mennonite subgroup, we share a common Swiss-German Mennonite heritage and ethnicity as well as, in some cases, kinship connections: in more than one interview the informants in my study discovered that we were distantly related.[10] In ethnographic terms this makes me a partial or "peripheral" member.[11] My challenge in this role was to work at what Jim Thomas calls "de-familiarization," that is, thinking critically about concepts formerly taken for granted.[12]

My partial membership status afforded me a beginning level of trust with conservative women. I was able to introduce myself as a friend of one of their relatives, some of whom either accompanied me on visits or phoned ahead on my behalf. In addition, because of my Mennonite connection I was less likely to make gross misinterpretations about the group.[13] On the other hand, I was enough of an outsider to their particular Mennonite denomination that I was excused for not wearing the "plain dress" these women adhere to.[14] My partial membership status encouraged informants to explain to me the full meaning of conservative dress, since I did not, in fact, understand their particular rationale for this outward expression of our common Mennonite beliefs. Ethnographically, in these ways I related as both insider and outsider.

My relations with informants also benefited from two additional factors. First, since this denomination places a high value on witnessing to one's faith, women were receptive to my requests for interviews. Second, my geographical residence gave us another common reference point, since I live in Lancaster County, Pennsylvania, where this denomination is centered. Although our perceptions differed—for example, I live and shop in Lancaster, a city of about 50,000, while the informants in my study consider the city dangerous and visit it only to pass out religious tracts—nevertheless my familiarity with their cultural landscape lessened the gulf between us.

Given my Mennonite connection, I certainly did not approach the data as a detached observer. Often after meetings with conservative women I came away disheartened by what seemed to me to be the limited choices imposed on them by their faith; but by the same token, I usually left with admiration for the sincerity and assurance with which they practice their understanding of our common religion. Certainly my Mennonite background influenced my subjective response to the women in my study, yet I doubt that objectivity is ever attainable, or even desirable. Ethnographer Ann Oakley, among others, rejects the falsely "objective" stance of the neutral interviewer as unsuitable, since meaningful research depends on empathy. On the contrary, I look to scientist and feminist Donna Haraway, who argues that we are always viewing things from some embodied position; our knowledge is always situated, our perspective always partial. Paradoxically, Haraway argues that only partial perspective promises objective vision.[15] We move toward objectivity when we first acknowledge our particular starting place, which I have taken to heart in explicitly identifying my own social location vis-à-vis my informants.

Finally, I wrestled with what ethnographer Pamela Cotterill describes as the dilemma of how a feminist researcher deals with data generated from interviews with women who are not feminists.[16] I often asked myself what was at stake for me in viewing these women as more contented or constrained than I was. Whose frame of reference should I use to describe their choices—theirs or my own? In the end, I labored to make respect and even-handedness my guiding principles, aiming to write in such a way that, in the words of Laurel Richardson, "the people who teach me about their lives are honored and empowered, even if they and I see their worlds differently."[17] These issues were background to my ethnographic data gathering, research, and interpretation.

DRESS AND IDENTITY FOR CONSERVATIVE WOMEN

I have never been out so far from Lancaster City in this direction, almost at the Susquehanna River, where farmland rolls in cultivated hills of corn and tobacco. Rebecca, an informant, told me over the telephone, "Just look for the gospel sign at the end of the lane. That marks the road." The hand-lettered sign proclaims, Fear God and Repent from Sin. Following Rebecca's instructions, I turn down her gravel lane.

At the first farmhouse I pass, smiling toddlers and their mother are shelling peas on the porch, surrounded by cats and a dog. The mother wears thick black stockings and a long-sleeved dress, which must be hot. Seeing them solves a question I had been meaning to ask about what clothing adaptations conservative Mennonites make to accommodate active children on hot summer days. The children are in short sleeves; the girls wear simple knee-length dresses, the boys' pants legs are rolled up to the knees, and both are barefoot. As one pastor was to tell me later, church discipline specifies only what must be worn in *public* life (where neither bare legs nor bare arms are permitted), but most families loosen restrictions at home.[18] I drive by slowly and smile, glad that my car, while not their regulation black, is at least a sedate gray, and wondering what explanation my informant will give her neighbors for my strange appearance on her doorstep. Evangelism, probably, since this group values mission outreach.

I park by the barn and approach a neat farmhouse flanked by tidy plots of herbs and flowers. Rebecca answers my knock, a light-brown-skinned young woman dressed in conservative dress, her kinky black hair pulled back in a bun under her white net prayer covering. Yesterday's informant has described her to me as, "a black girl, dear as can be."

Before we can sit down, Rebecca asks if I will follow her to leave her car at the garage for repair. It's the least I can do, though not the ethnographer's reciprocal "payback" I would have thought of first. Soon I am trying to keep up with Rebecca as she zips her car down hills and around bends along the winding country roads.

At the garage, Rebecca parks and unselfconsciously nods to the mechanic. While every Mennonite woman in plain dress attracts attention, surely Rebecca especially stands out because of her race. As she hops into my car, I am dying to ask her how she came to join this small, homogeneous band of white ethnic Mennonites.

Later we talk at her kitchen table, with the sounds of a tractor droning outside and an old-fashioned clock chiming inside. Rebecca tells me of her upbringing by a conservative Mennonite family as a foster child. She describes how the church has given her a sense of rootedness and a place to belong. These compensate, she believes, for the fact that she doubts she will ever marry because "even though church people say they believe in interracial marriages, very few of them actually would permit it for their own families." Rebecca smiles wryly, reflecting that she is more comfortable here than in any black church she has ever visited: "I guess belonging has more to do with the things you're used to in your culture rather than the color of your skin." Rebecca's race might seem to set her apart from the conservative Mennonite community, but on the contrary, like all of my other informants, the clothing she wears distinctively shapes her and cements her sense of identity as a conservative Mennonite woman.

Like Rebecca, every Eastern Pennsylvania Mennonite woman is mandated to wear a particular style of dress called a "cape dress" that, for modesty, includes an extra layer of fabric over the bust, attached at the shoulders and waist but open at the sides. The *Statement of Rules and Discipline* requires that cape dresses be "modest" and "without trimming," of "mid-calf length" and with "three-quarter length or longer sleeves."[19] As Lydia, another informant, told me, "We promise to dress this way. And if we don't then we forfeit membership." Dresses are sewn at home out of serviceable cotton-polyester fabrics; a knit material called "softique" is especially popular. Cape dresses are worn with prayer coverings, that is, white mesh head coverings. Black shoes and stockings complete the prescribed attire for women.

The head covering is made of two pieces of white net fabric, sewn together in the center and pinned to the hair with straight pins. Covering strings—approximately ten-inch ties that attach to the covering behind the ears and are usually left untied for decoration—are optional and may be white or black.[20] Women begin wearing the head covering when they make a public conversion and join the church, usually at about thirteen years of age, though sometimes as late as sixteen.

I explore below the multiple meanings that conservative women attach to their dress.

DRESS EXPRESSES SUBMISSION

The primary meaning that Eastern Pennsylvania Mennonite women intend through their apparel centers in the head covering, which symbolizes submission to God and subordination to male authority. Eastern Pennsylvania Mennonites refer back to the biblical injunctions in 1 Cor. 11:1–16 RSV, in which the apostle Paul states that "any woman who prays or prophesies with her head unveiled dishonors her head" and that "the head of every man is Christ, the head of a woman is her husband, and the head of Christ is God," which they take literally. Lydia described their philosophy this way: "God has an order set up, it's God, man, woman.

That's God's chain of command."[21] For conservative Mennonites, the head covering visually reinforces this ordained order.[22]

Eastern Pennsylvania Mennonites accept that men are to be the leaders at home and in church, a situation with which women claim to be quite content. Ellen describes the situation:

> We feel very strongly that the father is the head of the home. He has the final word. Um, we see the women's movement, liberation movement, as being completely contrary to God's plan for the family, where the father is the head of the home, even though he's not there all the time or maybe not as much as the mother. We've heard, just [sermons] all the time encouraging the fathers to take their proper responsibility, don't push it off on your wife, you know, it's actually your job. I think in the Bible almost all the commandments are to fathers. It hardly ever says, "Mother, do this." But it says, "Father," you know, "train up your children in the way they're to go," and, and ah, give them advice. So I think it's actually [the fathers'] responsibility to see that it's going to go right. Be the spiritual head of the home. And, and actually the discipline, disciplinary head, too.[23]

Although male dominance is evident in this quotation, in my observation the reality is somewhat more nuanced than the rhetoric. Women usually discipline children themselves, have decision-making power over the household budget, and give input into major family decisions. Similarly, Marie Griffith, in her study of the evangelical organization Women Aglow, argues that conservative doctrines that emphasize surrender to God through submission to male authority also encode women's personal power. Evangelical women "center their narratives on their own capacity to initiate personal healing and cultivate domestic harmony," forms of self-empowerment. Moreover, Griffith argues that the language of submission emphasizes "more word than deed" and valorizes women's "power to influence—or, in less flattering terms, manipulate—one's husband to one's own ends."[24] In these ways, religious conservatives like the women in my study may experience personal power despite the language of submission.

Nevertheless, for Eastern Pennsylvania Mennonite women the head covering manifests a visual marker of male dominance. Writing from her ethnographic study with conservative Christian and Orthodox Jewish women, Christel Manning has noted, "Maintaining traditional distinctions between men and women is therefore one of the things that makes religious conservatives distinct."[25] Thus, for women in my study, the head covering sartorially marks their membership in a particular, patriarchal religious subculture.

Because it is such a potent, visible symbol of women's submission, changing her head covering may be the first indication that a woman plans to leave. For example, when Dottie decided to leave her community she adopted a slightly smaller covering without strings, a change that was immediately noticed by her friends and family. Later she was told by an Eastern bishop, who saw this as the first step toward loss of faith, "Once you start making changes there's no convenient stopping place."[26] This seemingly minute change conveyed important meanings to insiders.

DRESS PROMOTES UNIFORMITY

A second meaning that conservative women in my study attach to dress is their belief that the church's uniform dress code promotes united thinking and confirms "a consistent witness," as Jane put it.[27] Kristina told me with satisfaction, "It expresses that we are one body."[28] In fact, the dress of Eastern Pennsylvania Mennonite women functions very much like a uniform, constituting a "symbolic shorthand" that is distinctive and easily recognizable.[29] Like the uniforms worn by nurses, police, or prisoners, the Eastern Mennonite women's "uniform" identifies group members, helps externalize standards for group behavior, and enables the group to exert authority over its members.

Because conservative Mennonite women's clothing functions as a uniform, little deviation is permitted. Male bishops in the denomination set dress standards and enforce women's dress codes. A girl will be "visited" (reprimanded) by the local ministry for failing to dress properly. The following violations were cited to me as examples: wearing loud colors or large print fabrics, putting a too-large collar on a dress, hemming a dress too short, putting extra trim or a wide ruffle on the sleeves, or topstitching with contrasting thread. As Ellen told me about these examples, "You know, it seems like such a small thing. But it's finally an expression of pride, or rebellion, that's really what it is. . . . Anything that attracts attention we feel is not consistent with our meek and quiet spirit, like the Bible says. . . . We feel, ah, the loud colors and the big prints would actually encourage attention to ourselves."[30] In these ways Eastern Pennsylvania Mennonite women willingly sacrifice individual self-expression for the larger goal of supporting a consistent witness.

DRESS EXPRESSES ANTIFASHION VALUES

Eastern Pennsylvania Mennonite women's dress is deliberately designed to mask many of the marks of identification usually revealed in clothing, suggesting a third meaning. For most people, clothing expresses one's economic class, social standing, and occupation. By contrast, their dress is deliberately designed to conceal these distinctions. When one is immersed in a sea of similarly dressed individuals, uniform dress lends near invisibility, muting the usual distinctions of class and status as well as obscuring individual idiosyncrasies.

In many ways conservative women's views on clothing fit what Fred Davis has described as "anti-fashion." Unlike indifference to fashion, sometimes called "nonfashion" (which Davis defines as being oblivious to or unconcerned with fashion trends), antifashion is oppositional dress.[31] According to Davis, antifashion is a form of deliberate disidentification with the cultural mainstream. Popular culture scholars Patricia A. Cunningham and Susan Voso Lab have defined antifashion as "clothing which goes against what is currently in fashion, . . . meant to communicate a message about the group that embraces it. [Antifashion] often reflects beliefs, attitudes, and ideas of subcultures of the larger culture. The dress functions as a sign of rejection of the norm and hence the status quo. . . . [It makes] a statement through its style that clearly says no to the hegemony of the prevailing style of fashion."[32] Antifashion, then, deliberately reacts against contemporary fashion trends, an accurate description of the practices of Eastern Pennsylvania Mennonites. In several places their *Statement of Rules and Discipline* specifically guards against fashionableness: for example, for men, "clothing or footwear shall not be of fashionable, sporty, or Western styles," and for women, "fashionable head dress shall not be worn."[33] Obviously, however, a member must have some sense of what the prevailing fashion *is* in order to dress *un*fashionably, thus making antifashion a conscious, deliberate choice.[34]

On the other hand, antifashion, as expressed by Eastern Pennsylvania Mennonite women, has much to recommend it. Rebecca illustrated the benefits of this attitude when she told me, "I don't have to worry about what's in style and what's not in style and I don't have to make sure I'm always all matching. And I spend very little money on clothing because, you know, I can wear the same dress for five years. I mean, to me it just cuts out a lot of the frivolous, frivolousness and the worry that I would have about dress otherwise. You know, I tend to be a practical person, and from that standpoint it's very convenient to dress this way."[35] Thus for conservative Mennonite women antifashion—because of its practicality and opposition to mainstream fashion trends—can be considered a modern-day equivalent of nonconformity, a traditional Mennonite value.

DRESS HIGHLIGHTS GENDER DISTINCTIONS

Just as clothing conceals, it also reveals, in this case highlighting gender distinctions. For Eastern Pennsylvania Mennonites, the sharp delineation of appropriate men's and women's apparel reinforces and rigidifies existing power differentials between the sexes. The primary clothing requirement for conservative men is the plain suit (a collarless suit jacket that buttons to the neck), worn with solid-color shirts and black shoes. Unlike women's clothing, which is sewn at home, men's suits are predominantly ready made (in China, according to the tags on the suits) and sold at a few select local stores selling plain clothing.[36]

The inconsistency about Eastern Pennsylvania Mennonite men's apparel, however, is that work clothes, which most men wear most of the time, are not regulated by the church, except under the general guidelines of modesty and proscription against fashionableness. Only a few men wear the plain suit to their jobs as accountants or teachers. Most are employed in blue-collar trades as mechanics, plumbers, masons, printers, and carpenters, where they wear work clothes during the week and a plain suit only on Sunday. This makes Mennonite men more easily able to pass in the wider world, leading to a double standard in dress that at least some informants are also aware of. Lydia described it this way:

> The men are to be the leaders, but in plain dress too often they aren't. In the workaday world, in the wintertime, you can't tell—my son goes off to work, he's a carpenter, he's out in the cold, so he has an insulated coverall suit, and, you know, an insulated pullover-hood jacket. Now, when my husband goes to work you *can* tell, he wears his plain suit in the classroom. . . . When you get to know one of our men who is consistent, you do *know* that they are separate,

because they don't wear some things that other people wear, but it's not, the
line is not as distinct [as for women].[37]

Overall in this church group, women bear the burden of cultural separation on their bodies to a much greater extent than do men, another indication of women's subordinate status in the denomination.[38]

In addition to clothing distinctions related to cultural separation, conservative Mennonite women are aware of gendered dress differences in
another way. Several informants alluded to "womanly virtues" that are
conveyed in part through modest, feminine dress. Such virtues include
submission, gentleness, maternalness, patience, and meekness.[39] According to Rebecca, if a woman were to exercise too much leadership or ini-
tiative, according to the "unwritten rules and assumptions" of the church
she would be seen as "uppity" or "lacking in modesty or in the graces that
are supposed to be associated with [Christian] womanhood."[40] These
womanly virtues are symbolized sartorially through the wearing of
dresses, never slacks. Many Eastern Pennsylvania Mennonite women
would agree with the evangelical women in Marie Griffith's study who
"validate and prize, as a rich source of female self-esteem, conventional
notions of women as more supportive, loving, and spiritual than men."[41]

Dress Provides Protection

Just as some Muslims view the veil as effective "anti-seduction devices,"[42]
so too do conservative Mennonite women view their own dress as a protection from society's dangers. Dressed as they are, conservative women
feel less susceptible to harm, as Rebecca indicates: "I guess I thought of
[my dress] more as a protection . . . from whether it be, um, violence or
abuse or anything like that, that you could meet out in the streets. . . . I
always thought of that as being a certain protection from physical harm
that God gives."[43]

Because of this belief in the protective qualities of clothing, dress restrictions in the denomination are extremely prescriptive. The *Statement
of Rules and Discipline* specifies the required thickness of stockings ("30
denier or its equivalent") and size of covering ("the front piece being at
least one and one-half inches wide").[44] Young women attending the denomination's winter Bible school are also required to sleep in head cover-

ings.[45] Following such rules seems to give women an added feeling of safety.

In addition, the church's restrictions on women's dress are related to its understanding of the dangers implicit in women's sexuality. Cape dresses are designed to conceal a woman's figure. Young girls begin wearing the cape dress, Lydia told me, when they "begin filling out."[46] Women who expose their bodies and are "improperly clothed" should not be surprised if they attract unwelcome male attention, according to Ellen. She continued, "We definitely feel that a woman dressed as we are does not encourage a man's attention. . . . We try to do our part in not encouraging it."[47] Another informant, Kristina, derives comfort from believing that her adolescent daughter's modest attire will deter male sexual harassment.

DRESS PROMOTES VIRTUOUS BEHAVIOR

The clothing of conservative Mennonite women not only offers them a feeling of protection but also provides internal motivation for upright, virtuous living. Lydia, a key informant, described the intent of Eastern Pennsylvania Mennonite women's dress: "We want people to look at us and think of God. And the way you dress changes how you feel about yourself. . . . Because I dress plain, people expect something from me that they wouldn't expect if I didn't dress different from everybody else, which is a challenge. . . . We believe very strongly that just because you dress plain . . . isn't the answer. It's the life that must back it up. But the dress, the plain dress, is a help to remind us of who we are."[48] As Lydia's quotation implies, wearing the prescribed clothing influences a wearer's identity and self-image. Designed to cause those who see them to "think of God," the clothing of conservative Mennonite women also reminds them of who they are, calling forth certain moral behavior. As Rachel told me, "Some people say there's no religion in clothes. But when I'm in them there is."[49] Beliefs as expressed through clothing thus become internalized as ethical norms for Eastern Pennsylvania Mennonite women.

Moreover, while Mennonite dress is important for the women who wear it, their apparel is also intended to project a desired image of the group to outsiders. The informants in my study view their dress as a form of witnessing. As Rachel said, "With your dress you can be a witness wherever you go. . . . Your clothes should help people to be God-conscious."[50] Mary carries religious tracts when she travels to give out to people who ask about her dress.

This sense of being a visible witness because of one's dress also influences women's behavior in another way. Conservative Mennonite women are aware of the expectations they believe outside observers have of them because they dress distinctively. As Lydia told me, "If I find myself going over the speed limit and oh! I remember that I have a covering on, you know [laughs], what, what are they going to think of Christ?"[51] In this way, as Nathan Joseph has written, uniform clothing enlists all onlookers as "norm enforcers."[52]

Dress Acts as a Sacred Symbol

The attire of conservative Mennonite women functions as a sacred symbol, a meaning conveyed most particularly through the head covering. Prayer coverings are the one article of plain dress that cannot be bought by outsiders; they must be custom-made by group members. Neither the particular net fabric nor a pattern for sewing it is available in retail stores.[53] Eastern Pennsylvania Mennonites shop at several variety stores in the Lancaster County area that sell plain clothing and are also frequented by non-Mennonites. I have visited three such stores. Every item of plain clothing—from footwear to undergarments to coats and sweaters to plain suits—is available for sale *except* prayer coverings. Here tourists may shop for suspenders or a Mennonite-style men's hat without profaning the symbolism of the article of clothing they buy as a souvenir. To sell a covering to a tourist, by contrast, would be sacrilege.

The sacredness of the covering extends not only to its purchase but to its wearing and disposal as well. Conservative women reserve new, Sunday-best coverings for church and special occasions and wear worn or frayed ones for housecleaning or other chores. One informant cuts up coverings when they become too old to wear so that outsiders cannot retrieve them and put them to any irreverent use.

Moreover, because the symbol is so imbued with sacred meaning, it is not easily laid aside. Dottie, who left the Eastern church ten years ago, still chooses to wear a covering when she goes out to work. As she says, "It's just been so much a part of my life that I can't throw it off abruptly."[54]

DRESS REFLECTS EMOTIONAL SECURITY

Eastern Pennsylvania Mennonite women adhere to narrowly defined, traditional female gender roles, of which dress is a primary outward indicator. Women's work, which takes place almost entirely in the domestic or private sphere, offers these women emotional security and belonging.[55] Most conservative Mennonite women marry and become full-time homemakers, although each congregation represented by my informants also included several unmarried women (predominantly referred to as "single sisters," a term that also includes widows and that women themselves preferred to "leftover blessings," which was occasionally used).

For Eastern Pennsylvania Mennonite women, their major investments of time and energy are expected to take place at home.[56] As Rebecca put it, "Women are supposed to be homemakers. . . . Our church would frown on women developing any kind of career. Definitely not if they're married."[57] Conservative Mennonite women shoulder unpaid but valuable tasks at home that feminist researchers such as Evelyn Nakano Glenn have referred to as the work of "social reproduction."[58] In the case of my informants this includes food production involving large gardens and hundreds of quarts of home canning, care and nurture of an average of five to seven children,[59] household cleaning and upkeep (most of the informants in my study live in older farmhouses), and sewing, laundering, and mending clothes. Some families also take in foster children (usually biracial and sometimes with special needs); other women are primary caregivers for aging parents who may live with them. The women I interviewed also take major responsibility for what Micaela Di Leonardo has called the "work of kinship,"[60] that is, maintaining family ties through such activities as planning family reunions and organizing visits to family members in other locations, corresponding with children on church mission assignments, and organizing "sisters days" (family work parties at the parents' family homestead).

Within these traditional, family-centered gender roles, Eastern Pennsylvania Mennonite women feel comfortable and secure. Janet Liebman Jacobs has speculated that women are attracted to conservative religious movements out of a "desire for community and family in a technocratic culture where such affiliations are difficult to maintain."[61] Moreover, Lynn Davidman's study of contemporary Jewish women's attraction to

Orthodox Judaism found that women choose conservative religions because they offer "valuable certainty concerning gender roles and family life that is unavailable elsewhere."[62] The informants in my study are comfortable with and committed to a traditional understanding of femininity that values family and defines women's roles as primarily domestic.

This valuation of traditional female roles and the accompanying sense of emotional security that conservative women derive from this gendered identity are confirmed and made visible through dress. Accepting the church's dress code is equivalent to accepting its prescribed roles for women. For Kristina, who converted to the Eastern Pennsylvania Mennonite Church with her husband and young children, the church's particular style of dress confirmed her identity as a Christian woman. As she reflected:

> I can say that in this kind of dressing, with the cape dress and, and the covering, I, I found my role as a Christian woman. I can say that. Because I was, always, for years and years, I was looking for something to express that I was a Christian woman. And I just wasn't satisfied with the way I looked. . . . Once I came to this church and they gave me some [cape] dresses, I felt some kind of—what can I say? It gave me a kind of *security* in a position I wanted to be. I thought, ah, now I'm, I'm living how Christ wants me to, to live.[63]

Dress Embodies Confinement

Just as comfortable, loose-fitting clothing enables freedom of movement and symbolizes autonomy and agency, so too does restrictive clothing restrain movement and exemplify confinement. To the outsider, Mennonite women's attire appears constrictive; women wearing long-sleeved cape dresses and thick black stockings lack the mobility and comfort of those who wear slacks. But to insiders, values of modesty and obedient faithfulness are more important than such considerations. However, while conservative girls and women do everything from playing softball to weeding the garden in cape dresses, their body movements are nevertheless more constrained than men's. Symbolically, this supports Susan Kaiser's analysis of men's clothing as emphasizing doing, or physical effectiveness, whereas women's clothing emphasizes being, or physical attractiveness.[64] In this way conservative Mennonite women's clothing reflects the feminine virtues and traditional gender roles described above even as it sends a sartorial message of confinement.

In addition to the physical confinement of constraining clothing, a psychological aspect of confinement may be inferred. In examining dress and gender roles among conservative Mennonite women, I had to consider the mental health strains of subordinate status and restricted life choices. Two informants suffered from depression: one had cyclical, ongoing episodes stemming from childhood sexual abuse, another experienced several years of depression after the birth of her fourth, and ultimately her last, child. A third informant described her mother as manic-depressive and chillingly remarked, "When my mom is most depressed she is most like women in my church are expected to be. . . . She's quiet and submissive."[65]

Feminist psychologist Dana Crowley Jack, who researches chronically depressed women, believes that for some women depression is a price they *choose* to pay in order to hang on to a particular view of self or valued relationships. Jack writes, "A woman may move into known depression rather than grapple with an unknown self that will, perhaps, destroy life as she understands it."[66] Thus a conservative Mennonite woman may accept depression rather than challenge the psychological confinement of her religious tradition.

As a feminist researcher I couldn't help asking why women remain part of confining, patriarchal structures when the obvious choice would be to leave.[67] When I discussed this with Rebecca she reminded me that leaving is difficult to do. As she put it, "Someone who left would be looked on as apostate, falling away. . . . Relationships would be strained." A woman may be fearful about where she will go or what she will do next if she leaves the church, having fewer options than men because of less activity in the public sphere. Moreover, as Rebecca mused, "You'd have to have something else out there to connect yourself with, otherwise you'd be totally alone."[68] For women, leaving their religion would mean leaving their social community as well, a daunting prospect that may make them more willing to live with confining aspects.

Eastern Pennsylvania Mennonite women themselves acknowledge these barriers of confinement, but they perceive them in a positive light.[69] As Jenny summarized it, "The Eastern Church is like a lush, green garden with a fence around it. And I like that fence."[70] As this quotation implies, confinement is by choice. Ellen used the analogy of a greenhouse to describe protecting her children from dangerous influences outside the community of faith. As she said, "What hothouse owner would put his little tomato plants out in the frost? You don't do it because you know it's not good for them. . . . We're actually deliberately protecting [our children] from those [negative] influences."[71]

The husband of a third informant, with her full support, subscribes to the daily newspaper and weekly news magazine but censors them before the rest of the family is permitted to read them, blacking out or cutting out offensive portions. As these examples illustrate, confinement—either physical or psychological—is embraced as a virtue by Eastern Pennsylvania Mennonite women.

Furthermore, my informants derive real benefits from this single-minded sense of confinement. Not only is leaving difficult, I have come to recognize that a woman might have valid reasons for remaining part of a conservative religious group. The depth of care and warmth of community found inside the Eastern Pennsylvania Mennonite Church is uncommon in contemporary society. This sense of community includes frequent visiting at the time of births and marriages; instrumental assistance such as sharing tasks (for example, getting together to can one hundred quarts of peaches); and occasionally financial assistance as well—one Eastern congregation was supporting a young widow to enable her to remain at home full time with her small children. Finally, expressions of support during times of tragedy can be especially meaningful, as Dottie describes:

> For instance, like when my father died, he died very suddenly of a heart attack and gee, you know, half an hour elapsed, and one neighbor was there bringing folding chairs and setting 'em up because they knew that persons would be coming very shortly and we probably wouldn't have enough of chairs for everybody that would be showing up. And persons were there with food, and persons came and cooked, . . . and they prepared a meal for the day of the funeral and ah, just, you know, that kind of thing. It was there automatically.[72]

Dottie's story illustrates the depth of sharing and community involvement found among Eastern Pennsylvania Mennonites—particularly in times of tragedy—which offers compelling, valid reasons for women to remain within the confines of community.

CONCLUSION

Dress for Eastern Pennsylvania Mennonite women carries many complex meanings. Sartorially, the women in my study are content with a wardrobe limited to several variations of essentially the same dress pattern. They find a single mode of all-purpose apparel to be life giving, not limiting; they strive for homogeneity, not individuality. Specifically, conservative dress reinforces women's subordination to men and highlights gender distinctions. In addition, it functions as a uniform, offers a feeling of protection from harm, motivates right living, and serves as a visible mark of separation from the larger society. Finally, plain dress offers women emotional security and reflects elements of confinement that they embrace.

Women's dress and gender roles are inseparably intertwined in the conservative Mennonite community. Dress influences women's identity, and their religious identity influences how they dress. The women in my study view their apparel as an outward expression of their commitment to integrity and faithful obedience and of their conviction about distinct and separate male/female roles.

NOTES

1. I use pseudonyms here and elsewhere to protect the anonymity of the informants in my study.

2. Church members take seriously the biblical mandate in Rom. 16:16, Revised Standard Version (RSV): "Greet one another with a holy kiss."

3. Grant McCracken, *Culture and Consumption* (Bloomington: Indiana University Press, 1988), 76–77, 60.

4. Joanne B. Eicher and Mary Ellen Roach-Higgins, "Definition and Classification of Dress," in *Dress and Gender: Making and Meaning in Cultural Contexts,* ed. Ruth Barnes and Joanne B. Eicher (New York: St. Martin's Press, 1992), 12.

5. In the three church districts represented by my informants, fewer than one-quarter of the families still farm. Most men are employed in blue-collar trades such as carpentry, plumbing, and auto repair. Unmarried women often

teach school, serve in church missions, or live in as a "mother's helper." Married women work full time at home.

6. The Eastern Pennsylvania Mennonite Church was formed when five bishops withdrew from Lancaster Conference of the (Old) Mennonite Church in 1968, later joined by eleven congregations totaling 469 members. See Robert B. Graber, "An Amiable Mennonite Schism: The Origin of the Eastern Pennsylvania Mennonite Church," *Pennsylvania Mennonite Heritage* 7 (October 1984): 2–10. Large family size—the average is five to seven children—is a reason for church growth, and the Eastern Pennsylvania Mennonite Church retains the great majority of its youth. A bishop I interviewed estimated that roughly 80 percent of their young people join the church. According to my informants, most young people join between ages thirteen and sixteen. Adult membership in 2001 was 4,206 members. See the 2001 *Directory of the Eastern Pennsylvania Mennonite Church and Related Areas* (Ephrata, Pa.: Publication Board of the Eastern Pennsylvania Mennonite Church, 2001), 28–31. By contrast, the Lancaster Mennonite Conference has grown by only 2.5 percent during the same period. See Steven M. Nolt, "The Mennonite Eclipse," *Festival Quarterly* 19 (summer 1992): 10.

7. *Statement of Christian Doctrine and Rules and Discipline of the Eastern Pennsylvania Mennonite Church and Related Areas, Sixth Statement* (Ephrata, Pa.: Publication Board of the Eastern Pennsylvania Mennonite Church, 1993), 15–21.

8. Mennonites base their belief in nonconformity on Rom. 12:2 RSV: "Do not be conformed to this world but be transformed by the renewal of your mind, that you may prove what is the will of God." Although conservative Mennonites express nonconformity through visible markers such as distinctive dress and rejection of modern technology, progressive Mennonites have tended to emphasize inward beliefs and subtler lifestyle differences.

9. Of this group, four informants were single, seven were married, and two were formerly married (one widowed and one abandoned). Interviews ranged from two to three hours.

10. Interestingly, the informants and I shared not only kinship connections but what I call departure connections. For example, some of them noted that their conservative Mennonite church and my more liberal Mennonite congregation were both splits off the same parent conference. We share a history of having left Lancaster Mennonite Conference, though for entirely different reasons. Their 1968 breakaway was toward greater discipline and regulation; the church that

formed on leaving Lancaster Conference in 1959 and ultimately spawned my home congregation did so to escape legalism and regulation. Nevertheless, our point of connection was in the act of leaving.

11. Patricia Adler and Peter Adler, *Membership Roles in Field Research* (Newbury Park, Calif.: Sage, 1987), 36–49.

12. Jim Thomas, *Doing Critical Ethnography* (Newbury Park, Calif.: Sage, 1993), 43.

13. As John Caughey has written, studying "at home" groups that one is already somewhat familiar with increases the chances of "getting it right." See "Epilogue: On the Anthropology of America," in *Symbolizing America*, ed. Hervé Varenne (Lincoln: University of Nebraska Press, 1986), 239.

14. In the vocabulary of my informants, "plain dress" is the generic term used to refer to the distinctive style of women's and men's clothing worn by Amish and conservative Mennonites (who are sometimes referred to as "plain people"). Plain dress lacks ornamentation and is designed to reflect values of simplicity and nonconformity to the world. Because the fault was with my parents for not having trained me in the virtues of wearing plain dress, I was not considered "backslidden" or apostate. My parents, however, were.

15. See Ann Oakley, "Interviewing Women: A Contradiction in Terms," in *Doing Feminist Research*, ed. Helen Roberts (New York: Routledge, 1981), 30–61, and Donna J. Haraway, "Situated Knowledges," in her *Simians, Cyborgs, and Women: The Reinvention of Nature* (New York: Routledge, 1991), 188–90.

16. Pamela Cotterill, "Interviewing Women: Issues of Friendship, Vulnerability, and Power," *Women's Studies International Forum* 15, nos. 5–6 (1992): 593–606.

17. Laurel Richardson, "Trash on the Corner," *Journal of Contemporary Ethnography* 21 (April 1992): 108.

18. One informant told me later that she tended to forgo stockings during the summer at home, although she worried that doing so when she walked to her mailbox at the end of the lane might weaken her witness to neighbors. Another informant referred to such loosened dress standards as "knockabout" clothing worn only at home.

19. *Statement of Rules and Discipline*, 17–18.

20. The presence of covering strings in this denomination seems to indicate somewhat greater conservatism or religiosity. In general, older and more pious women wear coverings with strings, although in one church district all ministers' wives are asked to wear them.

21. Interview with Lydia, Millersville, Pa.: 10 October 1993. All taped interviews are in my possession.

22. In fact, women's actual reality may be less patriarchal than the rhetoric above implies, since most women wield a certain amount of informal power in the domestic sphere. Unofficially, many women view themselves as "leaders in their homes," as one informant put it. In most Eastern Pennsylvania Mennonite families the fathers work away from home, and women exercise day-to-day control over children and household matters. Mothers seldom wait to discipline children until fathers come home but usually administer punishment themselves. In general the informants in my study control household expenditures, and in at least one case a woman took on extra work at home that gave her discretionary income: Lydia plants and tends a garden plot of lilies that she sells to a local greenhouse, using the money for trips to visit family.

23. Interview with Ellen, Denver, Pa.: 1 June 1994.

24. R. Marie Griffith, *God's Daughters: Evangelical Women and the Power of Submission* (Berkeley: University of California Press, 1997), 175, 185.

25. Christel Manning, *God Gave Us the Right: Conservative Catholic, Evangelical Protestant, and Orthodox Jewish Women Grapple with Feminism* (New Brunswick, N.J.: Rutgers University Press, 1999), 161.

26. Interview with Dottie, Lititz, Pa.: 8 November 1993.

27. Interview with Jane, Hinkletown, Pa.: 2 January 1995.

28. Interview with Kristina, Richland, Pa.: 25 June 1995.

29. Nathan Joseph, *Uniforms and Nonuniforms: Communication through Clothing* (New York: Greenwood Press, 1986), 105.

30. Ellen interview.

31. Fred Davis, *Fashion, Culture, and Identity* (Chicago: University of Chicago Press, 1992), 161. See Anne Hollander, *Sex and Suits: The Evolution of Modern Dress* (New York: Knopf, 1994), 17–18, for a fuller discussion of nonfashion. She equates nonfashion with traditional dress found in primitive societies.

32. Patricia A. Cunningham and Susan Voso Lab, eds., *Dress in American Culture* (Bowling Green, Ohio: Bowling Green State University Popular Press, 1991), 13–14.

33. *Statement of Rules and Discipline*, 17, 18.

34. In a similar way, John Caughey has discussed how the seemingly distinctive practices of Old Order Mennonites, whom he studied, are connected to mainstream cultural patterns through their opposition to them. See Caughey, 233.

35. Interview with Rebecca, Washington Borough, Pa.: 16 June 1995.

36. Men are restricted to black or navy plain suits, usually made of a stiff, machine-washable fabric called "Swedish knit." That the plain suit is standard wear for conservative Mennonite men is perhaps not surprising. Anne Hollander describes how suits came to convey authority and for this reason have historically (at least until recently) been limited to men. Even today, she writes, for men "the suit remains the uniform of official power." See Hollander, 101. Good's Store in Blue Ball, Pennsylvania, sells the largest selection of plain clothing in central Pennsylvania, including plain suits made in China. Coincidentally, plain suits bear some resemblance to Mao-style jackets.

37. Lydia interview.

38. Marlene Epp discusses this theme historically for Canadian Mennonite women. See "Carrying the Banner of Nonconformity: Ontario Mennonite Women and the Dress Question," *Conrad Grebel Review* 8 (fall 1990): 237–57.

39. According to an article in one church publication, the "ideal young woman" in the denomination is expected to be submissive, gentle, considerate, kind, with an abundance of common sense, sensitive and loyal to her husband, sympathetic, considerate, frugal, with a meek and quiet spirit, and a good household manager. See "Courtship: The Ideal Young Man and the Ideal Young Woman," *Eastern Mennonite Testimony* 2 (March 1970): 8–9.

40. Rebecca interview.

41. Griffith, 200.

42. Fatima Mernissi, *Beyond the Veil: Male-Female Dynamics in a Modern Muslim Society* (New York: Schenkman, 1975), 101.

43. Ibid.

44. *Statement of Rules and Discipline*, 18.

45. *Handbook of the Numidia Mennonite Bible School* (Ephrata, Pa.: Eastern Mennonite Publications, 1994), 12.

46. Lydia interview.

47. Ellen interview.

48. Lydia interview.

49. Interview with Rachel, Richland, Pa.: 30 March 1995.

50. Ibid.

51. Lydia interview, Millersville, Pa.: 15 June 1994.

52. Joseph, 50.

53. Eastern Pennsylvania Mennonite seamstresses special order the fabric in bulk from wholesale vendors in New York City.

54. Dottie interview.

55. By contrast, conservative Mennonite men dominate in the wider public sphere, including public roles in the church. On matters of church business, married women route their opinions through their husbands, who meet regularly with other men of the congregation to discuss the issues in "head of household" meetings. Then, according to informants in my study, the couple votes as a block. Single women, though voting members (and household heads), lack the background information available to married women and usually abstain from voting.

56. In general, church teaching prohibits wives and mothers from working away from home. An Eastern Pennsylvania Mennonite Sunday school lesson book admonishes, "Under normal circumstances, the wife and mother should not enter the job market." See *Building Christian Homes: A Manual of Bible Principles and Practical Instructions* (Lititz, Pa.: Eastern Mennonite Publications, 1991). However, Eastern women do contribute to their families' income through jobs done for pay at home. Examples cited to me of mothers' "home work" included binding quilts or quilting, baby-sitting, sewing clothes or women's prayer coverings for members in the local congregation, selling baked goods at roadside stands, or growing an extra family plot of strawberries or asparagus to be sold at local farmers' markets.

57. Rebecca interview.

58. Evelyn Nakano Glenn, "From Servitude to Service Work: Historical Continuities in the Racial Division of Paid Reproductive Labor," *Signs* 18 (autumn 1992): 1–43.

59. Some Eastern families have adopted children from church missions in Guatemala, Paraguay, or the Bahamas. Regarding family size, Martha described her family of six children as "small, but that's because we married late."

60. Micaela Di Leonardo, *The Varieties of Ethnic Experience: Kinship, Class, and Gender among California Italian-Americans* (Ithaca: Cornell University Press, 1984), 194.

61. Janet Liebman Jacobs, *Divine Disenchantment: Deconverting from New Religions* (Bloomington: Indiana University Press, 1989), 2.

62. Lynn Davidman, "Women's Search for Family and Roots: A Jewish Religious Solution to a Modern Dilemma," in *In Gods We Trust: New Patterns of Religious Pluralism in America*, 2d ed., ed. Thomas Robbins and Dick Anthony (New Brunswick, N.J.: Transaction Books, 1990), 405.

63. Kristina interview.

64. Susan B. Kaiser, *The Social Psychology of Clothing: Symbolic Appearances in Context*, 2d ed. (New York: Macmillan, 1990), 89.

65. Rebecca interview.

66. Dana Crowley Jack, *Silencing the Self* (New York: Routledge, 1992), 146.

67. Although no studies have been done on conservative Mennonites who leave their church communities, a related study of the Amish suggests that more men than women leave, as do more singles than married persons. (Both the women in my study who left were single.) See Thomas J. Meyers, "The Old Order Amish: To Remain in the Faith or to Leave," *Mennonite Quarterly Review* 68 (July 1994): 378–95.

68. Rebecca interview.

69. This is similar to Christel Manning's study of conservative Christian or Orthodox Jewish women, who were attracted to these faith traditions because they provided a "system of order that made sense of their lives" and "set clear guidelines for behavior." Manning, 152.

70. Interview with Jenny, Manheim, Pa.: 10 May 1996.

71. Ellen interview.

72. Dottie interview.

4

River Brethren Breadmaking Ritual

Margaret C. Reynolds

In traditional societies, how do women and men collaborate to sustain their communities in the battle against modernity? The breadmaking ritual, performed in silence by women, is unique to the Communion practices of Old Order River Brethren. In this account, written from the perspective of a participant observer, Margaret C. Reynolds analyzes how the breadmaking ceremony permits women to occupy a central ritual role that articulates the expectation that in their role as hearthkeepers they will serve as the primary bearers of a patriarchal tradition.

Behavior reveals the patterned language of a culture. Such is the case in ritual breadmaking, a unique worship rite centered on women in the Old Order River Brethren culture, encompassing foodways, using female images, and forming traditional female roles crucial to the cohesion of the community. On several occasions I witnessed this women's ritual that encodes the group's power relationships based on gender roles. In this exceptional ritual, River Brethren sisters who perform breadmaking learn far more than the patterned move-

A River Brethren deacon and his daughter. (Photographs in this chapter are courtesy of Louis Reynolds.)

ments of this ritual kitchen task. In breadmaking women learn their "place" in the social structure.

Old Order River Brethren refer to breadmaking in native terms as "preparation." It is a high point in the preparatory service for the most sacred of Old Order River Brethren rituals, love feast Communion.[1] Within the frame of the morning preparatory service, women mix, knead, and bake bread for evening Communion. Ordinarily a typical Sunday morning "experience meeting," as it is called, consists of singing, reading Scripture, prayer, and about an hour of men's and women's solo testimony, followed by about an hour of preaching on scriptural texts by five or six of the elders and ministers.[2] Breadmaking is different from the experience meeting because it is structured in two main parts: the breadmaking ritual, in which women prepare Communion bread while men preach, followed by a brief testimony period for women and men and about an hour of men's sermon discourse centered on headship, the women's prayer covering, and scriptural obedience.

Gender and women's roles are important issues in this essay. As a woman and an outsider, I was unconvinced by the one-dimensional image portrayed of women in plain groups. It was apparent from the literature on sectarian Old Order groups that scholars perpetuated stereotypes of women in plain society by devoting little space or thought to the symbolic and social significance plain women have in the construction of community.[3] I wanted to find out how River Brethren women met the needs of the community in practices that go deeper than the traditional roles of wives, mothers, and foodgivers.

Consequently I focused on questions about this apparent paradox, in which men in this particular culture assigned religious authority in breadmaking to women, who occupy a subordinate status in the culture. How does a small group with beliefs that run counter to those of surrounding groups preserve itself? What are the trade-offs between women and men who balance women's religious status? (Here I refer to women's power to integrate or disintegrate the community through symbolic ritual behavior.) What are the social restraints on women and the traditions that resolve this potential conflict?

Here I describe the patterned behavior of women creating ethnic identity by formalizing the ritual. First I explore the organization of space as an encoding of transition and liminality for women and as the temporal shift from sacred to profane space. Second, I analyze the social uses of breadmaking as a symbolic process by which women assent to their subordinate role to the community by remaining voiceless. Third, I interpret breadmaking as a source of feminine alliances and a channel for women to assert their power as potential agents of social change. Finally, I examine the relation of invented tradition to social stability.[4]

SPATIAL SETTING AND PERFORMERS

I observed spring and fall breadmaking events over a two-year period to record folkways, rituals, and beliefs.[5] I have been a participant observer at Brethren rituals and services. I tape-recorded personal interviews and sermon discourse and recorded notes on my own observations.

In September 1994 I attended a love feast at Andrew Hess's barn in West Hempfield Township, Lancaster County, Pennsylvania.[6] The deacon's wife courteously directed me to a chair near the rear of the threshing floor, close to the women's section where breadmaking tables were set up. She suggested that I could better observe the women and the ritual there. In other meetings I attended I was also seated in the center threshing area, just behind the younger, unbaptized women.

At the beginning of breadmaking ceremony, the men organized their seats in long rows facing the women's section. The brethren assembled long board trestle tables in the men's area with wooden folding chairs along the walls facing them in preparation for evening foot washing and Communion. Women sat along the open frame walls of the haymow, facing their tables, which served as a work area for making Communion bread. The wall framing behind the women was hung with plastic tarpaulins to conceal an area where women nursed and changed their babies, for women's modesty is a special virtue. The arrangement of women and men in the worship setting reveals something about the different ways they conceive of themselves in the gathered community. The rectilinear arrangement of elders facing the congregation connotes order, control, and hierarchy in Old Order River Brethren culture. Both fall and spring settings make use of linear rows and rectilinear seating groupings, which contrast sharply with the circular or elliptical configuration that women form as they gather around the tables to knead the bread. The closed ellipse of these feminine performers symbolizes wholeness and cohesion. This configuration among women working the bread reinforces the image of unity under obedience to the group, and as Mary Tew Douglas points out, "wholeness, [and] unity, . . . signify completeness in a social context," an equality among women in performance.[7]

Facing the forebay of the church, one sees the men's section with the Communion trestle. The far area is a liminal area for guests and visitors, women with babies, young girls, and unmarried women.

The use of space is highly structured and gender linked. Interior enclosed space in the barn is symbolic for Old Order River Brethren, and they divide interior space into gendered areas. They conceive of these spatial divisions as ritual and nonritual areas. Their worship structures have sacred and profane dimensions, and the congregation knows that sacred areas are divided into where men and women may sit.[8] Women do not trespass into the men's space in a ritual setting, nor do men venture into the women's breadmaking space.

The center section in the threshing area of the barn is particularly noteworthy, for it is a liminal area given over to the nonbaptized: outsiders, visitors, adolescent girls, small children, and infants.[9] By inclusion in this ungendered area, visitors, nonbaptized persons, young girls, and female children of all ages are beings without ritual gender or status. They are ritually ungendered, spiritually neither male nor female, nor are they adults in the sense of being baptized, "spiritually complete" beings.

Spatial boundaries in barn settings are definite and clearly divided for

The women's area with work table, chairs, and the Communion table at the far end. The tarps are hung to provide privacy for nursing mothers and personal care.

men and women except for this area in the threshing bay. Men and women visitors, being nonpersons ritually, may sit together, unlike the members of the group, who are segregated by sex. Young boys and un-baptized adolescent boys sit with the men rather than in the central threshing area. Even in various stages of toddlerhood to late adolescence, male children are in the men's section, while female children are in the liminal center section of the barn threshing floor. This seems to indicate that even before baptism, a special status is accorded to young boys by al-lowing them to sit in the men's section.

The community regards unbaptized women as liminal beings without ritual status. Through baptism, as a rite of passage, the woman is ritually engendered as a full social being.[10] As the woman was regarded as a non-person before baptism, she is accorded status as an adult female by be-coming baptized. She is now ready to assume a legitimate adult role as a sister, a performer in breadmaking. Thus the central threshing area may serve as a presexual, liminal space occupied by toddlers, young girls, and unmarried young women.

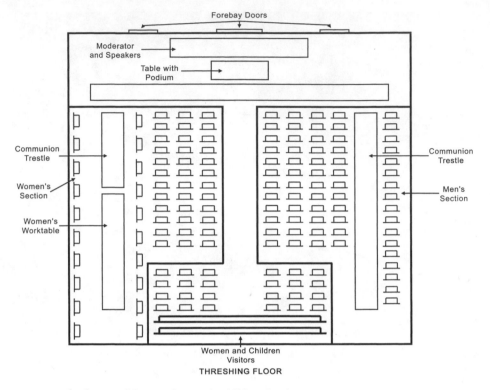

The design of the ritual space for fall breadmaking.

When women perform breadmaking in both fall and spring settings, women's space is sacred. Their ritual action sanctifies the space in which they perform. Their space is subjective, for when the ritual concludes, women rearrange their chairs to face the forebay, so that the space that but a moment before was sanctified by ritual action becomes, as Heilman observes, "ritually unattended . . . in the space but no longer really a part of what is going on in the space."[11] Indeed, this subjective space again becomes sacred in the evening love feast when the same segregated spatial structure is restored for the subservient ritual of foot washing and Holy Communion.

Sanctified space controls women's access to and movement in the area during ritual. It also controls seating arrangements. Women begin the service seated, facing their worktables. When the service commences, they are already sitting with those they feel closest to, either relatives or friends, and latecomers must find a place on the sidelines until the ritual begins and they may enter the ritual circle. The use of this space for breadmaking renders the space sanctified during the ceremony. Women shift their chairs to face the forebay when the men begin the preaching portion of the preparatory service. The men's section becomes sanctified only during the evening love feast, when, by the enactment of the men's rituals of impurity and purity, foot washing and Communion, their space is ritually consecrated. Foot washing is only for the baptized. Women wash women's feet, while men perform foot washing on the men in their section. While the congregation kneels facing the chairs, the deacons lead the opening prayer, concluding with the Lord's Prayer and a hymn. Men key the beginning of the women's performance by this impromptu portion of the traditional, formulaic two-part prayer: "As we are now coming upon the service concerning the making of the bread, Lord, we ask that you look down upon us as we perform this sacred part of the service. . . . We pray for the sisters as they now prepare this bread, Lord . . . as the sisters prepare and make the bread we will hear some brethren speak forth from the Word and share thoughts that would pertain to the preparation, breadmaking, and to the love feast service."[12] Immediately after the Lord's Prayer, women quickly rise and gather around the table to begin their patterned action.

In ritual, wives derive their spiritual leadership through their husbands' elite status as authority figures to the congregation. The senior deacon's wife takes a leadership position. She grounds the ritual in the preparation and mixing of dough. The other sisters in the hierarchy are wives of bishops, deacons, and ministers. They assist in the chores of rolling the dough and shaping it on baking trays. They score the dough into strips so that each sister can participate by pricking it with the fork. In orchestrating the breadmaking ritual, these wives of the male "elite" mirror their husbands' hierarchical status. They attain additional status through senior ritual experience and by mentoring younger women to whom they pass the skills of directing the ritual. Despite this limited women's hierarchy, all sisters have an essentially equal role in kneading, passing, and scoring the dough. The sisters themselves express this idea. Sister Anna declared that "anyone that is there [at the breadmaking service] is to be included . . . that every sister has a piece [of dough]. It's important to be in one mind . . . and fellowship and we feel that we should love one another, that we're concerned and help each other. [Breadmaking] is all our own, our work, we all had our part in it."[13]

Communion Bread

Needed Ingredients:
15 c. of unbleached flour   3 c. of milk (raw)
3 c. of unsalted butter (room temperature)

Mix Flour and butter until crumbly. Mix in Milk slowly, working with hands until well blended and smooth. May not need to use all the milk, depending on the temperature or the way the cups of flour are measured. Divide into four parts and roll directly onto ungreased cookie sheets slowly to prevent tearing the dough (1/4-inch thick). Mark into strips with a ruler. Perforate each strip from end to end with a fork, making sure to touch the cookie sheet to prevent bubbles when baking. This will make enough for 250 members. Bake at 350 to 375 degrees for 30 to 45 minutes.

Emma Sauder

This is the recipe for the Communion bread served at the love feast. (From *River Brethren Recipes*, published by Sonlight River Brethren School.)

Since the sisters remain silent throughout the ritual, the senior deacon's wife communicates with nonverbal signals to indicate when sisters must pass the dough. While the sisters perform the silent ritual in patterned movement, their men are situated so that they watch the women performing. Elders frame the women's ritual in turn by preaching didactic messages concerning headship and the purity of women's veiling.

Sister Sara prepares the ritual by arranging baking utensils on the tables and organizing the setting. She mixes the dough and subsequently makes sure it is properly baked in the host family's kitchen oven. Since purity is an issue in breadmaking, before the ritual the sisters wash their hands. During passing and kneading, the senior deacon's wife keeps count of the sisters to see that every woman handles each lump of dough.

The deacon's wife choreographs the ritual by tearing her prepared dough into small rounded pieces about three inches in diameter. She places them on a metal baking sheet in preparation for the opening prayer. After the congregation kneels for prayer, the women quickly and silently surround the tables and begin passing small pieces of dough to the sisters at the far end of the table.

Each sister accepts her piece of Communion dough and silently begins to knead it. At a signal from Sister Sara, each one passes the lump of kneaded dough to the sister on her right. They resume kneading. The process of passing and kneading is repeated as many times as there are sisters, so that each piece of dough is handled and kneaded equally by all sisters participating in the ritual.

The sister who formerly performed this ceremonial task noted that her predecessor "laid down a toothpick for every time it [bread] was passed." She declared, "Every time [the bread passed] she [the deacon's wife] laid down a toothpick to count. So that she knew how many times it passed, as many times as there were sisters."[14] The deacon's wife was careful to include each sister in the tradition of enacting unity in ritual. Using a metaphor that men commonly employed in sermon discourse, Sister Anna relates this sense of oneness: "Wheat—we don't know where it comes from . . . once it's together, there's no way you can take it apart. Like the sisters each working—after they're all together, having one lump of dough, there's no way you can take out the individual parts. That signifies unity. Nobody is better than anyone else, and we all have a part. It takes everybody. The refining that we go through spiritually . . . [makes us] pliable in God's hands."[15]

After all the women silently knead each of the individual pieces of dough during about a twenty-minute period, they place each piece on a tray that is passed down the center of the table, combining the dough into one large lump as it is passed. When they have all combined their small lumps of dough, each in turn comes to the head of the table and kneads the single large lump. Again, nonverbal signals from the senior deacon's wife—a nod, a beckoning motion—cue each woman to come forward to knead the large mass of dough. Using a "stick" resembling a straightedge, the deacon's wife then separates the dough into four equal portions, placing each quarter of the large lump on a baking sheet. Paired women shape the dough into a large rectangle on each pan, one sister holding the pan, the other rolling the dough. After the dough is shaped, these sisters score it horizontally with four wooden staves, marking it into strips about two inches wide. Sharing this task, every sister then chooses a single strip of rolled and flattened dough and scores it up one side and down the other with a fork, piercing through to the pan.

Women's distinctive language in ritual is exclusively gestural. The senior deacon's wife gives the nonverbal signals that cue the women to ac-

Communion bread to be used during the love feast ritual of the Old Order River Brethren. Piercing the bread, which represents the wounds of Christ, is ritualistically performed by all the sisters.

tion in this ritual. The sisters' physical actions of kneading and passing the dough use bodily motion to communicate with the community. Women's silent language embodies the character of their inner being, the folk processes that preserve and defend their cultural values and their religious views.[16] Breadmaking is a vehicle for transmitting the culture, and women serve as its tradition bearers. Sisters stand silent around their worktable with heads inclined. This gesture bespeaks humility and communicates submission to the "family" of watching men and community members. In ritual action, the women's very persons symbolize the values this society holds essential to their nonassimilation. By drawing themselves into postures of humility around the tables, these women give bodily form to the symbols they represent.[17]

Analogies in men's sermons, used as object lessons, instruct the congregation in living the holy life. Men's sermon rhetoric stresses two dominant themes: purity and obedience. "Brokenness," "being yielded," and "refining" are metaphors for obedience and "working" by God, and leaven is a symbol of impurity and sinfulness.[18]

Men's and women's narratives frequently refer to difficulties experienced in preparing the bread. The narrative referent, dough texture, is different for each breadmaking. For these women and men, bread functions metaphorically as a test of faith for the participants. Overcoming obstacles in preparing the bread for Communion is a gendered metaphor for life's trials and a testing of sisters' faith. The dough texture, either "sticky" (too pliable) or "brittle" (easily broken), is a Brethren metaphor for obedience. "Brokenness" is a proper attitude in the rigor of Brethren spiritual life. Therefore Brethren frequently refer to the softness or brittleness of the bread in sermons. The symbolism is variable, depending on the breadmaking experience and the dough texture itself. In the sisters' narratives, the bread takes on the characteristics of a living entity:

> Each breadmaking is different. One time we had [bread dough] so dry . . . it just took a lot of work to get it to go into one bowl. It didn't want to go into one bowl. . . . The last time it was so wet, and how did Martha word that? She said it was sticky, but "that's what I want to do, I want to stick to the Lord." I just needed that, because someone had suggested we add flour to it. And I said, "No, I just think if each of us pray, it's just not going to stick to the rolling pin." And it didn't. It didn't stick to our hand. And like, it came off of my hand. Although it was wetter than I've ever worked bread. And when [the dough] was harder, sometimes when the sisters worked it, it would get softer. The [resulting] texture was brittle. And so we're just all holding our breath. And I'm just saying, "It's the Lord trying to tell us this is how we are. We're all so brittle that we just . . . fall apart [without the Lord]."[19]

Men watch the sisters' mute performance and listen to the exhortation of the preaching brother. A larger framework of men's prayer, preaching, and singing encloses the sisters' silent ritual of breadmaking. Preachers' sermons focus on the women's role, and relationships between women and men outlined in the traditional role of headship in the life of this community. Sermon themes concern Paul's teachings on the husband as the head of the wife. Sermon discourse emphasizes the submissive wife as the keystone that supports the patriarchal framework.

Men in the audience physically signal their attentiveness to women's performance by turning their chairs toward the breadmaking ceremony. Men also cue the conclusion of the breadmaking ritual and the beginning of the headship sermon by rearranging their seats to face the forebay. The moderator keys this change in focus: "We'll take a break now as we turn our chairs around to face the front, and we're going to now listen to the prophetic importance of Jesus' sufferings."

Marking the conclusion of ritual action, women gather the pans of unleavened bread to bake in the oven. They collectively finish the kitchen tasks of cleaning the tables and gathering the utensils. Accordingly, the men rise and turn their chairs toward the speaker's table. This motion signals the conclusion of the women's part in the ritual. Where a moment before men focused on the women working in ritual union, they now refocus on the front, forebay end of the barn where the elders resume the usual order of service.

BREADMAKING: INVENTED IDENTITY AND ETHNICITY

Breadmaking had been an informal part of love feast weekend for two centuries before it became a formal women's ritual about 1980. In the early 1980s, just over a decade after the merging of the Strickler-Keller-Musser groups of the Old Order River Brethren, the group decided to include making Communion bread as a formal part of the service held Saturday mornings as preparation for evening love feast.[20] It was now a formal ritual with its focus on women, removed from the intimacy of the kitchen and situated within the preparation service for Communion, which is much more public.

A member speculates that the ritual ceremony was rescheduled for Saturday morning examination service for the convenience of members who traveled from Iowa, Ohio, and Franklin County, Pennsylvania.[21] But the changes occasioned in redefining the ritual go beyond mere convenience for traveling members. The reasons for changing this informal folk ritual to a formal ritual may be beyond the consciousness of the group, for it occasioned subtle but profound transformations in the dynamic interaction of women and men in structured ritual.

Breadmaking as a formal ritual has a brief history—only about twenty years. Alide Cagidemetro suggests in her concept of "invented identity" that the past must be included in the present examination of identity. Examining breadmaking today, one cannot divorce it from its historical past: "No contemporaneity can be written about or understood without recognition of the process that formed it in the past and is still active in the present."[22]

This link between past and present in analyzing the ritual is essential in understanding the social uses of breadmaking. In its history, breadmaking has served the ongoing function of unifying the group and keeping it together. One may question why an informal folk ritual traditionally performed in a farmhouse kitchen became ritualized within the context of the male-directed preparation or "examination" service for love feast Communion. As a result of transforming the ritual to a formal, structured preparatory service, participation in the ritual was now extended to all baptized women, married or unmarried, instead of the few whose husbands happened to be preparing the barn for love feast services. This change required baptized women to organize and orchestrate the ceremony so that it became restricted to patterned and coordinated movements divided into three essential motions within a given time frame: kneading singly and communally; rolling and cutting the dough (which now necessitated a limited women's hierarchy to perform these duties); and communal piercing of the dough before it was sent to be baked. Therefore breadmaking became a timed, spatially organized ritual of movement and action, tended and supervised by women in a matriarchal leadership role, accompanied most significantly by gesture and by absence of speech, an unprecedented cultural change situated in women's ritual silence. By framing women's silence with men's sermon rhetoric on the women's head covering, men ritually reduced any ambiguity of women's status in the society by clearly pointing out women's subordination to men in their society.

Why such an abrupt and stunning change in the 1980s, converting folk custom to folk religious ritual? In her discussion of purity and impurity in nonliterate cultures, Mary Tew Douglas points out that although rituals seem timeless and unchanging, there is reason to believe that they are subject to change.[23] Before the re-creation of breadmaking, River Brethren women met in the kitchen of the host family and "shared together" in the informal experience of making Communion bread and preparing food for the following day's love feast service. In the intimacy of this kitchen setting, women voiced aloud, in spoken testimony, their spiritual experience with the elements of Communion and their faith. Women talked about the emblems of Communion, the bread and wine, and the men said a "few words of exhortation."[24]

Old Order River Brethren have intensified their sense of belonging together by formalizing women's breadmaking. Ethnicity is a form of collective identity and group solidarity. Kathleen Neils Conzen argues that people have an essential need for belonging based on shared ancestry and culture.[25] Thus ethnic groups like Old Order River Brethren, having a shared history and ancestry, may "create" a tradition such as breadmaking to reinforce their ethnicity, as a shield against the enveloping Anglo "ethnoculture." Renegotiation of identity, such as the transformation from making bread in a housewife's kitchen to the formalization of ritual breadmaking, illustrates the extraordinary effort of Old Order River Brethren to accommodate changes yet keep mainstream American culture at arm's length.

What might an invented feminine tradition such as breadmaking signify for this group? For the Old Order River Brethren, breadmaking is looking back to what is meaningful in River Brethren women's tradition to form a new marker of ethnicity, helping to accommodate social changes into the group's world-denying stance. Redefining this kitchen task as a formal ritual provides an invented identity, a vehicle for change in the ethnic group, that allowed it to adapt to changes in core values in the host society. The formalization of this egalitarian women's ritual characterized by sisterhood and spiritual equality within an ordered hierarchical masculine culture grants an acceptable means for Old Order River Brethren women and men to cooperate in resisting the pressures of feminism from the host society. Women who see themselves as sisters in ritual equality perform a cultural trade-off with men who view them as wives and mothers. In addition, the ritual creates a legitimate ethnic identity in breadmaking that sets River Brethren apart from other Old Order groups and establishes them in opposition to modernity, with its pressures of feminism and its array of choices, materialism, and secularism.

As ethnic "others" in American society, Old Order River Brethren also invent ethnicity in this women's ritual to define their group in terms of what they are and are not.[26] In changing the folk ritual to ceremonial women's silence and expressing women's authority structures and egalitarianism through patterned movement, Old Order River Brethren changed the uses to which these people have put cultural rituals and symbols.[27] The ritual empowers women to know that they hold the key to group survival in the present—that they do not merely make the bread but, by accepting the subordinate role in breadmaking's symbolic behavior, publicly reassure the community that they will continue to enact traditional feminine roles. What once was an informal gathering for food preparation and making bread now has a broader purpose: to co-opt women in a ritual that affirms group ethnicity, separation, and world denial, in ritual symbolism that reaffirms women's subordinate role. In the intersection of gender with ethnicity in breadmaking, Old Order River Brethren women are the instruments of change, accommodation, and resistance to the host society as they create ritual, symbolic, and ethnic boundaries between themselves and other Old Order ethnic groups and between Old Order River Brethren and the host culture.

The Brethren's fashioning a formal ritual implies a threatening force from the host culture, since formalization and change in ritual are rare. Asked whether the women's movement threatens the Old Order River Brethren, the unofficial spokesman for the group admits that "women's lib" does pose a threat to the group.[28] Reasons for this response of the Old Order River Brethren are embedded in profound social change in the dominant culture. They perceive the women's movement as a threat to core values of the group, for Old Order River Brethren religion is based on the subordination of women in authoritarian culture. Mary Tew Douglas states that "ritual recognizes the potency of disorder."[29] If one views, as Old Order River Brethren do, the threat of the array of women's choices in the dominant culture as a source of extreme disorder, then transforming making bread into breadmaking as a woman's silent ritual is a way to reaffirm women's subordination in the River Brethren social order. Breadmaking as an invented tradition meets social and cultural needs of the group. Douglas points out that cultural themes are expressed by rites of bodily "manipulation," for example, the patterned movement in breadmaking. Thus the breadmaking ritual enacts the form of River Brethren social relations, and River Brethren women and their watching men "know their own society through the visible expression of the symbolic medium of the physical body."[30]

FEMININE ALLIANCES

Women's discourse about breadmaking illustrates their lack of assertiveness and their self-abnegation. These are core values for women in Old Order River Brethren culture. Women's self-examinations reveal these values: Sister Emily evaluates herself in the leadership position of senior deacon's wife:

> I'm not quite sure why I have the responsibilities I do, because I'm a better follower than I am a leader. . . . [In ritual] you're standing up in front of everybody, which is not my favorite thing. I think some people live or thrive on that type of thing, but not me. . . . Oh, I'd be so glad if someone else would just tell me what to do in some situations. You know, you'd just be so glad if someone else would tell you what to do, because then that would be all your responsibility is, just do it. I'd rather not make any of them [decisions], because then I'm responsible for them once I make them.[31]

So self-effacing are these women that one sister refers to the breadmaking ritual as "stealing time from [the men and from] testimony and speaking on [the covering in breadmaking]." Emily voices the anxiety she felt as the former leader of the ritual:

> Well, the first time I did the ritual, I never watched the clock when we made bread. There's been a couple of times Daniel [the minister and her husband] said to me, you know, please be done by ten. And all of a sudden you know, we had to make sure that it [the breadmaking paraphernalia] was out of there and the sisters were in their places for the worship. We had to pass the bread quicker, I believe.[32]

Several sisters admit anxiety in performing the ritual. They fear committing a blunder in performance, thus calling attention to themselves. Ritual goals are centered not in pride and self-assertiveness but in the implicit symbolic messages of self-effacement and humility that these women enact in this kitchen task. Individual sisters neither call attention to themselves nor focus on individual performance. In their use of posture and gesture and ritual patterned movement, they embody collective images of submission and humility.

Women compensate for these images of self-abnegation by forming alliances along intergenerational lines and within their own age-groups. The affection they voice for each other evinces a network that bonds them in a women's culture within the larger community. Characteristically, women's and men's views of ritual roles do not converge. Women see themselves as "sisters," but in sermon rhetoric men conceptualize women in maternal images. Separate apprehensions of breadmaking in this culture are based on women's and men's differing worldviews. These worldviews are based on their gender roles and on preserving order. Sisters see their breadmaking role as solely inclusive of women. They perceive themselves as a community, a sisterhood, a support network within a controlling patriarchal frame, governed by a God personally involved with each individual. Sister Anna relates the breadmaking metaphor to the sisterhood and God's role in each sister's life: "We're all one lump. We want to be one lump in God's hands . . . it's all our own work, . . . we [sisters] all had our part in it. . . . [We are] one body. I do think of it when I have that piece of bread in my hand, and I think of how I can handle that any way I want to handle it. . . . It just is in your hands and you can do as you want to it. And that's the way I think our lives should be. That God could work with us like that."[33]

Men view women in ritual as metaphorical mothers and wives. These distinctions are critical to Brethren cultural definitions of femininity. There are no analogous distinctions among Brethren men that are critical for defining their own masculinity.[34] This exclusively female ritual experience celebrating women's traditional domestic roles is absent in men's ritual experience. Men perceive women in subordinate, affinal kinship categories, as wives and mothers. Female alliances support men's religious-maternal structures, and this is particularly true for sisters who embody the mother-grandmother image in relating to one another.[35] Age and gender-linked alliances in ritual performance transfer the tradition intergenerationally. As a young novice, Sister Emily notes that older, experienced women mentored her and passed on their techniques in orchestrating ritual performance. It is noteworthy that men nonetheless validate this religious ritual exclusively for women that ennobles women in the sacred realm, despite gender asymmetry in the culture.

In contrast to men's ordered view of women as mothers and wives, women invoke sister images to describe their relationships in ritual.

Emily describes the oneness of sisters' devotion and her trepidation at leading them in ritual: "All these are my sisters, and this overwhelming responsibility of having so many sisters. . . . Each sister has a responsibility, but it's also a blessing."[36] Sister Martha notes these relationships connected to the ritual: "Each of us has our own portion of it [the dough, the ritual], and so I'm passing . . . to my sisters, [which] signifies to me that if there's anything [impure] in my life, it's probably going to affect my sisters. What I may fail to do, the sister next to me will do [in breadmaking and in life]. When it's all together [the dough], that shows you we're one . . . because you can't take it apart and say, "Now I did that." So we all have our part, but nobody can say that mine's better or say "That's what I did."[37] Public as it is, the ritual is yet an intense, private feminine experience. The intimacy engendered by this egalitarian ritual interaction among women in breadmaking and Communion creates cohesion, a feeling of sisterhood. Sister Martha describes this feeling: "It's always beautiful when you pass the bread to your sisters . . . it's just so meaningful and special that you can't talk about it."[38]

When I asked her to explain why breadmaking is a woman's devotion, Sister Martha said, "Traditionally the women always make the bread." She views the ritual primarily as a woman's event. Sister Anna describes breadmaking as "mainly a woman's task . . . because that's what a woman does, making food."[39] In making sacred food, traditional roles of woman as foodgiver conjoin with woman's maternal role as nurturer in the cultural sphere. The sisters in religious ritual provide "food" to "mother" their "family," the community. A sister's individual self is subsumed in the collective, in the feminine will and purpose of ritual that nurtures cohesion, but ultimately in the masculine will to perpetuate the patriarchal community.

Reintegration and Social Change

Women represent a final symbol of utmost importance in integrating their community: the image of woman as emotional leaven in Old Order River Brethren culture. Although in native terms leaven is seen as an impurity, in this context leaven is the potential for good in restoring and revitalizing the community. Sister Emily voices this in her description of how making bread is a metaphor for renewal in her life: "Every now and then you might work the bread one way and another way. . . . Yes, this could relate to such a circumstance in my life, and you think of natural things [women refer to their feminine domestic duties and culturally assigned roles as 'natural things'] relating unto spiritual things. You can relate [breadmaking] to a spiritual idea. So this is how the Lord is teaching me, and it doesn't matter which way I move this bread, I have to . . . make it good bread, and make it match my own life, too."[40]

It is women's collective sanctioning of their own sacrificial image that acts as the ferment of emotional leaven and imparts renewed life to the community. As potential agents of change in reintegrating the group, Old Order River Brethren women are returned to the margins of the group at the conclusion of the breadmaking ritual. Were these Old Order women to reject the actual and symbolic roles they play within both ritual and community, they would be a fearful source of disintegration. Women and men resolve this fear through the public ritual of breadmaking, in which men control the most powerful element of subversion, women's speech. Men appropriate control of women's verbal communication in breadmaking, and women accept this limitation of their religious status. By assuming religious and social authority over women, men encourage women to sustain orthodoxy. Women willingly acquiesce to the order of a patriarchal society by remaining silent. Their potential to threaten social order through the transformative powers of speech and teaching in the church is effectively muted in ritual. The River Brethren maintain the status quo with the help of women, by framing women's silence within men's sermon exhortations. This ritual restraint symbolizes women's and men's "place" in their culture.

Thus men in this traditionalist group depend on women to defend the culture. What appears to be a departure from the authoritarian tradition leads to a redefinition of gender roles in this sectarian culture. Although men preempt leadership roles in Old Order River Brethren society, it is women who have the literal power to make or break the group by accepting or rejecting social restraints and sustaining or discarding traditional customs and gender roles that allow this culture to persist in separation from the world. Women collaborate with men to keep order in the domestic sphere and in society. It is men who summon women from the domestic sphere, indeed, who appropriate the domestic sphere as the arena where the battle against modern American culture and assimilation is fought. Paradoxically, this is the source of River Brethren women's religious power: for a limited time, in this women's devotion, sisters create an egalitarian social structure with women at the center to preserve and affirm men's hierarchical social order. Breadmaking is an extension of the household into the community, a form of "social hearthkeeping." Symbolic of foodgivers who provide nourishment for their families, these women performing a ritual "kitchen task" nourish cohesion in the larger family of community. Sisters "keep house" by reinforcing men's authoritarian social structure in ritual by symbolic enactment of a women's humble kitchen task.

As transmitters of a "family" (community) tradition, women carry a heavy burden. Their ritual roles support cyclical reordering and reintegration of the Brethren to strict scriptural obedience, cultural tradition, and tribal feeling. Breadmaking ritual is a symbol of the kind of status revealed by women in this thrice-yearly performance. It is a means of teaching women their power and their "place" as "mothers" and hearthkeepers of the community.

The ritual also may obscure the realities of women's powerlessness. Breadmaking teaches women the limits of their power in willing submission to men and the community.[41] As a culture bearer, the individual woman enacts her symbolic role of submission silently. In surrendering her voice in the domestic and spiritual realm, she reassures the community that she will continue to affirm traditional values and ensure the continuance of her culture.

NOTES

1. Old Order River Brethren are a small pietistic Anabaptist religious group originating within the Pennsylvania German culture region of the northwestern corner of Lancaster County, Pennsylvania. They emerged in the eighteenth century from the Mennonites and incorporated the ordinances of the Church of the Brethren (Dunkers) and the United Brethren in Christ. Numbering about 350 members, the River Brethren, as they refer to themselves, are one of the least known of the several "plain" groups, which include the Amish, Mennonite, and Brethren Old Orders. See Stephen E. Scott, "The Old Order River Brethren," *Pennsylvania Mennonite Heritage* 1 (July 1978): 13–22, and Beulah S. Hostetler, "An Old Order River Brethren Love Feast," *Pennsylvania Folklife* 24 (winter 1974–75): 8–20, for a thorough treatment of River Brethren life and practice.

2. Testimony and preaching follow the breadmaking. Women and men rise,

line a hymn that has personal significance, and share individual testimony with the congregation. For women this testimony is affective and quietly emotional. Their testimony expresses gratitude to God, recounts blessings, often demonstrates self-effacement and feelings of unworthiness, and sometimes shares a personal experience that has spiritual meaning to the sister who narrates it. This is the sole voice women have publicly in ritual. Scriptural injunctions of Paul forbid women to teach or preach for edification; therefore women's testimonies reflect personal experience and emotion.

3. I refer here to benchmark works on the Amish by John A. Hostetler, *Amish Society*, 4th ed. (Baltimore: Johns Hopkins University Press, 1993), and Donald B. Kraybill, *The Riddle of Amish Culture* (Baltimore: Johns Hopkins University Press, 1989), and to works on the Mennonites by Calvin W. Redekop, *Mennonite Society* (Baltimore: Johns Hopkins University Press, 1989), and Redekop, *The Old Colony Mennonites: Dilemmas of Ethnic Minority Life* (Baltimore: Johns Hopkins University Press, 1969). These studies devote little space to women's roles and pay even less attention to the part women play in maintaining plain culture and society. These landmark works, long viewed by scholars as models for the study of plain groups, are written by men who are insiders to the patriarchal Anabaptist groups they write about. This orientation may account for the lack of insights in their works concerning women and the vital roles they silently assume for the good of their communities.

4. Several sources of theoretical literature underlie my description of women's behavior and creation of ethnic identity. Kathleen Neils Conzen et al., "The Invention of Ethnicity: A Perspective from the USA," *Journal of American Ethnic History* 12 (fall 1992): 3–41, discusses created ethnicity as a construct to bind groups. Samuel C. Heilman, *Synagogue Life: A Study in Symbolic Interaction* (Chicago: University of Chicago Press, 1976), informs my interpretation of spatial order and its connection to social organization. I draw on Marcia K. Hermansen, "Two-Way Acculturation: Muslim Women in America between Individual Choice (Liminality) and Community Affiliation (Communitas)," in *The Muslims of America*, ed. Yvonne Yazbeck Haddad (New York: Oxford University Press, 1991), 188–201, for the connections between liminality and community. Elaine J. Lawless, *Handmaidens of the Lord: Pentecostal Women Preachers and Traditional Religion* (Philadelphia: University of Pennsylvania Press, 1988), provides an excellent source for the study of female bonding and women's support of cultural subordination to maintain the fundamentalist religious community.

5. Love feast breadmaking (which is part of the River Brethren morning

preparation service for evening Holy Communion) is held in the fall and spring in Lancaster County. Members from Franklin County, Pennsylvania, and from Ohio and Iowa travel to Lancaster County for these love feasts. In May the Lancaster County and Iowa members travel to Franklin County for a love feast, the third in the calendar year. This schedule was a compromise worked out by River Brethren groups who, previously divided over issues of technology and acculturation, merged in 1977. See Margaret C. Reynolds, "Transmission of Tradition in the Old Order River Brethren: Gender Roles and Symbolic Behavior in a Plain Sect" (Ph.D. diss., Pennsylvania State University, 1996).

6. I conducted all the interviews myself, and I use pseudonyms for all informants to protect their identity.

7. Mary Tew Douglas, *Purity and Danger: An Analysis of Concepts of Pollution and Taboo* (London: Routledge and Kegan Paul, 1966), 52.

8. The terms "sacred" and "profane" refer to the subjective space Heilman discusses in *Synagogue Life.*

9. I draw on the theories of Arthur Van Gennep, *The Rites of Passage* (Chicago: University of Chicago Press, 1960), 184–89, and Victor Turner, *The Ritual Process* (Ithaca: Cornell University Press, 1977), 94–130. See also Hermansen.

10. Douglas, 96.

11. Heilman, 51.

12. Sermon tape recording, Mount Joy, Pa.: 23 March 1994.

13. Interview with Sister Anna Schubauer, Lancaster County, Pa.: 1993.

14. Interview with Sister Emily Schubauer, Lancaster, Pa.: 5 October 1993.

15. Sister Anna Schubauer interview.

16. Richard Bauman, *Folklore, Cultural Performances, and Popular Entertainments: A Communications-Centered Handbook* (New York: Oxford University Press, 1992), 29–30.

17. Ibid., 255.

18. In the Bible, leaven is considered an impurity in making bread; in the Passover meal bread must be unleavened or it is considered impure or unclean.

19. Interview with Sister Emma Schubauer, Lancaster, Pa.: 23 September 1993.

20. Earlier in the twentieth century these three groups divided from the parent group over issues of change and accommodation to modernity, especially owning cars. They put aside their differences to reunite in 1977, when it became evident that they faced extinction if they remained divided.

21. Interview with John Snyder, Lancaster County, Pa.: 17 March 1996.

22. Alide Cagidemetro, "A Plea for Fictional Historic and Old-Time 'Jewesses,'" in *The Invention of Ethnicity*, ed. Werner Sollors (New York: Oxford University Press, 1989), 14.

23. Douglas, 4.

24. Jacob Longenecker [pseud.], interview by author, Mountville, Pa.: 18 December 1995.

25. Conzen et al., 13–41.

26. Ibid., 31.

27. Ibid.

28. Stephen E. Scott, "The Old Order River Brethren," lecture delivered as part of lecture series "Minority Voices: Old Order Anabaptists in North America," Young Center for the Study of Anabaptist and Pietist Groups, Elizabethtown College, Elizabethtown, Pa., 17 March 1993.

29. Douglas, 94.

30. Ibid.

31. Sister Emily Schubauer interview.

32. Ibid.

33. Sister Anna Schubauer interview.

34. Sherry B. Ortner and Harriet Whitehead, "Introduction: Accounting for Sexual Meanings," in *Sexual Meanings: The Construction of Gender and Sexuality* (New York: Cambridge University Press, 1992), 21.

35. Lawless, 160.

36. Sister Emily Schubauer interview.

37. Interview with Sister Martha Schubauer, Lancaster County, Pa.: 23 September 1993.

38. Ibid.

39. Interview with Sisters Anna and Martha Schubauer, Lancaster County, Pa.: 26 October 1993.

40. Sister Emily Schubauer interview.

41. Robert Orsi, *The Madonna of 115th Street: Faith and Community in Italian Harlem* (New Haven: Yale University Press, 1985), 15–16.

5

The Chosen Women

The Amish and the New Deal

Katherine Jellison

How did women's work contribute to the perception of the Amish as models of stability during the American agricultural depression? Katherine Jellison analyzes records from the Bureau of Agricultural Economics to describe the centrality of Amish women's work to the economic success of Amish farms and document how government investigators idealized assumptions about strict gender divisions of labor as a recipe for stability.

*I*n 1994 cultural geographer Walter M. Kollmorgen looked back on his experiences in 1940 among the Old Order Amish of Lancaster County, Pennsylvania, and remembered what happened when the wife and mother of a local family suddenly died during threshing season. Her oldest daughter simply took her place and fed the large group of threshers the sumptuous meal they had expected. In Kollmorgen's words, "That fourteen-year-old gal had three sweets . . . three meats, three this, . . . three that, all right there. Now you find a girl like that today."[1] From the vantage point of the end of the twentieth century, Kollmorgen seemed to attribute the girl's industry and know-how to the values of a bygone era. At the time, however, Kollmorgen and other

The clean, orderly kitchen in this conservative Mennonite home was typical of those Amish and Mennonite women labored in throughout Lancaster County at the time of Kollmorgen's study. Amish woman Lydia Stoltzfus remembers, "We had an old blue range, which we bought for a little bit of money when we got married [in 1934]. It burned wood and coal. My kitchen sink was not very fancy." Photograph by Irving Rusinow, 1941. (Photograph 83-G-3/548, BAE Collection, National Archives II, College Park, Maryland.)

social scientists working for the United States Department of Agriculture's Bureau of Agricultural Economics (BAE) viewed the girl's behavior—and that of other Lancaster County Amish—as the product of a distinctive, superior rural culture that was vanishing from other regions of the United States. To these government-sponsored investigators, the Old Order Amish of Lancaster County represented the best of rural America, and Amish women—with their strong work ethic, emphasis on "family values," and respect for the land—were truly the "chosen women." In the eyes of BAE personnel, Old Order Amish women were appropriate role models for farm women throughout the nation. Members of the agency, therefore, chose to focus a portion of their investigatory efforts on the industrious Amish women of Lancaster County and their successful endeavors to preserve the family farm.

The BAE Stability-Instability Study

In 1940 Carl C. Taylor, head of the BAE's Division of Farm Population and Rural Welfare, sent a group of young social scientists, including Walter M. Kollmorgen, to investigate rural community stability in six economically, culturally, and geographically diverse locations across the United States. A chief objective of the project was to determine the impact of New Deal programs on these communities and to provide guidance for future government planning in rural America. From the beginning, Taylor and his associates envisioned the six communities as lying along a continuum from most stable to least stable, with the Old Order Amish of Lancaster County on one end and the Dust Bowl residents of Sublette, Kansas, at the other. Between these two extremes lay the communities of El Cerrito, New Mexico; Irwin, Iowa; Harmony, Georgia; and Landaff, New Hampshire. Taylor and his colleagues assumed that community stability and quality of life depended on a variety of cultural, historical, and sociopsychological factors in addition to the economic and geographical conditions that investigators typically examined in USDA studies. Taylor's "community stability-instability study," as he dubbed the project, would be more ambitious than previous investigations the BAE had undertaken and would require each young "participant observer" to conduct intensive fieldwork in his assigned community for nearly six months.[2]

Taylor and his colleagues developed a list of criteria to define community stability and instability. The stable rural community depended on a long-established economic base that had remained constant or had changed slowly over time, was isolated from outside influences and divergent cultures, practiced a system of values in which some noneconomic value dominated all others, and experienced little in- or out-migration. In contrast, the unstable rural community depended on a widely varying agricultural income, had experienced a disaster to its economic base and thus had shifted to a new means of support, had encountered disturbing cultural influences from the outside, had accepted new agricultural techniques or tools that disrupted the established class structure, and had experienced broad fluctuation in population. Given these criteria, the self-sufficient, highly religious Old Order Amish indeed seemed the very model of community stability, in direct contrast to the cash-dependent, drought-plagued residents of Sublette, Kansas.[3]

Taylor and his colleagues in the BAE viewed the Old Order Amish not only as a model of community stability but as a group of people who were living out Thomas Jefferson's agrarian ideal. In outlining his own philosophy on rural life to a colleague, Taylor clearly acknowledged his belief in the agrarian ideal when he stated that "there are inherently good traits in the rural way of life, . . . there are spiritual, cultural, esthetic, and social values which attach themselves to . . . the closer associations of family and community which are typical of the simpler rural cultures." In contrast, he noted, as a society "grows more complex, becomes more mechanical and more mercenary, it tends to lose its spiritual, cultural, esthetic, and creative nature."[4] When Taylor sent his young subordinates into the field in 1940, he was envisioning a series of studies that would ultimately demonstrate the merits of many aspects of the Amish people's belief system—their commitment to family farming, their rejection of expensive technology, and their view of farming as a superior way of life rather than as a mere business proposition. In instructing Kollmorgen how to interact with his often reluctant Amish informants, Taylor advised the young geographer, "Try to convince these Amish people that we believe that many of their characteristics are praiseworthy and that rather than pry into their individual beliefs, we are anxious to discover the good things in their whole system and reveal these good things to other people."[5]

WALTER KOLLMORGEN'S RESEARCH IN LANCASTER COUNTY

Incorporating this strategy, Kollmorgen informed his contacts among the Old Order Amish that Washington bureaucrats considered Lancaster County the "garden spot of the country," admired Amish self-sufficiency, and wanted to know the reasons for their great success as agriculturalists. Kollmorgen's appreciation for many aspects of Amish life was genuine. Having grown up in a German Lutheran farming community in Nebraska, he was sympathetic to the Amish preference for a well-ordered life on the land, safely removed from the "corrupt" confinement of the city. Kollmorgen, however, was not without his criticisms of the Amish. In particular, the young Columbia Ph.D. was troubled by their rejection of higher education; he realized, however, that the Amish considered this practice necessary to limit disruptive outside influences on their culture and community.[6] In fact, he largely attributed the high level of group cohesion among the Old Order Amish to their religiously motivated adherence to nonconformity and separation from the world. He closed his study of community stability among them with an analysis of their formula for success: "A group that has survived centuries of persecution in Europe and has so far resisted many of the onslaughts of factories, with their standardized products, and the appeals of higher education must have qualities that make for survival. Important among these qualities are a tradition of hard work, a willingness to make sacrifices for the good of others, and an enviable tradition of constructive diversified agriculture."[7]

Kollmorgen's study of the Old Order Amish achieved a positive reception both inside and outside the Amish community. Published along with the other five community studies in 1942, the report eventually went through two more printings and became the most popular publication ever produced and sold under BAE auspices.[8] Among those who wrote to BAE officials with words of praise for Kollmorgen's work were numerous members of the Anabaptist community, including the assistant director of a wartime Mennonite Civilian Public Service Camp, who reported that the Amish men under his direction considered his study to be "the best and most sensible evaluation of their sect that has ever been published. They [were] loud in their praise of the man who has done such a remarkable job in recording [the] innermost feelings of the 'Plain People' who are so often misunderstood."[9] No doubt one reason for the popularity of Kollmorgen's study among Amish readers was that their values and practices were being held up as a model for other farming communities. Even before publication of the study, Kollmorgen's Amish informants had expressed the opinion that they were appropriate models for the other communities the BAE was investigating in New Mexico, Georgia, and elsewhere and that if "the Mexicans, negroes, and other people followed the Bible, worked hard, didn't give their children too much schooling, and weren't interested in worldly things, there would be no difficulties."[10]

THE SIGNIFICANCE OF AMISH WOMEN'S WORK

Noted throughout Kollmorgen's study, however, was another key to the success of the Old Order Amish community—women's work. His emphasis on the importance of large family work units to the achievements of Amish agriculture and his acknowledgment of the significance of women's work in the garden and home demonstrated that he recognized

Baking bread was one of the important home production activities that Amish women undertook at the time of Kollmorgen's study. Photograph by Irving Rusinow, 1941. (Photograph 83-G-37556, BAE Collection, National Archives II, College Park, Maryland.)

the vital role women played as reproducers and producers within the Amish farm family. Nevertheless, in portions of his analysis he seemingly ignored his own evidence and instead bowed to conventional notions about appropriate gender hierarchies within the American family. For example, Kollmorgen stated at one point in his study of the Lancaster County Amish that the "man is distinctly the head of the household and in most cases directs the affairs of the family. Neither on the family level nor on the community level does the wife initiate or direct important activities."[11] These comments seemed to imply that women's gardening and food production efforts were not deemed "important activities" within the Amish farm family.

Such incongruous statements were not surprising, however, given the instructions Kollmorgen received from his superiors within the BAE. Since the USDA's establishment in the nineteenth century, members of its various bureaus and agencies had subscribed to a rural "separate spheres" philosophy, in which they viewed farm men strictly as agriculturalists and farm women distinctly as homemakers. Such a mind-set, even in the face of abundant evidence that farm men and women regularly crossed prescribed gender-role boundaries, often prohibited investigators from stressing the important part women actually played in the agricultural economy.[12] Kollmorgen's supervisors certainly did not emphasize women's unique concerns as farm producers when they briefed their "participant observers" before sending them into the field, although some evidence exists that there were those within the BAE who wanted greater attention not only to women's issues but to issues of race as well. One BAE bureaucrat suggested during the fieldwork stage of the project that the agency consider hiring "at least one woman and at least one Negro in order to provide materials which . . . [other] workers [were] not likely to get."[13] There is no evidence, however, that other BAE administrators ever considered following this advice, and the final community studies reflected research gathered and supervised by white males who emphasized the centrality of men's cash crop production to the success or failure of local farming operations. Working on the assumption that men's activities were paramount and noting that direct contact with women of the community would be considered morally questionable, Kollmorgen had made his primary contacts among the Amish with male religious leaders and prominent male farmers; most of his study therefore reflected the importance of men's work to the Amish success story.[14]

Nevertheless, Kollmorgen and the other young social scientists involved in the stability-instability study analyzed gender roles at least briefly in their final reports. As Kollmorgen later noted, that women were "very important in farming" was simply "taken for granted" by the BAE investigators and not given any special emphasis in their reports, although these young scholars duly documented women's activities in their published research as a matter of course. These community studies, along with other New Deal–sponsored research, clearly demonstrated the importance of women's work to the success or failure of an agricultural community, as is illustrated by a brief comparison of the "unstable" Dust Bowl community of Sublette, Kansas, and the "stable" Old Order Amish of Lancaster County.[15]

As BAE investigator Earl H. Bell found in his examination of Sublette, Kansas, residents there viewed farming largely as a money-making venture and relied on just one cash crop—winter wheat. Sublette-area families, many of whom had resided in the region only since the World War I wheat boom, found themselves at the mercy of fluctuations in the wheat market, and during the drought of the 1930s this meant they lived precariously, with few other home and farm production activities remaining to supplement their dismal income from wheat. With the exception of women in the area's small Mennonite community, which engaged in more diversified and traditional agricultural practices, female residents of Sublette did not contribute significantly to their family economies by garden and home production. The year before Bell's arrival in Sublette, one-fourth of the farms in the county had sold, traded, or used less than $250 worth of farm products. Women raised poultry on only 56.7 percent of farms in the region and tended gardens on only 13 percent. Instead, farm women spent scarce family resources to purchase dairy products, poultry, and produce at the local grocery store and frequently earned the necessary cash by holding wage-earning "town jobs" at the courthouse or in local retail establishments. And travel to these jobs required that scant cash resources be spent on gasoline and automobile maintenance.[16]

Women in Lancaster County also felt the strain of the Great Depression. One Old Order Amish woman remembered standing in the fields with her husband after the stock market crash and telling him, "Even the clouds don't look right."[17] Indeed, for residents of Lancaster County, as for most Americans, the depression affected all aspects of daily life. Farm prices were low and cash resources were scarce, but the Old Order Amish could at least fall back on a number of well-established survival strategies. For instance, Amish farm families raised most of the food they ate and also sold food in the local marketplace. As a result, in contrast to the dire situation in Sublette, Kansas, among the Lancaster County Old Order Amish annual value of farm products sold, traded, or used was $1,444 at the time of Kollmorgen's research. This figure included profits from the potatoes that women and children helped raise as a cash crop. Virtually all Old Order women also tended poultry and gardens. The average woman canned 345 quarts of fruits and vegetables a year and was responsible for raising and processing $422 worth of her family's total food supply for the year—nearly a third of all agricultural products exchanged or consumed by the typical Amish farm family. In addition, women provided numerous baked goods for their own families as well as for the market-

Eight hundred quarts of food were stored in this Amish cellar during the autumn of 1940. Photograph by Irving Rusinow, 1941. (Photograph 83-G-37532, BAE Collection, National Archives II, College Park, Maryland.)

place. One woman remembered her mother and sisters baking a hundred pies in a day and selling them for twenty-five cents apiece at the farmers' market or peddling them door to door.[18]

While Amish women's role as producers certainly aided their families, so too did their limited role as consumers. Unlike the women of Sublette, Kansas, Old Order Amish women purchased very few goods and services away from the farm. As one woman remembered the period, "We raised everything we needed on our own farm. In the garden. We made our own butter. We bought only staples at [the local store], and occasionally some candy. That's just how things were."[19] Amish women also cut family members' hair, made most of the new clothing for their family, recycled and mended old clothing, and made no investments in modern household, communication, or transportation technology. For example, one Old Order woman remembered using an "old Singer treadle sewing machine"

One way Amish women and their families survived the depression was by selling fruits, vegetables, baked goods, and other items here at the Southern Market in the city of Lancaster. One Old Order Amish woman remembers that her family "went to market" every Tuesday, Friday, and Saturday during the depression. They sold vegetables in the summer and cheese, butter, eggs, sweet potatoes, apple butter, and dressed chickens in the winter. Photograph by Irving Rusinow, 1941. (Photograph 83-G-37608, BAE Collection, National Archives II, College Park, Maryland.)

during the depression to make school clothing for her six children, including "twenty or more pairs of pants every winter."[20] Another woman frequently noted in her 1933 diary entries that she "was patching all day."[21]

Amish women's role in increasing home and farm production and limiting consumer purchases was obviously a key component of the Amish success story during the Great Depression—one that the women themselves recognized. As one Old Order woman noted in discussing her depression-era marriage, "Davie and me always worked together. I knew what was going on. I'm so thankful for that. We were very self-sufficient on this farm. One summer it was especially dry, but we didn't starve." In summarizing her work during the depression years, this particular Lancaster County woman was also characterizing the experience of many of her Amish sisters when she recalled: "I baked lots of bread. . . . We farmed potatoes and sold them for twenty-five cents a bushel. . . . I made pillow-cases, bedsheets, and tablecloths from feed bags. . . . We had a very large garden. And everything we needed was right here on the farm."[22]

Nevertheless, the important contribution of Old Order Amish women remained largely unpublicized to the larger American public. By the time Kollmorgen, Bell, and the other BAE investigators published their community studies in 1942, "Dr. Win-the-War" had replaced "Dr. New Deal." Kollmorgen himself was called away to war work and never again did any research among the Amish. Although 15,000 copies of Kollmorgen's study were eventually printed and distributed, the BAE was unable to keep up with demand for the report, particularly on college campuses and within the Anabaptist community, because additional printings were not deemed "necessary" to the war effort. The war also interrupted efforts to produce an additional volume in the stability-instability series that would have synthesized the six community studies and made clear the advantages of the Amish community's labor-intensive diversified agriculture over capital-intensive monoculture—and additionally would have reinforced the significance of Amish women's production. Wartime distractions likewise halted plans to publish an extensive volume of photographs to accompany each of the community studies.[23]

Among the images to be included in the volume on Lancaster County were photographs that documented Amish and Mennonite women's work in the kitchen, sewing room, garden, dairy barn, and farmers' market. According to one of Kollmorgen's Amish informants, these photos were "unexcelled," since the subjects were normally "camera-shy for the most part," but this visual testimony to Amish women's work remained largely unseen.[24] Hostile reaction to the BAE's praise for traditional family farming and its criticism of farming as big business also surfaced at this time among conservative members of Congress and among some other agencies within the USDA. This situation resulted in BAE budget cuts and censorship of some BAE publications and further ensured that the results of BAE research would not be widely disseminated after the war.[25]

THE MODEL AMISH WOMAN

In the years following World War II, most American women who remained on the farm followed more in the footsteps of the women of Sub-

During the depression, Old Order Amish woman Lydia Stoltzfus "baked sticky buns, bread, cakes, pies, and took [them] to the Southern Market in Lancaster." Among the many photographs that Irving Rusinow took to illustrate Kollmorgen's study was this portrait of women selling their goods at the Southern Market in March 1941. (Photograph 83-G-37609, BAE Collection, National Archives II, College Park, Maryland.)

lette, Kansas, than in those of the "chosen women" of Lancaster County, as American farming generally continued on the path toward greater specialization and capital investment and increasing numbers of American farm women began to define themselves more as consumers than as producers. Nevertheless, members of the BAE who had organized and participated in the stability-instability study remained fervent admirers of the Amish. Among those who continued to look to the Amish for guidance was senior agricultural economist O. E. Baker. Inclined, in Kollmorgen's words, to be an Anabaptist "at heart," Baker espoused a natalist philosophy, believing that successful farming required a large farm family labor force to produce agricultural products and sizable off-farm families to purchase and consume farm goods. Putting his ideals into practice, Baker married a Quaker woman and had several children, in whom he intended to instill "plain" values. After a visit to Kollmorgen while the geographer

Kollmorgen's informant Grant M. Stoltzfus told a BAE official that this portrait of his mother and aunt at their quilting showed two women who were usually very "camera-shy." Photograph by Irving Rusinow, 1941. (Photograph 83-G-37605, BAE Collection, National Archives II, College Park, Maryland.)

was conducting his fieldwork in Lancaster County, Baker decided that the Old Order Amish family would serve as a model for his own. Years later, after leaving the USDA and going to teach at the University of Maryland, Baker purchased a house at the edge of town, where he indoctrinated his family in the plain ways of Amish life. Focusing particular attention on

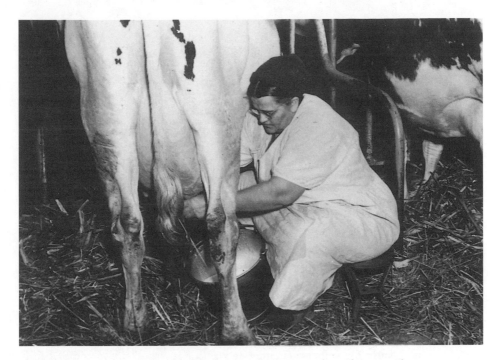

Milking was among the diverse chores that Amish women undertook to contribute to the success of Lancaster County farming. Photograph by Irving Rusinow, 1941. (Photograph 83-G-37585, BAE Collection, National Archives II, College Park, Maryland.)

one child, Baker made the girl raise chickens in the backyard and forced her to dress in simple homemade clothing, which she would discreetly exchange for more fashionable wear at school when safely out of her father's sight.[26]

The Old Order Amish women of Lancaster County obviously made a great impression on Kollmorgen, Baker, and other New Deal social scientists, particularly those involved in the stability-instability study. Unfortunately, wartime disruptions and conservative opposition prevented widespread distribution of their findings, which acknowledged—at least briefly—that women's productive and reproductive efforts were vital for the success of an agricultural community in the closing years of the Great Depression and the New Deal. In recent years scholars have rediscovered the rich community studies published by the BAE in 1942, and with careful attention to gender issues that scholars often ignored or took for granted in the 1930s and 1940s, they have publicized the importance of farm women's work to agricultural achievement during this era.[27]

With the entrance of more women into the disciplines of sociology, anthropology, and history, there have even been opportunities for female investigators to directly question the "chosen women" of Lancaster County, who readily acknowledge the importance of their work to Amish farming. For instance, when a female oral historian recently asked Lydia Stoltzfus to describe her experiences during the Great Depression, the elderly Amish woman confidently replied, "On our farm I did whatever needed to be done. I stripped tobacco. I mixed doughnuts. I papered the house. Whatever needed to be done, I did it."[28] With this testimony, Stoltzfus, the Amish insider, confirmed what the outsiders of the BAE had assumed all along: that women's labor was central to successful family farming.

NOTES

I thank Walter M. Kollmorgen, Steven D. Reschly, and Louise Stoltzfus for their assistance in the research for this chapter.

1. Walter M. Kollmorgen, interview with Katherine Jellison and Steven D. Reschly, Lawrence, Kans.: 20 March 1994.

2. Ibid.; Walter M. Kollmorgen, "Kollmorgen as a Bureaucrat," *Annals of the Association of American Geographers* 69 (March 1979): 84; "Opinions, Attitudes, and Values in Self-Sufficing and in Commercial Agriculture" (19 December 1939), and Carl C. Taylor, "My Memory of the Conceptual Development of the Community Stability-Instability Study" (28 August 1944), both in American Farm Community Study Project Files (1941–46), General Correspondence (1923–46), box 538, Records of the Bureau of Agricultural Economics, Record Group 83, National Archives II, College Park, Maryland. This collection of papers will hereafter be cited as AFCS Project Files.

3. Earl H. Bell to Carl C. Taylor (16 October 1944), AFCS Project Files. For discussion of Bell's study of Sublette, Kansas, see chapter 4 of Katherine Jellison, *Entitled to Power: Farm Women and Technology, 1913–1963* (Chapel Hill: University of North Carolina Press, 1993).

4. Carl C. Taylor to O. E. Baker (22 November 1937), O. E. Baker Folder (1936–40), General Correspondence (1923–46), box 62, Records of the Bureau of Agricultural Economics, Record Group 83, National Archives II, College Park, Maryland. This collection of papers will hereafter be cited as Baker Folder.

5. Carl C. Taylor to Walter M. Kollmorgen (8 April 1940), AFCS Project Files.

6. Kollmorgen interview.

7. Walter M. Kollmorgen, *Culture of a Contemporary Rural Community: The Old Order Amish of Lancaster County, Pennsylvania*, Rural Life Studies, vol. 4 (Washington, D.C.: Government Printing Office, 1942), 105.

8. Kollmorgen, "Kollmorgen as a Bureaucrat," 84.

9. Charles Suter to BAE (2 April 1943), AFCS Project Files.

10. Amish point of view summarized by Charles P. Loomis to Carl C. Taylor (22 April 1940), AFCS Project Files.

11. Kollmorgen, *Culture of a Contemporary Rural Community*, 78.

12. For further discussion of the USDA's separate spheres philosophy, see material throughout Jellison. For discussion of men's and women's shared labor and the transgression of strict gender-role boundaries on the family farm, see Nancy Grey Osterud, *Bonds of Community: The Lives of Farm Women in Nineteenth-Century New York* (Ithaca: Cornell University Press, 1991), and Mary Neth, *Preserving the Family Farm: Women, Community, and the Foundations of Agribusiness in the Midwest, 1900–1940* (Baltimore: Johns Hopkins University Press, 1995).

13. Conrad Taeuber to Ed Hulett, Charles P. Loomis, and John H. Provinse (5 July 1940), AFCS Project Files.

14. Kollmorgen interview.

15. Ibid.

16. See chapter 4 of Jellison. See also material in Pamela Riney-Kehrberg, *Rooted in Dust: Surviving Drought and Depression in Southwestern Kansas* (Lawrence: University Press of Kansas, 1994).

17. Anonymous Old Order Amish Woman A, interview with Louise Stoltzfus, 29 April 1995.

18. Anonymous Old Order Amish Woman B, interview with Louise Stoltzfus, 29 April 1995.

19. Lydia Stoltzfus, interview with Louise Stoltzfus, 17 April 1995.

20. Ibid.

21. Old Order Amish Woman B interview.

22. Old Order Amish Woman A interview. For further discussion of Amish women's work in this era, see Steven D. Reschly and Katherine Jellison, "Production Patterns, Consumption Strategies, and Gender Relations in Amish and Non-Amish Farm Households in Lancaster County, Pennsylvania, 1935–1936," *Agricultural History* 67 (spring 1993): 134–62. This article examines the results of a consumer survey conducted by the New Deal's Works Progress Administration.

23. Kollmorgen, "Kollmorgen as a Bureaucrat," 84; Peter H. DeVries to Charles Suter (27 April 1943), Carl C. Taylor to Charles P. Loomis (6 November 1941), Carl C. Taylor to E. W. Burgess (2 August 1944), Ralph R. Nichols to Wayne C. Neely (26 September 1944), and Conrad Taeuber to Ray E. Wakeley (22 June 1942), AFCS Project Files.

24. Grant M. Stoltzfus to Peter H. DeVries (14 September 1943), AFCS Project Files. Because members of the Old Order Amish community refused to have their pictures taken for this project, photographer Irving Rusinow apparently photographed Beachy Amish or Conservative Mennonites engaged in activities that were also typical of the Old Order Amish.

25. Kollmorgen interview. For further discussion of opposition to the BAE and its position on socioeconomic issues of the day, see material in Richard Kirkendall, *Social Scientists and Farm Politics in the Age of Roosevelt* (Columbia: University of Missouri Press, 1966). Evidence suggests that wartime budgetary concerns and staff cutbacks resulted in the elimination or reduction of some proposed BAE publications. There is also evidence that some BAE studies were altered before publication to soften or eliminate their criticism of other USDA agencies. In the case of Earl Bell's study of Sublette, Kansas, both wartime conditions and censorship of his criticism of the Agricultural Adjustment Administration resulted in major alterations of his manuscript before publication. See Kimball Young to Carl C. Taylor (29 June 1942), Kimball Young to Conrad Taeuber (2 August 1942), and Earl H. Bell to E. A. Ross (27 November 1942), AFCS Project Files. There is no evidence, however, that Kollmorgen's study of the Old Order Amish underwent such harsh censorship before its publication.

26. O. E. Baker, "Will More or Fewer People Live on the Land?" address delivered to the National Catholic Rural Life Conference, Fargo, N.D. (13 October 1936), Baker Folder; Kollmorgen interview; Kollmorgen, "Kollmorgen as a Bureaucrat," 84.

27. For modern scholarship on gender roles that incorporates material from the BAE community studies and related photographs, see Jellison, Reschly and Jellison, and Neth.

28. Lydia Stoltzfus interview.

Part 2

Creating

Gendered Community

6

Meeting around the Distaff

ANABAPTIST WOMEN IN AUGSBURG

Jeni Hiett Umble

How does a gendered analysis inform scholars' notions about the formation and spread of the Anabaptist community in sixteenth-century Europe? Jeni Hiett Umble's investigation of Augsburg court records shows that Anabaptist women came from a variety of social backgrounds, ranging from servant girls to grocers to wealthy widows. Anabaptism brought women of varying backgrounds together in small groups for Bible study and in larger groups for worship. The young, struggling community in Augsburg in 1527–28 illustrates that the religious enthusiasm of early Anabaptist women overcame social and economic boundaries.

Because her husband (who did not share her Anabaptist sympathies) was out of town, Susanna Doucher was able to host a meeting of the Augsburg Anabaptist community on Easter Sunday, April 12, 1528. Rich merchants, officials of the guilds, and prosperous craftsmen rubbed elbows with common grocers, day laborers, and servants as the congregation met to celebrate Easter. Despite Susanna's efforts to conceal the meeting by hanging blankets over her windows, the worshipers—possibly as many as two hundred—were betrayed. Soon after they had gathered, the Anabaptists received a warning that the police knew of the meeting. The ministers said that any believers who feared arrest could leave. Some heeded the warning, but eighty-eight Anabaptists were caught that day and others were subsequently arrested.

The Anabaptists were thoroughly interrogated by Konrad Peutinger, a humanist who was employed as the official city secretary.[1] Peutinger was determined to obtain full information regarding the members and activities of the congregation. After expelling the foreigners,[2] Peutinger carefully questioned each Augsburg resident. He first noted the name and occupation of each Anabaptist and then pressed for details regarding his or her baptism. His next area of interest was the number and location of all meetings attended and the names of others who were present. Finally, he asked for the names of those who gave food or lodging to other Anabaptists. A brief note at the end of the interrogations indicates that Peutinger used torture to ensure that his interrogants had not withheld any information.

The Easter meeting was the first to be hosted by Susanna Doucher, but during her interrogation she admitted she had attended several other meetings in the homes of believers and one meeting in a forest outside the city.[3] The wife of a prominent sculptor (and therefore belonging to the high-middle class), Susanna attended meetings hosted by common cobblers (Katharina and Simprecht Wiedemann), middle-class weavers (Gall and Elisabeth Vischer), a widowed grocer (Barbara Schleiffer), and the wife of a city messenger (Scolastica Stierpauer).[4] Other Anabaptists present at these gatherings included the wife of a town guard, the wife of a potter, her sister's maid, and the widow of a brickmaker. Six months before her arrest, Susanna had been baptized in the home of a lacemaker. She opened her own home to the wife of an itinerant preacher who made his living as a furrier and also hosted two unidentified foreign women overnight. Clearly, Susanna did not allow her higher social status to isolate her from middle- and lower-class believers in the congregation. The testimony of other Augsburg women also demonstrates the ability of these believers to cross social and economic boundaries for study and worship.

The interrogation records must be understood in the context of the life of the congregation.[5] Meetings of the believers were always shadowed by

The stories of Anabaptist martyrs were vividly depicted in etchings published in the *Martyrs' Mirror* (1685), a book that is found in many Amish and Mennonite homes today. This etching depicts Anabaptist hunters seizing an infant in its cradle along with women and men caught worshiping. (Reprinted by permission from *Mirror of the Martyrs*. Copyright Good Books, 1990.)

the possibility of persecution. A year earlier, Protestant preachers in the city had voiced opposition to the Anabaptists. City authorities became greatly alarmed when more than sixty Anabaptist leaders gathered in August 1527 for a series of evangelistic planning meetings that were subsequently labeled the "Martyrs' Synod."[6] During the next few weeks Augsburg authorities arrested many Anabaptists and sympathizers, releasing them only after they took an oath not to attend Anabaptist services. Those who had not yet been baptized were required to swear that they would not meet with the Anabaptists or seek rebaptism.

Despite the strict punishments threatened for those who reneged on their oaths, the council did grant the request of the Anabaptists for "two or

three" to meet together to read and discuss the Bible. This was the only le-
niency granted to the congregation. Those who would not swear the oath
were banished from the city. On October 11, 1527, the council mandated
that Augsburg residents refuse to heed or assist the "corner preachers"[7]
and instead be satisfied with ordinary church sermons. All children were
to be baptized, and rebaptism was forbidden. Punishment "in body or life
or possessions" was threatened for those who disregarded the mandate.

Most of the imprisoned Anabaptists were released, although their sentences were pending. Only the leaders, including Hans Hut, Jakob Gross,
Jakob Dachser, and Sigmund Salminger, remained in jail after the fall arrests of 1527. Hut was tortured and died of severe burns after a candle ig-
nited the straw in his cell. The remaining leaders spent over three years
in the dungeon before finally recanting.

Despite the imprisonment of these four leaders, the congregation in
Augsburg continued to grow throughout the fall of 1527 and during the
early months of 1528. Disregarding the ban on meetings, the faithful
gathered at least sixty to seventy times during these months.[8] Itinerant
preachers and local leaders held meetings and baptized converts.[9] Many
of the meetings consisted of only a few believers—probably in an attempt
to comply with council's concession that "two or three" could meet together. Yet other meetings were somewhat larger, and as the believing
community approached Easter, it seems their boldness increased.

The thriving congregation in Augsburg did not recover from the
Easter arrests and subsequent punishments. Peutinger's records note that
most of the believers were first questioned, then tortured, and finally exiled. A local leader, Hans Leupold, was beheaded. The sentence for four of
the most active women included branding their cheeks and beating them
out of the city. As punishment for blaspheming the Lord's Supper, one
woman also had her tongue cut out. Most of the remaining Anabaptists
were exiled—with or without a beating. By the summer of 1528 the few
remaining believers decided to disband their meetings.

Peutinger's meticulous records provide a wealth of information regarding the spread of Anabaptism in the Augsburg congregation. The testimony of the women in the congregation shows that the faith spread
from one family or guild member to another. Apparently the women disregarded differences in social class when they met for worship and mutual encouragement. Indeed, the portrait of the Augsburg congregation

that emerges from the interrogation records reveals a congregation very different from the traditional interpretation of Anabaptism—that it appealed to the masses but not to the wealthier members of a community.[10]

In a landmark statistical analysis of Anabaptism published in 1972, Claus-Peter Clasen reported that 98 percent of the Anabaptist believers he studied were "common people" and fewer than 2 percent were "intellectuals or noblemen."[11] In comparison, Clasen estimated that 71 percent of the Augsburg congregation belonged to the lowest classes, 16 percent owned limited or medium-sized property, 11 percent were well-to-do, and the remaining 2 percent were wealthy.[12] Acknowledging this wider range of rich, middle-class, and poor believers in the Augsburg congregation, he nevertheless noted that class distinctions did not disappear.

Despite his detailed analysis of the social position of the Augsburg Anabaptists, Clasen did not identify the specific believers who belonged to each social class.[13] From his data alone it is not possible to determine each woman's socioeconomic position. In addition to Clasen's data, therefore, the occupation of each woman (or her husband) is necessary to determine her social class. This classification of a woman's economic status based on her occupation should not be considered absolute, but neither is it completely arbitrary. Class distinctions based on occupation allow observations of the interactions of women within and across class groupings.

Clasen cited examples indicating that wealthy Anabaptists may have disliked attending meetings with their poor brethren.[14] In support of Clasen, Konrad Peutinger's interrogation records do reveal some tension between the extremely wealthy and those of lower classes. A cobbler, Simprecht Wiedemann, complained to Peutinger that the poor were arrested and often tortured, yet the wealthier Anabaptists were ignored or given minimal attention.[15] The records do not indicate, however, that a preponderance of poor Anabaptists deterred would-be believers from the higher classes. Indeed, a detailed examination of the various gatherings of women for Bible study and conversation shows that women from all social classes found creative ways to meet for mutual encouragement.[16]

Meetings among believers varied in size, style, and location. Finding adequate meeting places was a problem. Because many of the believers had sworn before the city council not to participate in gatherings of more than two or three, the Anabaptists frequently met in small conventicles. Sometimes larger groups of ten to twenty would gather, and on a few occasions as many as fifty to two hundred believers came together for worship. Meetings were held both inside and outside the city walls. The size of the meeting and the social class of both the host and those present reveals much about the spread of Anabaptism among Augsburg women.

Smaller meetings were the easiest and safest to arrange. The testimony of some women reports that their gatherings were accidental—or were contrived to appear so. Such was the report of Apollonia Widholtz regarding the baptism of Magdalena Mertz in her home. Apollonia told Peutinger that her sister, Felicitas Lautterwein, and a friend, Magdalena, visited her after the birth of her child. Finding itinerant minister Georg Nespitzer present, Felicitas asked him to read the Bible.[17] The three of them then left the room, and Apollonia only later learned that Magdalena had been baptized at that time. Apollonia hastened to assure her interrogator that neither Felicitas nor Magdalena knew they would find Nespitzer in her home at the time of their visit.[18] This apparently accidental meeting thus led to the baptism of a new believer.

Larger groups also found creative ways of gathering. Sometimes a woman would carry a distaff through the street, presumably as a kind of signal for a meeting or to legitimate her journey to the home of another woman.[19] The grocer Elisabeth Hegenmiller was invited to bring her distaff to the home of weaver Martin Wegman. Wegman's wife told her that someone would speak to them of good things, meaning that an Anabaptist leader would be present.[20] Katharina Weidenmann, wife of a cobbler, and Barbara Schleiffer, a grocer, also opened their homes for these meetings "around the distaff."[21] Groups of women met to spin or sew. Often, but not always, an Anabaptist leader was present to read or teach. Felicitas Huber, a lacemaker, mentions attending two of these meetings. Hans Leupold, a tailor and a local leader of the congregation, taught the women as they worked.[22] Presumably such a meeting would look innocent enough.

Secrecy was essential when the Anabaptists contrived to hold their largest gatherings. On several occasions they met outside the city in a forest or gravel pit. On April 4, 1528, as many as fifty to sixty Anabaptists met in Barbara Schleiffer's cellar to celebrate the Lord's Supper. The meeting took place at night and lasted several hours.[23] Several days later, about forty believers arrived in small groups for a meeting on Easter Eve at Gall Vischer's house. His wife sat behind the door, apparently to be certain that only believers were admitted.[24] As mentioned above, the blankets hung over windows at Susanna Doucher's home were not enough to conceal the large Easter meeting in her home.

New converts were brought into the faith as one believer talked with another. Naturally these conversations often took place among family members. A large number of those interrogated by Peutinger were blood relatives, showing that the faith spread throughout extended families.[25] This may not seem noteworthy, given the tendency for sixteenth-century households to follow the example of the male head of household,[26] but among the Anabaptists husbands and fathers were not solely responsible for the spread of the faith. Many examples demonstrate that Anabaptism spread from mother to daughter or son and between siblings. Several wives joined, with or without the knowledge and permission of their husbands.[27]

The baptism of Magdalena Mertz illustrates the spread of Anabaptism among family and friends. In a small gathering around the childbed of her friend Apollonia, Magdalena heard the teaching of an Anabaptist leader and received a private baptism. Except for a maid, all the women present were members of the high or high-middle class. It is not possible to determine whether this was a chance encounter or whether Magdalena knew in advance of the presence of Georg Nespitzer. Magdalena was almost certainly predisposed toward Anabaptism because of the religious influence of her mother, Honester Krafter, a wealthy believer. This further illustrates the spread of Anabaptism through family members.

Anabaptism also spread as the believers conducted business. Some believers, such as the cobblers Katharina and Simprecht Weidenmann, took advantage of the traffic through their home to spread their faith. The high number of grocers and weavers within the congregation suggests that evangelism spread throughout certain guilds. In the weavers' guild, the home of Elisabeth and Gall Vischer became a place of gathering and refuge. Elisabeth confessed to hosting several prominent leaders, some for several days. Other members of the Augsburg congregation came for short visits. On April 11, 1528, Elisabeth and Gall hosted a meeting of more than forty persons, many of them members of the weavers' or grocers' guild. Among those present were the guildmaster of the weavers, Benedikt Gnugesser, and his wife, Ursula. Although they never joined the congregation, Benedikt and Ursula stayed for about an hour.[28]

Sometimes the spread of the faith through family and its spread through guild connections are intertwined. One wonders if Elisabeth Hegenmiller first learned of Anabaptism through the grocers' guild and then spread it to her sister, Regina Weisshaupt, or if Regina converted Elisabeth, who then spread her beliefs through the grocers' guild. Certainly the grocers' guild was filled with believers, and Elisabeth Hegenmiller was one of the most active women.[29]

Naturally Anabaptism spread through the interaction of believers with their families and others from their guilds or social class. Several Anabaptist homes, however, were especially suited for the meeting of believers from all aspects of the socioeconomic range. A broader range of social classes was also represented as women found excuses to meet for Bible reading and encouragement.

Middle-class lacemakers Konrad and Felicitas Huber opened their home to Anabaptists of varied class status. Two maids, Elisabeth Leitl and an unnamed servant, were baptized there by Melchior of Salzburg. During the summer of 1527 an itinerant pastor, Jakob Gross, baptized another maid, Apollonia Schmid. The following October another pastor, Thomas of Waldhausen, baptized sisters who were both members of the high-middle class. Susanna Doucher was married to Hans Adolf, a prominent sculptor, and Maxentia Wisinger to a goldsmith. Scolastica Stierpauer, wife of a city messenger, was probably also present at the sisters' baptism in the Huber home.

Also from the testimony of Felicitas Huber and Susanna Doucher we learn of a meeting of several women in the home of Katharina Weidenmann, a cobbler's wife.[30] Probably the women brought their sewing, at least for appearances; Felicitas specifically mentions the distaff. The local Anabaptist leader, Hans Leupold, spoke to them for an hour. The socioeconomic makeup of this group, however, confirms that this was an Anabaptist meeting, not merely an afternoon of sewing. Anna Vischer, the wife of a potter, was also the sister-in-law of Katharina. Agnes Vogel, Anna's landlady and the wife of a town guard, was present as well. Anna seems to be a link between at least two of the women.[31] But what explains the presence of Susanna Doucher and Maxentia Wisinger, both married to prominent Augsburg citizens and with no apparent family or social links to the other women? Not only does this meeting demonstrate the cunning that Anabaptist women used to gather, it also illustrates the willingness of women across social class lines to meet together.

Clasen suggests that wealthy Augsburg Anabaptists avoided large gatherings within the city, and he infers that they preferred not to associate with their poor brethren. Specifically, he states that few wealthy persons were present at the large meetings hosted by Barbara Schleiffer and Susanna Doucher.[32] Based on the testimony of those present, however, Peutinger's records show that all but the very richest class of Augsburg society were represented as the believers celebrated the Lord's Supper in Barbara Schleiffer's cellar.[33] The arrest of the entire congregation, most of whom were present at Susanna Doucher's home for the Easter worship, also confirms that believers from all classes had met to worship in her home.

Clasen's prime example of a wealthy woman who avoided the lower classes was a widow named Honester Krafter. Presumably she was initially attracted to Anabaptism but became disenchanted when confronted by a congregation of poor believers. Peutinger's interrogation records, however, offer another view of Honester. Several women refer to her, indicating that she was well known among women of all social classes in the congregation.[34] She housed Anna Salminger, a seamstress and the wife of the imprisoned leader Sigmund Salminger, for several weeks.[35] Although she did leave the Easter worship service before the arrests took place, her departure was viewed in a sympathetic light by grocer Elisabeth Hegenmiller.[36] According to Elisabeth's testimony, one of the Anabaptist leaders learned that arrest was imminent and advised those who feared "the cross before the door" to leave the meeting. Elisabeth learned from other believers that Honester rose, confessed her weakness to the brothers and sisters, and asked them to pray for her. Such a confession, if heard and reported accurately by Elisabeth, would contradict Clasen's assertion that Honester disliked worshiping with the masses. Indeed, her appeal for prayer suggests she valued the spiritual support of this congregation, which included lower-class citizens.

Honester's own explanation of her interactions with the Anabaptists (noted in her letter of recantation) did not specifically refer to her feelings about lower-class believers. In an appeal to the city authorities, Honester emphasized that she had been privately baptized and had left the meeting in Doucher's home because it was too crowded.[37] Her recantation was carefully worded. Surely Augsburg city leaders would lend a sympathetic ear to her claim that "too many people were present." When it became clear the authorities would not tolerate Anabaptism within the city, Honester recanted, choosing words that would most likely restore her position in the community.

Had the Anabaptist community in Augsburg not been persecuted, historians would know very little about the congregation. Indeed, it is through the careful notes made by interrogator and persecutor Konrad Peutinger that one learns of the activities of female Anabaptists as they spread their faith through their natural contacts with members of their families and guilds. Careful scrutiny of these records also reveals that the appeal of Anabaptism was by no means limited to the lower classes of Augsburg society, nor did socioeconomic boundaries prevent believers from gathering. Indeed, the cross section of Augsburg society that was arrested on April 12, 1528, reflected relationships among the believing community that had been formed and strengthened as Anabaptist women gathered for study and worship.

APPENDIX: SOCIOECONOMIC STATUS BY OCCUPATION

   I. High, Rich

       Honester Krafter, merchant

       Regina Krafter, merchant

       Magdalena Mertz, merchant

  II. High-Middle

       Susanna Doucher, sculptor

       Ursula Gnugesser, guildmaster of weavers

       Maxentia Wisinger, goldsmith

       Apollonia Wildholtz, guildmaster of the grocers

       Scolastica Stierpauer, civic messenger

 III. Middle Crafts or Trades

       Magdalena Seitz, weaver

       Margareta Berchtold, weaver

       Dorothea, wool carder

       Anna Butz, weaver

       Veronika Gross, furrier

       Regina Weisshaupt, cabinetmaker

      Elisabeth Vischer, weaver
      Anna Vischer, potter
      Elisabeth Knöll, weaver
      Felicitas Huber, lacemaker
      Ursula Aurbach, weaver
      Petronella Teber, carpenter

IV. Common Crafts or Trades
      Elisabeth Schweizer, wool carder
      Martha Beck, baker
      Margareta Wiedenmann, baker
      Anna Klein, chicken dealer
      Elisabeth Hegenmiller, grocer
      Ursula Schleiffer, grocer
      Agnes Vogel, town guard
      Apollonia Thoma, blue dyer
      Katharina Wiedenmann, cobbler
      Afra Gabler, baker
      Anna Rauner, cobbler
      Anna Miller, grocer
      Anna Gabler, baker
      Anna Otlin, glassmaker
      Katharina Kunig, stonemason

V. Lower Crafts
      Anna Malchinger, laundress
      Dorothea Frolich, tile/brick maker
      Anna Haller Salminger, seamstress
      Magdalena Ziegler, gingerbread maker
      Anna Graber, carpet weaver
      Anna Baumänn (mother), embroiderer
      Anna Baumänn (daughter), embroiderer

VI. Servants (employers' occupations)
      Justina from Klein-Aitingen (merchant)
      Afra Schleich (baker)
      Anna Schuster (blue dyer)
      Barbara Dätz (cobbler)
      Elisabeth Leitl (lacemaker)
      Elisabeth Mair (grocer)

Radegundis Raiser

Apollonia Schmid (guildmaster of grocers)

Anna Custermann (gingerbread maker)

NOTES

1. Records of the interrogations were translated by Dr. Friedrich Roth and published in "Zur Geschichte der Wiedertäufer in Oberschwaben: III. Der Höhepunkt der wiedertäuferischen Bewegung in Augsburg und ihr Niedergang in Jahre 1528," *Zeitschrift des Historischen Vereins für Schwaben und Neuburg* (Augsburg) 28 (1901): 1–154; hereafter cited as Roth. These records provided the data used for this chapter.

2. Apparently the Augsburg congregation provided refuge for fellow believers from outside the city. I treat this topic in detail in "Mutual Aid among the Augsburg Anabaptists, 1526–1528," in *Building Communities of Compassion: Mennonite Mutual Aid in Theory and Practice,* ed. Willard M. Swartley and Donald B. Kraybill, 103–18 (Scottdale, Pa.: Herald Press, 1998).

3. Roth, 51–53.

4. See appendix for the list of class rankings of Augsburg women by occupation.

5. For a concise history of the Augsburg congregation, see Christian Hege, "Augsburg and the Early Anabaptists," in *Mennonite Encyclopedia: A Comprehensive Reference Work on the Anabaptist and Mennonite Movement,* 4th ed. (Scottdale, Pa.: Mennonite Publishing House, 1982), 182–85, and Paul J. Schwab, "Augsburg and the Early Anabaptists," in *Reformation Studies: Essays in Honor of Roland H. Bainton,* ed. Franklin H. Littell (Richmond, Va.: John Knox Press, 1962), 212–28.

6. Hege, 183.

7. Hege, 184. Corner preachers were probably those who preached in secret; they certainly did not have the sanction of the local civic or religious authorities.

8. My collation of the information provided in Peutinger's records indicates that between sixty and seventy meetings were held from the summer of 1527 until the Easter arrests in 1528. I define the term "meeting" very broadly by including any mention by an Anabaptist of a gathering of fellow believers. The exact number and nature of these meetings are difficult to determine owing to the secretive nature of the movement and the prisoners' desire not to divulge to Peutinger more information about fellow believers than necessary. Indeed, for some of the gatherings I include, the very persons who confessed to being pres-

ent denied that they were "meetings." For the purpose of examining the spread of Anabaptism through the socioeconomic strata, however, I consider even small and possibly chance meetings significant.

9. John S. Oyer counts "at least twenty who baptized others [Anabaptists] in Augsburg from 1526 through April 1528; another eleven preached but did not baptize." See "Anabaptist Women leaders in Augsburg: August 1527 to April 1528," in *Profiles of Anabaptist Women: Sixteenth-Century Reforming Pioneers*, ed. C. Arnold Snyder and Linda A. Huebert Hecht (Waterloo, Ont.: Wilfrid Laurier University Press, 1996), 83.

10. This view was challenged first by Paul Peachey in *Die soziale Herkunft der Schweizer Täufer in der Reformationzeit: Ein religionssoziologische Untersuchung* (Karlsruhe, Germany: Schneider, 1954), and also to some degree by Claus-Peter Clasen in *Anabaptism: A Social History, 1525–1618* (Ithaca: Cornell University Press, 1972).

11. Clasen, 323.

12. Clasen, 325.

13. With direction from John Oyer, I placed the women into social class categories based on their occupations. See appendix for Oyer's complete list of occupations and his divisions into high, high-middle, middle crafts or trades, common crafts or trades, lower crafts, and servants. Oyer acknowledges that these categories are not sacrosanct but contends they are an accurate guide to social groupings of the time. A more complete understanding of socioeconomic status would be gained by correlating occupation, education, and wealth. Such analysis is hampered by lack of pertinent sixteenth-century records.

14. Clasen, 323, 326–27.

15. Roth, 97. A weaver named Matheis Huber also complained that the rich were given special treatment (Roth, 101).

16. Whenever possible, I listed the meetings chronologically, noting the location and the name of the leader who baptized or taught. I then listed the names of all Anabaptists present, highlighting those who confessed to being at a meeting to distinguish them from believers whose presence was known only from the testimony of others. Sometimes the testimony of one Anabaptist corroborated the confession of another. In many cases, however, the presence of a particular woman at a meeting is known only by either her own confession or the testimony of another. Faulty memory or the desire to avoid incriminating others—or both—may have caused some prisoners to add or delete names when Peutinger questioned them about the presence of others at Anabaptist gathering. I paid particu-

lar attention to the occupations of the women in attendance. Many women were known only as "wife of—" and those women were therefore classified by the occupation of their husbands. Each woman was assigned to one of six socioeconomic status groups based on her (or her husband's) occupation. After I color-coded the name of each woman based on her socioeconomic status, meetings of women in similar positions were readily apparent, as were the gatherings of women from very different class backgrounds.

17. The term "read" implies that the Anabaptists were obeying the stipulation set forth by the city council, although the term probably included both reading and exegesis of the biblical text.

18. Roth, 114.

19. Distaff: a staff for holding the flax, tow, or wool in spinning. In Roth, see the testimony of Anna Butz (41), Elisabeth Hegenmiller (54), and Felicitas Huber (110), for examples of the distaff used as a signal or as an excuse to meet with other women.

20. Roth, 54.

21. Roth, 110, 41. For examples of other sewing meetings, see the testimony of Scolastica Stierpaur (50) and Konrad Miller (79). Several women—Veronika Gross, Anna Salminger, and a woman named Kicklinger—were identified as seamstresses. Two women, a mother and daughter both named Anna Baumänn, were embroiderers.

22. Hans Leupold also testifies to this meeting in Roth.

23. Schwab, 225; the testimony of numerous believers in Roth, 62.

24. Reported by Anna Butz in Roth, 39.

25. Clasen notes the spread of Anabaptism among the Nespitzer family, 56. Georg Nespitzer, an important leader and the baptizer of many in the Augsburg community, was the brother-in-law of fellow Augsburg believer Thoma Paur and of Eukarius Kellerman, an associate of Hans Hut. Brigitta Nespitzer, Ursula Nespitzer, and the wife of Thoma Paur were sisters.

26. Lyndal Roper notes that the Reformation gave a married craftsman more control over his extended household, yet Anabaptism flourished because the woman had some measure of control over the household. See *The Holy Household: Women and Morals in Reformation Augsburg* (New York: Oxford University Press, 1989), 3, 253–54.

27. For example, the testimony of Elisabeth Hegenmiller reports that her husband never joined, but he helped her distribute groceries to needy Anabaptists. See Roth, 54–55. In contrast, Susanna Doucher was married to a prominent

sculptor, Hans Adolf. He was adamantly opposed to Anabaptism. She was able to host the Easter worship service in her home only because he was out of town. See Roth, 51–53.

28. Ursula insisted that she went to the meeting to look for her maid. Roth, 108–9.

29. Grocers included Elisabeth Hegenmiller, Anna Klein (mother), Anna Klein (daughter), Anna Miller, Ursula Schleiffer, and Apollonia Widholtz (wife of the guildmaster).

30. Roth, 51, 110.

31. Testimony of Anna Vischer and Agnes Vogel; Roth, 81–83.

32. Clasen, 327.

33. My listing of the believers present indicates that there were three women from the high-middle class, four from the middle class, four from the common crafts, two from the lower class, and one servant. Not all the believers present at that meeting can be identified.

34. See the testimony of Anna Butz, who reports that the wife of a baker, Martha Beck, came to her home looking for the itinerant leader Claus Schleiffer to take him to Honester's home. Anna describes the location of Honester's home. From Anna's testimony, it appears that a refugee farm wife from Bavaria, Elisabeth Sedelmair, frequently stayed with rich members of the congregation, one of whom was possibly Honester Krafter. Roth, 40.

35. Testimony of Anna Butz and Anna Salmiger; Roth, 40, 70–71.

36. Roth, 55. Elisabeth was the only woman who mentioned to Peutinger that Honester was present at the Easter meeting.

37. Roth, 119–21.

7

"Weak Families" in the Green Hell of Paraguay

Marlene Epp

The Paraguayan Mennonite communities of Volendam and Neuland, settled primarily by women and children who were refugees from Ukraine after World War II, offer a sobering picture of immigration and settlement. Carving out farms and villages from an area known as the "green hell" took on heroic dimensions as female-headed families struggled to survive, often without male assistance or adequate help from Mennonite church relief agencies.

O n February 1, 1947, the *Volendam* left the port of Bremerhaven, Germany, bound for Argentina. On board were 2,303 refugees, most of them Mennonite. Donna Yoder, an American relief worker in Europe, described the makeup of the passengers: "The first person to go on board on Monday was a little old lady and her daughter. The lady is not well and we wonder if she will stand the journey, but she has determination. There were little babies too. . . . There were twins, little kiddies with wooden shoes, old grandmothers, young folks and all. Not many men though, but some young boys and a few young men."[1]

Twenty-one days later the *Volendam* arrived in Buenos Aires, the first of four large transports that moved a total of 5,616 refugees from war-

An elderly grandmother and her daughter prepare to sail from Germany to Paraguay. (Photograph courtesy of Mennonite Central Committee Photograph Collection, Archives of the Mennonite Church, Goshen, Indiana.)

torn Europe to South America in 1947 and 1948.[2] Approximately 4,500 of these refugees were Mennonites destined for Paraguay, where they joined an existing Mennonite population of about 5,000.[3] Here land had been purchased by the North America–based relief agency Mennonite Central Committee (MCC) specifically for settling the newcomers in two new colonies called Volendam and Neuland.[4] The migrants were a small part of close to 100,000 Mennonites who had been displaced from their homes in the Soviet Union and Eastern Europe during the Second World War.[5]

The Discourse of Weakness

As the relief worker's quotation suggests, the demography of the Mennonite migrants destined for South America was characterized by a high percentage of fatherless families and an overall ratio of two adult women to each man.[6] The sex imbalance was due to a number of factors. Several waves of arrests, disappearances, and deportations during the 1930s and in the early years of the war had severely depleted the men in Soviet Mennonite communities. Others—some as young as sixteen—were killed, missing in action, or conscripted into the German armed forces.[7]

Besides the small number of adult men, families in general were fragmented by prewar and wartime circumstances. Many households could be characterized as "grab bag families," a phrase Sheila Fitzpatrick used for individuals with or without a blood relationship who share housing, food, and other resources to survive in wartime.[8] For instance, sampling in the Volendam village of Tiefenbrunn in 1949 shows that not even 20 percent of the 52 family units were intact. Of these, 13 were headed by widows and none by widowers.[9] In Neuland colony, 253 of 641 families, or 40 percent, were headed by widows.[10]

This amazing story of female-headed families starting anew in an unfamiliar land contrasts with an early historiography of immigration in which women were typically "non-migrants who wait in the sending areas for their spouses to return or . . . passive reactors who simply follow a male migrant."[11] Women and children have frequently been grouped together as "dependents" while the active decision-making and breadwinning roles are assumed by the male head of household. Writing on the female experience of migration, particularly that of single women immigrants, has increased significantly, yet the migration of an entire community dominated numerically by women and children represents a fascinating anomaly. The story of postwar Mennonite migration to Paraguay has the potential to contribute new insights to the history of migration, the roles of widows in small communities, and the understanding of family in the context of fragmentation and displacement.

The refugee families that migrated to Paraguay are frequently described in the correspondence, minutes, and published reports of relief workers as *schwache*, or weak, families. Their feebleness was directly attributed to the absence of fathers or other adult males. But their described weakness was in sharp contrast to the harshness of the environment— sometimes called the "green hell"—that they now called home. As women and their families cleared land, built homes, grew food, and attempted to sustain themselves with minimal resources and limited outside aid, the characterization of frailty was really an abstraction from reality. For the new immigrants pioneering was in many ways a continuation of the previous two decades, in which they developed strategies of physical and emotional survival in situations of inescapable hardship. As a result of the past and present demands placed on them, refugee families were in many respects "stronger" than the average whole family. As an analyst of contemporary displaced women has observed: "The women refugees who have endured the horrors of war, dislocation, loss of loved ones, hunger, humiliation, and still opted for life and safety of their children are not weak women."[12]

Yet Mennonite refugees lacked certain elements that may have been deemed essential to a strong person or family unit, that is, the father figure as head of the family and the formal structures and practices of institutionalized religion. Weakness thus meant first of all the absence of a father figure and male provider. However, the term had multiple meanings. It defined refugee women as weak economically and, of even more concern to North American Mennonites, weak spiritually and morally. The main agenda of North and South American workers entrusted with supervising the resettlement was thus a combination of material assistance and religious rehabilitation.

SETTLING IN THE WILDERNESS

The two new colonies, although very different environmentally, represented equal, if distinct, challenges and hardships for the new immigrants. In Volendam colony, in eastern Paraguay, dense forest had to be cleared with machete, saw, and ax before roads and villages could be laid out. The bush was so dense that in some cases settlers had to crawl on hands and knees from the main path to their building sites. Trees a meter in diameter and climbing vines as thick as a person's arm had to be cut with the few hand tools available. The hardships of pioneering were exacerbated by new and strange dangers in the form of wild antelope and ostriches, rattlesnakes, jaguars, and "vicious zebu bulls."[13]

In Neuland, about 500 kilometers northwest of Volendam, the terrain was divided between grassland and bush. Clearing the land was somewhat easier because there were fewer trees, but the wood was so hard that axes would often bounce off, and it became necessary to burn the trees out. The soil was sandy and relatively easy to plow, but it was not amenable to the kinds of fruits and vegetables that could be grown in Volendam. Beans, cassava, and sweet potatoes were the main crops in the early years. The

A Mennonite mother making bricks in Volendam during the spring of 1950. (Photograph courtesy of Mennonite Central Committee Photograph Collection, Archives of the Mennonite Church, Goshen, Indiana.)

climate was hot and dry, and the settlers were plagued with all manner of insects and pests.

It was thus in a strange and mostly untouched environment that the refugees, with minimal equipment and provisions, set about creating new homes. Even with outside assistance, the task was daunting and dispiriting. One young woman recalled that she and her younger sister broke down and cried when they saw what lay ahead of them in Paraguay: "We didn't know what we should do. But crying didn't help anything. We had to do what we could do."[14] Doing what they could meant first of all clearing enough bush to build small houses of adobe brick and planting sufficient grains, fruits, and vegetables to sustain the household.

Visiting the household of widow Margareta Enns and her four children, MCC worker John W. Warkentin was "gratified" to find, after about six months, a house that was almost complete, right to the whitewash on the inside walls, and that the family was eating watermelon, beans, and other vegetables from its own garden. He further observed that "the family was very happy and contented." And apparently a neighboring woman had told Warkentin, "Never before have we been as poor as we are now, but we have never been happier."[15]

To what extent Warkentin accurately assessed the state of mind of these two women is open to question. His statements may have in part been aimed at defusing the concern of both immigrants and North American Mennonites that perhaps MCC had made a big mistake in settling the refugees in the green hell of Paraguay. In that respect his description was a public relations statement. On the other hand, the women may have indeed felt the happiness that arises from pride in accomplishment. This pride is evident in the photograph of an "old mother of eighty years" standing beside one of two cookstoves and a baking oven that she constructed entirely on her own out of mud and sod. Canadian businessman and MCC worker C. A. DeFehr remarked, "It must be admitted that she did her work very well."[16] Another noteworthy photograph depicts two women, wearing dresses, atop a scaffold surrounding a house under construction. The caption says: "Their husbands and brothers in Siberia, these women are building their own homes with adobe brick in the Chaco."[17]

DeFehr was not the only relief worker who was struck by the daunting obstacles facing female-led families in Paraguay and also by their ability to meet the challenge. In her report on a visit to the new colony of Neuland, MCC worker Ella Berg made several comments about the sex imbalance there. In the six villages she visited, only once was she hosted in a home where the husband and wife were together—"a rare thing." In one home the mother of four children had become a semi-invalid when she broke her leg while loading a tree soon after arriving. Berg commented, "Do you wonder that the future looks dark to them?" At the village of Halbstadt, she "saw again how bravely a mother and two daughters carry on. One of them had charge of the land work and did some topnotch plowing with Fred and Charlie, the oxen."[18]

Even after the first year or so of constructing basic shelter and planting a few crops for food, household maintenance continued to be intensive and difficult. Writing in the early 1950s, sociologist J. Winfield Fretz commented after visiting the Paraguayan colonies: "People who have not experienced the life of the Mennonite housewife in Paraguay have little idea of the burdens under which she lives and labors."[19] Several years later his views had only intensified, and he commented that the women looked old at forty and completely worn out at sixty.[20] Fretz made a public plea for kerosene-burning refrigerators to ease the workload of women in Paraguay. Although he was perhaps erroneously setting up a strictly gendered division of labor that was not as applicable to Neuland and Volendam as to the older colonies, Fretz nevertheless suggested it was time to give "at least one big push to help the women." After all, "we have helped the men in the colonies with loans for tractors, land, cattle, seeds, and industrial equipment."[21]

Many families received small and larger amounts of money from relatives in Canada and also from Mennonite women's organizations and churches in North America, but this direct financial assistance did not begin immediately. For the first months up to several years, the settlers received material assistance from Mennonite Central Committee and the earlier Mennonite colonists in Paraguay. At the outset, residents from Menno, Fernheim, and Friesland colonies provided accommodation for the "weaker" families for several months while land was cleared and houses were built; Fernheim reportedly carried out its part in maintaining five hundred persons "free of charge" for three months.[22] Building units were formed in Fernheim whereby groups of six farmers were responsible for erecting houses for "the poor women [who] were justly concerned who would help them build their houses."[23] Vernon Neuschwander reported that forty-one houses for widows in Neuland were built "in record time" by Fernheim colonists.[24] Fernheim colonists also lent each family a cow for five years, provided a pair of work oxen for each complete farm, and gave each family six chickens and thirty kilograms of peanuts for seed. According to DeFehr, Fernheimers also wanted to place the "very weak" families, one per village, in the older colony.[25]

Mennonite Central Committee was a key provider of material support at the outset. It was initially expected that settlers in Volendam would be self-supporting by December 1, 1948, less than two years after their arrival. Warkentin reported in August of that year that they planned to keep the immigrants on full maintenance until October 1, gradually reduce their allowance in the following six months, and they hoped, discontinue it entirely by March 31, 1949. Full maintenance was the equivalent, in United States dollars, of twenty cents per person per day in both Volendam and Neuland.[26] MCC also supplied a minimal amount of household and farm implements and some basic garden tools. At the same time, however, Fernheim resident Jakob Isaak made a public plea that support for Volendam settlers be extended at least until after the harvest of 1949, stating: "Keep in mind the women and mothers who must feed as well as train their children without a husband and father. . . . If, in addition to the hard labor, these poor souls must bear the worry of what they shall eat or wherewithal they shall clothe themselves in the immediate future, the burden will be unduly heavy."[27]

In addition, the maintenance allowance for food was barely adequate for some families, and before the first planting in the fall of 1948, there were numerous reports of hunger and in some cases of families going without food for several days. The food shortage was exacerbated by the difficulty of transporting supplies to the remote colonies.

A WOMEN'S VILLAGE

The outstanding example of female strength and self-sufficiency occurred in the creation of a village of women. For the most part, villages were organized according to the wishes of the refugees themselves and frequently following patterns that had existed in Russia.[28] In some cases relief workers intervened to ensure that "strong" individuals—men—were well distributed among the "weak" families. In one instance there was concern over the "pettiness" of a group of eight strong men who resisted efforts to separate them, rendering one village very weak by their absence.[29] That some men may have been reluctant to settle near widows and their families is corroborated by the experience of one Volendam family. This widow with four children under age twelve was upset to learn that her male neighbor was annoyed because she lived next to him. He thought she would not keep up with him in clearing the surrounding forest, thus inviting in wild animals.[30]

The village of Friedensheim in the Neuland colony was more commonly called the Frauendorf (women's village) because in its earliest form all of the 147 adult inhabitants were women. The eldest male was a thirteen-year-old boy. The women had come together as a group while fleeing the Soviet Union. Initially the "committee of men" responsible for or-

The entire "Frauendorf," or village of women, in Neuland colony attended a church service on Easter Sunday morning in the spring of 1950. This was Friedensheim, the village made up largely of families where husbands and fathers were missing. (Photograph courtesy of Mennonite Central Committee Photograph Collection, Archives of the Mennonite Church, Goshen, Indiana.)

ganizing the new settlement reportedly balked at the idea of a village of women; they said, "You can't do that, you won't survive." The women countered, "Weren't we told that we were free to group ourselves into villages as we pleased?" When asked how they would manage such heavy tasks as cutting trees, digging wells, and building houses, the women responded that they would help each other.[31]

In helping each other undertake the hard tasks of settlement, the women created a community joined by common experience and shared suffering and, to a certain extent, free from the suspicions, sexual tension, and traditional patterns of authority that exerted themselves in villages with even a few adult men. It may be that mutual support and cooperative efforts came more easily in the Frauendorf, where all the households were woman headed. In her study of female-led households, Joan Chandler found that single-parent families are obliged to depend on one another and that lone women often need to borrow other people's husbands for help with certain tasks. "But the capacity of women to engage in such borrowing, even if it is meant in the most innocuous of ways, is limited. Women without husbands are viewed with reserve, if not suspicion, or are targeted by men with sexual ambitions. The very absence of a husband may then inhibit the inter-household exchange."[32] In the Frauendorf, where there were no husbands to borrow, women were more free to assist one another than in other villages, where the problems associated with husband borrowing may have forced female-headed households to be more self-sufficient, as Chandler suggests.

Beyond the physical labor that was shared in the Frauendorf, women supported one another emotionally and psychologically in a way that may not have been possible had some of them lived with husbands. Peter Dyck, an MCC worker who helped arrange the migration to Paraguay, recalled meeting a woman who had lived in the Frauendorf and later immigrated to Winnipeg, Manitoba. She remarked that despite her personal prosperity and her flourishing church life in Canada, she felt a great sense of loneliness, having lost this community of women. For her the informal spirituality nurtured by singing by the fire, the shared pride of accomplishment in building mud houses for themselves and their children, and the removal of status barriers based on either material goods or the presence of a husband had all filled a void that a more prosperous and stable environment could not assuage.[33] This example is from the Frauendorf, but it is probable that similar feelings of community existed in other villages where women and children predominated. One woman, not a resident of the Frauendorf, commented that the severe poverty in the new colonies drew people together. She said that in her village people were "united" in helping one another. "We loved each other so much," she recalled.[34]

Despite declarations of independence by the residents of the Frauendorf, there were ongoing concerns for the development of the village. Frequent references in the records of settlement workers regarding the poor progress being made by the widows of Friedensheim suggest that this village, more than others, was under scrutiny and was expected to fail. Statistical summaries of the new colonies by village, listing amounts of livestock, buildings, acres cleared and sown, and so on, suggest otherwise.

However, the workers' reports tend to focus on the helplessness of Friedensheim's residents rather than to praise their amazing accomplishments in the face of obstacles. For instance, MCC worker Vernon Neuschwander wrote in November 1948 that the "plowing is not going too good with the widows."

> In the first place many of them that did buy a team of oxen bought young ones and they are not able to do very much work. A. Loewen told me of one instance where three women were trying to plow with a team of oxen and they were some of the young ones [and] they were just not getting anywhere, when the plow would hit a small root the oxen would not pull any more and maybe the ox would lie down and so it went, that naturally was hard for the women they said what shall we do we don't get any thing done. In time this situation will probably work out better as the oxen get older and stronger and then some man can come and help for a day or two it will go better.[35]

To what extent the problems the widows experienced were unique is difficult to ascertain, given that the same attention is not focused on some of the villages with more men. It is evident, however, that the workers were quite unprepared to deal with the tremendous needs in this village and in others where "man" power was limited.

Particular concern for the unruliness of the children of Friedensheim also suggests that family discipline was correlated with a father's presence. Anxiety existed foremost over the lack of school and religious training for the children of the immigrants. Although instruction of any kind was a lesser priority for all families struggling to establish themselves at a subsistence level, it seemed there was particular concern for villages where there were fewer men. In June 1948, C. A. DeFehr wrote to an MCC colleague about Friedensheim, particularly about the village's lack of both a schoolteacher and a minister. DeFehr was trying to find a solution that would address the problem of fifty-two school-aged children who were "to this day still running around" without any instruction.[36] Several months later he used Friedensheim as an example of how loose the young people could become if they were not given religious instruction. He was gratified that after the arrival of a teacher-preacher, all the youth in the village were participating in a choir.[37]

THE FATHERLESS FAMILY

The gender-role disruption that occurred within female-headed refugee families did not relate only to the widowed mother's assumption of roles hitherto held by the father-husband. In many families without a father, the eldest son would assume leadership, often well beyond his actual years. As one Neuland immigrant described it, "The family unit as a whole was considered the unit of operation. If there didn't happen to be [an adult] male, then the son would take his place."[38] For instance, in one family the oldest son at thirteen and a half years became the "symbolic head."[39] This meant attending town meetings and voting on behalf of his family. In a semifictional account of a widowed family settling in Neuland in 1947, the author makes a similar observation: "Boys not yet twelve stepped into the places left empty by their fallen or exiled or executed fathers, and took the burdens of sustenance upon their young, suntanned shoulders, smiled with slow confidence, and did what had to be done."[40] Competition for the scarce resource of male labor increased as the number of able-bodied men in the colonies increased. This occurred as boys grew older and as some men were released from prison camps in Europe in the early 1950s. Widows happily saw their daughters get married, because "when you have a man in the family it was so much easier."[41] Young men then often worked "day and night" for two families. A Volendam woman, in an oral history source, could not understand why her widowed mother had slept in the same room with her and her new husband on their wedding night. Although she assumed that it was because the other room in their two-room house had been used for visiting after the wedding, the mother may also have subconsciously viewed this new man in their household as a symbol of her husband and two grown sons, all lost in the war, and thus wanted to be as close to him as possible.[42]

The need for male leadership, even if only symbolic, may have been more acute for refugees in South America than for those who went to Canada. This would relate to the highly patriarchal nature of family life among Paraguayan Mennonites, in which, according to Fretz, "The father is the unquestioned head of the family, and in case of death is normally succeeded by the oldest son."[43] Fretz continued his gender analysis of the South American Mennonite family observed during his visit there in the early 1950s:

The mother appears to defer to the father in the matter of discipline, as in most other things. A North American visitor is likely to be impressed with the way the woman of the house plays the role of servant. In the writer's many home calls, the woman was seldom present during the visit, and in most instances, where the visit took place over mealtime, only the husband and the guest were seated at the table. The wife generally served the food but only in a few instances did she take part in the conversation.[44]

An immigrant woman who settled in Volendam with her widowed mother and three siblings recalled that "it was a man's world, still is, but at that time it was much more."[45] In a setting where rigidly patriarchal family values were prominent, as was the case for the earlier colonists in Paraguay, the fatherless nature of many refugee families was that much more pronounced. In this context strength became synonymous not only with physical ability but with the presence of a male head. The identification of those that were dead or exiled in the Soviet Union as "the strong and able-bodied and those possessing qualities of leadership" set up a sharp contrast with the refugees, frequently characterized in general terms as "the old, the weak, the crippled, some women and children."[46] The dichotomy between male strength and female weakness was especially strong in Paraguay, where there were in fact more physically weak refugees than had emigrated to Canada, a country with stricter medical requirements for immigration. In observing that the "manhood" of the Mennonite fellowship had been severely weakened, one MCC overseer was speaking not only of numbers of men, but of qualities of maleness that included strength, virility, and dominance. The family itself was also emasculated. This was evident in the comment of one MCC worker who described a village in which only three of forty-two families had a father: "Because of this unfortunate circumstance, it will take a number of years before the group will grow strong again through the children who will eventually fill the present gaps."[47] Growing male children were expected to fill the shoes of their absent fathers and thereby make the family unit strong again.

RELIGIOUS AND MORAL REHABILITATION

The discourse of weakness focused most explicitly on the physical and economic condition of refugee families. However, there was evident concern for the moral and spiritual strengthening of the new immigrants as well. One observer made what was a typical characterization of the postwar refugees: "For almost 30 years, they have been encouraged to loosen family life and engage in immoral sex experimentation, and have been constant witnesses to brutality, bestiality, radical change, disobedience of children to parents, and glorification of the mechanical and material achievements of life."[48] Beyond the task of assisting the new immigrants economically, North American Mennonite organizations saw as their mandate the "religious rehabilitation" of the refugees, who, given the repression of religion in the Soviet Union, had been without formal church institutions for almost two decades. This rehabilitation operated at a number of levels. First of all, for Mennonite denominations it meant planting churches and saving souls.

For many of the refugees, formal church life was not the first priority. Most refugees had established an informal religion based on private ritual that had sustained their spiritual needs over the past two decades. With the building of churches, the appointment of ministers, and the reinstitution of such formal rituals as baptism, religion took on the forms and norms of North American and other Paraguayan Mennonite churches. This formalization, which also followed the prevailing male-ordered hierarchy, made for some incongruous results given the sex imbalance among the refugees and accentuated the absence of men. For instance, the General Conference Mennonite Church in Volendam in 1952 had 147 members: 42 men and 105 women.[49] A common practice in Mennonite churches in Paraguay at the time, and in some churches in Canada, was that women and children sat on one side of the church and men on the other. Thus churches in the new colonies were visually unbalanced because the left side—where the women and children sat—was always full while the right side had only a few men and older boys.[50]

As had been the case during the German occupation of Ukraine and in the refugee camps of Germany, church choirs and their directors were mainly women. At the outset, when there were too few male ministers to serve all the immigrant settlements, women continued to undertake worship services on their own. In one instance this caused some consternation for a female relief worker accustomed to male leadership in this realm. While distributing Christmas bundles in Neuland colony, Ella Berg, an MCC worker from North America, was surprised and reluctant when she was asked to lead worship services in one village. "At Saturday night prayer meeting and Sunday morning service, I was asked to take charge. At first I protested, but they assured me they were mostly among themselves (women) and someone had to do it."[51]

Aside from performing baptisms, building churches, and instituting formal religious practice, rehabilitation also addressed issues of morality. Part of the concern for the morality of the new immigrants lay in minor aspects of external conduct and deportment. Fashion was one of these. Although the refugees were welcomed and received material assistance from the earlier settlers, different historical paths had also created significant gaps in experience and outlook between the first pioneers and the newcomers. As would happen to a degree in Canada as well, the refugees were viewed as worldly because of their short dresses and cut and curled hair. C. A. DeFehr, when confronted with this, suggested that women in refugee camps curled their hair "to pass the time," but fortunately "here in Paraguay they will be so busy they won't have time to curl it again."[52] Styling their hair was not just a way for refugee women to alleviate the boredom; in fact many had cut their hair after leaving Ukraine to reduce the problem of lice.[53]

If fashion did not vex relief workers as much as it concerned the resident colonists, other issues were more troubling. After the first transport to Paraguay, MCC subjected potential Paraguayan settlers to moral screening. Although the screening was directed at men and women alike, given the demography of this migrant group the guidelines were definitely gendered in their implications. Among a variety of points to be considered in determining the eligibility of a refugee was the moral problem of common-law marriages.[54]

RECREATING FAMILIES

The existence of "companionate marriage," as Mennonite Central Committee chief William Snyder termed it, caused ongoing headaches for relief workers and denominational leaders and ministers in both Europe and South America.[55] Perhaps unintentionally, Snyder was offering the perfect definition for those relationships that developed between men and women who had lost their first spouses through death or disappearance but had no confirmation of death. Such relationships grew out of the need for companionship, physical intimacy, material practicality, and greater economic security.

In their 1991 memoir, Peter and Elfrieda Dyck deal with the issue in a candid manner that has hitherto not been present in published writing about the Paraguayan Mennonite experience. They describe the experiences of a young woman named Elizabeth whose husband had been arrested by the Soviet secret police eight months after their marriage and who immigrated to Paraguay with a seven-year-old son. In a conversation years later she had told the Dycks that the Chaco was a green hell in a double sense for widowed refugees. She meant that the women had to cope not only with the harsh natural environment but also with their own natures as women. She pointed out that church ministers, stuck in "their traditional thinking about morality," assumed that common-law marriages were based primarily on sex, when in fact Elizabeth argued that loneliness and economic necessity were more fundamental reasons for men and women to join households.[56]

In describing the morality of the ministers as "traditional," Elizabeth was indirectly and conversely referring to the situational morality of necessity adopted by many refugees under wartime conditions.[57] In oral interviews, immigrants to Paraguay freely acknowledged the existence of companionate marriage as an almost logical outcome of the circumstances. A typical beginning of the companionate marriage was one in which "William" helped "Helen," who was struggling to get the center beam of her house in place, and she in turn replaced some missing buttons on his shirt; he might help her break in the wild ox, and she would return the favor with some freshly baked bread; soon William and Helen were sitting on each other's porches, and before long they were sharing a house.[58] Precedents for such relationships were established in unions between Mennonite women and German soldiers during the occupation of Ukraine, and also between Mennonite women and men during the refugee trek and in displaced persons camps. One woman stated: "Now it is very hard for us to understand. But during the war so many things happened that otherwise never would."[59] She clearly acknowledged the creation of a situational morality that was at odds with the normative standards of the Mennonite church.

A refugee who had been a young man growing up in the Neuland colony also acknowledged that "retroactively, it's natural that [common-law relationships] would have developed." He recalled one serious incident early in the life of the colony when an immigrant minister who had lost his wife began to spend a great deal of time at the home of a widow and her family, initially to obtain various household services such as cooking, sewing, and laundry. Seemingly the relationship progressed further, and because of his status, the man was "kicked out of the church pretty fast" and returned to Germany. The woman, who didn't know the fate of her own husband, had to publicly apologize in church.[60] In the young man's memory, this incident was a deterrent to much more "hanky-panky" in the colony; however, sources indicate that the "problem" did not go away.

That companionate marriage was a reality, but nevertheless a problem to be dealt with, was keenly felt by religious workers and other Mennonites in Paraguay who considered the situation not only immoral but acutely "embarrassing."[61] To take action on the situation, a conference was convened in Fernheim, Paraguay, in July 1949, with church representatives from Paraguay, Uruguay, Brazil, and North America. The ruling that resulted permitted remarriage for those who had been separated forcibly by the war and who had not heard from their spouses for seven years. Remarriage was also allowed after one year of obtaining proof that a still-living spouse had remarried in the Soviet Union or Europe. The guidelines condemned common-law marriages if the seven-year waiting period had not passed or if either man or woman had knowledge that a previous spouse was still alive and not remarried.[62] The outcome of this decision was mixed. The ruling seemed to cover all situations in which one member of the couple had been missing before 1942, which would have represented the majority. In cases where a couple was separated within the seven-year period or where a husband or wife was found to be living unmarried in the Soviet Union, existing common-law relationships would have been subject to discipline. For some couples it meant terminating a relationship in order to maintain their standing in the church. Others chose excommunication rather than endure yet another separation from a loved one. That there were enough cases standing outside the guidelines to cause extensive heartbreak is suggested by some oral sources. And though the ruling provided a clear statement on a gray issue, it nevertheless clearly placed companionate marriage in the realm of moral aberration and categorized the new immigrants.

Although the new immigrants in Paraguay altered the norms for unofficial marriage, they also deviated from certain accepted patterns for legal marriages. First of all, the family fragmentation among the refugees, as well as precedents set in the Soviet Union and later in Germany, led to a "greater than usual" tendency toward marriage between Mennonite women and non-Mennonite men, mostly of German stock. This exogamy was evidently viewed as a problem by Fretz, who remarked: "This situation may correct itself as the ratio of men to women tends to equalize within the next generation."[63] Also, the curiously termed "intermarriage" between Mennonite groups—specifically between General Conference Mennonites and Mennonite Brethren—became more common after the arrival of the refugees, for whom denominational divisions had little relevance. In North America, however, the Mennonite Brethren prohibited such marriages unless the General Conference member of the couple was willing to be rebaptized in a form acceptable to the former.[64] Gradually this taboo on "mixed marriages" exerted itself in Paraguay as local ministers complied with North American pressures in order to maintain "good relations." In one case "considerable ill feeling" arose when a young woman was forbidden to pray in public or to take communion within her own church because she had a boyfriend from the other conference.[65] In this, as in other examples, postwar Mennonite immigrants in Paraguay were compelled to conform to standards held by other Mennonites that had little relevance to their own experience.

Conclusion

The perception that female-headed refugee families were weak was not entirely inaccurate. With more than a decade of loss, starvation, violence, and displacement behind them, many widows and their families undoubtedly felt an overwhelming sense of defeat at seeing their new homes in the Paraguayan wilderness. Although they had left the instability of war-torn Europe behind them, the prospect of starting from scratch had the effect of weakening both body and spirit for many new immigrants, women and men alike. However, the weakness ascribed to them meant more than just the physical and emotional realities of their immediate lives. The discourse surrounding the reception and settlement of the postwar refugees suggests that they were viewed as weak, first of all, because many families lacked what made for "strong" families—a husband

and father. The language of rehabilitation further suggests that the refugees were considered weak at the moral and spiritual level as well. Although many of the new immigrants eventually migrated to Canada, in the first few years of settlement the strength that predominantly female communities displayed in sustaining themselves with limited resources was a vivid contradiction of the image of weakness ascribed to them.

NOTES

I acknowledge financial assistance from the Social Sciences and Humanities Research Council of Canada, the University of Toronto, and the Quiring-Loewen Trust.

1. Donna Yoder, "Mennonite Refugees Leave for New Homeland," *MCC Services Bulletin* 1 (March 1947): 1.

2. This total is from "Table 20—Distribution of Refugees Arriving in South America, 1947–48," in Frank H. Epp, *Mennonite Exodus: The Rescue and Resettlement of the Russian Mennonites since the Communist Revolution* (Altona, Man.: Friesen, 1962), 390. Descriptions of the four transports can be found in Peter Dyck and Elfrieda Dyck, *Up from the Rubble: The Epic Rescue of Thousands of War-Ravaged Mennonite Refugees* (Scottdale, Pa.: Herald Press, 1991). The three major sailings that followed the *Volendam* were the *General Heintzelman* (February 1948), *Charlton Monarch* (March 1948), and *Volendam II* (October 1948).

3. Previously established Paraguayan colonies of Mennonite immigrants from Canada and the Soviet Union were Menno (Canada, 1928) and Fernheim (Russia, 1930) in western Paraguay, in an area called the Chaco, and Friesland (offshoot of Fernheim, 1937) in eastern Paraguay. A recent study of Mennonite settlement in Paraguay is Edgar Stoesz and Muriel T. Stackley, *Garden in the Wilderness: Mennonite Communities in the Paraguayan Chaco, 1927–1997* (Winnipeg, Man.: CMBC, 1999).

4. Mennonite Central Committee (MCC) was established in 1920 with the initial purpose of providing material aid to Mennonites in the Soviet Union in the wake of civil war and famine. During and after World War II, MCC coordinated a variety of relief efforts in Europe and also helped approximately 12,000 Mennonites immigrate to North and South America. On the history of MCC see, for instance, John C. Unruh, *In the Name of Christ: The Story of the MCC from 1920 to 1951* (Scottdale, Pa.: Herald Press, 1952); "Mennonite Central Committee, 1920–1970," special issue of *Mennonite Quarterly Review* 44 (July 1970); and

Frank H. Epp, ed., *Partners in Service: The Story of Mennonite Central Committee Canada* (Winnipeg, Man.: Mennonite Central Committee Canada, 1983).

5. Of the 35,000 Mennonites who actually left the Soviet Union during the war, approximately 23,000 were repatriated or died on the front. Including Mennonites who were residents of Poland and Prussia, 12,000 refugees emigrated to North and South America, most to Canada. The material in this chapter is also part of a larger study: Marlene Epp, *Women without Men: Mennonite Refugees of the Second World War* (Toronto: University of Toronto Press, 2000). Oral interviews I conducted in 1993–94 are cited by number.

6. The age and sex breakdown on board the *Volendam* was as follows: children (under age sixteen), 909, men (age sixteen and over), 444, women (age sixteen and over), 950. Statistics are from *Canadian Women's Activities Letter* (Canadian office of Mennonite Central Committee) 32 (1 March 1947): 2.

7. For background on the Russian Mennonite experience during the Soviet era and World War II see, for instance, Epp, *Mennonite Exodus*, chaps. 18 and 23; George K. Epp, "Mennonite Immigration to Canada after World War II," *Journal of Mennonite Studies* 5 (1987): 108–19; Ingeborg Fleischhauer and Benjamin Pinkus, *The Soviet Germans: Past and Present* (London: Hurst, 1986); Victor G. Doerksen, "Survival and Identity in the Soviet Era," in *Mennonites in Russia, 1788–1988: Essays in Honour of Gerhard Lohrenz*, ed. John Friesen, 289–98 (Winnipeg, Man.: CMBC, 1989); John B. Toews, *Czars, Soviets and Mennonites* (Newton, Kans: Faith and Life Press, 1982); and "Mennonites and the Soviet Inferno," special issue of *Journal of Mennonite Studies* 16 (1998).

8. Sheila Fitzpatrick, *Stalin's Peasants: Resistance and Survival in the Russian Village after Collectivization* (New York: Oxford University Press, 1994), 221. Fitzpatrick suggests that the "grab bag family" was not at all uncommon in the Soviet Union during the 1930s.

9. These statistics were tabulated by George K. Epp, who as a young man was one of the immigrants to Volendam. See Epp, "Mennonite Immigration to Canada."

10. This was according to Peter Derksen, the mayor of the Neuland colony, in Dyck and Dyck, 332. Peter P. Klassen states that 264 of 636 Neuland families were female headed; he does not say for what year. He also says that in Volendam the situation was much the same. See *Die Mennoniten in Paraguay: Reich Gottes und Reich dieser Welt* (Bolanden-Weierhof, Germany: Mennonitischer Geschichtsverein, 1988), 291. According to sociologist J. Winfield Fretz, in Neuland in 1951 there were still 177 women who were in some way separated from

their husbands and not remarried, compared with 32 men. See J. Winfield Fretz, *Pilgrims in Paraguay* (Scottdale, Pa.: Herald Press, 1953), 70.

11. Caroline B. Brettell and Rita James Simon, "Immigrant Women: An Introduction," in *International Migration: The Female Experience*, ed. Rita James Simon and Caroline B. Brettell (Totowa, N.J.: Rowman and Allanheld, 1986), 3. See also Betty Bergland, "Immigrant History and the Gendered Subject: A Review Essay," *Ethnic Forum* 8 (1988): 24–39; Donna Gabaccia, "Immigrant Women: Nowhere at Home?" *Journal of American Ethnic History* 10 (summer 1991): 61–87; Gabaccia, *From the Other Side: Women, Gender, and Immigrant Life in the U.S., 1820–1990* (Bloomington: Indiana University Press, 1994); and Sydney Stahl Weinberg, "The Treatment of Women in Immigration History: A Call for Change," with comments by Donna Gabaccia, Hasia R. Diner, and Maxine Schwartz Seller, *Journal of American Ethnic History* 11 (summer 1992): 25–69. A particularly useful and specifically Canadian treatment of the issue is Franca Iacovetta, "Manly Militants, Cohesive Communities, and Defiant Domestics: Writing about Immigrants in Canadian Historical Scholarship," *Labour/Le Travail* 36 (fall 1995): 217–52.

12. Sultana Parvanta, "The Balancing Act: Plight of Afghan Women Refugees," in *Refugee Women and Their Mental Health: Shattered Societies, Shattered Lives*, ed. Ellen Cole, Oliva M. Espin, and Esther D. Rothblum (New York: Haworth Press, 1992), 127.

13. John W. Warkentin, "Carving a Home out of Primeval Forest," *Proceedings of the Fourth Mennonite World Conference*, 1948, 196–99; C. A. DeFehr, "Our Visit to Colony Volendam," *MCC Services Bulletin* 1 (December 1947): 2.

14. Interview 8.

15. Warkentin, 197–98.

16. DeFehr, 2. This article also provides descriptive details of clearing the land and building houses in the new colony. See photo in Epp, *Mennonite Exodus*, 382.

17. "Volendam and Neuland," *Mennonite Life* 5 (January 1950): 28.

18. Ella Berg, "My Visit to the Chaco's New Colony," *MCC Services Bulletin* 2 (June 1948): 2, 6.

19. Fretz, *Pilgrims in Paraguay*, 67.

20. J. Winfield Fretz, "Paraguay—Where Women Carry the Heavy End of the Load," *Canadian Mennonite*, 18 December 1958, 4–5.

21. Ibid.

22. C. A. DeFehr, "Report of the Work Done in the Past Year in Connection with the Immigrant Group, 2,305 in Number, Which Landed in Buenos Aires,

February 22, 1947," 3, Center for Mennonite Brethren Studies (hereafter CMBS), C. A. DeFehr Collection, box 3.

23. John W. Warkentin, "New Settlers Receive Much Help from Older Colonies in Paraguay," *MCC Services Bulletin* 1 (January 1948): 2; Fretz, *Pilgrims in Paraguay*, 43.

24. Vernon Neuschwander, "Mennonite Settlement in the Chaco," *MCC Services Bulletin* 1 (November 1947): 2.

25. DeFehr, "Report of the Work Done."

26. Warkentin, "Carving a Home out of Primeval Forest," 199.

27. Jakob Isaak, "The Settlement in Paraguay from the Point of View of the Colonist," *Proceedings of the Fourth Mennonite World Conference*, 1948, 192–93.

28. Interview 1.

29. H. Duerksen to C. A. DeFehr, 9 November 1948. Mennonite Heritage Center (hereafter MHC), XXII-A.1, Canadian Mennonite Board of Colonization (hereafter CMBC) Collection, (205), 1367/1358.

30. Interview 26.

31. Dyck and Dyck, 332. See also Robert Kreider, *Interviews with Peter J. Dyck and Elfrieda Klassen Dyck: Experiences in Mennonite Central Committee Service in Europe, 1941–1949* (Akron, Pa.: MCC, 1988), 188.

32. Joan Chandler, *Women without Husbands: An Exploration of the Margins of Marriage* (New York: St. Martin's Press, 1991), 121.

33. Peter Dyck, in Kreider, 378. Michael Roe, who has analyzed the experiences of refugee women displaced from their homes in the Philippines and Central America, similarly observes that "cooperative efforts in which the violently displaced organize themselves according to their own needs and priorities can be quite successful in meeting physical, safety, and psychosocial needs." See Michael Roe, "Displaced Women in Settings of Continuing Armed Conflict," in *Refugee Women and Their Mental Health: Shattered Societies, Shattered Lives*, ed. Ellen Cole, Oliva M. Espin, and Esther D. Rothblum (New York: Haworth Press, 1992), 98.

34. Interview 8.

35. Vernon Neuschwander to C. A. DeFehr, 1 November 1948, MHC, CMBC (205), XXII-A.1, 1367/1358.

36. C. A. DeFehr to J. A. Warkentin, 11 June 1948, CMBS, C. A. DeFehr Collection, box 3.

37. C. A. DeFehr, "Ein kurzer Ueberblick, betreffs der Immigranten-Gruppen, die im Jahre 1948 mit den Schiffen: Heintzelmann, Charlton Monarch

und Volendam nach Paraguay und teilweise nach Uruguay gekommen sind," 9 December 1948, CMBS, C. A. DeFehr Collection, box 3.

38. Interview 1.

39. Interview 1. Similar sentiments are expressed in interview 24. A young man aged about twenty recalled that because he "felt even more mature than his age," he assumed much of the leadership in his family.

40. Ingrid Rimland, *The Wanderers: The Saga of Three Women Who Survived* (St. Louis, Mo.: Concordia, 1977), 233–34.

41. Interview 8.

42. Interview 8.

43. Fretz, *Pilgrims in Paraguay*, 62.

44. Ibid., 64.

45. Interview 26.

46. J. Winfield Fretz, "Mennonite Aid Section, Report of the Chairman to MCC Annual Meeting," 8 January 1948, MHC, CMBC (205), XXII-A.1, 1367/1356.

47. Report of C. A. DeFehr to "Dear Teachers and College students," at Goshen College, Goshen, Indiana, 6 January 1948. MHC, CMBC (204) XXII-A.1, 1366/1353.

48. Fretz, "Mennonite Aid Section, Report of the Chairman," 1367/1356.

49. From CMBS, C. A. DeFehr Collection, box 3. It is important to remember that these numbers did not include children and other unbaptized church attenders.

50. Interview 1.

51. Berg, 6.

52. This incident is described in Dyck and Dyck, 330–31. The narrator in Interview 1 also stated that the immigrants were thought to be worldly and that this resulted in little ongoing support after the first few months of settlement.

53. See Kreider, 329–30.

54. From minutes of meeting of MCC workers at Frankfurt, Germany, 4 January 1948, MHC, CMBC, XXII-A.1, 1369/1366.

55. William T. Snyder to C. A. DeFehr, 16 September 1948, MHC, CMBC, XXII-A.1, 1369/1366.

56. Dyck and Dyck, 332–40.

57. I discuss the issue of wartime morality in greater detail in Marlene Epp, "The Memory of Violence: Soviet and East European Mennonite Refugees and Rape in World War II," *Journal of Women's History* 9 (spring 1997): 58–87.

58. Dyck and Dyck, 334–35.

59. Interview 8.

60. Interview 1.

61. Isaak, 192.

62. This is from Dyck and Dyck, 341.

63. Fretz, *Pilgrims in Paraguay,* 70–71.

64. The General Conference Mennonite Church and the Mennonite Brethren Conference were the two largest Mennonite denominational bodies in North America. Although the two conferences had similar ethnic roots, their theological emphases and church practices differed in certain areas. There was also substantial competition between the two groups to baptize individuals and plant churches among the postwar Paraguayan immigrants.

65. Fretz, *Pilgrims in Paraguay,* 70–71.

8

"The Parents Shall Not Go Unpunished"

PRESERVATIONIST PATRIARCHY

AND COMMUNITY

Steven D. Reschly

How are gender systems constructed and reconstructed? New communities offer opportunities to observe the process. Amish leaders during the first half of the nineteenth century in the United States stabilized their communities by placing increased authority in the hands of male household heads. In one Iowa community this larger process played out around issues of household simplicity and subordination, and in 1865 it became visible in decisions to take or refuse Communion.

The problematic relationship of household and community has exercised religious and political leaders across centuries of Western history. Male authority has most often served to correlate and articulate segments of an idealized social order— individual, family, household, church, community, state. In particular, during times of instability (and in the right hands what situation cannot

About 1862 Susie Miller Umble, Henry Umble Jr., and their friend Mary Stoltzfus pose in their Amish attire for their portrait in Lancaster, Pennsylvania. By 1870 the Umbles joined the Millwood Amish Mennonite Church, a new, more liberal Amish group. (Photograph courtesy of Lancaster Mennonite Historical Society, Joanne Hess Siegrist Collection, Lancaster, Pennsylvania.)

be portrayed as unstable?) male authority has fixed social relations and assuaged anxieties.

Amish immigrants from Europe to eighteenth- and nineteenth-century America confronted nearly insoluble threats to their very survival. Immigration from Europe in the early eighteenth century had created scattered clusters of Amish families in the English colonies, leading to intermarriage with non-Amish neighbors and to variations in prescribed and proscribed behavior. It seemed clear to Amish leaders that their communities were in danger of losing their distinctive identity.

The early American republic, racked by a powerful market revolution, presented a difficult environment for the survival of patriarchal rural producer communities.[1] One cluster of responses to the new urban marketplace and resulting anxieties about the patriarchal household centered on religious revival and reform, often led and shaped by women. Another cluster focused on patriarchal preservation, attempting to maintain an ancient order in the face of change perceived to be out of control. The commonsense practice of national and communal identity made appeal to paternal authority virtually instinctive as the preferred means of connecting individuals in households with the community's sense of itself. The Amish joined in the cultural recovery of male leadership by including a version of preservationist patriarchy in their repertoire of community.

Their search for means of self-preservation in the early nineteenth century led Amish religious and social leaders in the United States to strengthen the household, and paternal authority within the household, as the core of community. These leaders, including Jacob Swartzendruber, first Amish bishop in Iowa, were able to call on a long-standing tradition of patriarchal household authority in European Christianity, a legacy left unchallenged by the social radicalism of the Anabaptist movement.[2] This pattern of male leadership made sense within the Amish tradition of community when leaders found it necessary to clarify communal distinctiveness against American society.

Anabaptists and their descendants accepted the European custom of "housefather" dominion in the family. Amish disciplines in Europe include no specific reference to fathers' responsibility to enforce communal norms, likely because gathered Amish ministers could assume the ubiquitous presence of paternal rule. The disciplines do mention parents' general duty to socialize children. Ministers and elders are usually held responsible for resolving conflict and keeping order in congregations.[3] In North America, however, Amish leaders could no longer assume universal awareness and acceptance of housefather authority, and they found themselves forced to attempt to re-create housefather rule in their new circumstances. Amish ministers and bishops constructed more and more elaborate cultural distinctions, and they relied on parents, especially fathers, to patrol the borders they constructed.

CRISIS AND PATRIARCHAL INNOVATION

The crisis of Amish survival stretched across the late colonial and early national periods of American history. Many immigrant families found themselves isolated and lacking support for Amish group identity. Kinship ties took precedence over responsibility to communal duties within and among these scattered family clusters. Traveling bishops accomplished little more than performing marriages, administering Communion, and officiating at baptisms. Amish historian Joseph F. Beiler has maintained that the Revolutionary era nearly destroyed the tiny Amish communities in Pennsylvania: "For quite a few years we have noticed that most of our initial ancestor families in America have not raised more than one son to remain in the old faith. Some have not kept any sons in the church, some have kept a few, but not one record do we have that kept the whole family within before the revolution. After that there are some. It is evident that many sons who came to this land of freedom were overwhelmed with the air of freedom in America during the revolution period."[4] Similar isolation, combined with harsh persecution and destructive warfare, resulted in the complete extinction of the Amish in Europe by 1937.[5]

According to anthropologist John A. Hostetler's interpretation, in the early nineteenth century church supervision gradually superseded family autonomy in the effort to preserve Amish communal identity. As settlements slowly grew in size—the Lancaster County Amish did not divide into two congregations until 1843, about a century after the first Amish arrived in the county—Amish family clusters "ordained resident bishops [to replace itinerant bishops], and thus church control began to be exercised over family and kinship rule." Church regulation of lifestyle resulted in the gradual emergence of a reconfigured identity "as Amish were distinguished from non-Amish" in the American context. However, with increasing congregational control over families and individuals, "both religious and secular controversies began to plague the Amish people."[6] Communal directives made effective through family authority deposed individualism and family autonomy in Amish practice, thus preserving a unique ethnoreligious identity based on group dominion.

Historian Paton Yoder followed and expanded Hostetler's interpretation. Yoder used several recorded Amish church disciplines, or *Ordnungen*, behavior-oriented versions of the more familiar Confession of Faith, to trace the elaboration of communal regulation in antebellum Amish communities. Yoder pointed to the enforcing of community standards through traditional Anabaptist practices of the ban (excommunication) and shunning (*Meidung*, or social avoidance) as the means by which "the authority of the church over the Amish community" was strengthened.[7]

Developments in Amish communities during the first half of the nineteenth century can be interpreted as asserting church control *through* the family rather than over it. Or more accurately, one can say that Amish disciplines tightened the connections among individual, family, household, and community by bonding all four elements in a common patriarchal framework to maintain traditional Anabaptist values of separation from and nonconformity to the world. Paternal authority was the blessed tie that bound households to community, forged in the imperative linkages of parents, children, and religious community. Regulation of marriage and household formation, especially restrictions on traditional courtship practices, were the avenue for strengthening paternal household management.

Historian Helena Wall has argued that colonial Americans believed in an essential relationship of family and community and "accepted the preeminent right of the community to regulate the lives of its members" in the interests of community order. Family behavior required special attention, since a well-ordered family was a microcosm of orderly society. The right of community oversight, expressed in neighborly supervision of marital and child-rearing practices, eroded during the second half of the eighteenth century. Principles of patriarchy and hierarchy were replaced by republicanism in politics, individualism, and contractualism.[8] Wall probably overemphasized how completely patriarchalism disappeared and underestimated the continuation of patriarchy in post-Revolutionary ideals of republican motherhood. She was hardly the first to place individualism at the center of an American ethos.

If Wall is correct in finding a disconnection of the family-community nexus in the early American republic, then the Amish found they could no longer set their community against a larger community, as they had learned to do in Europe. Maintaining communal distinction against a set of individuals became more difficult, especially since American ideas of society seemed to be moving toward the Anabaptist and Amish practice of voluntarism. Like the society around them, Amish leaders attempted to preserve the patriarchal household as the bulwark against extremist American individualism. But whereas Americans believed in the necessity of a universal social order, the Amish wished to preserve communal order without recourse to a coercive state. The lack of coercion made patriarchal leadership seem even more essential if Amish communities were to retain their cohesion.

The Amish in Europe and North America practiced congregational autonomy and local control, traditions developed in response to persecution and scattered households. Distance and decentralized organization made it difficult to impose conformity, and Amish leaders often resorted to ad hoc local or regional ministers' meetings to resolve disputes and connect distant settlements. Jacob Swartzendruber attended several ministers' meetings during the first half of the nineteenth century, and he gathered an extensive personal library of handwritten disciplines and ministers' manuals.[9] While always seeking to preserve traditional Amish religious values, Swartzendruber and his fellow ministers innovated by reemphasizing housefathers as a crucial link in the chain of authority devised for community continuity.

The first recorded gathering of Amish ministers in America occurred on October 17, 1809, most likely in the Berks-Chester-Lancaster settlement. According to Bishop Jacob Frederick Swartzendruber (grandson of Jacob), his great-grandfather Christian Yoder, bishop of the Glades Congregation in Somerset County, Pennsylvania, wrote the discipline agreed on by the assembled ministers. The nine points regulated the relationship of individual, church, and world. Members who left the Amish must be banned and shunned, with provisions for disciplining those who did not follow the rule of shunning; swearing of oaths and jury service were prohibited; ministers could preach at the funerals only of Amish members, not of outsiders; and all members could take part in the council (*Abrath*) of the church, that is, participate in setting community standards and maintaining communal harmony in preparation for Communion services. Personal grooming and clothing also fell within the purview of Amish maintenance, as article 7 of the 1809 discipline prohibited cutting hair and beard, and article 9 reads, "Proud dresses, proud trousers, hats, and combs in the hair, and similar worldly clothing shall not be tolerated in the church."[10] Both male and female deportment came under scrutiny, but this discipline did not yet specifically appeal for parental exertion on behalf of general Amish standards.

By contrast, the 1837 discipline drawn up by the three congregations in Somerset County, Pennsylvania, on March 18 (at a meeting attended by Preacher Jacob Swartzendruber) did entreat parents to enforce the lengthening list of concerns. The first article of the twelve encouraged use of the ban and shunning and blamed neglect of the ban for the "decline" that had "set in" among Amish members. Other articles prohibited holding political office, excessive driving of sleighs, and painting vehicles with two colors and required church members to keep the Sabbath and avoid fashionable clothing in favor of the "old style."

The ninth article prohibited bundling, the courtship practice in which a male and female sleep together while fully clothed:

> With regard to the excesses practiced among the youth, namely that the youth take the liberty to sleep or lie together without any fear or shame, such things shall not be tolerated at all. And when it takes place with the knowledge of the parents and something bad happens on account of it [that is, a pregnancy], the parents shall not go unpunished.

By making parents responsible for their children's sexual behavior, the assembled ministers hoped to cement the bond between parental authority and community moral precepts. Control over courtship and marital practices was a keynote of the 1837 discipline, which Jacob Swartzendruber signed.

The second and third articles specifically mentioned mothers and implied that their tendency to adornment must be curbed, both in clothing themselves and their children and in decorating their houses:

Second: It is noted that there is awful pride in clothing, namely with respect to silken neck-cloths [*Halstuecher*] worn around the neck, so that mothers tie silken neck-cloths on their children, and make high collars on their children's shirts and clothing, and the mothers permit their daughters to wear men's hats and go with them to church or other places, or that even the mothers have them themselves. Decided that such things shall not be among us.

Not only fashionable clothing, but the tendency to confuse gendered clothing received special attention. Parents were given responsibility for socializing their children into Amish values.

Third: Decided that there shall be no display in houses, namely when houses are built, or painted with various colors, or filled with showy furniture, namely with wooden, porcelain, or glass utensils (dishes), and having cupboards and mirrors hung on the wall, and such things. . . .

Eleventh: Likewise, the cabinetmakers are not to make such proud kinds of furniture and not decorate them with such loud or gay [*scheckich*] colors.

The second, third, and eleventh articles dealt with the "feminine" domain of raising children, running the kitchen, and guiding domestic activities. Fashion and color were temptations to pride, the opposite value of humility and lowliness prized by Amish tradition. The potential disobedience of mothers and children in dress and household fashion required careful prevention.

The sixth and seventh articles regulated marriage with persons outside the Amish faith, and both advocated more stringent requirements for accepting partners into fellowship. Specifically, non-Amish partners were to be brought "into Christian discipline," meaning submission to the Amish *Ordnung,* and they had to "promise before God and the brotherhood to fulfill the obligations of Christian marriage," in effect holding a second wedding in the church. The ad hoc disciplines of 1809 and 1837 used the politics of gender to enhance community discipline and uniformity. Male authority became the conduit for creating communal distinction, and patriarchy remained the preferred communal principle for confronting uncertain social challenges.

These written disciplines with their renewed paternal authority were not mere documents to be ignored. Jacob Swartzendruber, for example, moved first to Maryland and then to Iowa to escape the practice of bundling in Somerset County, Pennsylvania.[11] He wished to become part of a new community where the ideal of housefather leadership, symbolized by eradicating bundling, could be put into effect. In 1851 he bought 560 acres of land in Johnson County, Iowa, and immediately began settling his adult children on farms of their own, enacting the new church discipline in order to protect his children from worldly influences. One indicator of the anxiety he felt about retaining his family in the faith appears in the form of a dream he had a few years after his move to Iowa.

While Jacob Swartzendruber was staying with his stepson, Daniel P. Guengerich, the night of April 27–28, 1858, he dreamed an enemy took a position nearby and shot fiery arrows and bullets at him. All flew by and none found its mark, but the patriarch finally perceived his danger and moved away from his attacker. Daniel appeared in front of his stepfather and, as Swartzendruber wrote to him later, "I pushed you before me away from the fire because there was danger, but you were so heavy that I almost could not get you away; you turned your face from me, and I had both my hands square in your back and pushed with all my strength." Then Swartzendruber awoke, perhaps an hour and a half before daylight, and could not find sleep again.[12]

Swartzendruber wished to warn his stepson about the dangers of associating with a member of his congregation he considered dangerous and unproductive. Earlier in the letter, he admonished Guengerich not to help Levi Miller in any way.[13] He was willing to expend great effort to keep his kin out of harm's way. It appears he perceived his stepson as uncooperative and unappreciative of this warning. But the aging bishop was following a prescription for housefather leadership and responsibility that he himself helped to develop and that he argued for repeatedly among his fellow Amish ministers.

Another indicator of Swartzendruber's firm commitment to family life was his emotional farewell to his first wife and his subsequent remarriage. Barbara, his first wife, died on January 24, 1856, an event that distressed him greatly. He wrote a moving tribute to his departed wife in October, noting that her commitment to the Amish church was so strong she insisted he attend a Communion service in 1853 at William Wertz's house, some eight miles from home, even though she was seriously ill. Swartzendruber was ordained bishop that same Sunday in 1853. In 1860, during a trip to visit churches in the East, he was married again, to Mary Miller, widow of Daniel Miller, a full deacon in Indiana.[14] During this trip he continued to gather copies of older disciplines and ministers' manuals, and he returned even more prepared to institute the new discipline of housefather administration.

Swartzendruber wrote impassioned essays in 1863 and 1865 condemning bundling and appealing to parents to stop the traditional courtship practice.[15] In his August 1863 essay on bundling, he recalled the local ministers' meeting in the Glades congregation in Somerset County on October 3, 1830, which condemned bundling and made parents responsible for enforcing the injunction. No printed discipline survives from this meeting, unless Swartzendruber meant 1837 instead of 1830, but he recalled language similar to the 1837 discipline: "If something evil results" from young unmarried people lying together during the night, meaning a pregnancy, "then the parents should not remain unpunished." Therefore parents should be careful to "keep good order in their households," since "every House-father and House-mother is responsible before God for their children." By addressing both fathers and mothers, Swartzendruber extended the obligation of adult married women to enforce community moral standards. The essay continued with many biblical citations concerning purity and separation of the church from the world, especially in terms of sexual behavior, and asserted that ministers were not warning their children with all prophetic seriousness. "What must an outside honorable man think of us," Swartzendruber continued, when he hears that "our young people lie together at night and perhaps can be seen going home in the gray light of dawn."

He also worried about outsiders gossiping about weddings and frolics. Neighbors were hearing about Amish failings. Young people should not "make secret vows" without consulting parents and sending a minister to ask for a woman's hand in marriage. Swartzendruber considered parental control over marriage decisions part of the Amish confession of faith and Christian practice; loss of control was represented by bundling and fashionable marriage ceremonies. In Swartzendruber's view, weddings should not be conducted with such great excess, where even English songs and rough talk appear, but should reflect spiritual care and consciousness of marriage under God. He called on both parents and ministers to control weddings and courtship practices among Amish congregations.

In fact, marriage and the administration of households constituted a central issue in the *Diener Versammlungen* (ministers' meetings), which met annually from 1862 to 1878, except in 1877. Several progressive leaders called these meetings and invited representatives from every Amish community in North America in an attempt to resolve conflicts in several local Amish communities.[16] At the first ministers' meeting in Wayne County, Ohio, in June 1862, the first order of business was "the difficulties between the Elkhart and Lagrange congregations" in northern Indiana. Tradition-minded and change-minded factions had already parted company by 1857, but there was still some hope for reconciliation. The assembled ministers turned the matter over to a committee of six to attempt a settlement. As the proceedings continued, some ministers pleaded for toleration of individual conscience, while others argued for stricter attention to the traditional principles of separation from the world and nonconformity to the world. Levi Miller, a traditionalist bishop from Holmes County, Ohio, spoke against lightning rods, photographs, lotteries, meetinghouses, and insurance and the innovation of baptism in streams rather than in houses. Then, in response to a plea for tolerating differences from John K. Yoder, a change-minded bishop from Wayne County, Ohio, someone produced a letter from Jacob Swartzendruber.

> The letter said that he was minded to stay with the articles of faith as they are recorded in the prayer booklet; he is against all innovation. He is against recommending the office of full deacon for a [regular] deacon right at the beginning [before he has gone through a probationary period of some years]. [He] speaks strongly against outsiders [unbaptized young people, not yet members] sitting in a [congregational] council meeting, and against the marriage of near relatives, such as grandchildren [first cousins]. He wants to be patient concerning baptism in water if that is what the assembled ministers approve.[17]

Swartzendruber seems to have been particularly concerned with maintaining traditional Amish social values. His special concern with faithful families and marital ethics appears in the brief minute from 1862, when he wrote against consanguineous marriage.

At the next ministers' meeting, held in Mifflin County, Pennsylvania, in May 1863, Abner Yoder served as chair. Again the first order of business was attempting to reconcile factions in the local Amish community. Jonathan Yoder, a change-minded bishop from McLean County, Illinois, raised the question whether a member who was banned because of marriage outside the church could be taken back "without his spouse joining our church."[18] A committee recommended discontinuing the ban if the member demonstrated repentance, without specifying what would be required.

Jacob Swartzendruber attended the following ministers' meeting in Elkhart County, Indiana, in June 1864, the only one he observed in person. Once again the first order of business was to attempt a reconciliation between the change-minded and traditionalist factions in the local Amish churches. After a report recommending local decisions on whether to ban members who left to join another nonresistant denomination (such as Mennonite), Swartzendruber asked, "Is it not immoral if a person leaves the [Amish] church?" He seemed to express traditionalists' frustration when he asked shortly thereafter, "Shall the other side not be heard?" Later, he said he stood "in favor of shunning without regarding the person" and added his intention "to hold to Holy Writ."[19]

The assembly also dealt with the issue of marriage outside the Amish faith and again recommended great caution in applying the ban, especially if the member married into another nonresistant denomination. Jacob Swartzendruber addressed himself to the report, but his words were not recorded; his son, Frederick, noted the "bad results which generally come from marrying outside the denomination."[20] Issues involving marriage arose again later in the conference, leading John K. Yoder to present a lengthy discourse on marriage and the necessity of not mingling church and world. Yoder stated that "those who are in the church of God have no permission to marry outside the church with those who stand in unbelief" and advocated punishment with the ban. Yoder also said, "A marriage in the Lord between a believer and an unbeliever is surely impossible." When Yoder finished, according to the minutes, "Jacob Schwarzendruber witnessed forcefully to what Johann K. Joder had presented with respect to marriage."[21]

Marriage is a most difficult locale to enforce separation from the world. How can a congregation ban one partner and keep the other in the church? Powerful issues of sexual ethics, bundling in courtship, household order, discipline of children, and reproduction of community are involved. Marital mores were not the central issue of the ministers' meetings, but family life was clearly an important and recalcitrant subject, to which Jacob Swartzendruber gave his special attention.

Swartzendruber did not attend the 1865 ministers' meeting, held in Wayne County, Ohio, in June, the one that finalized the Great Schism between the tradition-minded and the change-minded.[22] Tradition-minded leaders set forth a manifesto that was virtually ignored by the other faction, and very few tradition-minded leaders attended any ministers' meetings after 1865. Jacob's son, Frederick, attended in 1865, as did future Iowan Abner Yoder, still in Somerset County, Pennsylvania. And Jacob Swartzendruber penned a lengthy letter to the 1865 gathering. He offered his position on whether Amish members who left and joined the Dunkers or Mennonites should be shunned (they should); whether anyone should marry closer than second cousins (they should not); the practice of bundling (no one should); the ongoing issues of fashionable clothing, represented by fancy weddings (in his mind an excessive practice and offensive to Amish simplicity); and the $300 commutation fee as an alternative to Civil War military service (frivolous if done to stay home and live in comfort while others died in battle).

As in his 1863 essay, Swartzendruber wrote passionately against bundling and quoted the same 1837 discipline on parental responsibility if a pregnancy occurred from the courtship practice. "The parents should take care" regarding "the young people lying together, pre-marital intercourse," and if "something bad" results, "the parents should not remain unpunished." He lamented occurrences when "the boys go into the beds with the girls when they perhaps have drunk too much and evil consequences follow," as evinced by illegitimate children and acts of church discipline. "Oh what a great sin it is if ministers and parents and all members do not take enough care for the youth, or the mother of a house perhaps herself helps to prepare the beds." He considered bundling a hindrance to "right knowledge" among Amish youth, an "evil which has rooted itself in all the congregations" that prevented young people from submitting to the truth. He wrote sternly, "How sad it is that old people say, I cannot forbid this because I myself did it."[23]

Swartzendruber also wrote at length against what he called "the abuse" of holding weddings, expanding his 1863 call for spiritual wed-

dings without revelry. He again advocated that young people take counsel from their parents when they want to marry, then send a minister to
carry a proposal of marriage from young man to young woman, "and not
make promises in advance whereby the young people play the hypocrite."
Excessive meals and secular music should be condemned, and all members
should be responsible to "pay sufficient attention to order," especially
ministers, "the watchmen who are to warn the people."[24]

Jacob Swartzendruber's vigorous opposition to bundling brought a response from the 1865 ministers' meeting. According to the minutes,

> A letter from an old and experienced minister from Iowa was handed in. But
> since it was noted that the main thrust of the letter is encompassed in the first
> ruling [of the 1865 session, on not conforming to the world], it was considered
> superfluous to vote on the total contents of the letter. But it was considered
> highly important to lay the following [proposed] ruling before the assembly,
> which was unanimously adopted:
>
> Ruled [*beschlossen*] that we fully agree with Brother Schwarzendruber's
> views concerning the vulgarities [bundling] of single people of opposite sexes
> and we herewith give full support, and admonish all Christian house-fathers
> to prevent all improprieties of the youth in their houses.[25]

Legislating against the traditional courtship practice did not stop
bundling, of course, but the issue makes the connections between household authority and communal norms more explicit.

Another question answered during the 1865 ministers' meeting spoke
even more directly to the situation in Johnson County, Iowa. Someone
asked how to deal in a "scripturally appropriate" way with a member who
refuses to take Communion for several years. The assembly responded
that the Lord's Supper is not to be neglected. If a member does not respond after being "admonished in love with God's Word," that person
may not continue as a member of the congregation. In nineteenth-
century Amish theology and practice, Communion was the central symbol and embodiment of congregational accord. Nothing less than unani-
mous agreement with the *Ordnung*, tested the week before Communion
in congregational council meeting (*Abrath*), would suffice as preparation
to hold Communion. Indeed, the term of choice for Communion was *Die
Einigkeit,* the union or unity.[26] To stay away from Communion meant ex-

treme disagreement with the *Ordnung*, and according to the logic of congregational discipline, continuing to abstain could be treated as equivalent to voluntary withdrawal from fellowship.

SHOULD FATHERS RULE?

The question of participation in Communion existed in Johnson County because of a conflict focused on Preacher Joseph Keim and Deacon John Mishler. Indications are that the issues focused on household management, since Keim complained of colored or decorated dishes, and on male household leadership.[27] Owing to the lack of community consensus, no Communion could be held from 1863 to 1865; and when Jacob Swartzendruber finally did conduct a Communion service, it served as an occasion to express disunity more than harmony. The dissension challenged Jacob Swartzendruber's religious leadership in the Amish community, his personal authority within his own extended family, and the principle of paternal household administration.

On Easter Sunday, April 16, 1865, some six weeks before he wrote to the 1865 ministers' meeting, Jacob Swartzendruber held Communion in the Sharon Township congregation for the first time in three years. The service took place at the home of John Kempf in section 33, at the south edge of the township. According to a list recorded by Swartzendruber, sixty-six members took Communion and sixty refused. The following Sunday in the Deer Creek congregation, Washington Township, thirty-eight participated in Communion at the Peter Brenneman residence, again at the southern end of the township, while forty-eight did not. The nearly even division between those who considered themselves in harmony with the Amish church and those who did not reveals a community at odds with itself. Only one week after General Lee surrendered to General Grant at Appomattox Court House in Virginia on April 9, and only two days after John Wilkes Booth shot President Abraham Lincoln on April 14, the Amish of Johnson County, Iowa, continued their own internecine struggle over the meaning of union.

Swartzendruber's cryptic list presents problems in identifying who took Communion and who refused. He often used nicknames or first names and seldom wrote any women's names. Two generations later his grandson, Elmer G. Swartzendruber, identified most persons on Jacob Swartzendruber's list in response to a query from historian Melvin Gingerich.[28] About 70 percent of the names mentioned can be identified from the 1860 and 1870 federal censuses for Sharon and Washington Townships. The rest lived in Washington County or Iowa County, arrived after 1860 and left before 1870, or may have been missed by census takers.

Most of the persons Jacob Swartzendruber listed are married couples. Only adult children appear, in keeping with the Amish practice of considering only baptized adults full members. A number of names appear alone, mostly older widows and widowers. More females than males chose to refuse the symbol of community unity. In the Sharon Amish church, besides married couples, eleven men and three women broke bread while five men and twelve women refused. The next weekend, ten men and five women partook while one man and six women refused. Twenty-one men and eight women participated while eighteen women and six men refused, about a 75 percent majority in either direction based on gender. In addition, at least twelve married couples parted company for these Communion services, and in no case did the wife participate. While most women demonstrated their consent to Jacob Swartzendruber's program, a significant number refused their support, and a disparity appeared between the backing of men and the discomfort of women. This gender gap is all the more remarkable given the expectation that husbands and wives be unified in the congregation and the sanctions against those who married outside the faith or the ambiguities created when one partner was banned and shunned.

Three of the married women who refused to follow their husbands to the Communion table were Jacob Swartzendruber's own daughters-in-law: Barbara, married to Jacob's eldest son, Joseph; Elizabeth, married to Christian; and Mary, wife of George. Jacob's nephew, Peter Swartzendruber, saw his wife, Barbara, refuse Communion; and Jacob's daughter, Lena, wife of Joseph Bender, also stayed away. Mary Shetler Swartzendruber gave birth to twins, Amelia and Lovina, on April 8, and Elizabeth Eash Swartzendruber gave birth to Simon on March 12. Since both families lived near the northwest corner of Washington Township, while the service at Peter Brenneman's took place toward the southeast corner, this may explain why neither attended. Joseph Swartzendruber attended both Communion services, and his wife, Barbara Brenneman Swartzendruber, attended neither. Her youngest child, Noah, was born the previous August. Given the importance of the biennial Communion ceremony in

Amish theology and practice and the fact that no Communion had been held for three years, severe extenuating circumstances would have been required to allow members to miss the service. Twins eight days old would likely excuse the mother, but not the rest of the kin network. It appears that the struggle to define household authority reached to the patriarch's own extended family.

Henry Hostetler, the only household head older than forty-five whose wife refused Communion, was accompanied to the Communion service by three of his sons. His wife, Susannah, stayed home. One of Henry's sons, Emmanuel, had served in the Union army and met his death at Vicksburg; another son, Christian, had also served in the military but survived the war.[29] Hostetler was one of the wealthiest farmers in southwestern Johnson County in 1860 and could have paid the $300 commutation fee several times over, but for some reason his sons joined the great national conflict. Perhaps Susannah avoided the symbol of community union because of her grief and the uncertain status being the mother of a veteran would carry within a nonresistant ethnoreligious group.

Three couples from Sharon Township went separate ways in their Communion service: John J. and Sarah Plank, Samuel and Ann Hostetler, and John and Sarah Petersheim. With the exception of Henry Hostetler, age sixty in 1865, all the male household heads were between twenty-six and forty-five years old. Three of Henry Hostetler's adult male children attended Communion, and other cases in which children did not follow parents appear in the record. Three children of John and Magdalene Rhodes took Communion, even though both their parents refused; and three children, one a daughter, of Joseph P. and Sarah Miller did not attend even though both their parents participated in Communion. Both gender and generation divided partakers and nonpartakers.

There are few extant materials written by nineteenth-century Amish women. No document has yet been discovered, for example, in which the women who stayed away from Communion explained what they were doing. Silence is a traditional Amish demeanor, especially in church conflicts. A first-person letter or article in which an Amish woman explains her nonparticipation in Communion is virtually unthinkable.[30] Indirect access through quantitative methods must suffice to examine why some members refused Communion in 1865. Compared with partakers, nonpartakers of Communion were younger and more oriented to new technology and agricultural production for cash markets, but they owned less land and spent more on personal consumption. The fundamental issue may have been transmitting Amish household structures to the next generation. In the 1860 population and agricultural censuses, nonpartakers owned less landed wealth and more personal wealth; their household heads were slightly older, and they produced more hay and wheat, owned less value in agricultural implements, and produced less butter. They were more oriented to personal consumption, new technology, and less involvement by women in agricultural production. The younger households of nonpartakers were not in as secure an economic position in 1860 as the older and wealthier partaker farm households. Principles of personal frugality, balancing production for home and marketplace, cautious adoption of new technology, and paternal household leadership were imperfectly transferred. The prescriptions of Amish leaders for ethnoreligious recreation in new settlements that Jacob Swartzendruber helped to formulate and defend, such as careful control over household formation and paternal administration of family and church, came into question in the 1865 refusals to take Communion.

By contrast, data from the 1870 census reveal a more successful transfer of values from the older generation to the younger. By 1870, those who refused Communion in 1865 actually owned more value in real estate and nearly as much farmland. Those households that were divided in 1865 owned the most real estate and the largest farms in 1870, and women in those households produced by far the most children and even the most butter. The greater wealth of all three groups compared with all Amish households in 1870 likely indicates a large number of new households since 1865 because of migration from eastern Amish communities. The most significant variable in an analysis of the 1870 census is number of children, with nonpartakers producing almost two more children per household than partakers despite being more similar in age than in the 1860 census figures. Partakers continued to own more implements in 1870, which may indicate greater orientation to new technology and cash production within the mainstream Amish community rather than utilizing the kin network for paid farm labor. Value of farm was higher for partakers, likely due to more developed buildings and fields. Partaker households still produced more butter, but the disparity was growing smaller.

Comparison of the 1860 and 1870 censuses substantiates the impression of an Amish community that succeeded in resolving conflicts capable of destroying it. Transfer of wealth and the re-creation of the Amish farming and household system by a new generation had been accomplished. The generational and domestic crises of 1865 seem to have dissipated by 1870, producing a community in greater harmony with itself.

But this harmony was not without personal and communal costs. Many Amish families who could not reconcile themselves to the directions the Johnson County Amish had taken chose to move to other Amish communities, and Melvin Gingerich reported faint echoes of hostility among families as late as the 1930s resulting from the bitter disputes of the 1860s. Preacher Joseph Keim and Deacon John Mishler moved to other Amish communities. Mishler was "silenced" (he could no longer serve as deacon) on March 6, 1864, and moved to Polk County, Iowa, in 1868. Keim moved to Douglas County, Illinois, where he became the first Amish bishop in that state.[31]

Abner Yoder, an ally of Jacob Swartzendruber, moved to Iowa in the spring of 1866 from Somerset County, Pennsylvania. A Communion service in 1868 showed more harmony, at least in the Deer Creek congregation, where eighty-eight observed the ceremony and only nine refrained, although the Sharon Township congregation saw sixty-four communicants and fifty-seven who refused.[32] Jacob Swartzendruber died on June 5, 1868, completing the transition to a new set of community leaders.

There may have been an emphasis in the Iowa Amish community, led in its early years by Bishop Jacob Swartzendruber, on founding as many strong households as possible, with an accent on male household heads' safeguarding the Amish way of life. Raising believing, obedient children, after all, was considered a prerequisite to holding the office of bishop, and "keeping house" was a central metaphor for maintaining congregational discipline.[33] Swartzendruber did put pressure on his family to help "keep house" in the congregation, a peculiarly feminine idiom in English but a phrase that in German implies "ruling the household."

The effort to suppress bundling may have been an especially sensitive issue. Courtship practices such as bundling and night courting likely offered mothers and daughters greater control over mate selection in eighteenth- and nineteenth-century America. When Jacob Swartzendruber attempted to strengthen household authority and create a structure of preservationist patriarchy—a stable standard of female subordination to male household heads on behalf of the community—it seems logical to conclude that renewed paternal authority threatened female autonomy. Gendered authority models faced resistance during the nineteenth century, but they were also strongly defended as an essential levee to restrain the rising flood tide of American individualism.

NOTES

1. Jacksonian America has long been portrayed as a period of rapid social and economic change. The Amish, despite their sense of isolation, were not immune from the atmosphere of upheaval. See Charles Grier Sellers, *The Market Revolution: Jacksonian America, 1815–1846* (New York: Oxford University Press, 1991), and Paul E. Johnson and Sean Wilentz, *The Kingdom of Matthias: A Story of Sex and Salvation in Nineteenth-Century America* (New York: Oxford University Press, 1994).

2. Keith Sprunger, "God's Powerful Army of the Weak: Anabaptist Women of the Radical Reformation," in *Triumph over Silence: Women in Protestant History*, ed. Richard L. Greaves (Westport, Conn.: Greenwood Press, 1985), 45–74.

3. Harold S. Bender, "The Discipline Adopted by the Strasburg Conference of 1568," *Mennonite Quarterly Review* 1 (January 1927): 57–66; Harold S. Bender, "An Amish Church Discipline of 1779," *Mennonite Quarterly Review* 11 (April 1937): 163–68.

4. Joseph F. Beiler, "Revolutionary War Records," *Diary* 7 (March 1975): 71.

5. John A. Hostetler, *Amish Society*, 4th ed. (Baltimore: Johns Hopkins University Press, 1993), 68–70.

6. Ibid., 64.

7. Paton Yoder, *Tradition and Transition: Amish Mennonites and Old Order Amish, 1800–1900* (Scottdale, Pa: Herald Press, 1991), 29–34; quotation on 29.

8. Helena M. Wall, *Fierce Communion: Family and Community in Early America* (Cambridge: Harvard University Press, 1990): ix, 8, 148.

9. John S. Umble, "Catalog of an Amish Bishop's Library," *Mennonite Quarterly Review* 20 (July 1946): 230–41.

10. Harold S. Bender, trans. and ed., "Some Early American Amish Mennonite Disciplines," *Mennonite Quarterly Review* 8 (April 1934): 90–98. This article includes the disciplines of 1809, 1837, and 1865.

11. Melvin Gingerich, *The Mennonites in Iowa: Marking the One Hundredth Anniversary of the Coming of the Mennonites to Iowa* (Iowa City: State Historical Society of Iowa, 1939), 244; notation in a notebook kept by Jacob Swartzen-

druber's grandson, Jacob Frederick Swartzendruber, in Archives of the Mennonite Church, Goshen, Indiana (hereafter AMC), Daniel Bender Swartzendruber Collection, Hist. MSS. 1–144, box 1, folder 3. The grandson states explicitly that bundling was the reason Jacob Swartzendruber left Maryland and claims that Iowa was one of the first Amish communities in America where bundling was not allowed.

12. Jacob Swartzendruber to Daniel P. Guengerich, shortly after April 1858, AMC, Daniel Bender Swartzendruber Collection, Hist. MSS. 1–144, box 1, folder 23.

13. Miller evidently accused Swartzendruber of unspecified mistakes, and eventually Swartzendruber was obliged to make a confession before his congregation. Jacob Swartzendruber to Jonathan Yoder, Andrew Ropp, and Christian Ropp, 18 October 1866, AMC, Daniel Bender Swartzendruber Collection, Hist. MSS. 1–144, box 2, folder 5.

14. Swartzendruber's tribute to his deceased wife and notes on his remarriage can be found in AMC, Daniel Bender Swartzendruber Collection, Hist. MSS. 1–144, box 2, folder 20.

15. Harold S. Bender, trans. and ed., "An Amish Bishop's Conference Epistle of 1865," *Mennonite Quarterly Review* 20 (July 1946): 222–29; original letters in AMC, Daniel Bender Swartzendruber Collection, Hist. MSS. 1–144, box 1, folder 16.

16. Yoder, *Tradition and Transition*, 137–203; James Nelson Gingerich, "Ordinance or Ordering: *Ordnung* and the Amish Ministers' Meeting, 1862–1878," *Mennonite Quarterly Review* 60 (April 1986): 180–99.

17. *Verhandlungen der Diener-Versammlungen der deutschen Täufer oder amischen Mennoniten*, translations and pagination from *Proceedings of the Amish Ministers' Meetings, 1862–1878*, ed. Paton Yoder and Steven R. Estes (Goshen, Ind.: Mennonite Historical Society, 1999), 8; hereafter cited as *Proceedings*.

18. *Proceedings*, 1863, 30, 32.

19. *Proceedings*, 1864, 47, 49.

20. *Proceedings*, 1864, 51–53.

21. *Proceedings*, 1864, 54–56.

22. Yoder, *Tradition and Transition*, 153–70.

23. Bender, "Amish Bishop's Conference Epistle."

24. Ibid.

25. *Proceedings*, 1865, 63–64.

26. A term used by Jacob Swartzendruber in his letter to Jonathan Yoder, Andrew Ropp, and Christian Ropp; see note 13 above.

27. An oral tradition reported by Melvin Gingerich in *Mennonites in Iowa*. In the 1890s Jacob Frederick Swartzendruber noted with disapproval the presence of porcelain dishes. See his copybook, AMC, Daniel Bender Swartzendruber Collection, Hist. MSS. 1–144, box 1, folder 3.

28. The original list may be found in AMC, Daniel Bender Swartzendruber Collection, Hist. MSS. 1–144; work by Elmer G. Swartzendruber and Mary Gingerich on the identity of persons listed may be found in Iowa Mennonite Historical Society Archives, Kalona, Iowa (hereafter IMHSA).

29. Emmanuel Hochstetler to Peter Swartzendruber, 29 November 1862, IMHSA; letter published in Iowa Mennonite Historical Society *Reflections* 5 (summer 1991): 3–4.

30. Hostetler, 387–90.

31. Willard H. Smith, *Mennonites in Illinois* (Scottdale, Pa.: Herald Press, 1983), 132–33.

32. Gingerich, *Mennonites in Iowa*, 125–26, 129. The issue in 1868 in the Sharon Township congregation was communal responsibility in the disposition of private property; see chapter 5.

33. David Beiler to Jacob Swartzendruber, AMC, Daniel Bender Swartzendruber Collection, Hist MSS. 1–144, box 1, folder 12; Yoder, *Tradition and Transition*, 99–112.

9

Mennonite Missionary Martha Moser Voth in the Hopi Pueblos, 1893–1910

Cathy Ann Trotta

In Mennonite historiography missionary women's contributions to indigenous cultures and communities are often overlooked. Through diaries and thousands of photographs left by Martha Moser Voth and her husband, Heinrich R. Voth, Cathy Ann Trotta recovers how Martha's experience as a woman enabled her to establish herself as an insider among the Hopi. Trotta examines how domestic duties associated with late nineteenth-century womanhood helped Martha gain access to the Hopi community, access that was denied to men. Gender was an important consideration in the Hopi matrilineal culture.

In 1893 the United States Department of the Interior and the General Conference Mennonite Church Board of Missions authorized Heinrich R. Voth and his bride, Martha Moser Voth, to establish a mission in the Hopi pueblo of Oraibi, on the Hopi Mesas in Arizona. Over the next decade the Voths and their daughter, Frieda, established a household and a Mennonite mission at Oraibi

Martha and her daughter, Frieda. (Voth collection, 90. All photographs in this chapter are courtesy of the Heinrich R. Voth Collection, Mennonite Library and Archives, Bethel College, North Newton, Kansas.)

and became active and trusted members of Hopi society for a time. The Voths also regularly shared hospitality with other missionary families and corresponded with friends in other parts of the country, who sent great quantities of medical supplies, food, clothing, agricultural equipment, and money to aid the mission.

Besides mission activities, Heinrich Voth also came to be recognized for his thorough documentation of late nineteenth-century Hopi religious life, language, and culture. His meticulous records and publications are the single most used and recognized source on the subject. Voth's photographs also are well documented and constitute an unprecedented record of the structure and functioning of a cohesive indigenous matrilineal culture during a period of transition. How could Heinrich have

Heinrich Voth preaching in the Oraibi plaza and pointing to a picture of Jesus. The men to the right are standing near a Hopi subterranean kiva. (Voth Collection, 1133.)

accomplished so much while still establishing and maintaining the mission at Oraibi?

RECORDING HOPI HISTORY

The enigma is solved when we recognize Martha Moser Voth's contribution. It is more accurate to ascribe Voth's accomplishments to a partnership of Voth and his wife. The Voths' recently translated diaries reveal her pivotal role in establishing them as insiders in the Hopi pueblo community.[1]

Until now, however, Martha Moser Voth's role has been ignored, although she participated actively and directly in creating the historical record. For example, Martha and her daughter Frieda—not Heinrich—developed most of the more than two thousand photographs taken among the Hopi. Indeed, without his wife Heinrich could not have gained the intimate access to Hopi society required to create this record.

While the Voths lived in Oraibi, their roles became increasingly complex. This is the time and the historical process that the Voths, at once participants and observers, recorded in their diaries and photographs. One hundred years later the Hopi would call this time *Naahoynaninwa*,[2] the time of separating or breaking away. Their diaries, together with their correspondence and photographs, are the single most significant archival source for Oraibi history during this period. Together the photographs and the Voths' diaries record not only the major disruptions that affected Hopi life—the land allocations, the forced schooling, the diseases brought by outsiders—but also the mundane tasks that were necessary to run the mission and help the community survive in this arid, drought-stricken land and the conscious dedication of the Hopi matrilineal community to affective and effective human relationships.

An important part of the Voths' daily routine was to write in their journals.[3] Martha's entries represent a traditional nineteenth-century Mennonite woman's viewpoint. She carved out and occupied a public and community space that was midway between the realms of domesticity and politics. At times she became a leader as she introduced new sewing techniques to the Hopi men and women. At other times she blended in with the Hopi matrilineal society and shared in their communal concerns.

Her entries are primarily an account of her daily activities and those of her family, her correspondence, travels, visitors, and the people she met and assisted. Important events are recorded in her diary along with trivial ones such as the weather, daily chores, and social calls. Her notations of visitors to their home show the Voths' direct involvement with government agents, school superintendents, and the first generation of anthropologists, including Jesse Walter Fewkes, Frederick Hodge, Harry James, and George Dorsey of the Chicago Field Museum. She also wrote about other missionary families at the Hopi Mesas, including the Stauffers, Mennonite missionaries working at the government school at Keams Canyon, and the Russells, Baptist missionaries at Oraibi, as well as making occasional references to unidentified Mormon missionaries. Martha Voth commonly discusses women's activities, whereas Heinrich Voth does not. On the whole, Voth overlooked the influence of women on land issues and village politics, sometimes leaving him perplexed about the way important decisions in these areas were made.

The photographs Martha developed are historically and culturally priceless. As anthropologist Colin M. Turnbull observed, the measure of a culture's worth is the extent to which communal harmony and social order are emphasized over individual needs, rather than the sophistication of its technology, longevity of the population, or production of material comforts and goods. In such societies, individuals live in full consciousness, constantly reinforced, of their worth to society. The Voths' ethnographic and photographic record is important because they note the importance of Hopi communal values before the acceptance of the cash economy of capitalism, industrialization, and urban migration that outsiders brought to the pueblos. (The Hopi later considered Voth's kiva photographs intrusive.)[4]

The 1890s were a time of great change in the Oraibi pueblos, a time in which the pueblo people's isolation ended both as a matter of United States government policy and because of the increasing numbers of European and American visitors, including ethnographers, journalists, settlers, and the merely curious, who came to the Hopi Mesas by rail. For the Hopi this was a period of health and environmental crises: serious illnesses, including smallpox, influenza, and pneumonia, were endemic; famine was a constant threat; and the cycle of episodic droughts followed by flash floods reduced the amount of productive farmland and ultimately altered forever the topography of Oraibi wash.[5] The land allotment and socialization provisions of the Dawes Act (1887), designed to assimilate Indians to white cultures by encouraging individual landownership, added to these crises by undermining the matrilineal clan system of land use and removing children from their families.

At the turn of the century, Oraibi was the largest and most important Hopi village and the center of resistance to the government's land allotment and educational policies; after 1906 Oraibi was abandoned for a time. The 1890s were a critical period in the growth of the Hopi factions and in the strengthening and enforcement of traditional Hopi cultural control mechanisms and teachings (prophecy) that led to the Oraibi split in 1906.[6]

During this period the government made a concerted effort to acculturate and assimilate native peoples by supporting Christian missionary efforts, supplanting traditional teachings with those of the American educational system, and replacing communal landownership with individual holdings. Implicit in the government's designation of missionary groups and the authorization of missions was the expectation that missionaries

Soldiers camped near Oraibi during the 1890s. The soldiers helped protect the mission against raiding by other tribes. The soldiers also arrested "hostile" Hopi leaders. Hostiles were those who opposed United States government land distribution plans and educational policies that forced Hopi children to attend boarding schools. (Voth Collection, 27.)

would act as business agents of the government and assist, as outlined in President Grant's peace policy, in the acculturation of Native Americans, turning them into "civilized farmers."[7] The General Conference Mennonites viewed mission work as an opportunity for Mennonite people to leave their rural isolation behind and expand their knowledge into the realms of service, mission, and education.[8]

The Voths found the Hopi living close to their traditions, bound together by kin relationships and by their membership in the religious societies that overlay lineage, phratries, and clans. The complex system of clan relationships in the matrilineal society dictated land use, guided temporal land distribution, and helped to ensure individual as well as collective survival. Religious ceremonies were a highly integrative force bring-

Hopi women watch a *katsina* ceremony from a pueblo rooftop. The ceremony was performed with the intention of uniting all the villages and bringing about harmony (*na'okiwquatsi*). Unmarried maidens wear their hair in whorls (*poli'ini*), also called the "butterfly hairdo." (Voth Collection, 456.)

ing Hopi together across village lines and kiva groups and joining them in a community of belief that was the basis for resisting secular challenges from outsiders.

A devout Mennonite, Martha grew up in an agrarian communal society whose values, representing nineteenth-century Mennonite women's culture, closely paralleled those of Hopi matrilineal society. Atypically for Mennonite women of this time, she had received a public education in Alexanderwohl, Russia. This background, and her willingness to work alongside her husband and with Hopi women and children, created bonds that offset Heinrich Voth's patriarchal formality.[9] Her diary and correspondence show her to be a compassionate and selfless worker with both Voth and the Hopi community. These qualities allowed her to move with ease within Hopi matrilineal society and gave her access to knowledge and direct interaction with the most powerful men and women in the Hopi pueblos.

Chief Loloolma was friendly to the Voths. (Voth Collection, 331.)

The Voths dealt with leaders whose ceremonial significance and economic and political control were vested in clan sovereignty. As their connections spread beyond Oraibi to other Hopi villages, they came to know Hopi of both the *sukavungsinom* (commoners) and *pavansinom* (elite) classes.[10] Through their activities, the Voths became woven into the fabric of Oraibi society and were brought closer than any other *paahana* (white) family to the most sacred, fundamental, and ordinary characteristics of Pueblo culture. Crossing these cultural boundaries into Hopi knowledge and secrecy placed them in a position of responsibility among the Hopi that would directly affect the results of their mission.

MISSION PARTNERSHIP

Establishing the mission and their household entailed the cooperative teamwork of Martha, her daughter Frieda, and Heinrich, and each had well-defined roles in caring for their daily needs and those of the mission. Heinrich became ill shortly after they arrived in August 1893, and until January 1894 a series of ailments left him bedridden for weeks at a time. Thus it fell to Martha to take on all the chores in the early months of establishing the mission. She quickly learned the Hopi language, and in turn she delegated some duties to Hopi villagers who volunteered to assist in their household. Wickwaya, a Hopi priest from First Mesa, taught Hopi to the Voths (as he had done for ethnologist Alexander Stephen). He also collected firewood, picked up the mail, loaded supplies from the train onto the wagon, and helped distribute them. Martha found Wickwaya's help essential when Heinrich took a turn for the worse in early November. By November 23, 1893, Martha had begun to fear that he would not recover from a swollen gland in his throat, which she referred to as a tumor: "He still had a high fever in the morning and a very fast pulse. Oh how inconsolable it would be without him in the strange surroundings here. Hopefully, God will hear our prayers and keep him with us. We only trust in his help."[11] Heinrich had largely recovered by January, but he suffered from numerous other ailments throughout the years at Oraibi, complaining (in his or Martha's diaries) of kidney, bladder, lung, and heart problems. In later years Heinrich wrote that he had forgotten how ill he had been until he read his wife's diary for 1893–94.[12]

In addition to Heinrich's bouts of illness, Martha had to deliver and raise her family in extremely harsh conditions. Without access to a hospital or nearby physician, childbirth became the responsibility of family members. Heinrich recorded in his diary the birth of his son "Little Albert" in Oraibi and also attempted to explain the events to his young daughter Frieda. On October 9, 1895, Heinrich wrote that he "set up the oven in the bedroom. M. thought this morning that she might act ill. . . . M. suffered from pain all day. Her delivery seems to be close. In the evening at 8 o'clock I took Frieda to Russells. She wanted to know why she had to go there. I told her not to ask questions now that tomorrow we will see and might have a surprise for her." The next day, Heinrich reported:

It was a difficult night, particularly for Martha although she was very brave. I became concerned that I would have to apply forceps, but it went without it. The little boy arrived at 5:30 in the morning. At first he looked lifeless. Mrs. Stauffer and I did not get any sleep at all. Sister Susie slept approximately one half-hour. We are all very tired. When I got Frieda in the morning and told her she would get a doll, she answered that she thinks that she knows what I mean and later she remarked to Sister Susie that she had expected it to be something like this.[13]

"Little Albert" was frequently ill with diarrhea, earaches, and fever that left him weak and frail. Heinrich noted, "It seems that he has bad digestion and is not growing. Does the Lord want to take him away from us? That would be a very great sacrifice for us."[14]

Heinrich often got up in the evenings to care for the children when they were ill, and he and Martha shared the child rearing. Frieda was severely ill in May 1895, and Heinrich wrote, "We got very worried that it could be croup or scarlet fever." Her illness lasted about a week, and then she was back to her chores and preparing to teach Sunday school classes with her mother because Heinrich was then bedridden with a sore, cramping right leg.

Simply meeting basic necessities of life required a great deal of the Voth family's efforts. The daily gathering of wood for cooking and heating, caring for livestock, and carrying water from the spring occupied a major part of their day. Martha and Frieda did not have a source of water nearby until Heinrich brought in drilling equipment for wells in 1893. He commented: "Except some occasional help by some government employees at the wells and the house and some Indian labor I had to do all the mason, carpenter and other work myself assisted by a young Hopi named Tabo and my faithful wife."[15] Working hard with the Hopi in the fields brought them closer to the Oraibi residents. When water was scarce, the Voths' wells supplied the pueblo community. Working together to solve the water problems solidified the Voths' friendship with the Oraibi residents.

FEMALE RECIPROCITY AT THE ORAIBI MISSION

Martha was actively involved in the community exchange and reciprocity system, receiving food and "trinkets" in return for assistance or for tending the ill. For example, Martha noted on September 14, 1893, that

Moshunganya brought mutton, and on the eighteenth that "the Indians brought beans, cabbage and tomatoes. Honanie brought trinkets to trade." The Voths welcomed the Hopi into their home to trade, to share meals, and also to discuss whatever was of immediate concern, embracing the pueblo community as theirs to minister to by evangelizing and giving aid. They became close friends with a number of Hopi families. On November 25, 1893, Martha recorded that "Wickwaya, Qwachequa, Talasnimithwa, Kayanginawa . . . our best friends visited with us." Throughout their sojourn at Oraibi, Hopi people came to the Voths for medical assistance, such as Chief Loloolma's 1897 visit to get medicine for his wife and child.

Martha's Mennonite values and attitudes paralleled those of Hopi society. Hard work, selflessness, humility, pacifism, and her enduring perseverance enabled her to become an integrated part of the pueblo community. Although she came to the pueblos as a young bride, she seemed to know instinctively how to work within the Hopi matrilineal structure.[16] By establishing her household as a subsistence-producing economic unit within the Oraibi village, she became intimate with the Hopi exchange system of trading produce. She learned the Hopi language, and she took charge of her family's produce, as Hopi women did, and brought it to trade with others. When peaches were abundant, she used the Hopi method of preservation, cutting up the peaches and setting them out to dry. As early as September 1893 she wrote: "All day the kitchen was crowded with Indians. I traded quite a number of peaches." However, like the Hopi women she struggled with the problem of sandstorms that covered the peaches with grit so that she had to clean them. Tired from all her chores, she wrote in her diary that she hoped this wouldn't happen again. Martha made peach jam with what remained.

Women's missionary groups sent her canned goods when they had a surplus. On one occasion Martha used some slightly spoiled canned peaches to make peach butter; a few days later she recorded that they were ill, but apparently she made no connection. (Unfortunately it was not then known that cooking alone will not inactivate toxins produced by spoilage.) The Voths greatly appreciated twenty pounds of butter and a gallon of vegetable oil sent by express from Kansas. Preparing the butter was extremely time consuming; Martha spent an entire day salting it. She presented this precious commodity to other missionary wives as a gift

Hopi women and children drying peaches on rocks in Oraibi. In the 1890s drying was the Hopi's preferred method of preserving produce. (Voth Collection, 1742.)

whenever Heinrich had disagreements with their husbands—in particular the Baptists. "Martha has sent butter to Russells with a brief friendly note. We are curious if they will accept it." On Sunday Heinrich reported, "The Russells acted as if nothing had happened, what [which] in my opinion takes the skin of a Rhino."[17]

Domestic Evangelizing

On December 12, 1893, Martha noted that "numerous Indian women were here today to learn how to sew. They did very well." Early in her first year at the Hopi Mesas Martha had colorful calico material sent to her from missionary wives in Kansas and began a sewing circle. In this area in particular, her partnership with her husband served their mission well. The sewing bees were social occasions and also gave Martha an opportunity to preach the gospel. In a sense she established a new women's society based on domestic evangelizing. The Hopi women's societies functioned in a similar way, since they often got together to weave bas-

Hopi women and children gather outside the mission house for a sewing bee. Martha Moser Voth established a sewing circle where she taught Christian songs as well as sewing. (Voth Collection, 96)

kets and simultaneously practice songs for upcoming ceremonies.[18] Martha introduced new Christian songs. The women enjoyed the new information and probably recognized Martha's sincere spirituality, but they did not convert to Christianity.[19] Martha crossed gender barriers in her sewing circle, which held the interest of men as well as women, since in Hopi culture men commonly wove garments, spun cotton, and produced the bride's wedding dress. Martha and Frieda were invited into Hopi homes to observe these operations. Martha notes in her diary that "in the afternoon we went to the house of an Indian neighbor to watch how 16 Indian men were spinning wool. It was Nawini's house. They worked hard and sang their heart out. Most of the spinners paid us a visit in the evening."[20]

Children were required to wear appropriate Victorian dress to school, and Martha made shirts and trousers and dresses for men, women, and children. One day she completed six shirts. On December 4, 1893, Martha noted that "after the Indians learned that we had received sewing material, they did not leave us alone." On their frequent trips to the Canyon

Diablo depot for the colorful sewing supplies, they were accompanied by interested Hopi and Navajo.

Martha's contact with Hopi men and women of the *pavansinom* elders brought her into daily interactions with the religious elite. She created a peace quilt and gave it to one of the Hopi leaders. The visits continued throughout their stay. In 1896 "Lomahungyoma, [leader of the hostiles] came to get his calico and we gave him a quilt *which he accepted*" (emphasis in the original).[21] By generously offering her hospitality and sharing her knowledge about sewing, as well as supplying the Hopi men and women with colorful materials and listening to their concerns, Martha became the most important link for the Voths as an insider in the Hopi matriarchal society.

The trusting friendship that Martha established among the Hopi in her household is revealed in her husband's diary. They wrote and translated letters on behalf of family members to the Hopi leaders who had been imprisoned at Alcatraz and communicated their responses. The diary entry of October 3, 1895, noted a visit from the released prisoners immediately on their return to Hopi: "Fifteen of the captured people returned. They were all here and were nice and friendly. The poor people were very tired and hungry."[22] This entry is revealing, because this celebration is exactly the customary hospitality that Hopi themselves would offer friends. Indeed, Martha usually had food prepared for guests, and in this way she too shared hospitality. Both Heinrich's and Martha's diaries continually speak of "a houseful" of Hopi visitors. The Voths rarely had one day of complete privacy; either they were working with pueblo villagers in the community or Hopi were visiting them in their own household.

TREATING ILLNESS: NINETEENTH-CENTURY PHYSICIANS

It is evident that throughout the time the Voths lived at Oraibi, the pueblo villagers were devastated by illness and severe food shortages owing to drought and flash floods that reduced essential farmlands and destroyed crops. The Voths greatly supplemented supplies through their contact with other missions and thus protected the Hopi population from complete devastation in these marginal times.

The first government medical service was not established until 1913 at Keams Canyon, and during the early years the Voths' medical attention helped to save lives and solidify their standing at the Hopi Mesas. Each

Heinrich and Martha on their way to distribute food and medical supplies to the Pueblo villages. (Voth Collection, 483.)

morning, Martha tended to sick and indigent pueblo people who came to their home, and she also made "house calls" to even the most remote pueblos in a mule-drawn wagon. The wagon provided mobility, which the average pueblo dweller did not have, as well as the ability to carry goods and food to villagers in need. By 1896 the Voths considered themselves part of the pueblo community. "Our work was essentially a pioneer work, and my dear wife and myself were practically alone to do it. Many times villages on the other mesas were visited, very many visits to families were made. Many sick people were looked after and treated. One time I treated 80 cases of measles."[23] Heinrich noted in his diary on February 23, 1896: "In the canyon school they have the measles. They will get them here too."[24] On February 24 he noted: "I now believe that Lomahungyoma's son who I treated about a week, and even little Albert had them. The latter had it only lightly if it should have been measles. Some came for medicine."[25]

Ailments previously unknown to the Hopi had devastating effects. Every pueblo man or woman could remember someone who had died during an epidemic of smallpox (variola virus), since these epidemics

The Voths picking up supplies for the Hopi from the Canyon Diablo train station. (Voth Collection, 85.)

occurred about once in the lifetime of each generation. Edmund Nequaptewa, a member of the Sun Forehead clan living at Shipaulovi village on Second Mesa, recalls being told of the smallpox outbreak after the Spanish left the mesas: "There was a small pox epidemic. This of course took most of the people at all the towns of the Hopi country. There were so few people left on Second Mesa that for a while the complete service of annual ceremonies was only held at Shungopavi."[26] In his own family, Nequaptewa recorded that an outbreak "soon spread all over the Walpi village and over to Second Mesa. . . . My mother had one spot on her breast, and my father had a spot on his hands. Two of my aunts died with the small pox: Vivian's mother and my father's sister."[27]

Outsiders became aware of the smallpox affecting native communities only when it struck large groups of the population, but small outbreaks had serious consequences for the stability of the Hopi religious and political structure when key religious elders died without passing on ceremonial knowledge. The Voths recorded the individuals who succumbed to illness and their clan and village relationships. The first documented smallpox epidemic in the southwest occurred about 1780–81, and other outbreaks were documented in 1892, just before the Voths' arrival, and again in 1898.[28]

The continual episodes of disease among the pueblo villagers devastated and weakened the population over time. Smallpox had the most enduring consequences,[29] far greater than government assimilation policies, because the disease did not differentiate between the Hopi *pavansinom* and *sukavungsinom*. As a consequence, important religious positions were left unfilled when the elders who controlled the necessary ritual knowledge died suddenly, with no time to apprentice replacements. Since knowledge is fragmented among clan members, the disease had a significant impact on the continuity of Hopi ritual and religious society membership. The Voth diaries seem to indicate that among the pueblo villagers infections occurred constantly from 1893 to 1898, although the epidemic was not considered significant until it was labeled as such in 1898.

During the eight years that the Voths lived at Oraibi they were able to note certain regular cycles of illness. Every summer both the Voths and the Hopi were affected by what Heinrich called the "summer illness." The symptoms were fever, exhaustion, and sometimes diarrhea. Heinrich commented that "so many Indians are suffering from the summer illness." On June 19, 1896, he wrote, "The Indians come frequently to get medicine for the summer illness." The Voths requested shipments of quinine from the government and missionary auxiliary groups and anxiously waited for them to arrive at Canyon Diablo, Winslow, or Holbrook rail station.

Delivering medicines and treating patients from other villages brought the Voths into contact with Hopi from a number of villages and familiarized them with intervillage relationships, and as they became more fluent in the Hopi language they also came to understand the interaction between village and clan relationships. Evidence of the Hopi's acceptance of the Voths is given by the notations of visitors in Martha Voth's diary. For example, on September 17, 1893, she reported that a Mr. Kayaningawa had brought a sick man to her for medicine and that they "had quite some Indian visitors today." Kayaningawa of Water, Coyote clan, was head of Soyal until 1883. He was the father of Loloolma and Shockhangyama and detested Euro-Americans; in accepting the Voths' help, he placed them in a different category from other outsiders. Other Hopi who were considered to be hostiles also accepted the Voths' assistance. Martha notes in her diary, for example, that she and Frieda took a poultice to Shockhangyama for his ailing leg,[30] and they made frequent follow-up visits.

Martha's compassion for sick children and the elderly is frequently illustrated in the diary. On December 9, 1893, "In the afternoon we visited Totasimtiwa's sick child. We brought him some food and clothing. I washed the child and put clean clothes on him but the child is very ill and seems doomed to die."[31] Hopi men and women conversed in her home about their losses. Martha sewed clothing for Hopi children as part of her daily chores. Concerned and sensitive about the family losses, she made trousers for Nawini's son, and Nawini and her son picked up the clothing at the Voth house. (Martha noted that "the mother still talked about her deceased child.")[32]

Comforting both fathers and mothers who lost children to unknown illnesses became one of Martha's responsibilities throughout their stay in Oraibi. "Komaestiw . . . was here this morning and cried over his [oldest] daughter's loss. Oh, the poor people don't have the hope that they will meet again their loved ones on the other side."[33] As the December temperatures dropped, Martha gave responsibilities to her daughter Frieda. "Frieda spent the afternoon on the mesas distributing clothes for the naked children."[34]

On a cold December 31, the last Sunday of the year, near the well she found a half-frozen old woman who had become sick while gathering wood. Martha brought her into her home, prepared a meal for her, and gave her dry, warm clothing. She later arranged for Wickwaya to take the woman home to her pueblo.[35]

The Oraibi villagers brought gifts of food in exchange for medical assistance, the same as would be given to traditional Hopi healers. Martha notes, for example, that "Kew..nebuinewa brought corn, and beans in gratitude that Heinrich had helped him with medicine." The Voths also participated in other exchanges. Hopi helped with chores such as getting the mail and bringing Martha much-needed firewood for cooking and heating.

For numerous reasons, including his and Martha's aid to the sick and indigent, in 1894 the Hopi priest Wickwaya gave Heinrich Voth the honor of distributing seed corn to the villagers, a responsibility usually reserved for the *kikmongwi*, the village chief. Wickwaya's mother, also a frequent visitor to the Voth household as a participant in Martha's sewing circle, held the position of chief priestess of the women's Marau society. Seed corn and cornmeal are ceremonially distributed by certain *katsinam* during the plaza and kiva dances. During ceremonies the father of a *katsina* offers prayers and blessings with cornmeal to the *katsinam*. Heinrich was also given permission to visit the kiva and view the sacred sprouts growing in the pottery containers. Voth was so comfortable with his position among the Hopi by this time that he visited the kiva with his daughter Frieda and photographed the sprouts.[36]

Connecting Scholars to Hopi Cultural Practices

Martha shouldered mission responsibilities when Voth interrupted his regular mission schedule to meet with visitors. Visitors who sought to collect artifacts or information or who traveled as tourists usually planned their trips in August. The following citations represent typical August days during the ceremonial dances. These visits required additional work to prepare and serve food to the parade of guests who took advantage of the Voths' hospitality as they escorted them to plaza dances and the homes of villagers. But for the Hopi these ceremonies involved serious prayer and participation in the dances for the well-being of all.

These are the conditions under which individuals such as Jesse Walter Fewkes and George Dorsey gathered information about the Hopi during their summer visits. Fortunately for them, Voth maintained collegial correspondence, reviewing their notes and generously sharing his own. Martha supplied photographs for their publications.[37]

> August 25, 1897 Albert is worse so I couldn't go along for which I was very sorry since we wanted to go to the Grand Canyon together. So Qom went with Brother Peter. It was so quiet after everyone left. Martha and I had just laid down to rest awhile since we were tired when someone knocked and here was another group. G. A. Dorsey and E. P. Allen from [the] Field Columbian Museum and their driver. They were without supplies so they simply stayed at our place. They came from Alaska where they wanted to make excavations. For this I surely didn't encourage them nor would I help them. That is not my line. Drove with them to the mesa and interpreted for them.
>
> August 26 Martha washed. Looked at some trinkets upstairs and then was in Oraibi with the guests. They bought several trinkets. Our supplies are not too plentiful.

Many visitors like George Dorsey, who later became a most helpful colleague to Voth, were not prepared for the trip and the Voths had to assist them. The Voths changed their pattern of daily life during the summer to accommodate tourists and scholars. Their household served as a central gathering place, and their generous hospitality was similar to the hospitality the Hopi had shown them. Some of these guests were international scholars, such as Aby Warburg from Berlin. That the Hopi brought food (melons and other things) for the Voths' guests demonstrates the communal ties they had to the villagers through 1901.

Their failure to secure converts may have been because things did not get better: children and elderly people died from unknown illnesses, and Hopi farmers continued to face difficult times. When important religious elders who also had responsibilities for farming were arrested, Hopi women were left to struggle without the necessary labor force. The loss of shared religious positions for the continuity of the ceremonial cycle in all villages also created dislocations. Collectively the Hopi may have been overwhelmed by their serious problems and considered the Hopi teachings as they interpreted their destiny. The Voths confronted the failed mission, as represented in Heinrich's diary entry of June 20, 1897: "There are dark times for me here. I am discouraged, sick nervous and agitated. Oh if I could just leave this place. I become so angry at these people. The doors are not open for mission work here. Not yet! The people don't want to, not at all."

Martha's endurance also was tested by her struggle to balance her multifaceted roles during the social disruption created by the secular challenges the assimilation policies brought to the Hopi traditional society, where the religious and political relationships of the culture were inextricably linked. In particular, she took on all the responsibilities related both to her family and to the mission, including distributing medicines and caring for the ill, keeping the Hopi women's sewing circle,[38] and maintaining the photographic record while Voth took ill for months at a time. Martha's positive attitude, strength, confidence, and faith are reflected in her diary;

> Although we feel the solitude here often very much, it seems to us that time passes faster now. It seems that time flows like water down a river and we rush along with the flow. May we arrive at the proper destination at a place where time does not eat into our life with biting teeth! Looking back reminiscing the

Martha Moser Voth's grave in Oraibi, 1901. (Voth Collection, 2072.)

past year, during our stay here we must acknowledge that God, in spite of leading us often on difficult roads was merciful and loving toward us. We give praise and thanks for everything.[39]

So integrated was the Voth partnership on the mission field that when Martha died in 1901; Heinrich left the Hopi mission field with their children and immediately returned to Kansas. Heinrich describes the events that led to his wife's death:

On May 3, 1901 a daughter was born to the Voths in Oraibi. Three days later Martha was "suddenly seized by an attack of puerperal eclampsia which continued without interruptions for about 12 hours, leaving her in an unconscious state with the exception of one time for about half a minute. The doctor was 35 miles away and before a message could reach him and he could get there in a buggy she was beyond help. We buried her the following day.[40]

Heinrich Voth recognized Martha Moser Voth's devotion to the mission, "I knew that the seed sown by my sainted wife and myself, in our simple way had taken root and was sprouting in some hearts because we had the proofs."[41]

Martha Moser Voth's contribution to Hopi history as presented in her diary reveals the integrative role of the Voth family within Hopi matrilineal society. Her influence in working with the pueblo community during a critical historical moment is clear. The period is characterized in her notes by a weakening and demise of the population after continuous bouts of disease that led to the loss of important people in households and the land struggles that caused stress among the Hopi matrilineal society and between the Hopi and representatives of government policy.

NOTES

1. The Heinrich Voth and Martha Moser Voth original diaries written in German can be found in the Mennonite Library and Archives, MLA.MS.21, North Newton, Kansas. The diaries provide rich detail on issues pertaining to daily life in the Hopi villages and the activities of outsiders. The diary materials include Martha Moser Voth's journal for 1893–94 and Heinrich Voth's diaries for 1895–98. The translation of the Voth diaries, currently being edited by Cathy Ann Trotta, would not have been possible without the dedication of my colleague and friend Ilse Kohler Grimm, a native of Germany, who generously gave of her time and talents for this academic endeavor. She passed away on 21 January 1997.

2. *Naahoynaninwa*, "the time of separating away," is the term designated in personal communications with Emory Sekaquaptewa, of the University of Arizona, on 24 March 1995. Also, the name was discussed with a Third Mesa clan woman age sixty-nine, April 1995, Flagstaff, Arizona.

3. Martha's diary, written in German and translated by Ilse Kohler Grimm, was relatively easy to translate, since the writing was legible and her writing style was direct and unembellished. One complication in comparing Martha and Heinrich's references to Hopi individuals is that they both transcribed the names phonetically, and care is required to avoid confusion. When excerpts from her journal are quoted, I have used the common Hopi spelling. Heinrich Voth's diaries were much more difficult to translate. The diaries were written in archaic German script interspersed with occasional Russian, English, or Hopi terms. Entries were written in a shorthand peculiar to Voth, with fragmented phrases and sentences, and in nearly illegible handwriting. His common practice of abbreviating Hopi names, proper names, and place names, his failure to include the Hopi male or female gender suffix, and his characteristic interchangeable use of Hopi

birth names and initiated names for the same individual were additional complications.

4. See Colin M. Turnbull, *The Human Cycle* (New York: Simon and Schuster, 1983), 272–75; Victor Masayesva and Erin Younger, *Hopi Photographers, Hopi Images* (Tucson: Sun Tracks and University of Arizona Press, 1984), 22–23.

5. Scott Rushforth and Steadman Upham, *A Hopi Social History: Anthropological Perspectives on Sociocultural Persistence and Change* (Austin: University of Texas Press, 1992), 92–96.

6. Peter M. Whiteley, *Deliberate Acts: Changing Hopi Culture through the Oraibi Split* (Tucson: University of Arizona Press, 1988); see also Richard O. Clemmer, *Roads in the Sky: The Hopi Indians in a Century of Change* (Boulder, Colo.: Westview Press, 1995); and Mischa Titiev, *The Hopi Indians of Old Oraibi: Change and Continuity* (Ann Arbor: University of Michigan Press, 1972). For information on the growth of factions, see Shuichi Nagata, "Accommodative Context of Moenkopi Factionalism," paper presented at the Joint Meeting of the Central States Anthropological Society and the American Ethnological Society, 1968, and Elizabeth A. Brandt, "Internal Stratification in Pueblo Communities," paper presented at the annual meeting of the American Anthropological Association, Washington, D.C., 1985.

7. Regarding the efforts to Christianize the Hopi, see discussions of President Grant's peace policy in Francis Paul Prucha, *Documents of United States Indian Policy* (Lincoln: University of Nebraska Press, 1975), 141, 157. Regarding socialization efforts and individual landownership, see Francis Paul Prucha, *The Great Father: The United States Government and the American Indians* (Lincoln: University of Nebraska Press, 1986), 224–34. See also William.T. Hagen, *The Indian Rights Association: The Herbert Welsh Years, 1882–1904* (Tucson: University of Arizona Press, 1985), 219, 221, and Cathy Ann Trotta, "Crossing Cultural Boundaries: Heinrich and Martha Moser Voth in the Hopi Pueblos, 1893–1906" (Ph.D. diss., Northern Arizona University, 1997).

8. Marlin Wayne Adrian, "Mennonites, Missionaries, and Native Americans: Religious Paradigms and Cultural Encounters" (Ph.D. diss., University of Virginia, 1989). See also the work of James C. Juhnke, *A People of Mission: A History of the General Conference Mennonite Overseas Missions* (Newton, Kans.: Faith and Life Press, 1979).

9. The rigid gender-role differentiation that characterized American society in the mid-eighteenth and mid-nineteenth centuries led to emotional segregation of men and women. Such was also the case in Hopi pueblo society. Hopi females

helped each other with domestic chores, supported each other in times of sickness and sorrow, and created strong bonds between women regardless of cultural differences. Martha Voth's attitudes reflected the values of both Mennonite and Victorian society. For an analysis of Victorian women see Carroll Smith-Rosenberg, *Disorderly Conduct: Visions of Gender in Victorian America* (Oxford: Oxford University Press, 1985). For an analysis of Mennonite attitudes see Cornelius Dyck, *An Introduction to Mennonite History: A Popular History of the Anabaptists and Mennonites,* 3d ed. (Scottdale, Pa.: Herald Press, 1993): 174–86.

10. *Sukavungsinom* refers to commoners within the society; *pavansinom* represents the elite.

11. Martha Moser Voth Diary (hereafter MMVD), 23 November 1893.

12. Heinrich R. Voth, autobiographical notes hand typed by Voth at Goltry, Oklahoma, 29 January 1923, contained in the Bethel College Mennonite Library and Archives, Newton, Kansas, later excerpted in Heinrich R. Voth, *Historical Notes of the First Decade of the Mennonite Mission Work among the Hopi of Arizona, 1893–1902* (North Newton, Kans.: General Conference Mennonite Church, 1920).

13. Heinrich R. Voth Diary (hereafter HRVD), 9 and 10 October 1895.

14. HRVD, 4 January 1896.

15. HRVD, autobiographical notes.

16. The matrilineal structure in the Hopi pueblos also included the customary matrilocal residence where women, their daughters, and sometimes their granddaughters occupied the same residence throughout their lifetimes. The pueblo also served as an economic unit. See Whiteley; Titiev; and Fred Eggan, *Social Organization of the Western Pueblos* (Chicago: Unversity of Chicago Press, 1950).

17. HRVD, 6 and 7 July 1895.

18. John Wesley Powell of the Bureau of American Ethnology in his "Suggestions on the Management of these Reservation" advised giving women fabric to sew to help them achieve self-sufficiency. See Curtis M. Hinsley, *Savages and Scientists: The Smithsonian Institution and the Development of American Anthropology, 1846–1910* (Washington, D.C.: Smithsonian Institution Press, 1981), 149.

19. Indeed, the Voths made no converts, not for lack of effort, but because Hopi traditions were strong and conversion was alien to the Hopi belief system, whose origin myth holds that one is born into a particular Hopi clan and initiated into societies and kiva groups. Some outsiders over the years may have taken part

in some rituals and thus became adopted by the Hopi, but to have landholding rights, fully participate in Hopi political and religious life, and permanently occupy a pueblo, one must have descended from a matrilineal clan.

20. MMVD, 28 September 1893.

21. HRVD, 27 January 1896.

22. Voth uses the word "people" or "Indians" to designate the Hopi rather than "savages," as was common terminology for the late nineteenth century. When he was tired and frustrated, however, he occasionally used "savage" in some of his correspondence to the Mission Board. Unfortunately these are the passages most often quoted by scholars.

23. Voth, *Historical Notes*, 8.

24. HRVD, 23 February 1896.

25. HRVD, 24 February 1896.

26. Cited in David P. Seaman, *Born a Chief: The Nineteenth Century Hopi Boyhood of Edmund Nequaptewa as Told to Alfred F. Whiting* (Tucson: University of Arizona Press, 1993). Shongopavi is a Hopi village on Second Mesa.

27. Ibid., 108.

28. H. H. Bancroft, *Arizona and New Mexico, 1530–1888*, vol. 17 of *The Works of Hubert Howe Bancroft* (San Francisco: History Company, 1889). See also Rushforth and Upham, 68–96, and Whiteley, 90–92.

29. Similar effects occurred among Indians in Mexico during the Spanish occupation. See Frances Karttunen, *Between Worlds: Interpreters, Guides and Survivors* (Piscataway, N.J.: Rutgers University Press, 1994), 15.

30. Shockhangyama was identified as a "hostile" by government officials, and Heinrich and Martha Voth's daily interactions within the Hopi villages included individuals identified as both "hostile" and "friendly." These terms meant more to the government agents then to the Hopi themselves, who identified their clan relationships and membership in religious societies as most significant. Members of both groups individually and together visited the Voth household. For information on the significance of clan relationships, see Heinrich Voth, *Traditions of the Hopi*, Publication 96, Anthropological Series 8 (Chicago: Chicago Field Colombian Museum, 1905). See also Titiev; Whiteley; Eggan; and Helen Sekaquaptewa, *Me and Mine: The Life Story of Helen Sekaquaptewa as Told to Louise Udall*, ed. Louise Udall (Tucson: University of Arizona Press, 1985).

31. Martha's attention to the sick child also followed the Hopi clan women's ritual of ceremonial washing in preparing an individual to enter the next world.

32. MMVD, 20 October 1893.

33. MMVD, 30 April 1894.

34. MMVD, 9 December 1893.

35. MMVD, 31 December 1893.

36. This privileged status given Voth came with responsibilities—in particular with the hope that prayers for rain would be answered. One Hopi later expressed anger at his relatives for allowing Voth to take photographs of ceremonies, observe the ceremonial life, and later have Hopi altars replicated in Chicago's Field Museum. Don Talayesva's words are often quoted by scholars: "I do not blame the whites for buying them as much as I blamed the old Hopis, the head Soyal priest, Shokhungyoma, and Chief Lolulomai. There even was a picture of my great uncle, Talasquaptewa, who acted as Star Priest. If those chiefs had not permitted Voth to take the pictures and watch those ceremonies they would never have been published." Quoted in Leo W. Simmons, ed., *Sun Chief, the Autobiography of a Hopi Indian* (New Haven: Yale University Press, 1942), 344. Also cited in Leah Dilworth, *Imagining Indians in the Southwest: Persistent Visions of a Primitive Past* (Washington, D.C.: Smithsonian Institution Press, 1996), 53. The Voth diaries reveal that the Voths' actions, in particular their humanitarian efforts to aid the sick by having medical supplies and food shipped in by the trainload and their support of indigenous landholdings (actually working with Indian rights groups) placed them in a trusted position. It would have appeared to the Hopi that the Voths gained no personal benefit. Voth recognized that he did not get converts; however, he did not abandon the Hopi by failing to assist them with their physical needs. And as correspondence reveals, he was losing financial support from the Mennonite Board.

37. The Voth diaries indicate a great deal of note sharing between scholars, who were characterized as gentlemen who used the team approach to produce the most accurate scholarly pieces.

38. The sewing circle Martha established continues at the Hopi Mesas one hundred years later.

39. MMVD December 1894.

40. See Heinrich Voth, "Missionary Reports: From Our Station in Arizona," *Mennonite* 12 (April 1923): 6. Puerperal eclampsia was not uncommon at the turn of the century. Many women died during childbirth from the onset of high blood pressure, causing seizures that resulted in a semiconscious state until death.

41. Ibid.

10

Schism

WHERE WOMEN'S OUTSIDE WORK AND
INSIDER DRESS COLLIDED

Kimberly D. Schmidt

What happens when conservative women refuse to wear the uniform as keepers of religious tradition? Controversies over women's work and dress punctuated history in the Conservative Mennonite community of Croghan, New York, during two times of economic crisis: the Great Depression of the 1930s and the farm crisis of the 1980s. During both times women worked outside the home in unprecedented numbers, and many of them challenged church traditions by rejecting religiously sanctioned regulation dress. In Croghan, dress became a site for debate and conflict over women's place in this conservative community.

The Conservative Mennonites in Croghan, New York, once called themselves Amish Mennonites. This change in self-identification in part represents their gradual acceptance of once prohibited cultural practices. These changes have not come without significant resistance, however, especially when women, the erstwhile keepers of tradition, were seen as the initiators. One such series of

A Croghan bridal couple in 1947. He wears a plain suit and she is dressed in a dark cape dress. Note the length of her prayer covering ribbons. One way for women to express their religious inclinations was through the length of the ribbons and size of the covering. A smaller covering and short ribbons usually denoted a less conservative church. (Photograph courtesy of Nelda Steria.)

changes in women's work and dress culminated in a schism in 1941. Women began working outside the home and wearing typical American clothing instead of plain dresses. Later, during the farm crisis of the 1980s, a fierce debate occurred over women's refusal to wear the prayer covering, their perceived lack of submission toward men, and their place on the farm, in church, and at work. Both controversies over women's work and dress, one buried in history and one contemporary and painfully fresh, are still unresolved.

The continuing debate about the 1941 schism and the 1980s controversies raises a number of questions. Were women's work responsibilities undergoing fundamental transformations during these periods, and did these transformations raise community tensions? Or, to frame the issue differently, were women just responding to the harsh economic climate, and did their choosing to work off-farm make them scapegoats for a generalized anxiety about community survival during the worst years of the depression and the farm crisis? Additionally, what do these periodic controversies over women's dress and work reveal about women's place in the community?

DRESS AND NONCONFORMITY

As with other Amish groups, a key belief of Croghan's Amish Mennonites was "nonconformity," or "being in the world but not of the world."[1] They created close-knit farming communities to separate themselves from the world[2] and keep the farm, church, and community safe from negative "worldly" influences. Husbands and wives worked together on the farm. By rarely leaving home, women were protected from the outside world. Older women often recalled during interviews how the father or husband would do all the family shopping, including choosing fabric for women's dresses.

One symbol of nonconformity was dress.[3] Men wore plain coats, and women wore cape dresses and prayer coverings. Plain coats were made of black or tan cloth and had no collar or lapels. Cape dresses included a triangular piece of material draped over the bodice of a loose fitting dress and pinned at the waist.[4] Women wore their hair tightly pulled back in buns under prayer coverings—little white mesh caps with ribbons attached. Cape dresses and prayer coverings symbolized a woman's nonconformity to the world and her subservient place within Amish Mennonite society.

Rejecting plain apparel is one way women dissent or even rebel in these highly regulated cultures.[5] Women who disagree with church teachings become less plain in their appearance. The cape disappears, and floral patterns and lighter colors replace dark solid fabrics. The coverings

The graveyard outside the Conservative Mennonite Church in Croghan. Headstones are small and uniform. Even in death church beliefs called for uniform nonconformity, favoring plain headstones over more elaborate styles. (Photograph courtesy of Kimberly D. Schmidt.)

lose their strings and become smaller and smaller. Some women crochet small brown doilies that match their hair color to replace the more visible white mesh of traditional coverings. In certain cases one can hardly tell whether a woman is wearing a covering. Sometimes a woman will stop wearing her covering every day and save it only for Sunday worship.[6]

In Croghan, plain dress was a way of promoting group solidarity and identity in addition to visually confirming nonconformity with the

A Croghan Mennonite family poses for a picture in 1938. The second young woman from the right is not dressed in a cape dress. Her hair is pulled back, but her covering is not visible as are the older women's. Perhaps she had yet to join the church and was not required to wear regulation dress. Young children, who are not baptized members of the church, are dressed in fashionable clothing. (Photograph courtesy of Ruth Widrick.)

world. Any move away from dress regulations was a move toward "worldliness" and threatened the solidarity of the community and its separation from the world.[7]

Debates over Women and Authority in the 1941 Schism

In 1941 Bishop Jacob Gingerich of the Conservative Amish Mennonite Church in Croghan, New York, was presented with a resolution that supported the reluctance of recently elected Sunday school leaders to wear the plain coat routinely (see appendix). Unhappy with the rigid enforcement of dress regulations, the dissenters felt many church members wore the plain coat for the wrong reasons, that is, "people were beginning to live by the rules, rather than the spiritual teachings of Jesus."[8] The resolution so divided the church that Communion rituals ceased for the duration of the year-long conflict.[9] Repeated meetings, including a series held with prominent church conference leaders, brought no solution. In fact the acrimony between former fellow church members had risen to a level

A wedding party photographed in 1948. Both men and women wear regulation dress; the men are in plain coats and the women in cape dresses and head coverings. Their dress could indicate slightly more assimilated or "worldly" views than those of the couple in the figure on p. 209. Although the men are in plain suits, the women's dresses are a lighter color and the prayer covering ribbons are not visible. (Photograph courtesy of Nelda Steria.)

where the committee needed to gently remind them to restrain themselves verbally as well as to physically separate themselves at worship. The final negotiating committee drafted recommendations to recognize the schism and to heal hurt feelings, including the following two: "1) That care should be exercised in conversation 'Let your speech be always with grace seasoned with salt that ye may know how to answer every man,' 2) That the Croghan house legally belonged to the Croghan-Lowville Congregation, those dissenting from the main group legally forfeit their right to the Croghan house."[10]

On October 10, 1941, after the committee's report, sixty-seven members presented Bishop Gingerich with a statement of their intention to form a new congregation. By November the group had purchased land for a new church, and by April they dedicated the church building for the

First Mennonite Church of New Bremen, New York. The following May the newly formed congregation called a new pastor, J. Lawrence Burkholder.[11]

In church documents and local histories, the primary reason given for the schism was men's objections to wearing the plain coat. But there is another side to the story that does not appear in the official church histories. During oral interviews, some narrators insisted that written accounts of the schism excluded women's role in it. According to these reports, the debate over dress was started by young women who took jobs in nearby factories. They rejected wearing regulation dress to work and were the main culprits in the move away from it.[12] The women started the debate over dress, and those who were most adamant left the church. However, an interview with a daughter of New Bremen dissenters counters these views: "It was men and women, but they [Croghan leaders] were striking out more at the men, really. I think at the time they thought that women would pretty much follow their husbands."[13]

After more than fifty years, there remains a provocative controversy over women's dress and how important the question was in shaping the schism. Two community historians, Arlene Yousey and Kathleen Zehr, differ in their opinions. Croghan church historian Yousey argued that women's dress was an important part of the controversy. Zehr, the New Bremen church historian, rebutted Yousey's position, saying that the woman's dress issue was unimportant. Another New Bremen woman, however, admitted she would not join the Croghan church because she refused to wear the cape dress.[14] She remarked that she was "kind of an outsider." This same woman's parents, leaders of the dissenters, paid for her college education at a non-Mennonite school in spite of community criticism. Harriet L. Burkholder, wife of the first minister and perhaps a more impartial observer, since she was not directly involved in the schism, acknowledged that women's dress was a shaping factor in the schism:

Women's dress was truly an important part of the break, but more importantly there lay behind an imphasis [sic] on rules and regulations for women, a power struggle between the old bishop, Bishop Noftsier, and the leaders of the break away group. The bishop insisted . . . that the women be dressed uniformly—dark, plain dresses with capes, black coverings tied with ribbons under their chins, and of course black stockings and shoes. . . . By the time we arrived [in 1942], however, all the younger women wore regular dresses and suits as found in dress shops.[15]

Different interpretations over whether women's dress served to pull the community apart are ongoing, with Croghan members arguing that women's part in the schism was instrumental and New Bremen members countering that women were marginal.

WORK AND DRESS PATTERNS DURING THE DEPRESSION

The men who presented Bishop Gingerich with the petition and most of those who signed it did not wish to wear the plain coat, nor did they follow the Amish Mennonite nonconformist practice of independent farming, "separate from the world." During the 1920s and 1930s employment patterns for Croghan men underwent a fundamental transformation. By 1940 many of the dissenting men had abandoned the Amish Mennonite ideal of working and living away from the world on small family-owned farms.

A quick glance at the 1920 Federal Manuscript Census for Croghan Township shows that Amish Mennonite male heads of households were mostly farmers. Of the ninety-one male and six female heads of households, sixty-three men (69.2 percent) and two women (33.3 percent) were listed as farmers, as were thirty-one sons and one daughter. The secondary occupation of Amish Mennonite heads of households in Croghan was work in lumber or paper mills. Eighteen heads of households (18.5 percent) worked as laborers in the local mills, as did fourteen sons. Other types of employment for Amish Mennonite male heads of households included working as owners of shops (three), teachers (two), and hunting guide (one). The census data show that in 1920 most of Croghan's Amish Mennonite men upheld the nonconformist practices in separation from the world by working on family-owned farms.

By 1940, however, this picture of male employment had changed. Unlike 70 percent of the men in the Croghan church, most of the dissenting Amish Mennonite male heads of households were in primary occupations other than farming. With three exceptions, they worked off-farm. They owned businesses and worked as painters, electricians, salesmen, and mill hands. Two dissenters owned auto dealerships, and one owned a local lumber company. In this way they rejected the belief in nonconformity. Reconstruction of history through taped interviews, census data, and lists of women's occupations at the time of the schism reveals that changes in women's work responsibilities during the late 1930s and early 1940s also may have contributed to increased community tensions.

In the late 1920s women and men in Croghan still wore plain dress, and women who worked off-farm mainly were domestics before they married and had children. One newspaper account describes the "Hook and Eye Baptists" in Croghan.

> The Amish Mennonite women are as plainly clad as the men. Their best dress is invariably of black and closes tightly about the throat. It is a sin for a woman to cover her ears with her hair. It is braided and made to cling tightly to the back of the head with a coarse net. As for bobbed hair, this is unheard of. The women wear a black sunbonnet in the summer and a black hood in the winter and this custom is rigidly adhered to. . . . Many of the girls are . . . put to work as domestics in Lewis county families and invariably they make excellent servants doing their tasks well and faithfully.[16]

Thus, according to observers, Amish Mennonite women in the late 1920s were "rigidly adhering" to the plain styles. Other accounts from the time describe them in a similar fashion, and one adds that women did not wear coats but instead used heavy woolen capes during the winter.[17]

The newspaper article also pointed out that the main source of income for young Amish Mennonite women in the 1920s was domestic work. The 1920 census data confirm that their employment in Croghan was limited to domestic work. In 1920 only twenty-four (15.8 percent) out of 151 Amish Mennonite women of employable age (fifteen years and older) worked off-farm for wages. The census listed only three married women as working off-farm, and these were all housekeepers in the domestic sector. The remaining twenty-one were single daughters or relatives of the male head of household. These women also worked primarily in the domestic sector. One single woman was listed as a farmer and another as a laborer at a paper mill.[18] But like the men's situation, by 1940 this picture had changed. Wives, daughters, and single relatives of the dissenting males were educated and held jobs that reflected their education and regularly took them into the world. Dissenting women were nurses, nurse's aides, elementary and secondary schoolteachers, secretaries, and mill workers.[19] Their work experiences and education distinguished them from other Croghan Amish Mennonite women who remained on the farm.

Many narrators recalled how younger women had limited employment opportunities and were discouraged from working outside the community. Instead they were expected to contribute to the family income by working as domestics for other Amish Mennonite families. Often teenage girls would work for a month or two at each job, helping a wife with a new baby and doing the worst chores. Of her work during the 1940s, one woman said:

> I went to school until I was sixteen, and then I started working for other people, . . . people would call Ma and Pa and ask for someone to help them. And so I had worked for other people from sixteen to twenty-one. And had my first job when I was only fourteen. . . . Usually we worked at a place probably about six weeks. . . . The woman was going to have a baby and so you went there . . . a few days before . . . and then stayed there and helped her afterward. . . . Very often you housecleaned the house while you were there because that was cheap labor. . . . In fact I remember housecleaning six houses in one year.[20]

Bishop Richard Zehr recalled that during the 1930s his older sisters regularly worked away from home:

> it would have probably been a year or two before they were married, often they worked household work. If a farmer was having another child, my sisters often went and worked in a home where there was a new baby. Probably worked there a month. And then from there they went to another home. . . . My two older sisters . . . that's mostly all they did, and housecleaning in the spring, that kind of thing. [The] girls got sick of doing that kind of work. You got all the hard work, that's what you'd get.[21]

Another woman compared her job as a post office clerk with that of a domestic worker: "I liked [clerking] much better than going from place to place for a couple of weeks, I didn't like that. You did everybody's hard work. And everything was unfamiliar."[22]

Partly because of the potential for exploitation as domestic workers, some women during the depression preferred jobs in the local mills and factories. Richard Zehr, who was a child in the 1930s, explained, "Women, many in our generation and older, many of the women would work out in the paper mill even after they were married and maybe even on the farm worked that way for a while until their first child came along or so."[23] One woman fondly recalled working in a nearby basket factory for a few years before marrying in 1945.[24] After her marriage she did not work outside the home. The most often cited source of off-farm work was the Climax Paper Mill in Casterland, about five miles from Croghan.

According to oral reports, leaving Amish Mennonite farms to work in the paper mills was the reason behind young women's rejection of plain dress and their consequent involvement in the 1941 schism. It is clear that at least some in Croghan identified off-farm employment for women as a source of tension that erupted in the schism.

The repercussions of the schism were strong and long lasting. Many of Croghan's working women left the old ways behind when they formed the New Bremen church. They continued to work as nurses, teachers, at the Climax Paper Mill, and at other places of employment after the schism and made sure that cape dresses and prayer coverings were not required apparel in the New Bremen congregation. When asked about cape dresses and prayer coverings, one dissenter said, "We never had either one of those things here [in the New Bremen church], and I went to church all the time."[25]

Croghan church members saw this change and concluded it was exposure to the world that corrupted young women and caused them to reject the cape dress. Young Amish Mennonite women left the religious and domestic sphere behind and entered the secular workforce.[26] During World War II they mirrored the "Rosie the Riveter" experience of many American women when they replaced men in the factories. For some of these Rosies, the dominant American culture was too alluring. After venturing out into the world, they became of the world. Besides distinguishing Amish Mennonite women from other women in their communities, the cape dress symbolized humility, submission to men, and women's commitment to their religious communities. By working in the world and rejecting the cape dress, the female dissenters challenged these religious beliefs.[27]

DRESS CONTROVERSY RENEWED

After fifty years the issues that shaped the cape dress controversy persist. The Croghan church is no longer "Amish Mennonite," for in 1954 the Conservative Amish Mennonite Conference, with which it was affiliated, peacefully dropped "Amish" from its title and became known as the Conservative Mennonite Conference.[28] After fifty years the cape dress has gradually having fallen out of favor, and most women no longer wear it. However, during the 1980s a renewed debate over women's work and dress engaged the community. Instead of a concern over single women's working outside the home, the debate was over married women's working off-farm, especially those with small children. And the emphasis shifted from the cape dress to the prayer covering. Since Croghan church members no longer wear the cape dress or the plain coat, for many Croghan members the prayer covering is the only remaining sign of nonconformity and community solidarity. Once the prayer covering is rejected, Croghan church members will be outwardly indistinguishable from their non-Mennonite neighbors.

Interviews with contemporary dissenting women indicated that dress was once again a site for conflict over a range of issues including the transformation in women's work, women's submission to men, and anxiety over community survival in the face of economic stress. Abrupt shifts away from traditional work and dress patterns occurred as women took jobs to save their farms from the economic devastation of the 1980s farm crisis. Some church leaders were adamantly opposed to the new practices. One minister wrote that women should "work away from home less, be more conservative in their dress."[29] A woman noted that during church councils and meetings some male church leaders stressed the importance of wearing the prayer covering at all times (in the workplace), not just on Sundays.[30]

Anxiety over women's changing dress was apparent in church documents. Every year church bulletin announcements implored men to keep their female relatives in line: "We urge husbands & fathers to encourage the sisters to faithfully respect God's order by wearing the veiling with uncut hair. I Cor. 11:1–16."[31] In spite of church admonitions there was a wide range of responses and practices among women. These responses reflected a dilemma forced upon women by a changing local economy and a handful of intransigent church leaders who opposed changes in women's dress

The local bishop, Richard Zehr, his wife, Eileen, and their daughter, Rosemarie, on Sunday morning outside the Croghan Conservative Mennonite Church in 1992. Note that Bishop Zehr is wearing the plain coat whereas his daughter is dressed in "modern" clothing. (Photograph courtesy of Kimberly D. Schmidt.)

and work. Some women strove to assure themselves and conservative leadership that outside work would not compromise their tacit acceptance of female subordination, one manifestation of which was nonconformist dress. Other women, unwilling to submit any longer, were in the process of discarding the prayer covering, the last visible vestige of submission. The church has been unable to accommodate women's challenges to traditional beliefs. Ministers from the Conservative Mennonite Conference were called in to mediate disputes over conservative church leadership, and so far schism has been avoided. During interviews, some women said that if tensions continued the church might undergo another schism.

Women at Work and under Submission

In many ways history seems to have repeated itself during the farm crisis of the 1980s. Its effects in Croghan were staggering. In 1988 a seven-page questionnaire was administered to the Croghan congregation.[32] Of the 106 men and women over age eighteen who responded, 96 percent said they grew up on a family farm, defined as a farm from which all or most of the family income was derived. But by 1988 barely half of the men listed their occupation as "farmer," and only seven out of twenty-two men aged eighteen to forty said they farmed. Of these, four wrote that they farmed only part time. They supplemented farm income by working as loggers, truck drivers, and carpenters or in nearby mills or factories. Families were not leaving the farm en masse, but young people saw no future in farming. As a consequence, land that had been in the family for generations was not passed on because of lack of interest. The countryside revealed these changes. Route 12, the major road into Croghan, was dotted with neglected farms. Bishop Zehr commented that there were abandoned farms all over the county that used to be owned and operated by Mennonites. I asked if the people moved to town. "No," he responded, "the children grow up, and after they go to college many just don't come back. And if they do come back, they don't want to farm."[33]

During the 1980s the mixture of religious belief with the farm crisis had important ramifications for women. Young married women in Croghan, feeling the pinch, took off-farm jobs to supplement farm income. Except for a full-time nurse in her fifties, all the married women who worked full time were young, in their late twenties or early thirties, and felt they had to work to save the farm from foreclosure. The nurse was an exception because of her age, but also because of her education and profession. She was a registered nurse and had worked off-farm most of her adult life.[34]

The questionnaire also asked about women's responsibilities in the home and with the children. Men and women in Croghan agreed that a woman's primary place is in the home with the children. In response to "What do you think of the sentiment that women's place is in the home, with the children and in the kitchen?" 66.7 percent of women and 73 percent of the men agreed. However, the questionnaire also showed that by 1988, 56.1 percent of women had some off-farm work experience, including 40.9 percent who said they were employed full time. A survey taken in 1990 showed that 43 percent of married women in the Croghan congregation worked off-farm at least part time.[35] The conflict between community beliefs that women should work on the farm with their families and women's off-farm work stirred up a storm of controversy.

Many people in Croghan believed women should not work off the farm. As one young farm wife saw it, some women had to work outside because the family needed the money, but many were working for added luxuries. "Well, some has to [work outside]. Some has to, not as many as what do. I don't know, I'm old-fashioned. I would still like to see the woman on the farm. Just because they want to have a higher standard of living, that's a poor excuse, but if you have to, I'll sympathize. There's cases where they have to."[36] All the women working off-farm who were interviewed said they felt discriminated against by other church members. A woman with no dependents said, "Not a Sunday goes by that I don't hear some comments about my working out."[37] Another young mother keenly felt other church members' disapproval. She said, "If I were a nurse or a teacher, or some acceptable profession they wouldn't bother me as much. Since I got my license I get an earful all the time. I get up at four in the morning to milk the cows, make breakfast and then get my daughter ready for nursery school. I'm usually at the office around 9:00. . . . I always help chore in the evening even when I don't feel like it. . . . I'm hardworking."[38]

Croghan church members were forced because of economic circumstances to tolerate new work responsibilities for women. Since such tolerance did not come easily, many women were struggling with how to work cooperatively with their mates, be good Mennonite mothers, and hold down off-farm jobs at the same time. Much of the discussion about women's off-farm work centered on a perceived lack of female submissiveness at home.

One might expect that religious beliefs in women's submission would hinder women from making decisions on the farm, but this was not the case. Many of the women interviewed were upset with themselves and other women who did not assume a properly submissive attitude. A number mentioned that women ran not only the house but the farm as well. A common complaint was that their husbands were too passive. One woman said, "I do feel we have a little bit of a problem in this area. The wives, the women do tend to take over. . . . I feel sometimes we step out of our place. . . . Too many times the women run the show and I'm not sure I like that."[39] Another woman agreed but added that her husband, like many other men, "won't say anything. I ask him for money, he says 'go ahead.' He doesn't care how much money I take. He can't balance a checkbook. He's always forgetting to write in the amount. I have to do all the work and he should do it. He's the man."[40] Yet another woman commented on the situation in Croghan: "The men do not run the homes around here. What that woman says goes. The guys need to be more assertive. A lot of the women run the checkbooks." She added proudly, "It's not that way in my house. He takes care of all the bills and makes the decisions, and I have to toe the line."[41]

WOMEN'S SUBMISSION AND SILENCE IN THE CHURCH

The rhetoric on women's submission and male authority became even more heated when the topic included women's participation in church functions. Croghan traditions required females to keep silent in the church and to wear the prayer covering as a symbol of their submission to men. However, church members were not united in their opinions about women's submission or wearing the prayer covering. In answer to an item on the questionnaire about women's keeping silent in the church, the responses of Croghan Mennonites showed some diversity of opinion between men and women. A substantial majority of men thought women should keep silent in the church, whereas women were divided equally: 70.5 percent of men and 50.9 percent of women agreed when asked, "What is your reaction to the passage in the Bible that says women should keep silent in the church?" Almost half of the women (49.1 percent) and almost a third of the men (29.5 percent) disagreed.

Written comments on the questionnaires show that many Croghan members were uncomfortable with any female outspokenness or leadership. "Women has her place when to be silent" was a popular saying, and a number of people wrote it in the questionnaire's comment section. These people thought women should "speak their opinions through their husbands"[42] and gently recommended that wives "[be] meek and submissive persons and loyal to [their] family and helping in the church and community in times of need."[43] Others were quite strong in their opinions. One man wrote, "They should stay out of discussions in the church [community]. They should *Dress, act,* and *Live* according to the Bible [his emphasis]."[44]

Although some church members complained about assertive female behavior, others expressed confusion and even defiance toward teachings that required female submission. Regarding women's keeping silent, one woman wrote: "Honestly, I hate to pick verses out and say I don't believe in them so I guess I have to swallow pride and be quiet. Then again maybe women [in biblical times] weren't educated and didn't have anything to say. But some men aren't educated either so it can't be that. As you can probably tell the issue is very confusing for me at this time."[45]

Others, less confused, were clearly impatient or angry with the church's "old-fashioned" traditions. One upset woman wrote: "I was just told that I had no right to tell a man what to do because he had more 'authority' than me. I just walked away before I slapped him. I feel if men aren't taking their roles then we should step in. I don't feel we should be a doormat or a slave."[46]

Women maneuvered around keeping silent by not taking the Bible literally, by putting the biblical passage in a historical context, or by citing other biblical teachings that encouraged church participation and visibility. For example:

I'd like to see what the Greek or Hebrew word for "silent" really is. I don't take that verse literally.[47]

I don't believe it means a literal silence—women are needed in the church and have many roles to perform.[48]

It was appropriate in Biblical times when women were less educated, however now women are often as educated, or more so then men, and have many good ideas to contribute![49]

What does the Bible say about having gifts and not using those gifts?[50]

A Symbol of Submission

Croghan church members were divided over the issue of women's silence in the church. This debate grew stronger when it shifted to the issue of women's prayer coverings. The most visible sign of female submission to men was the prayer veiling or covering. Women understood the symbolism of the covering and the implications of not wearing it. When asked about the meaning of the prayer covering, one woman explained, "She is under submission, submission to man, submission to God."[51] A seventy-year-old woman said, "Well, it's a symbol of man is above woman, and I just feel that we've been brought up to respect it. I know it's gotten to be a big issue. It's gotten to be a big issue. I don't wear it all the time. When I'm praying, I put it on at home. I always wear it when I go to church."[52]

Respecting tradition by wearing the prayer covering crossed generation lines. A thirty-year-old woman wrote, "I feel that there are areas such as dress, [and] cut hair that we are neglecting. The Bible is clear on these areas. I can see myself that we are very worldly, and need to get back to the Bible."[53]

Many women adhered to church teachings and wore the covering at all times. Others, however, were in the process of discarding the tradition at their workplaces. Church members saw a connection between off-farm work and not wearing the prayer covering. One woman said, "Now we still have many women . . . who . . . still wear the covering all the time, and whatever. But most of those women don't work outside the home."[54] Women who worked off-farm confirmed this statement. For example: "I don't dress as a Mennonite. I never wear dresses or skirts to work, I always wear slacks. I never wear my covering at work or when I'm out in the field. And I have led more people to Christ with slacks than I ever did with a dress and covering. . . . I don't wear the covering to work. . . . I work with a very elegant lady, and she's been a big influence on me. She compliments me a lot, and it makes me feel good. . . . If I feel like wearing nail polish, I do. If I feel like wearing earrings, I do."[55]

Most women who worked off-farm often felt embarrassed by the covering and wore it only to church. They said it had the undesirable effect of separating them from their coworkers. "I used to teach. I taught with it [the prayer covering] for a long, long time. . . . I wore my prayer veiling, because I felt I should. It wasn't any problem. No one said anything to me about it. But then, after some newer teachers came in, some younger teachers, I always felt like there was a barrier there. They didn't know me. . . . So I dropped my prayer veiling when I taught school, and I always felt like I could communicate better."[56]

One young mother who wore her covering to her off-farm place of employment said fellow employees were often confused by her decision. "I wear my covering to work so I really look conservative. They'll ask if I'm from another group in the area and I'll explain I'm from the Conservative Mennonite Church. And then, 'Well why do you wear a covering and there's a girl that works in the Croghan Bank here and who's from the same church and she doesn't.' Well, this is where the individualism really comes in. Sometimes I think it's detrimental to us to be so individual that we're so different [from one another]."[57]

Even if women continued to wear the prayer covering, the attitudes toward it changed. One woman said a main reason she wore her covering was convenience: "I can comb my hair in three or four minutes. I'm finished and that's all there is to it . . . and so that's probably the most, one of the biggest reasons why I wear it the way I do."[58] This woman also said that she felt better, more herself, when she was not wearing the covering. Some women expressed a quiet defiance. Even if they wore the covering to church they did not believe in its symbolic implications and were often less than reverent during interviews. "I keep it in my car. I get to church, and I put it on my head, and I come out of church, I stick it in my car. It's not a big tradition with me. But it is to a lot of other people, so I do it."[59] This young woman wore her prayer covering to church in deference to other community members. However, like some of her peers, at her workplace she chose not to wear it.

Conclusion

Debates over women's dress and keeping silent crystallized the effects of the 1930s economic stress and the 1980s farm crisis in this small ethnoreligious community. Unlike the women described in Beth Graybill's chapter in this book, for whom dress was a site of community stability and cohesiveness, in Croghan dress was a site of conflict. Swirling around the dress controversies were anxieties over changes in farming, economic pressures, and community longevity, as well as outright opposition to female assertiveness. Those who opposed women's working off the farm and abandoning the prayer covering seemed to think that if only women would revert to wearing plain dresses and stay on the farm everything could get back to normal. These people, however, did not see the contradiction or double standard of forcing women into traditional roles while allowing men free access to the outside world. One elderly man in the church expressed it this way:

> ELDER: I really feel that we have lost our witness in the community by dropping off some of the things that we dropped off. There was a time that you knew our members when you saw them on the street.

AUTHOR: You could tell by women's prayer coverings and men's plain suits?

ELDER: Well, probably in the menfolks there wasn't that much difference. But in the womenfolks, there were. Today, the majority of them you, you would never know. . . . I really feel it would have been better for our congregation at Croghan if we would have remained more conservative in our appearance. I don't think some of the things out there that are enticing us now would have had that much of a hold on us.[60]

Although the exact nature of the "things out there that are enticing" was never made clear, this man and his wife described as idyllic the days when families worked together on the farm and women stayed in the home and kept silent in the church.

When it came to women, some of Croghan's leaders, with the support of men and women in the congregation, were averse to change. The resistance to change for women was nowhere more apparent than in the anxiety over the move from on-farm to off-farm work and the resulting debate over women's dress. The challenge to reject nonconformist dress tendered by the Amish Mennonite Rosies of fifty years ago appeared again in the face of renewed economic pressure and off-farm work opportunities for women. The position modern Croghan women found themselves in was not unlike that of their predecessors fifty years ago. Working women were again being blamed for the rising tensions in the Croghan congregation. Women's taking off-farm jobs and subsequently refusing to wear the prayer covering to work challenge church beliefs in female silence and subordination. The controversies over dress, both the cape dress of fifty years ago and the prayer covering of more recent times, continued to engage the local community as a reflection of the unresolved relationship between Croghan's religious and economic life and of the central place of women in both.

APPENDIX: RESOLUTION ADOPTED BY THE GROUP AT A MEETING HELD AT THE CROGHAN CHURCH OCTOBER 10, 1941

We, the undersigned, deeply regret the change in some of the policies of the Lowville Am.M. [Amish Mennonite] Church to which we felt we could not submit and be true to our convictions and that as a result it seems best for the cause that we seek a church home with some other conference.

We, however, want to maintain our former brotherly feelings for all of you, and ask your forbearance and forgiveness for any grief we may have caused the ministry and the church as well as for the wrong attitudes we may have taken, or for things that we have said.

Signed by the following people:

Harold Chaffee	Chris Lehman
Ernest Zehr	Mrs. Chris Lehman
Benjamin H. Martin	Mrs. Benjamin Martin
Joe Switzer	Vera Lehman
Daniel Zehr	Mrs. Lydia Zehr
Reuben Zehr	Mrs. Addison Lehman
Leon Widrich	Earl Lehman
William Lehman	Mrs. Mary Zehr
Benjamin F. Zehr	Mrs. Marion Zehr
Addison Lehman	Samuel H. Lehman
Susiana L. Zehr	Arthur Farrance
Martha Chaffee	Mrs. Arthur Farrance
Mrs. Kate Zehr	Mrs. Benjamin Lehman
Benjamin Lehman	Mrs. Leon Widrich
Lloyd Chaffee	Mrs. Samuel Lehman
Mattie Kennel	Quinten Martin
Simon W. Lehman	Aaron M. Zehr
Ralph Lehman	Mrs. Aaron M. Zehr
Samuel Yantzi	Mrs. Nina Moser
Mrs. Samuel Yantzi	Ezra J. Lehman
Mrs. Wilber Lehman	William Litwiller
Pearl Lehman	Jacob Moser
Kenneth Lehman	Erwin Lehman
Andrew Lehman Jr.	Mrs. Erwin Lehman
Andrew Lehman Sr.	Gorden Gingerich
Helen Lehman	Mrs. Ezra Lehman
Reuben Lyndaker	Mrs. Kenneth Lehman
Mildred Lehman	Mrs. Reuben Lyndaker
Mrs. Joseph Lehman	Joseph Lehman
Hilton R. Zehr	Lois Zehr[61]

NOTES

Many thanks to Paul Boyer, Kathryn Kish Sklar, Anne B. W. Effland, Steven D. Reschly, Levi Miller, Melvin D. Schmidt, and David Navari, who read and commented on earlier versions of this chapter. I especially acknowledge the wonderful assistance of Croghan's church historian, Arlene Yousey, whose generosity and knowledge greatly aided my research. A grateful thank you also to Richard and Eileen Zehr, who on numerous occasions graciously fed and housed me and who answered all my questions whenever I visited Croghan.

1. This belief is based on the New Testament verse, "And be not conformed to this world: but be ye transformed by the renewing of your mind, that ye may prove what is that good, and acceptable, and perfect, will of God" (Rom. 12:2, King James Version).

2. Gertrude Enders Huntington explains how Amish communities create separate spaces for themselves in "Bounding the Community—Mechanisms of Isolation" and "Interaction With the World," in "Dove at the Window: A Study of an Old Order Amish Community in Ohio" (Ph.D. diss., Yale University, 1956), 101–29, 347–430.

3. John A. Hostetler discusses dress as a symbol of Amish beliefs in nonconformity in "The Symbolism of Community and Custom," in *Amish Society*, 4th ed. (Baltimore: Johns Hopkins University Press, 1993), esp. 237–40.

4. For a detailed description of female and male clothing see Donald B. Kraybill, *The Riddle of Amish Culture* (Baltimore: Johns Hopkins University Press, 1989), 49–60, and Melvin Gingerich, *Mennonite Attire through Four Centuries* (Breinigsville, Pa.: Pennsylvania German Society, 1970), esp. chap. 7.

5. Clifford Geertz's *The Interpretation of Cultures* (New York: Basic Books, 1973) and his "Religion as a Cultural Symbol," in *Anthropological Approaches to the Study of Religion*, ed. Michael Banton (London: Tavistock, 1966), 1–46, were helpful in assessing the importance of symbols (in this case dress) in religious cultures. Treatments of how dress embodies and internalizes gender roles and expectations can be found in Ruth Barnes and Joanne B. Eicher, eds., *Dress and Gender: Making and Meaning in Cultural Contexts* (New York: St. Martin's Press, 1992).

6. Over a four-year period I was able to observe a few women in Croghan who were starting to reject the prayer covering. Beth Graybill, Julia Kasdorf, and Jane Marie Pederson also mention how women's rejection of plain dress can signal changed attitudes about women's submission to men and their place in the church. See their chapters in this volume.

7. Donald B. Kraybill analyzes sacred symbols of the Amish in "Symbols of Integration and Separation," in *The Riddle of Amish Culture*, 46–68, and "Mennonite Women's Veiling: The Rise and Fall of a Sacred Symbol," *Mennonite Quarterly Review* 61 (June 1987): 298–320.

8. Kathleen Zehr, "History of the First Mennonite Church, New Bremen, New York," unpublished paper, chapter 4. Hereafter referred to as Zehr, "History, New Bremen."

9. The cessation of Communion is highly symbolic. One tradition among many Amish and Mennonite groups is that one should participate in Communion rituals only if one is at peace with God and other community members. Ceasing to take Communion manifests the depth of the conflict.

10. Zehr, "History, New Bremen," 9.

11. Kathleen Zehr, "First Mennonite Church, New Bremen, New York: A Brief History, unpublished paper, Lowville, N.Y. This was J. Lawrence and Harriet Burkholder's first ministerial position. J. Lawrence went on to become president of Goshen College, a Mennonite institution in Indiana, before assuming a professorship of theology at Harvard University.

12. Interviews 1 and 17, Croghan, N.Y.: 23 October and 20 October 1992, respectively. Seventeen interviews are quoted in this chapter. To protect the identity of the informants and to reference the interviews for future use, all interviews are numbered and dated. Please note that I conducted them all and that all tapes and transcripts are in my private collection.

13. Interview 2, Lowville, N.Y.: 21 October 1988.

14. Interview 3, Lowville N.Y.: 21 October 1988.

15. Letter from Harriet L. Burkholder to author, 24 February 1995.

16. Harry F. Landon, "Some of [the] Customs and Habits of 'Hook and Eye Baptists': Costumes of Women of Amish Colony Rigidly Restricted—Five Hundred Members of Little Known Sect in Lewis County Universally Respected," *Lowville Journal and Republican* [1926]. In 1926 the Croghan church hosted a conference that generated newspaper articles in the local papers including the *Lowville Journal and Republican* and the *Watertown Daily Times*. Landon, a historian and journalist, worked for the Lowville paper during the late 1920s and wrote a series of articles on the local Amish Mennonites and conference proceedings. Arlene Yousey, local church historian from Croghan, believes the 1926 conference generated the article. Another source, a handwritten note in the scrapbook of Magdalena Schrag, attributes the article to 1926.

17. Arlene Yousey, *Strangers and Pilgrims: History of Lewis Country Mennonites* (Croghan, N.Y.: Privately published, 1987), 213.

18. U.S. Department of Commerce, Bureau of the Census. *Fourteenth Census of the United States* (Washington, D.C.: Government Printing Office, 1920): Population, Croghan Township, Lewis County, N.Y. (series T625, reel 1117).

19. Personal correspondence and genealogical records of Doris Lehman, retired executive secretary of the Climax Paper Mill and relative of many of the dissenters, and Arlene Yousey.

20. Interview 6, Croghan, N.Y.: 21 October 1992.

21. Interview 4, Croghan, N.Y.: 15 July 1989.

22. Interview 7, Croghan, N.Y.: 21 October 1992.

23. Interview 4.

24. Interview 8, Croghan, N.Y.: 21 October 1992.

25. Interview 3.

26. This analysis has benefited from "separate spheres" theory as found in United States women's histories, which explains how the domestic sphere (female) and public sphere (male) were divided into distinct entities. See, for example, Nancy F. Cott, *The Bonds of Womanhood: "Women's Sphere" in New England, 1780–1835* (New Haven: Yale University Press, 1977); Carroll Smith-Rosenberg, *Disorderly Conduct: Visions of Gender in Victorian America* (Oxford: Oxford University Press, 1985).

More recent scholarship, especially that focusing on rural and farm women's experience, has contained arguments against separate spheres theory. See Nancy Grey Osterud, *Bonds of Community: The Lives of Farm Women in Nineteenth Century New York* (Ithaca: Cornell University Press, 1991), esp. "No Separate Spheres," 1–15. However, Croghan's Amish Mennonite religious belief in nonconformity was informed by gender in that men and women adhered to the principle of separation from the world in different ways. Separate spheres theory may indeed have relevance for the study of conservative Anabaptist groups. An assessment of separate spheres theory and its usage in United States women's history is provided in Linda K. Kerber, "Separate Spheres, Female Worlds, Women's Place: The Rhetoric of Women's History," *Journal of American History* 75 (June 1988): 9–39.

27. Beth E. Graybill and Marlene Epp argue that some Amish and Conservative Mennonite women were more constricted in their dress styles than men. Epp explained that "resistance to the plain dress was particularly acute when it was

apparent that standards were applied more rigorously to women than to men," and Graybill has argued that it was easier for men in transitional groups to "pass" into the rest of society, since their clothing was not as distinctive. See Marlene Epp, "Carrying the Banner of Nonconformity: Ontario Mennonite Women and the Dress Question," *Conrad Grebel Review* 8 (fall 1990): 237–57. See also Beth E. Graybill, "Gendered Interpretations: Toward a Feminist Reading of Mennonite Tradition," paper presented at the National Women's Studies Association conference, 17 June 1993.

28. Ivan J. Miller, "Conservative Amish Mennonite Conference," in *The Mennonite Encyclopedia: A Comprehensive Reference Work on the Anabaptist-Mennonite Movement,* 4th ed. (Scottdale, Pa.: Mennonite Publishing House, 1982), 1:700–702.

29. Croghan questionnaire 044 (see note 32 below). Another male leader consistently advocated moderation. When I asked him about his moderate views he explained that being a parent taught him not to resort to rigid rules (interview 4).

30. Interview 5, Croghan, N.Y.: 10 October 1992.

31. Croghan Conservative Mennonite Church bulletin, 9 October 1988.

32. The questionnaire asked for opinions about issues affecting the church, men's and women's on-farm and off-farm work, and women's place in the church as well as information on education, age, marital status, number of children, and income. All questionnaires are in my private collection.

33. Interview 4.

34. Interview 6.

35. The 1990 church directory listed 127 families. Of these, 55 (43 percent) of married women worked off-farm.

36. Interview 9, Croghan, N.Y.: 20 March 1988.

37. Interview 10, Croghan, N.Y.: 24 October 1992.

38. Interview 11, Croghan, N.Y.: 19 March 1988.

39. Interview 12, Croghan, N.Y.: 19 March 1988.

40. Interview 13, Croghan, N.Y.: 20 March 1998.

41. Interview 11.

42. Croghan questionnaire 033.

43. Croghan questionnaire 046.

44. Croghan questionnaire 058.

45. Croghan questionnaire 014.

46. Croghan questionnaire 094.

47. Croghan questionnaire 019.

48. Croghan questionnaire 006.
49. Croghan questionnaire 057.
50. Croghan questionnaire 022.
51. Interview 5.
52. Interview 14, Croghan, N.Y.: 22 October 1992.
53. Croghan questionnaire 015.
54. Interview 6.
55. Interview 15, Croghan, N.Y.: 24 October 1992.
56. Interview 5.
57. Interview 12.
58. Interview 6.
59. Interview 10.
60. Interview 16, Croghan, N.Y.: 21 October 1992.
61. Zehr, "History, New Bremen," 10.

Part 3

(Re)creating Gendered Tradition

11

Speaking up and Taking Risks

Anabaptist Family and Household Roles in Sixteenth-Century Tirol

Linda A. Huebert Hecht

In recent years scholars have debated at length whether the Protestant and Catholic Reformations improved conditions for women in the church. Rather than merely asserting that Anabaptist women were "emancipated" or "oppressed" to match modern sensibilities, Huebert Hecht develops a more nuanced argument. Anabaptist women contributed substantially to their movement, but most often within their expected social and family roles.

In the past there have been certain "windows of opportunity" when women participated more actively and visibly in religious life. Historians Bonnie S. Anderson and Judith P. Zinsser refer to these times as "interludes of equality." They have been associated with the turning points of history, with times of reorientation, upheaval, and crisis. The early phase of the sixteenth-century Reformation was one of these windows.[1]

At the beginning of the twentieth century sociologist Max Weber recognized a pattern when he hypothesized that women were more active and visible in the early phase of a religious movement, before the "routinization and regimentation of community relationships set in."[2] The prominent Anabaptist and Reformation scholars Harold Bender, George Williams, and Roland Bainton in essence agreed with Weber, but their critics Claus-Peter Clasen and Joyce Irwin did not. The new social history approach of the 1970s introduced by Clasen, who surveyed more Anabaptist records than any earlier historian, provided little information about Anabaptist women. And Irwin, who focused on the history of women mainly using the writings of men, stated that opportunities for religious women were not expanded until the Quaker movement of the seventeenth century.[3] However, none of these historians, whether they agreed or disagreed with Max Weber, systematically examined women's participation in the Anabaptist movement, particularly in terms of how they functioned within their communities in their social roles as wives, mothers, daughters, sisters, widows, maids, and single women. Discussion of the centrality and contribution of Anabaptist women as members of the family and the household is just beginning.[4] The choices made by sixteenth-century Anabaptist women in the Austrian territory of Tirol during the three brief years of their window in time will be the focus of this chapter.

In order to go beyond assumptions and impressions about Anabaptist women as well as the idealized hagiography of women in the most-used traditional source—the *Martyrs' Mirror*[5]—gender must be the main category of analysis. Whereas historian Joan Wallach Scott proposed this for historical analysis in general,[6] Reformation historian Merry Wiesner addressed the meaning of gender for the sixteenth-century Reformation specifically. Wiesner contends that gender was more important than class during the Renaissance and the Reformation.[7] In Tirol most of the population lived in rural areas. A few of the Anabaptist families in Tirol engaged in mining and the crafts, but most by far were farmers.[8] They were part of the classes referred to as the common people (ordinary folk). Very few women of noble birth jeopardized their social position, wealth, and property as Helena von Freyberg did when she and her servants were rebaptized in her castle at Münichau in 1527. Sixteenth-century women's roles differed from those of today in that women were "defined" and spoken of as wives, mothers, daughters, widows, sisters, or single women— that is, in relation to their position in the family. Women worked in the domestic economy, being responsible for childcare and running the

This etching from the *Martyrs' Mirror* depicts two Anabaptist women being led to death in 1550. (Reprinted by permission from *Mirror of the Martyrs*. © Good Books, 1990.)

household. Families were often large, and the preindustrial household was labor intensive. In most cases women participated in the same occupations as their fathers or husbands. If the male head of the household was a peasant farmer, they worked on the farm; if he was a weaver or a shoemaker, they worked with him in the craft industry. Younger women often were maids in the households of relatives or neighbors, assisting in childcare and household duties. That a high percentage of the members in the Anabaptist movement of Tirol were women can be interpreted as a positive response to Wiesner's question whether there was a "revolution of the ordinary woman."[9]

In her discussion of the Reformation in Strasbourg another Reformation historian, Miriam Usher Chrisman, explains: "Reaction to the Reform was an individual matter." In Chrisman's view "The Reformation did not make any fundamental change in the position of women in urban society—their role continued to be within the family and household. The significant change was the overthrow of the celibate ethic."[10] This major change not only affected women's marital status but also challenged them to rethink old ideals and religious beliefs in both urban and rural environments. It required women to make choices. (Agency is a crucial issue in the study of gender.) In regions like Tirol where Anabaptist ideas were widespread, information about the women who affirmed their faith before court officials and were not afraid to risk life and limb was documented by the officials who arrested them for heresy. Thus their choices can be studied in detail.

To succeed, the Anabaptist movement required the participation of everyone, particularly the women who were part of the household and family settings where Anabaptists held their meetings and won their followers.[11] But not all women acted on their Anabaptist faith in the same way. Their choices during the initial phase of Anabaptism in Tirol, between 1527 and 1529, can be categorized according to their different levels of participation. A total of 268 women were named in connection with Anabaptism in Tirol during these three years.[12] Most of these women (172) are classified as believers or rebaptized members (approximately two-thirds of all direct participants); close to fifty—a large group—were martyrs, forming 40 percent of the total number of martyrs in Tirol in these three years;[13] and more than fifteen were lay leaders and missionaries, engaged in preaching, teaching, and proselytizing. A smaller number of the women named in the records (thirty) were indirect participants. It is not certain whether they had been rebaptized, but they were suspected because other members of their family or household were involved with the Anabaptists. Some women chose to recant at their arrest: it was a way to "buy time" and return to their families as well as to the Anabaptist movement. For recanters arrested a second time, punishment was immediate and severe. We know that the number of Anabaptist women in Tirol constituted nearly half (46 percent) of the total membership between 1527 and 1529.[14] Here the choices Anabaptist women made in these different categories of believer, martyr, missionary, lay leader, and indirect participant will be discussed from the point of view of their social roles in the family and household.

Anabaptism took root in the Austrian territory of Tirol between 1527 and 1529, though Reformation influences had reached this region several years before and were a major factor in the unrest among the common people that reached its climax in the Peasants' War of 1525 and 1526.[15] Ferdinand I, ruler of Tirol, put down the revolt. But the resistance of the common people to a government that sought to centralize political and religious control over its subjects remained and found a new form of expression after 1526 in the antihierarchical, anticlerical, and decentralized but outlawed Anabaptist movement.[16] By 1528 the activities of families like the Gassers, who had been leaders in the Peasants' War and now organized Anabaptist meetings, were being discussed by the authorities.[17] Persecution of Anabaptists was more severe in Tirol than in other regions of Europe because of the links between Anabaptism and the Peasants' War and because of Ferdinand's determination to stamp out all opposition to the orthodox church.

Owing to the arrest of both Anabaptist women and men by Ferdinand I and his officials, a rich source of information is available to us today in the form of government documents or court records (*Täuferakten*). Testimonies transcribed by male court secretaries and reports and directives sent to and from government officials at the central and local levels relate details about the speech and actions of Anabaptist women arrested on suspicion of heresy.[18]

Essentially these sources are those of "outsiders," since they are records created by people who were hostile to Anabaptists. As such they provide a more realistic picture of what women did than the idealized and hagiographic portrayal of women in the *Martyrs' Mirror.*[19] The martyrology, basically an "insider" source, linked Anabaptist martyrs to those of the first century and was intended to edify readers and provide models of faith. It has been the only source on female Anabaptists available to the English-language reader, and it is rightly valued, since one-third of the martyrs—a high proportion—were women. On the other hand, the court records are transcriptions of legal proceedings and actions taken against Anabaptists that include information not only about Anabaptists who were executed but also about those who escaped or recanted. The disadvantage of using information from the court records is that it is sometimes frustratingly incomplete and many of the stories are left unfinished. Some of the punishments were intended to frighten people into leaving the Anabaptist movement, but the authorities did not always have the staff needed to carry out their threats, and so it remains unclear whether sentences were always administered. Despite these problems (and the fact that many of the records were summarized by the editor, Grete Mecenseffy, who collected and published the ones for Austria), the court records are a more detailed and more objective source of information about Anabaptist women than the martyrology and contain the names of many more women.

In the sixteenth-century courtroom, women had to have a guardian speak on their behalf in a civil or property matter, but for a criminal offense such as heresy a woman was required to speak for herself. Although the court records for Tirol contain few of the actual testimonies of Anabaptist women, we know that they did speak for themselves because of references in the government reports to their testimonies (*Urgichten*). On several occasions Ferdinand's government instructed local officials to be sure each one spoke for himself or herself and that each accused person was treated individually. Phrases like "each with their own mouth" indicate that all confessions and recantations were to be given by the individual offender and not by the legal guardian, even if the accused person was female, since, as the government mandates stated, "each of these persons individually have allowed themselves to be baptized."[20]

Considering the restrictions in general on the public activity of sixteenth-century women, it is remarkable that Anabaptist women chose to live by their faith so fully and to defend it no matter what the consequences. Indications are that they were not unique in this. In a reference to the letters of Anabaptists facing death recorded in the *Martyrs' Mirror*, Brad Gregory tells us that "such resolve was not limited to Anabaptists, however, as many Protestant and Roman Catholic martyrs expressed the same ideas and demonstrated perseverance by their actions in the sixteenth century."[21] But the decisions of Anabaptist women in Tirol to speak up and to take risks for their religious faith are a significant and heretofore neglected foundation for modern-day women in the free church traditions.

ANABAPTIST WIVES

Most of the women mentioned in the court records of Tirol between 1527 and 1529 were married, and thus the largest number of women (137) categorized as believers, lay leaders, missionaries, martyrs, and indirect participants were wives.[22]

For some of the married women named in the court records we know only that they were baptized at the same time as their husbands. Their given names are often excluded; the phrase describing them is "and his wedded housewife" (*und seine eheliche Hausfrau*). Unlike Anabaptist men, wives have often been seen as mere followers "who had accepted Anabaptist ideas, but had not expressed them openly."[23] However, the wives named in the court records clearly had chosen to be rebaptized and thus were committed Anabaptists; otherwise their names would not have been entered in the records.

A classic case of similarity between the testimonies of husband and wife is that of Wolfgang and Martha Wynnter. Wolfgang was a tailor from a village near Vienna, and it was in that city that he heard the preaching of Hans Hut, the missionary leader from Augsburg, and was baptized by him. Following Wolfgang's brief testimony is a single sentence that reads: "Martha, Wolfgang's housewife, states the same." We do not know why Martha did not make a statement of her own. What is important, however, is that by this one sentence she affirmed her own Anabaptist beliefs.[24]

In February 1528, less than a month after the execution of the prominent south German Anabaptist leader Leonhard Schiemer, Jörg Held and his wife, from Hall, east of Innsbruck, were mentioned for the first time. Both were to be questioned. They were among a group of Anabaptists who had received instructions from the priest and wanted to recant.[25] Again the choices of husband and wife were the same. But the case of Christian and Barbara Pernhappel, who were in prison in June 1528 along with two other couples, illustrates that when husbands and wives undertook similar actions, they did not always receive similar treatment from the authorities. The request for the pardon of the Pernhappels and those imprisoned with them had the support of the judge himself, the mining company that employed the men, and the whole community of Rattenberg. It was to their advantage that Barbara and her husband had reported to the authorities during the grace period (*Begnadigungsfrist*).[26] However, Christian was punished with a public beating at the town pillory (*Pranger*) for having allowed an Anabaptist meeting to take place in his home.[27] We do not know whether he was more involved in Anabaptism than his wife or whether the government chose to punish only the head of the household.[28]

WIVES OF ANABAPTIST LEADERS

A second group of Anabaptist wives were those whose husbands were leaders in the movement. The variation in the actions they took reflects both their individual choices and their differing situations. The government mandates or laws made it clear that leaders were to be arrested first and punished more severely than other prisoners. In this way the civil authorities hoped to stop the spread of Anabaptism by eliminating its leaders. Thus the families of leaders were in greater danger than other Anabaptist members, and their actions could either help or hinder the growth of the movement.

Several of the men in the Taurer family from around Kitzbühel were Anabaptist leaders, including the father, Cristian, and his sons. When the men fled, their wives and two of their maids were arrested. The authorities threatened the women with torture while questioning them. In addition, the central government instructed local authorities to take an inventory of their property.[29] We do not know if these orders were carried out, but we do know that one of the women from this family, the wife of Paul Taurer, fled and left her child behind; she was later executed.[30]

The wife of an Anabaptist leader in Klausen named Messerschmidt assisted her husband in a different way. She could write, and this made her an accomplice in the crime of composing a threatening letter to the town priest, who did not approve of the radical evangelist the local Anabaptists were promoting.[31] In another case the wife did more than support her husband's activities. The wife of Mathis Waldner was her husband's coworker. She perceived God's call to be as binding for her as for her husband and participated with him in leadership, for the records state that she was to be arrested along with three other "key baptizers and seducers" (*Pinzipaltäufer und Verführer*). One of them was a woman named Gallpüchler, who was already familiar to the authorities in regard to the peasant revolt.[32]

In some cases, when male leaders were exiled their wives suffered the same fate. This was true for Peter Egger's wife, Cristina. However, she received a pardon after recanting because of the number of children who required her care, though we are not told exactly how many she had.[33]

When Jörg Blaurock was exiled from Switzerland, he and his wife Els both came to Tirol. In their case no children were mentioned.[34] Barbara Schützinger, wife of Jacob Hutter's coworker in Moravia, was not exiled with her husband but voluntarily left behind her home and her children in Tirol to join her husband in Moravia.[35] Thus the care of infants and children complicated the lives of Anabaptist wives whose husbands were leaders.

PREGNANCY AND CHILDBIRTH IN ANABAPTISM

In the sixteenth century pregnancy and childbirth carried high risks for women, and death was a possibility to be faced by every expectant mother. Prayers for pregnant women were continually offered to Saint Margaret, particularly when a difficult birth was anticipated.[36] Perhaps because pregnancy itself already put expectant mothers at risk, they were willing to face the additional risks of imprisonment and possible execution that came from joining the Anabaptist movement. A mandate Ferdinand I issued from Vienna in December 1527 stated that mothers who were nursing infants and women who were pregnant who returned to the orthodox church were to be released from prison after a sum of money had been paid on their behalf.[37] As the following cases demonstrate, not all pregnant women made the same choice.

As the mandates dictated, depending on the severity of her crime, interrogation and punishment were often postponed until a woman had given birth. This was the case for the wife of Treibenreif and the wife of Martin Nockh (whose husband was an Anabaptist leader) as well as for Hans Scheuring's wife, although she had to remain in prison until her child had been born. The trial of an unnamed pregnant woman whose case was discussed in February 1529 was also postponed until after she had delivered her child. Likewise, in December 1529 orders were given to postpone dealing with three pregnant Anabaptist women until they had given birth: Katharina Widmauer, Ursula Egger, and Cristina Sunschwennter.[38] Some pregnant Anabaptist women recanted and were pardoned, but others stubbornly persisted in their faith. Five women we know recanted were the Schlosserin, Anna Rinnerin, Waldpurga Ameiser, Anna Krätlerin II, and the wife of Jörg Schweitzer.[39] Anna Gasteiger may have been in the early stages of her pregnancy at her arrest, since the government called in another woman, possibly a midwife, to examine her. Her child was to be brought up according to the orthodox faith, but Anna herself was to be executed.[40]

In two cases women who had just given birth were involved in Anabaptism. The wife of Lorenz Vitzthum made a request to the government for her husband's pardon. It was reported that he was a simpleminded man who had lived a pious life. They had eight children, all underage.[41] The case of Wolfgang Schneider's wife is more unusual. Just three days after giving birth, this woman left her home and her newborn child, who became a ward of the state. Evidently the wet-nurse had baptized the child, a point on which the father was specifically questioned. His reply to these unusual proceedings was that a "proper" baptism was not necessary, since he believed the child to be "baptized by God."[42]

A number of pregnant Anabaptist women were arrested near the end of their pregnancies, as was Margret Kobl, whose husband was a leader in the Peasants' War and later in the Anabaptist movement. Fortunately she was released from prison at her first arrest because of her condition.[43] The wife of Hans Viltzurner from Gufidaun was not as fortunate. She was also near the end of her pregnancy when she fled with her husband, leaving a number of children behind. Her husband was accused of "evil talk" (*böse Rede*), probably meaning he had been speaking to others about Anabaptism. Hans sent a letter to the crown administrator (*Pfleger*) of Gufidaun informing him that indeed he was not guilty of such speech and asked the local administrator to write a supplication on his behalf, pleading his case to the court of Ferdinand I. Local authorities were instructed to appoint someone to supervise their property and care for their children. No further mention is made of this couple.[44]

For reasons unknown to us, Barbara Velcklehner came back to prison of her own free will shortly before she was due to give birth. She and her husband had already escaped from prison once. Did her action reflect personal guilt or a spiritual crisis as the time drew near for her to deliver her child? In her interrogation she insisted that her beliefs concerning the sacrament were not heretical. Fortunately for Barbara, she was released and allowed to rejoin her husband and children.[45]

One of the most striking cases of persistence among pregnant women was that of Anna Weltzenberger. The territorial judge, her father, and her husband all spoke earnestly to her, trying to persuade her to relinquish her

Anabaptist faith. But none of their arguments had any effect; she did not change her mind. The local authorities were not to release her from prison under any circumstances. She was to be kept there until her child was born. If after the birth she still persisted in her belief she was to be tried and sentenced. Since there are no further references to her, we do not know whether she was actually tried and whether the sentence was carried out. In any case, pregnancy did not excuse this woman from imprisonment.[46]

SINGLE ANABAPTIST WOMEN

A significant number of the 268 women linked to Anabaptism in Tirol (54) were not married. Many were younger and employed as maids in Anabaptist households. They were not servants in the contemporary sense. As was common practice in the sixteenth century, parents sent their children to live with other families in the same parish to receive training in household and farm management.[47] It was a form of apprenticeship, similar perhaps to what Old Order Mennonite families still practice today.

In the Gasser family from Klausen, both Anna and her husband were implicated as rebels in the peasant revolts of 1525 and 1526, but they were not arrested as Anabaptists until two years later. Anna Gasser had two maids, Lucia and Agatha. Lucia was arrested along with other members of the Gasser family and household in August 1528 and admitted being an Anabaptist.[48] Agatha's involvement was not discussed until the spring of 1529, when she was arrested with two male servants. The court decided that Agatha and the two youths were too young to be tried but that they should be punished as an example to other young persons. The government was concerned by this time about the number of young people involved in Anabaptism.[49] Margret Kobl also had two maids, Bärbl (Barbara) and Els, both of whom supported the Anabaptist faith. Barbara's name was given to the authorities by Margret herself. We know more about the participation of Els. She brought some things to the prison that enabled Margret's husband Ulrich to escape.[50]

Anna, the maid who worked for the Jacob Koler family residing on the Ritten Mountain near Bozen, was the only one from her household who was an Anabaptist. She was arrested in January 1529 at the same time as another man (not her employer) from that region. The government made it clear that despite the contrite attitude of the two prisoners, they would be tried. Fortunately it did not come to that, because the jurors were related to the male prisoner and refused to serve.[51] The persecution became more intense during 1529, and the maid working for a family named Gschälen was not so fortunate. She too was the only one of her household to be rebaptized, and she was arrested in September 1529 at Rattenberg. Like the other twelve prisoners, she was questioned several times; for some of these prisoners interrogation included torture. The authorities hoped to reeducate these Anabaptists with the help of knowledgeable priests, since the prospect of execution did not seem to deter the heretics. Whether the priests succeeded in reeducating the Gschälen maid remains a mystery, since there are no further references to her.[52] In the same month, the maid of the Schueler family was arrested together with the male servants from the household. In her case the link to Anabaptism was not the family she worked for but the other hired help. These servants, as well as the other prisoners with them, would not desist from their beliefs. Orders were given to question them in the presence of witnesses concerning a recent nocturnal meeting of Anabaptists.[53]

MOTHERS AND DAUGHTERS IN ANABAPTISM

Anabaptism offered its members a community, and as such it may have had a strong appeal for young and single women whose work separated them from their own families. At the same time, persons who had been rebaptized naturally were eager to see fellow family and household members do the same. Anabaptist influences within families are apparent in Tirol in the number of cases between 1527 and 1529, ten in all, where both mothers and their daughters joined the movement. Leonhard Schiemer baptized two daughters along with their parents.[54] We also know that Elsbeth Gesslerin and her daughter Katharina, Gross Enngerle and her daughter, an unnamed mother and daughter who were executed in 1528,[55] Margreth Wiser and her daughter Dorothea, Agnes Kassian and her mother Katharina from the Puster Valley,[56] and the Gallpüchlerin and her daughter from Bozen, were all Anabaptists.[57] Although there are several cases where only the daughters became Anabaptists—Pentzel's daughter, Hans Reck's daughter (her father submitted a request for her pardon), and Cristina from Scheyern, the daughter of a farmer[58]—this is less common than instances where both mothers and daughters were Anabaptists.

ANABAPTIST WIDOWS

In the same way that Anabaptism provided single women with a group to relate to, it seems to have functioned as a caring community for widows. Unfortunately, however, as with most of the other women involved in Anabaptism, we have no information about the motivations or feelings of widows. In many cases we have little more than their names. Sebastian Ampos and his mother were two of fourteen prisoners arrested in St. Petersburg in May 1528. They were accused only of rebaptism, so their punishment was not severe.[59] For the following spring the court records of Tirol reveal that several more widows were involved in Anabaptism. The widow of Lienhard Kofler was arrested on May 21, 1529, and imprisoned at Michelsburg, not far from her home. Two days later eight more people were arrested, among whom was another widow, Agnes from Erspan, near St. Lorenz. All we know about Agnes is that she was interrogated along with the other prisoners. The widow of Lienhard Kofler was ready to recant after two months in prison.[60]

When persecution increased in the spring of 1529, government officials at Innsbruck were eager to get information about Anabaptist leaders and those who supported them in the Inn River Valley. The civil authorities had reason to be alarmed. In one area alone, the mining town of Schwaz, the authorities estimated that 800 of the 1,200 inhabitants were Anabaptists, which is not surprising, since the first armed revolts against the government had taken place there in January and February 1525.[61] Several widows were named in 1529. In Rattenberg, which was close to Schwaz, the widow of Leonhard Lackner was acquainted with a woman (perhaps single) who had in her possession a register of 800 Anabaptists.[62] However, both the widow and the woman with the book of names eluded the authorities. Other widowed women who were Anabaptists were Katharina Kunz, whose husband was an Anabaptist martyr, and Jörg Tollinger's widow.[63] The former was arrested in September 1529, the latter in December of that year.

Not all women who became widows when their husbands were executed as Anabaptists adhered to the movement. Dorothea Frick's husband was an Anabaptist martyr, but she herself was pardoned by the government in April 1528. It seems she had been arrested only because of her husband's involvement in the sect.[64] Thus she is one of the women categorized as an indirect participant. Margarethe Gschäll also belongs in this category. She and her Anabaptist husband had been innkeepers in Rattenberg. Margarethe made an appeal for her half of the confiscated property that belonged to her as a deserted wife and for a daughter's inheritance from her parents.[65]

SISTERS IN ANABAPTISM

Of the different types of influences within Anabaptist families, those between siblings are evident in several of the cases discussed by the authorities of Tirol. Elisabeth Wolfram and her brother both belonged to the movement, but their parents did not. At first Elisabeth staunchly refused to recant, for which she might well have forfeited life and limb. Instead she received a pardon from the king and a milder punishment. Eventually she was absolved of even this, after her own request to the government as well an appeal from her brother and the intercession (*Fürsprache*) of friends and the whole district of Völs. The reprieve was granted on condition that she recant, do penance, and pay for the costs of her imprisonment. Her penance took place in the local church and consisted of holding a burning candle while kneeling during mass. After that she publicly recanted.[66]

Ursula Nehspitzer Binder was the sister of Jörg Nehspitzer, an Anabaptist leader in Augsburg. She testified in November 1527 that she and her husband had been sent out by Hans Hut, the Anabaptist leader in southern Germany and Vienna. They were to inform people in Salzburg that Hut had a book with seven seals that the prophet Daniel was given by God. This book would not be opened until the "last day" (*jüngsten Tag*). Ursula's testimony illustrates not only that she, like her husband, had been influenced by the apocalyptic beliefs of Hans Hut but that she also, like her husband, felt called to do mission work.[67]

Agnes, sister to Jacob Hutter, founder of the Hutterites, may have been working in Saalen close to their native hamlet of Moos in the Puster Valley. She was arrested for the second time in December 1529. Despite the attempts of both secular and sacred authorities to reconvert her, she remained firm in her faith.[68] Three years later she and Agnes Kassian were part of a group of prisoners taken to Brixen. We know nothing further about Agnes Hutter except that she was questioned a second time. Agnes Kassian's story is likewise not complete. All we know is that she was fleeing with her father and two brothers at the time of her arrest. Her mother had already been executed.[69]

A report of May 1529 informed the authorities in the Puster Valley about a group of seven Anabaptists that included two sisters. The group had been meeting secretly in a hillside hamlet, preaching the forbidden teachings, and peddling books up and down the Puster Valley. We do not have the names of these two women, the only females in the group; the report merely states that they were sisters of the tailor Caspar Schwartz. However, they had a significant role in proselytizing in this region.[70]

The sister of Hans Velcklehner also proselytized actively, but in a different region, the district of Hertenberg, west of Innsbruck. She was forced to flee, and it was reported in May 1528 that she came to her brother in Telfs and also spent time with the baker Lamprecht Pens. She persuaded two women to become Anabaptists, her sister-in-law Barbara and Barbara's sister, the wife of Lienhard Platten. It is possible that Hans Velcklehner's sister was influenced by another single women, Anna Egger, who is described briefly as the "one-eyed" sister of Peter Egger the baker. In April 1528 Anna Egger had accompanied her brother and another man on a preaching and baptizing tour in this same region.[71]

CONCLUSION

The persecution of Anabaptists in the Austrian territory of Tirol was very severe. Yet the court records illustrate that without a doubt women were central figures in the Anabaptist movement there. They spoke publicly in court when required to and acted deliberately in support of their choice to be rebaptized as adults. In the context of their social roles in the family and the household, they participated in the Anabaptist movement as wives, mothers and daughters, expectant mothers, widows, maids, and sisters. Without their participation the Anabaptist movement could not have survived in this region. As members of the class of common people, Anabaptist women in Tirol were indeed pillars in the Anabaptist movement.

The more than two hundred women who joined Anabaptism during the early years of its development between 1527 and 1529 attest to a high level of female participation in the movement as believers, martyrs, lay leaders, and missionaries. Whether this intensity of participation continued and for how long remains a question for further research. The stories of the foremothers discussed here demonstrate that women made their own religious decisions and defended them ably to judicial and political authorities. They stepped beyond the bounds set for women in sixteenth-century society. Their history is a window in time and an important precedent that religious women today can look back to. But they are more than foremothers in the Anabaptist faith. For women in the various free church denominations that developed from Anabaptism, their stories provide a historical memory so that, as Adriana Valerio has said, women no longer need to create their history and their identity anew in each generation.[72]

NOTES

This chapter is dedicated to the memory of my mother, who died 25 October 1994. The material used is taken from profiles in my "Data Base on Anabaptist women in Tirol (1527–29)." Funding for the development of these profiles came from a grant of the Quiring-Loewen Trust Fund, to which I extend my thanks. I also thank Sigrun Haude, Elfrieda Schroeder, Marilyn Färdig Whiteley, and the editors of this book for their helpful comments on various drafts of this chapter.

1. Bonnie S. Anderson and Judith P. Zinsser, *A History of Their Own: Women in Europe from Prehistory to the Present*, vol. 1 (New York: Harper and Row, 1988), 243–44.

2. Max Weber, *The Sociology of Religion*, trans. Ephraim Fischoff (Boston: Beacon Press, 1922), 104, 105. See Shulamith Shahar, *The Fourth Estate: A History of Women in the Middle Ages*, trans. Chaya Galai (New York: Methuen, 1983), 256, 258, for a similar pattern in medieval heretical movements. Regarding the factors that gave sixteenth-century Anabaptist women a "window in time" and the validity of Weber's thesis for their experience, see Linda Huebert Hecht, "Faith and Action: The Role of Women in the Anabaptist Movement of the Tirol, 1527–1529" (M.A. cognate essay, University of Waterloo, 1990), 2, 22–23, 59.

3. Key references to Anabaptist women are found in Roland Bainton, *Women of the Reformation in Germany and Italy* (Minneapolis: Augsburg, 1971), 145–58; George Huntston Williams, *The Radical Reformation*, 3d ed. (Kirksville, Mo.: Sixteenth Century Journal Publishers, 1992), 762–63; Keith L. Sprunger, "God's Powerful Army of the Weak: Anabaptist Women of the Radical Reformation," in *Triumph over Silence: Women in Protestant History*, ed. Richard L. Greaves (Westport, Conn.: Greenwood Press, 1985), 45–74; Joyce L. Irwin, *Womanhood in Radical Protestantism, 1525–1675* (New York: Edwin Mellen, 1979),

xvii; Claus-Peter Clasen, *Anabaptism: A Social History, 1525–1618* (Ithaca: Cornell University Press, 1972), 207; Marion Kobelt-Groch, *Aufsässige Töchter Gottes: Frauen im Bauernkrieg und in den Täuferbewegungen* (New York: Campus Verlag, 1993); Linda Huebert Hecht, "An Extraordinary Lay Leader: The Life and Work of Helene of Freyberg, Sixteenth Century Noblewoman and Anabaptist from the Tirol," *Mennonite Quarterly Review* 66 (July 1992): 312–41; M. Lucille Marr, "Anabaptist Women of the North: Peers in the Faith, Subordinates in Marriage," *Mennonite Quarterly Review* 61 (October 1987): 347–62; Lois Y. Barrett, "Wreath of Glory: Ursula Jost's Prophetic Visions in the Context of Reformation and Revolt in Southwestern Germany, 1524–1530" (Ph.D. diss., Union Institute, 1992). A review of all relevant literature is found in C. Arnold Snyder and Linda A. Huebert Hecht, eds., *Profiles of Anabaptist Women: Sixteenth-Century Reforming Pioneers* (Waterloo, Ont.: Wilfrid Laurier University Press, 1996), 406–15.

4. Regarding the social history of the Reformation, see Miriam Usher Chrisman, "Women and the Reformation in Strasbourg, 1490–1530," *Archive for Reformation History* 63 (1972): 143–68; Susan C. Karant-Nunn, "Continuity and Change: Some Effects of the Reformation on the Women of Zwickau," *Sixteenth Century Journal* 13 (summer 1982): 17–42, and her "The Transmission of Luther's Teachings on Women and Matrimony: The Case of Zwickau," *Archive for Reformation History* 77 (1986): 31–46; Natalie Zemon Davis, "City Women and Religious Change," in *Society and Culture in Early Modern France: Eight Essays* (Stanford: Stanford University Press, 1975), 65–95; Lyndal Roper, *The Holy Household: Women and Morals in Reformation Augsburg* (New York: Oxford University Press, 1989); Merry E. Wiesner, *Women and Gender in Early Modern Europe* (New York: Cambridge University Press, 1993), and her article "Beyond Women and the Family: Towards a Gender Analysis of the Reformation," *Sixteenth Century Journal* 18 (fall 1987): 311–21; and Sherrin Marshall, ed., *Women in Reformation and Counter-Reformation Europe: Public and Private Worlds* (Bloomington: Indiana University Press, 1989). For the Radical Reformation the only two published longer works are Kobelt-Groch, *Aufsässige Töchter Gottes*, and Snyder and Huebert Hecht.

5. Thieleman J. van Braght, *The Bloody Theater, or Martyrs' Mirror of the Defenseless Christians Who Baptized Only upon Confession of Faith, and Who Suffered and Died for the Testimony of Jesus, Their Savior, from the Time of Christ to the Year A.D. 1660*, trans. Joseph F. Sohm (Scottdale, Pa.: Herald Press, 1950).

6. Joan W. Scott, "Gender: A Useful Category of Historical Analysis," *American Historical Review* 91 (December 1986): 1053–75.

7. Wiesner, "Beyond Women and the Family," 317–18.

8. There are only about thirty references to the occupations of husbands of Anabaptist women in the early court records for Tirol. They include two bakers, a blacksmith, a bookseller, a city judge (*Stadtrichter*), a civil servant (*Hofraiter*), a hatmaker, three innkeepers, a mayor, a merchant, two millers, three miners, a painter, two crown administrators (*Pfleger*), three shoemakers, a silversmith, a water carrier, and a tailor. See Huebert Hecht, "Faith and Action," 29–30 and appendix B.

9. Wiesner, "Beyond Women and the Family," 320.

10. Chrisman, 166.

11. In *Women of the Reformation in Germany and Italy*, Roland Bainton said of the Reformation: "The women constituted a half of the population, and had they boycotted the movement, one may be sure that would have been the end" (9).

12. For a complete list of their names and categories, see Huebert Hecht, "Faith and Action," appendix A, 126–30, and 30–31.

13. Linda Huebert Hecht, "Women and Religious Change: The Significance of Anabaptist women in the Tirol, 1527–29," *Studies in Religion: A Canadian Journal* 21, no. 1 (1992): 61.

14. For a discussion of how this percentage is derived, see Huebert Hecht, "Faith and Action," 33.

15. Werner O. Packull, *Hutterite Beginnings: Communitarian Experiments during the Reformation* (Baltimore: Johns Hopkins University Press, 1995), 161–63. See especially 364 n. 1, where Packull refers to earlier studies.

16. Natalie Zemon Davis refers to the Anabaptists as having a "less professional, less bookish, less hierarchical order" (84), which gave women greater opportunities.

17. Regarding the peasant revolt in Tirol, see Walter Klaassen, *Michael Gaismair, Revolutionary and Reformer* (Leiden: Brill, 1978); James M. Stayer, *The German Peasants' War and Anabaptist Community of Goods* (Montreal: McGill-Queens University Press, 1991); and Packull, *Hutterite Beginnings*, 169–71. For a discussion of women in the Peasants' War see Marion Kobelt-Groch, "Von 'Armen Frowen' und 'Boesen Wibern': Frauen im Bauernkrieg zwischen Anpassung und Auflehnung," *Archive for Reformation History* 79 (1988): 103–

37. See also Linda A. Huebert Hecht, "Anna Gasser of Lüsen," in Snyder and Huebert Hecht, 144–45.

18. Grete Mecenseffy, ed., *Quellen zur Geschichte der Täufer,* vol. 13, *Österreich,* part 2 (Gütersloh, Germany: Gerd Mohn, 1972). A few of the cases that will be discussed from this volume are from neighboring regions, but most are from Tirol. Hereafter this source will be referred to as TA, Ost. II, with the page number followed by a colon and the line number referred to in the record or the number of the document. All translations from the court records are my own.

19. Van Braght.

20. TA, Ost. II, 68:6–7 and 18:14 ff.

21. Brad Gregory, "Soetken van den Houte of Oudenaarde," in Snyder and Huebert Hecht, 370.

22. The group of single women totaled 54, widowed 7, deserted 3, and "other" 3. However, for 64 of the 268 women there is no reference to a male guardian, so this group cannot be categorized by marital status. See Huebert Hecht, "Faith and Action," table 1, 30a. In her 1987 article "Beyond Women and the Family," Wiesner states that "it is occasionally difficult to tell if an identity is a name or an occupation, especially for women, whose marital status is also often unclear" (315).

23. Marion Kobelt-Groch, "Divara of Haarlem," in Snyder and Huebert Hecht, 298.

24. TA, Ost. II, 26:12–15.

25. TA, Ost. II, 77:25 ff. and 80:20.

26. TA, Ost. II, 147:1–8.

27. This information is from Eduard Widmoser, "Das Täufertum im Tiroler Unterland" (doctoral dissertation, Leopold Franzens Universität, Innsbruck, 1948), 70. Mecenseffy published only the summary of this record; see TA, Ost. II, 159:2–5. Widmoser explains that the Pernhappels were mentioned once more in the records, when the Anabaptist leader Conntz Streicher used their names along with those of other Anabaptists (*Freundschaft*) to appeal for a pardon.

28. Two other couples, Margreth and Wolfgang Katten and Thomas and Barbara Reschl, are worthy of mention. They were in a group of twenty Anabaptists that included nine other women besides these two wives. That three priests were sent in to persuade the prisoners to relinquish their Anabaptist faith indicates that these Anabaptists were articulate in expressing their beliefs as well as being staunch believers. TA, Ost. II, 309:34, 35, 38; 310:1–3, 5 ff.

29. TA, Ost. II, 82, document 81; 96, document 99. See also Grete Mecenseffy,

"Anabaptists in Kitzbühel," *Mennonite Quarterly Review* 46 (April 1972): 99–112.

30. TA, Ost. II, 266:11; 421:20 ff.; 422:1–2.

31. See the testimony of Wölfl, the radical evangelist, published in Matthias Schmelzer, "Jakob Huters Wirken im Lichte von Bekenntnissen gefangener Täufer," *Der Schlern: Monatszeitschrift für Südtiroler Landeskunde* 63 (November 1989): 616.

32. TA, Ost. II, 183:29. Kobelt-Groch, *Aufsässige Töchter Gottes,* 191 n. 14, refers to her being accused by the authorities of "sinful talk" in June 1526 during the Peasants' War. They ordered her arrest and the search of her house for letters. Claus-Peter Clasen suggests that she was an Anabaptist leader in "The Anabaptist Leaders: Their Number and Background, Switzerland, Austria, South and Central Germany, 1525–1618," *Mennonite Quarterly Review* 69 (April 1975): 145. On female Anabaptist leadership, see Linda Huebert Hecht, "A Brief Moment in Time: Informal Leadership and Shared Authority among Sixteenth Century Anabaptist Women," *Journal of Mennonite Studies* 17 (1999): 52–74.

33. TA, Ost. II, 170, document 216; 192:10 ff.

34. TA, Ost. II, 81:10–11.

35. TA. Ost. II, 99:25; 266:11; 414:28 ff.; 422:28 ff.; 423:1–3; 480:24–28. See also *The Mennonite Encyclopedia: A Comprehensive Reference Work on the Anabaptist and Mennonite Movement* (Scottdale, Pa.: Mennonite Publishing House, 1959), 4:485, and *The Chronicle of the Hutterian Brethren,* vol. 1, trans. and ed. Hutterian Brethren (Rifton, N.Y.: Plough, 1987), 103–4.

36. *New Catholic Encyclopedia* (New York: McGraw-Hill, 1967–96), 9:200.

37. Grete Mecenseffy, ed., *Quellen zur Geschichte der Täufer,* vol. 11, *Österreich,* part l (Gütersloh, Germany: Gerd Mohn, 1964), 54, document 30.

38. Regarding the wives of Treibenreif, Martin Nockh, and Hans Scheuring, see TA, Ost. II, 90:30; 179:24 ff.; 182:32; 218:30 ff. Regarding the unnamed pregnant woman, see TA, Ost. II, 193:7–10, 17–19. And for Katharina Widmauer, Ursula Egger, and Cristina Sunschwennter, see TA, Ost. II, 310:26 ff.

39. TA, Ost. II, 99:26; 154:4 ff.; 158:31; 283:4; 283:27 ff.

40. See TA, Ost. II, 265:21–26 regarding Anna Gasteiger. Anna Krätlerin I, TA, Ost. II, 144:20 ff., is another pregnant Anabaptist woman who likely was executed.

41. TA, Ost. II, 172–73, document 219.

42. TA, Ost. II, 266, document 381. Anabaptists sometimes argued that they

had been baptized "by no man" but directly by God. See C. Arnold Snyder, "Agnes Linck from Biel," in Snyder and Huebert Hecht, 33.

43. TA, Ost. II, 136:4–8.

44. TA, Ost. II, 154–55, document 193.

45. TA, Ost. II. 196, document 269; 201–2, document 280.

46. TA, Ost. II, 212, document 296.

47. See Elise Boulding, *The Underside of History: A View of Women through Time* (Boulder, Colo.: Westview Press, 1976), 552; Nancy Chodorow, *The Reproduction of Mothering: Psychoanalysis and the Sociology of Gender* (Berkeley: University of California Press, 1978), 4.

48. TA, Ost. II, 164:28.

49. TA, Ost. II, 203, document 282; 213, document 298; 222, document 318.

50. TA, Ost. II, 164, document 207; and 165:11 ff. These two maids are categorized as indirect participants.

51. TA, Ost. II, 189, document 253.

52. TA, Ost. II, 284, document 402; 289:14. She is also referred to as Magdalena von Futtereith.

53. TA, Ost. II, 287, document 408.

54. Schiemer named a young woman (*Dirn*) who had joined with her mother and father and the daughter of Hanns Wennter, who had joined with her parents. See TA, Ost. II, 55:17 and 55:24.

55. See TA, Ost. II, 156–57, document 198; 142:14 and 138:10–14; 174:7, respectively.

56. Regarding these four women who were part of the same group from the Puster Valley, see TA, Ost. II, 244:32; 272:35–36; 273:7; 244:40, 44. Margreth Wiser had witnessed the burning of a crucifix, a sacrilegious act.

57. TA, Ost. II, 81:11. The Gallpüchlerin became an Anabaptist leader after the failure of the peasant revolt. See note 32 above.

58. TA Ost. II, 184:20; 230:18–20; 256, document 363; 147:12 respectively.

59. TA, Ost. II, 142:13. This group of prisoners included an older woman, referred to as the "alt Phlegerin." TA, Ost. II, 142:15. Two other women named elsewhere may have been widows, namely, the mother-in-law of Bartlme Dill, arrested with the other members of the household (see TA, Ost. II, 80:8; 117:34; 181:1), and a woman referred to as the (alt) Müllerin, perhaps named Ursula. She was arrested in July 1529. See TA, Ost. II, 263:25.

60. TA, Ost. II, 244:29; 244:31.

61. Peter Blickle, *The Revolution of 1525: The German Peasants' War from a New Perspective,* trans. Thomas A. Brady Jr. and H. C. Erik Midelfort (Baltimore: Johns Hopkins University Press, 1981), 120.

62. See TA, Ost. II, 239, document 342; 249, document 350, regarding Lackner's widow and the woman with the book of names.

63. TA, Ost. II, 289:15–16; 313:24.

64. TA, Ost. II, 119:25; 128:14 ff.

65. TA, Ost. II, 293–94, document 421; 300:17 ff. Other wives who did not flee with their husbands also appealed to the government for property ownership. This was the case with Jörg Vasser's wife and with Dorothea Angstwurm, both indirect participants. TA, Ost. II, 31:5; 423:5–9; 129:6–11.

66. TA, Ost. II, 183:14–15, 34; 201, document 279. This is an example where only the daughter, not the mother, was an Anabaptist.

67. TA, Ost. II, 25:21 ff.; 26:7–11.

68. See TA, Ost. II, 311–12, document 447. The second reference to her is in Grete Mecenseffy assisted by Matthias Schmelzer, eds., *Quellen zur Geschichte der Täufer,* vol. 14, *Österreich,* part 3 (Gütersloh, Germany: Gerd Mohn, 1983): 68:25, hereafter TA, Ost. III. Agnes Hutter was one of the prisoners being transferred to the prison in Brixen.

69. TA, Ost. II, 244:40 ff. and TA, Ost. III, 65.

70. TA, Ost. II, 237–38, document 340.

71. TA, Ost. II, 133, document 150; 119, document 120; Huebert Hecht, "Brief Moment in Time," 63.

72. Adriana Valerio, "Women in Church History," in *Women, Invisible in Church and Theology,* ed. Elizabeth Schüssler Fiorenza and Mary Collins, Concilium, 182 (Edinburgh: T. and T. Clark, 1985), 65. Valerio's statements can be seen as a response to Harold Bender's discussion twenty-six years earlier on Anabaptist women. See Harold S. Bender, "Women, Status of: Anabaptism," in *The Mennonite Encyclopedia* (Scottdale, Pa.: Mennonite Publishing House, 1959), 4: 972. See also note 3 above.

12

Household, Coffee Klatsch, and Office

THE EVOLVING WORLDS OF

MID-TWENTIETH-CENTURY

MENNONITE WOMEN

Royden K. Loewen

Definitions of "traditional" gender roles change over time. That fundamental insight from gender construction theory informs this chapter, in which Loewen ties rural economic shifts to Mennonite farm women's changing self-understanding over three generations. Gender has a history.

I made butter, sewed and set ten hens"; "I worked hard at 'keeping Saturday'"; "I worked hard at cleaning the chicken barn"; "I and Helena sewed and did the chores": these were daily descriptions in the German-language diary of fifty-five-year-old Helena Doerksen Reimer of Meade County, Kansas, in March 1949.[1] In 1952 another group of Meade County Mennonite women organized the "Cheerful Homemakers" Home Demonstration Unit and met regularly for all-day meetings to discuss an array of issues: topics such as "table arrangements," "smart shopping," "dressing attractively," and "global awareness" were followed with "coffee and dainties" or "coffee and chiffon cake," and more information on these issues could be obtained from the *Meade Globe News* column "Coffee Chatter." By the 1970s a third group of women reported to the local history committee that now that their children were grown they spent most of their time at their professions in Meade City. They were teachers and nurses, but also bookkeepers, hairdressers, motel managers, cooks, gift shop owners, dental assistants, and business secretaries.[2] The three texts—the farm household diary, the "Coffee Chatter" columns, and the history book notes describing women's professions—illustrate three distinct patterns of work and leisure in Meade County between 1945 and 1975. They also demonstrate a sequence of cultural worlds of rural women: the symbols, systems of meaning, views of life, and values of women in this Mennonite community changed dramatically in the middle decades of the twentieth century.[3]

The changing role of farm women over time has been the focus of much feminist literature. A controversial but widely accepted argument has been that the very social context of the pioneer or frontier family farm gave women an important level of power and status. The argument continues that this basis for autonomy was lost as agriculture became more commercialized and technologized and as urbanization undermined the old farm community. Almost two decades ago Martine Segalen posited that although women in the French countryside were in a subordinate position legally, the household economy produced a particular "man-wife relationship . . . [that was] based not on the absolute authority of one over the other, but on the complementarity of the two."[4] Numerous works in North America have reflected this reasoning.[5] Other works, however, have questioned this dichotomy. Veronica Strong-Boag in Canada, for example, has argued that the farm household's productive side did not mean that men and women "pulled in double harness"; it meant that women "pulled a double load." Deborah Fink in the United States has questioned her own earlier dichotomous assertions: although "the economic autonomy arising from women's participation in production has been a necessary ingredient in their gaining control of their lives . . . [t]he organization of labor within the nuclear family undermined [the farm household's] liberating potential."[6]

A Kansas farm woman rests against a tree while churning butter. (Photograph courtesy of Mennonite Library and Archives, Bethel College, North Newton, Kansas.)

This chapter engages this ongoing debate in four ways. First, it focuses on women of a single locality; Meade County in western Kansas, with its semiarid climate and its distance from large urban centers, may have affected the position of farm women in a particular way. Second, it isolates women of a particular historical, religious, and ethnic background to determine how such cultural variables may have tempered the construction of gender. Third, it focuses on a telescoped conjunction of three generations, 1945 to 1975, during which rural society in the United States underwent an especially rapid transformation. John Shover dubbed this period, characterized by sudden rises in mechanization, commodity specialization, and government controls, "the Great Disjuncture."[7] Fourth, this chapter seeks to understand not only behavioral patterns but also cultural constructions by which women gave voice to these social changes. They clearly sought symbols, systems of meaning, and cosmologies to explain their positions and ways to exert female autonomy and contest overt male power. The lives of farm women in the twentieth century were not static but changing, and in the course of those changes women's own status was affected by local economic conditions and by evolving religious and ethnic repertoires that could both limit and enable them in their struggle.

In Meade County those local conditions were in part environmental and economic. This wheat-producing region had come through the disheartening terror of the Dust Bowl during the Great Depression, and now in the postwar period it faced an unstable wheat economy. Farmers here shifted from wheat production to mixed farming during the depression and then to a highly mechanized commodity specialization during the 1950s. But demography and ethnicity also affected Mennonite women's lives. Meade County Mennonites had traditionally venerated the maintenance of social boundaries and household self-sufficiency. The Mennonites who first came to Meade County in 1907 from established Dutch-Russian Mennonite settlements in central Kansas and southeastern Nebraska were rigorously conservative.[8] This conservatism was maintained in part because both of the church congregations, the Kleine Gemeinde and the Bruderthaler, emphasized an agrarian life and communitarian theology. During the first half of the twentieth century, however, the Mennonite congregations went through remarkable changes: new names—Emmanuel Mennonite Church and Evangelical Mennonite Brethren—pointed to a "symbolic ethnicity" that allowed for the adoption of North American evangelicalism and an easier interaction with the wider world. The nature of the local economy as well as a new sense of ethnicity affected the construction of gender in Meade County in the 1950s and 1960s.

THE HARDWORKING FARM WIFE

Helena Doerksen Reimer's *Tagebuch* (diary) described a life centered in the Mennonite household. The numerous suffixes of *sehr* (very much) that followed descriptions of tasks signified hard work directed to the economic strength of the Mennonite farm. Helena's diary clearly was intended to outline the contours of the farm household; it was the economic record of the entire family and even of a wider kinship network. Her 1949 diary documented the work of her fifty-seven-year-old husband, Klaas, a farmer and carpenter who spent days each month building in nearby Meade City, Fowler, and Dodge City. The diary also listed the work of her teenage sons, Bernard, Gerhard, and Johann, including the seasonally varied work of fencing in winter, planting rye and sorghum in spring, harvesting wheat in June, endless days of "one-waying" (disking) in July, planting winter wheat in September, and repairing equipment in November. And the diary described the many times that her married children— her twenty-five-year-old daughter Helen and her husband, Martin Bartel—came to help out.

More important, the diary placed Helena's own work within the context of the household economic unit. Her descriptions, for example, of Monday washing, Tuesday ironing, and Saturday dusting and baking were placed on the same line in the diary as the tasks of Klaas and the boys. Moreover, much of the work Helena described was also overtly productive, generating direct income for the family. Her view of the house was both domestic and economic: here, as she described it, eggs were cleaned and prepared so that Klaas, or Klaas and Helena together, could take them to the market in Dodge City. Here too Helena used the DaLaval cream separator to generate another commodity that was taken to the creamery in Meade City. And old methods were used to "butter" and prepare yet another commodity. Helena secured the raw material of these commodities in the barnyard. Each day she would begin milking the ten cows until the boys finished their chores and continued the task, then she fed the pigs and tended the two barns of chickens, which included collecting eggs from the layers, feeding the fryers, and as time required, "setting" the brood hens on hatching eggs and cleaning the barns.[9]

A second document, the financial account of the Reimer household, kept by Klaas, undergirded Helena's implicit perception of mutuality. The farm was typical of western Kansas Mennonite farms; it comprised 420 acres, 230 planted to winter wheat and 50 to feed grains—maize, kaffir, oats, and barley. Moreover, the Reimers kept ten milk cows, 150 chickens, and fourteen pigs and maintained an orchard of ten peach and ten cherry trees for home consumption and local markets. By the end of the year the sector of the farm Helena was involved in—producing the chickens, eggs, cream, and hogs—earned $1,549.26. This was less than 20 percent of the $9,534 derived from grain and cattle sales, but it was twice as much as Klaas brought home from carpentry ($766). Arguably the net profits of the barnyard were proportionately larger than the gross figures indicated; they required little technology and tapped little of the $1,191 spent on fuel and oil for the tractor, truck, and car. Finally, another of Helena's contributions to the family income appeared in the line totaling $559 in oil and gas royalties from land she had inherited in Haskell County. Both Helena's diary and Klaas's account book suggest that the couple saw their roles as interdependent.[10]

The strong identification with household production that Mennonite women held in the 1940s was at least in part ethnically determined. First, it was an identification rooted in the dialectic between historical events and old ethnoreligious values that espoused an agrarian existence.[11] The historical contingencies of the depression, with its terror of the Dust Bowl, and of World War II, with the siege mentality of this German-speaking pacifist group, seems to have compelled Mennonites of Meade County to return to traditional religious values of farm household self-sufficiency. Second, Helena's diary links her household work with that of women in the semi-isolated, self-sufficient Mennonite community; almost daily she encountered neighboring Mennonite women—"Sam Friesche" and "Menno Wiensche" and "Gerhard Doerksche" (identifying each by her husband's first name and a feminine version of the surname). Sometimes Helena sold them products that she produced or that husband Klaas had purchased in bulk, sometimes she assisted at hog butchering, and sometimes she sent daughter Helen to work for one of them. A third ethnically determined factor that linked women with the productive side of the household was the Mennonite practice of bilateral, partible inheritance. Interviews and tax records indicate that Meade County families provided both boys and girls with land when they married or when the parents retired from farming. Feminist scholars have linked landownership and status among women.[12] In Meade County this system allowed some unmarried women to farm productively, other women to help their husbands become farmers, and others still to encourage their husbands to settle matrilocally in Meade County.[13] Bilateral inheritance provided Helena Reimer with her oil and gas royalties from Haskell County.

The description of Helena Reimer's life, ordered by interdependent work roles in the farm household, reflected a broad social reality in the Mennonite district of Meade County. Family histories of farms in the 1940s frequently allude to husband and wife working together and sharing an identity with the farm: "Following their marriage [in 1943] . . . they took up farming and raised cattle . . . [milking] a few cows, [and raising] chickens and hogs."[14] Farm census records suggest that the sector of the farm associated with women continued to be important until the 1950s. The percentage of families who owned a few milk cows, for example, dropped only slightly between the Great Depression and the early 1950s, from 94 percent in 1937 to 82 percent in 1950, despite a decade of good crops and high prices. There were similar signs of continued household self-sufficiency in patterns of chicken production; the percentage of farms tending flocks of two hundred or more dropped insignificantly, from 78 percent in the depression year of 1937 to 62 percent in 1950.[15]

The world of Helena Reimer in the 1940s was grounded in that farm household. Women saw their work as economically productive and complementary to the men's. Both Helena's diary and Klaas's financial record reflected female production of commodities and land inheritances. Mennonite religious values of an agrarian existence and a simple lifestyle led Mennonite women to react to depression and war with a commitment to mixed farming. The culture of bilateral inheritance similarly encouraged mixed farming by providing women with land and ensuring that each of the children of most families received a small acreage. Womanhood was intrinsically tied to the idea of gender mutuality within the household. As memories of the Great Depression and World War II began to dull, as a burgeoning wheat market provided new financial resources, and as a new round of mechanization and the lure of consumerism entered the picture, Mennonite ethnicity and ideas of gender began changing substantively.

THE CHEERFUL HOMEMAKER

One night in October 1963 on Highway 23, just outside Meade City, a "family vehicle" driven by thirty-year-old Mrs. Bea (Bessie Mae) Morrow Cornelsen struck a cow. It was a serious accident; Bessie Mae, who had left the high-school football game of the Meade Buffaloes early with her six children, ages three months to eleven years, had to have them "checked out" at the Meade City hospital. And the injured cow had to be killed. For the local *Meade Globe News* the accident was shocking, but for the purposes of social history the event illuminated the new world women lived in. Bea Cornelsen was not an economically productive farm-based woman; her life centered on children and included greater mobility and new forms of leisure. This tragic meeting of woman and cow on Highway 23 reflected this set of new social realities. Since women no longer milked cows daily, this may have been the only cow Bessie Mae encountered in 1963. According to 1961 records, she lived in Meade City with her husband Anthony and the children.[16]

The social basis of Bea Cornelsen's world lay in a new economic reality: the woman's sector of the farm declined in importance at the very time that the man's sector increased. Larger and more mechanized farms made the small dairy and chicken sectors seem insignificant, altered the culture of labor, and generated a cash flow that was more easily directed to store-bought products. During the 1950s total land acreage per Mennonite farm in Meade County rose by 27 percent (from 462 acres to 588), and the number of beef cattle more than doubled to thirty-four head. During this decade the percentage of farms with a few milk cows plummeted from 82 percent to 15 percent, and the number of farms owning small flocks of chickens dropped from 62 percent to 39 percent and would decline further, to just 7 percent in 1975.[17]

In this context a new description of women rose. Meade Mennonite women who began their households in the 1950s and 1960s more often referred to themselves as "homemakers" and "housewives." The family vignettes in the local history book bear this out. The history of Pete and Katherine Friesen, written by Katherine, notes that they "purchased their first home on 160 acres in 1954 . . . and called it Horseshoe Farm," and it further describes Pete as "active in farming" and Katherine as "a homemaker, enjoy[ing] added talents of painting and various crafts."[18] Similarly, the family history of John and Katie Bartel, written by daughter Arlene, noted simply that after moving from Manitoba in 1960 John became "a carpenter" and did "some farming" while Katie was "a housewife."[19] When women did work on the farm now in the 1950s, it was more often as assistants to men in male-dominated sectors: they hauled grain but did not comment on the wheat's yield; they drove the tractors while the men operated the balers; they brought food to the fields for the men who ran the combines.[20] The house of the housewife was separated from the farm in a new way.

The new economy also introduced a new level of consumerism, and it in turn affected the social patterns and culture of women's lives. The switch from wind-driven Delco plants to continuous power of the Rural Electrification Agency in 1947 and the construction of natural gas pipelines through the county in the 1950s brought significant changes to the inventory of household appliances. The local manager of CMS Electric Co-operative, Carl Zink, had promised that subscribing to the co-op's service would make "farm life more pleasant."[21] Evidently he was right. The April 1948 auction sale of the Isaac household included a mangle, an oil stove, a wood stove, an "Oak Heater," a gasoline-powered washing machine, and equipment for producing cream, butter, cheese, and meat. Compare it with the May 1960 auction sale of the Ediger household, which listed not only wares reflecting a more affluent life—a living room suite, "steel kitchen cabinets" with "'formica' . . . tops," and a riding lawn mower—but appliances requiring heavy electrical usage, an Admiral air conditioner, and a Maytag oven range fueled by natural gas.[22] Mennonites also began to patronize other stores, such as Ideal Grocer and Marrs Clothing Store, and judging from the new vogue of "permanents" cited by church elders, perhaps the hairdressers in Meade City too.[23]

Falling fertility revealed a third change in the cultural and social lives of Meade County Mennonite women during the 1950s. The birthrate had already dropped during the Great Depression and World War II, and now, in contrast to the "baby boom" in the rest of the country, they experienced an uninterrupted fertility decline: in the eight short years between 1953 and 1961 the number of children per Mennonite household fell by 22 percent, from 2.7 to 2.1.[24] At the same time, the average age of a woman bearing her first child rose from 23.1 years in 1953 to 25.6 in 1961.[25] One of the reasons for this decline is certainly economic, but there is also a cultural explanation. At least one historian has linked fertility decline with the rise of pietistic evangelicalism, a change that encouraged women to think of having "fewer children of 'greater spiritual quality.'"[26] This reality was reflected in Meade County, where most Mennonites acquired this sense of evangelicalism only in the 1930s and 1940s. In 1944, after the evangelistic Emmanuel Mennonite Church was founded from the remnants of the old Kleine Gemeinde, a new view emerged that children should be converted, or at the very least that it was the church's duty to mold their Christian life. Within months of the church's inception a Youth Meetings organization was begun, and over the next decade the issue of youth involvement in church programs was repeatedly raised.[27] In 1955 the congregation even discussed the new practice of "dedicating children," described as a "public dedication of children to the Lord by parents."[28] Mennonite women now also began employing the language of "child psychologists" to explore "correct ways" of child rearing.[29] In at least one meeting in June 1954, Meade Mennonite women concluded that while "love [was] the most important" in child rearing, it was also important to "recognize him, make him feel wanted and needed, and not forgetting the spiritual element."[30] As "housewives," Mennonite women had begun thinking differently about "motherhood."

The decline of household self-sufficiency, the rise of consumerism, and the plummeting of fertility occurred in the context of a significant change in the very notion of womanhood. Feminist scholars have long designated the 1950s as a decade of domesticity, when the "feminine mystique" placed women in economically unproductive roles in homes, turned them from producers to consumers, and separated and alienated them more completely from the world of men. On one level this is true for Mennonite women in Meade County. Compare the obituaries of mothers in the 1930s with those of the 1960s, and in exchange for the staid concept of "duty" there appear virtues of goodness, gentleness, dedication, and spiritual nurture of children.[31] Observe the new wedding parties in Meade County and one sees the creation of men and women as "incommensurable opposites," in the language of Thomas Laqueur, different not only biologically but ontologically, with bride distinguished from the groom by color and elaborateness of dress.[32] A June 1957 wedding report of a Meade Mennonite couple described the bride not only as "lovely" but as wearing a gown of "frost white silk organza and venice lace over taffeta, fashioned with molded basque bodice, shirred short sleeves and scoop neckline edged with lace . . . [and] a chapel-length train." It further reported that the bride had been given in marriage by her father and that the groom, wearing a "dark tuxedo," waited to receive her.[33]

As Mennonite women left the house for consumer goods and made child rearing more public, they also began joining and actively participating in publicly funded, secular Home Demonstration Units. The HDUs in Meade County, as elsewhere, were supervised by special "home demonstration agents" who worked closely with the school superintendent, county agricultural agent, and county health nurse to advance the cause of "homemaking, health and safety." Recent scholarship has suggested that the HDUs arose in part because government and business believed that farms would become more productive if women turned their attention from farm and neighborhood to house and nation.[34] It is significant that Meade Mennonite women resisted joining HDUs from 1918, when the first unit was established in the county, until 1952, at the very time female farm production in Mennonite households dropped. Significantly, too, when Mennonite women did join the HDU movement they avoided established units and organized their own distinctly Mennonite chapters. The "Cheerful Homemakers" and "Live 'n Learn" clubs that were founded in 1952 comprised almost entirely Mennonite women.[35]

These Mennonite units reflected the new social reality of increased mobility and leisure. They also provide the student of Mennonite gender with a text of a new perspective of womanhood. In a sense the language of the units differed little from that of the Mennonite sewing circle that Helena Reimer would have attended in the 1940s; women met monthly, they opened meetings with prayer, and they often adopted community service projects. But overriding these older features were a new agenda and a new language.

The language was, first, that of a new middle-class, consumer-oriented, and domestic femininity. In fact the core of ideas expressed through the HDU reports suggest that Mennonite women had exchanged a view of themselves as household producers for a view of themselves as consumers. The women, for example, used many of their meetings to discuss table settings, interior decorating, creating home spaces, and organizing domestic chores; there was no recorded discussion of farm work, even in the poultry or dairy sectors. The Cheerful Homemakers also demonstrated a new concern with physical appearance and fashionable dress. Representative of their lessons was the one from February 1957 in which "Mrs Corny Classen and Mrs Herman Harder" spoke on "How to Dress More Attractively." The women were introduced to the concept of "counterdressing" to improve the appearance of those who were "too tall or too short," and then they discussed more informally the "problems . . . that different members had."[36] And there was a set of symbols acquired from the wider commercial world to script their more domestic, genteel lives— symbols that farm women of the past would have rejected. One set of these symbols reflected their views of marriage. At one of their meetings each woman brought a wedding photo to show during roll call, at another meeting they all wore their wedding dresses, and during yet another meeting, a "Valentine's Day Special," they made the "heartshaped jello."

Ironically, the Cheerful Homemakers used a public forum to legitimize their new lives of domesticity. But like women elsewhere who engaged in what historians have dubbed "maternal feminism," these women extended their domestically based virtues to the public arena. Their own newspaper reports point to a new preoccupation with a wider world, beyond their immediate neighborhoods: the women heard lessons on "global awareness," discussed "my favorite radio program," and attended regional meetings of HDUs. They opened meetings by "singing 'America,'" and they met to discuss "our voting privileges and responsibilities as citizens of our country." The women also extended their services to the world outside their homes. The official histories of the Cheerful Homemakers and Live 'n Learn clubs suggest that the unit members thought of themselves as servants not of the poor, as in the older sewing circles, but of public institutions: the senior citizens' home, the hospital, the 4-H clubs.[37] In some instances they actively spread the word of the new virtues of happiness and discretion. Indeed, the women prescribed a standard of behavior and female virtue that the women of the more difficult, physically strenuous, and communitarian world of the 1930s and 1940s would have found odd. In February 1957 when the Cheerful Homemakers presented a program to the Meade Bible Academy, they began with two songs, "Always Cheerful" and "Kind Words Never Die," and followed with "a comical skit . . . by six ladies [suggesting] . . . not to say things we don't want repeated."[38] Ironically too, the women of the 1950s used these new images of nurturers and custodians of moral virtue to begin gaining entry into the public world in and around the Meade Mennonite community.

This is most apparent in the overtly public, although subservient, roles that women assumed in the increasingly evangelistic Mennonite churches, especially in the new Emmanuel Mennonite Church founded in 1944. In the old church tradition, lines of patriarchal authority from the male bishop to the all-male council of ministers and deacons to the general male brotherhood were clear and simple, and women held no official position. The birth of Emmanuel Church signaled a more subjective and individualized theology and a more complex church structure, and both presented women with new, more public roles. By becoming evangelicalized the church implicitly signaled that it had given up its moral suzerainty over the community and would henceforth compete for souls, and this new challenge required committed service from all members, women as well as men. Between 1944 and 1964 Emmanuel Mennonite women became Sunday school teachers, participated in church elections, served in the Mission Extension Department, and most important, entered mission service. By the 1950s the all-male council of the Emmanuel Church noted that "if a sister feels the call to enter into the Master's service . . . the minister or church board [shall] . . . give her their attention."[39] Clearly women "felt the call," and when they volunteered for missionary work the church hailed them in a special public forum, such as the August 1964 "farewell for Lena Isaac who is leaving for service in Morocco."[40]

During the 1950s Meade Mennonite women also began translating their public identity as nurturers into off-farm professions. As the number of women farm producers waned, the number of female students in secondary and postsecondary education waxed. Women who had pursued professional degrees in the 1930s and 1940s recall having to resist older agrarian notions of women's work and marriage. When in the late 1930s Minnie Classen announced her intention of becoming a registered nurse, she is said to have "tested the system," facing "great opposition. . . . great reluctance and admonishment from ministers and Grandma Friesen." Opposition was so strong that she, as a Mennonite, was forced to covertly join "the U.S. Cadet Nurses Corps" to obtain "help with expenses and tuition" until she "graduated in 1946."[41] Other women resisted old ideas that only farm households guaranteed security and fulfillment: "I had to ask for permission to attend high school," recalled one 1948 graduate of Meade Bible Academy, then "when I wanted to go to Tabor College for teacher's training, Dad suggested that this would be unnecessary if I wanted to get married."[42]

By the mid-1950s this culture had changed. At the Mennonite private high school, the Meade Bible Academy, it was said that the "most pleas-

ant and best equipped room. . . . [was] the home economics room," with
the latest in electric and gas cook stoves, refrigerators and electric sewing
machines.[43] Still, in a 1956 poll, students gave the school a low rating for
preparing them for family life, and—shockingly—of the approximately
thirty female students, only five said they wanted to become "housewives." Young Mennonite women had for some time been schoolteachers
in Mennonite-dominated rural districts of Goodwill, Lilydale, Sunrise,
and McNutty.[44] By the 1950s the vocational choice for most women was
nursing; the 1956 poll counted nineteen women intending to pursue this
vocation. Professional work was a new venture that did not contradict the
current culture of domesticity in the 1950s.[45] This was also apparent in
that the women who officially declared a vocation other than "homemaking" frequently returned to that very life after marriage.[46] Indeed, it was
inconceivable that women could both pursue professions and raise families. Thus when Morocco missionary Elsie Regier was courted by Peter Z.
Friesen of Meade in 1949, Elsie's colleagues objected that her "Arabic was
too good to waste . . . time raising children."[47]

The Meade women of the 1950s had made consumption and nurture
the hallmarks of true womanhood. They had exchanged a productive role
on the farm for a life of domesticity; they also turned this new conception
of womanly duty into a highly publicized role, first as homemakers and
then as Mennonite church workers and service professionals. Here were
signals that in limited ways these public roles could be turned to economically productive work.

THE PROFESSIONAL WOMAN

From the vantage point of the 1970s the period of the "homemakers"
must have appeared short-lived, for by this time an increasing number of
married Mennonite women in Meade County were returning to work. It
was the third part of a pattern, severely telescoped perhaps, but not unlike
the one described by Louise Tilly and Joan Scott as "a U-shaped pattern of
female productive activity—from relatively high in the pre-industrial
household economy, to a lower level in the industrial economies, to a
higher level with the development of the modern tertiary section."[48] The
western Kansas farm economy that had made wheat and cattle production
profitable in the 1940s and 1950s had also created a restricted farm economy, reflected in land inflation, higher input costs, and increasingly ex-

pensive equipment, all in what John Shover describes as an economy of "diminishing returns."[49] In this economy women's productive work once again became necessary. At the same time an increasingly complex society, with an increasingly sophisticated social safety net for the elderly and for farmers, and a consumer society that produced more medical services and offered more stores of food, clothes, and home furnishings, provided more spaces for working women.

The increase of the service industry and government offices significantly altered patterns of female employment in Meade County. These patterns are apparent in county and state records. They reveal, for example, that women in their twenties more often than men left the county to acquire postsecondary education and that these same women returned to work in the county. In 1970, for example, 22 percent more women than men in Meade County had college educations (355 to 290). In this context the number of women working in public places increased slowly and steadily from 13.2 percent of the total paid workforce in 1940 to 28.3 percent in 1960 and 33.8 percent in 1970.[50] More significant was the rapid entry into the workforce of married women, their numbers rising by almost 50 percent during the 1960s, from 27 percent to 39.8 percent of all married women.[51] Although quantitative data are not available to document the percentage of married Mennonite women returning to work, family biographies note this as an increasing tendency. They suggest, too, that Mennonite farm families, once committed to agriculture as a religiously sanctioned way of life and to an ethnically homogeneous rural community as a safeguard against "worldliness," were turning to town life for economic security.

There were several subpatterns in women's return to work in the 1970s. Some women found productive roles on farms that were similar to those of their mothers during the 1930s and 1940s. A few Meade County farms had pursued an avenue of commercialization not through growing winter wheat and ranging cattle, as the physical environment in southern Kansas encouraged, but through specializing in hog, dairy, and poultry production. Although men assumed primary roles in these barnyard-based farm economies, women seem to have played more crucial roles here than on wheat farms. Ike and Anna Reimer, who married in 1958, established a farm that illustrates this pattern: theirs was one of two Meade Mennonite farms specializing in hogs, with 250 sows by 1975. A family history notes that Anna assumed the multivariate tasks of "housewife . . . help[ing] with the hog chores and quilting . . . in her spare time."[52]

More women, however, seem to have found work as a direct result of an increasingly restrictive farm economy. Sometimes they worked the small farms, averaging less than 250 acres, while their husbands found work in nearby Meade City.[53] In 1961 Martin and Helen Reimer Bartel, for example, owned a small farm that had one hundred swine, twenty beef cattle, 120 acres of wheat and sorghum, and five milk cows: John recalled later that while "I worked for Meade [City] Manufacturing [Company], Helen ran the mixed farm, teaching all the boys to drive the tractor."[54] More often women contributed to the household economy by working in town, reactivating professions they had acquired in the 1950s. The story of John and Anna Siemens, who married in 1941 and had five children between 1943 and 1951, is not atypical. Their farm was relatively small; in 1975 they harvested 160 acres of wheat and marketed twenty-six head of cattle, but they had no hogs or dairy cows, and John worked for the local Friesen Windmill Company. When the two youngest children—twins Lois and Loel—turned sixteen in 1967, Anna went to work as a "medication aide" at Lone Tree Lodge, the senior citizens' home in Meade City.[55]

Most often, however, the couple left farming altogether, and both husband and wife drove to town to work or moved into town to be close to their jobs. The story of Herman Harms and Esther Wiens illustrates this pattern. After they married in 1945, they moved to a small farm, where in 1951 they raised 158 acres of wheat, marketed four head of beef, milked three cows, and raised fifty chickens. A family history notes, however, that after "1954, Herman was employed at Meade Manufacturing [where he worked] until September 1978 [when the plant closed]"; it adds that "in 1970 [after raising three children] Esther started to work at Lone Tree Lodge as cook on a part time basis."[56] Married women, especially those with school-age children, also found roles in family-based town businesses. Thus Betty Isaac Friesen of Friesen's Machine Shop worked as a "secretary" and Phyllis Grunau Rempel of Rempel's Auto Repair as a "part time book keeper."[57] During the 1970s, as women began to work in any position in the growing tertiary service sector—as business managers, hairdressers, novelty shop clerks, dental assistants, secretaries—the number of married working women rose even higher. A few married Mennonite women, like Mary Klaassen, played even more active roles, "manag[ing] the Meade Motel . . . and later own[ing] Mary's Variety and Fabrics, all in Meade."[58] As the number of women in the labor force increased, there were social developments. Fertility continued falling for Mennonite women; the number of children per family in the countryside, which had fallen from 2.7 to 2.1 children during the 1950s, now fell even further, reaching just 1.6 children per household in 1975. Similarly, the age of a woman bearing her first child, which had risen by two years in the 1950s, from 23.1 to 25.5 years, rose by a full year in the 1960s and early 1970s, to 26.7 years. The number of women who lived in town rose precipitously, from ten married women to fifty-nine in a matter of nine years, 1961 to 1970.[59] The everyday language of the last of the older Mennonite women began to be English; Helena Doerksen Reimer, for example, moved into town in about 1963, and on the very day of the move she changed the language of her diary from German to English.[60] The number of elderly Mennonite women who lived with their children after their husbands died decreased too, as homes became even more private and as the social safety net spread to establish a Mennonite-run senior citizens' home in Meade City. Mennonites were moving beyond old ethnic boundaries. The mostly Mennonite Cheerful Homemakers and Live 'n Learn clubs still met, but Mennonite women were now joining other women's organizations—the interethnic Sunnydale Homemakers, the Sirosis Club, and even the Meade Business and Professional Women's clubs.

The very evidence for these new social realities also points to a new culture of Mennonite womanhood. The one hundred or so biographies of Mennonite families in the local Meade history books reflect a new female representation. It is significant that the data rarely mention the family's ethnicity, its church affiliation, the name of the Mennonite minister who married or baptized the couple, or the children's birth dates, which would have been the signposts of community legitimacy in an earlier time. What are noted in these texts are the work and professions of family members, including married women. Sometimes women's work and, more important, their pilgrimage to work through difficult times of child rearing receives more script than men's work. Thus the biography of Roy and Alma Regier, married in 1956, notes in two lines Roy's employment at Meade Manufacturing and CMS Electric; it devotes four lines to how "Alma taught two years . . . and after their marriage taught one year . . . [and] while the children were growing up Alma did substitute teaching, custom sewing and taught piano." Finally, it adds that "Alma is now in her fifth year of teaching first grade." Similarly, the historical section of John and Anne Reimer's biography notes in three lines that before their marriage "Anne graduated from the Gretna Mennonite Collegiate and from the Tuxedo Teacher's College [and] after that she taught for three years in her home school" and adds in a single line that "John attended the McNulty School near Meade."[61] The Mennonite woman's legitimacy now lay not in her lineage, her effort in the farm household, or her domestic life, but increasingly in her publicly recognized profession.

CONCLUSION

Women's lives changed during the course of the post–World War II rural transformation. Farm mechanization, commodity specialization, and state-sponsored Home Demonstration Units changed the social configuration for Meade County women. As farms shifted from mixed farm operations to large, specialized businesses for grain or cattle production, women lost their production roles; but in the meantime they acquired the resources to engage in a new middle-class society. With the continued evolution of the farm economy, residents faced the early period of an agriculture of "diminishing returns." In this scenario women returned to productive work, usually by finding work in Meade City, sometimes as wage laborers and sometimes as professionals in jobs for which they had earlier received training. Commensurate with these changing work patterns were changes in social networks, falling fertility, and increased levels of education. Clearly, Scott and Tilly's idea of a "U-shaped" trajectory in which economically productive farm women of an earlier time set a pattern for later professional and town-based women reflects the social reality in Meade County.[62] Clearly too, women were leaving the privacy of the household for increased participation in a public world, comprising secondary relationships and easy associations with a wider community.

Mennonite women in Meade County, however, did more than change patterns of work. They adopted a new cultural meaning of "womanhood." The central text of the lives of women in the 1940s was the diary and account book. The very way the quotidian remarks were recorded by women suggested a mutual relationship between husband and wife. The diary was a record of the entire household, in which the activities of both men and women were indiscriminately recorded. Moreover, the male-written account books accorded equal representation to the incomes of men and women. There was a deeply interwoven sense of cooperation, even in an overtly patriarchal society. The central text of the women from the 1950s was the newspaper columns that recorded the activities of the local Home Demonstration Units. There was a remarkable confidence by which a new generation of women exhibited their preoccupation with establishing middle-class homes, complete with new houses, appliances, fashionable clothes, and time to arrange domestic space. Their own representation also emphasized their public service roles and their duties to community organizations, including their churches, all amid new virtues of joyfulness, nurture, and gentility. The third text, the local history book and its family biographies, reveals a new set of values. These short scripts, often written by women, not only emphasize their public professions but make their personal treks through college and post–child raising years into central aspects of the biographies. Significantly, women defined themselves in terms of economic activity.

Tempering and molding these constructions of gender, however, were not only the economic conditions of Meade County and the increasingly public forum in which gender was constructed, but the particular Mennonite ethnicity of these women. It mediated their economic responses and their cultural constructions, but it was not a static variable supporting the evolution of a particular idea of gender. Ethnicity too is dynamic, and as "being Mennonite" changed during this time, so too did the concept of being a woman. During the 1940s the idea of agrarian self-sufficiency was still a preached value in the Mennonite churches. It discouraged social integration with the broader world, censured overt consumerism, and warned against town life. The old Mennonite values of a landed existence, undergirded by bilateral inheritance, encouraged both mixed farming and women's participation in the farm household economy. During the 1950s the very concept of Mennonite peoplehood changed. Mennonites themselves realized that social stability and continued identity as a religiously devout and conservative people required that they appropriate institutional models from the outside. Ethnicity now changed from being grounded on a communitarian, linguistic, and economic base to being symbolic and celebratory, and the churches turned their attention from boundary maintenance to social integration. Womanhood was now expressed publicly, through the local newspaper and through attending high school and participating in a Mennonite-dominated Home Demonstration Unit. More important, Mennonite women now assumed that a religious imperative of the Mennonite churches was for women to extend virtues of clean living and nurture to a wider society. Finally, the women of the third generation entered a public world but continued identifying with local Mennonite churches and, more often than not, worked in Mennonite family businesses or Mennonite-sponsored social institutions. They would not participate in the language of the wider society's "second wave of feminism," but they justified their professional activities with reference to household economic imperatives.

The history of women in rural society in the twentieth century cannot, of course, be written without reference to dramatic social transformation. Their lives were radically altered by shifts in technology, education, state intrusiveness, and popular culture. But it is important to recognize that the very nature of those lives was affected by local variations in environment and economy and the interweaving repertoire of community practice and ethnic identity. The gender roles of women in Meade County continued to evolve as these variables interacted. Each group of women, however, continued to fashion elements of domesticity and autonomy from their circumstances. It is not a simple matter of measuring the nature of their gender by economic activity. Their own representations of what they considered important and autonomy producing is crucial in understanding their worlds. Each group of women found new ways to assert lives that they found autonomous and meaningful within societies that continued to produce new expressions of male dominance. The women of the 1940s did so by pursuing economically productive lives within the domestic unit, the women of the 1950s by exhibiting domestically oriented lives in the public sphere, and the women of the 1970s by combining elements of both.

NOTES

1. Helena Doerksen Reimer, "Tagebuch, 1949," George D. Reimer, Meade City, Kansas.

2. Larry Beard, ed., *Centennial History of Meade, Kansas* (Meade, Kans., 1985); Meade County Historical Society, *Pioneer Stories of Meade County* (Meade, Kans.: Meade County Historical Society, 1985).

3. Meade County Historical Society.

4. Martine Segalen, *Love and Power in the Peasant Family: Rural France in the Nineteenth Century*, trans. Sarah Matthews (Chicago: University of Chicago Press, 1983), 9.

5. Louise Tilly and Joan Scott, *Women, Work and Family* (New York: Holt, Rinehart, and Winston, 1978), 54; Jane Marie Pederson, *Between Memory and Reality: Family and Community in Rural Wisconsin, 1870–1970* (Madison: University of Wisconsin Press, 1992), 159; Deborah Fink, *Agrarian Women: Wives and Mothers in Rural Nebraska, 1880–1940* (Chapel Hill: University of North Carolina Press, 1992); Sally McMurry, *Transforming Rural Life: Dairying Families and Agricultural Change, 1820–1885* (Baltimore: Johns Hopkins University Press, 1995); Jane H. Adams, "The Decoupling of Farm and Household: Differential Consequences of Capitalist Development on Southern Illinois and Third World Family Farms," *Comparative Studies of Society and History* 30 (July 1988): 453–82; and Mary Neth, *Preserving the Family Farm: Women, Community and the Foundations of Agribusiness in the Midwest, 1900–1940* (Baltimore: Johns Hopkins University Press, 1995). See my previous work, "Farm Women and Town Ladies," in my *Family, Church and Market: A Mennonite Community in the Old and the New Worlds, 1850–1930* (Urbana: University of Illinois Press, 1993), 218–36, and "'The Children, the Cows, and My Dear Man': The Transplanted Lives of Mennonite Farm Women, 1874–1900," *Canadian Historical Review* 73 (September 1992): 344–73.

6. Veronica Strong-Boag, "'Pulling in Double Harness or Hauling a Double Load': Women, Work and Feminism," *Journal of Canadian Studies* 21 (fall 1986): 32–52; Fink, 10.

7. John L. Shover, *First Majority — Last Minority: The Transforming of Rural Life in America* (DeKalb: Northern Illinois University Press, 1976).

8. See G. S. Rempel, ed., *A Historical Sketch of the Churches of the Evangelical Mennonite Brethren* (Rosthern, Sask.: D. H. Epp, 1939); Kevin Enns-Rempel, "The Fellowship of Evangelical Bible Churches and the Quest for Religious Identity," *Mennonite Quarterly Review* 63 (July 1989): 247–64; Delbert F. Plett, *The Golden Years: The Mennonite Kleine Gemeinde in Russia, 1812–1849* (Steinbach, Man.: DFP, 1985); Plett, *Storm and Triumph: The Mennonite Kleine Gemeinde, 1850–1875* (Steinbach, Man.: DFP, 1986); Henry L. Fast, "The Kleine Gemeinde in the United States of America," in *Profile of the Kleine Gemeinde, 1874*, ed. Delbert F. Plett (Steinbach, Man.: DFP, 1987), 87–140; and Daniel J. Bartel, *The Emmanuel Mennonite Church of Meade, Kansas* (Meade, Kans., 1975).

9. Reimer, "Tagebuch"; interview with Martin and Helen Bartel, Meade City, Kansas, July 1992.

10. Klaas Reimer, "Account Book, 1950," Helen Reimer Bartel, Meade City, Kansas.

11. Interviews conducted with twenty-four Meade Mennonites between 1992 and 1995 suggest that as late as the 1940s most Meade Mennonites held town life, higher education, and professions to be less virtuous than a life on a self-sufficient family farm within a homogeneous Mennonite community.

12. For arguments based in Africa, North America, and Europe, see Ester Boserup, *Women's Role in Economic Development* (London: Allen and Urwin, 1970), 53 ff.; Sonya Salamon and Ann Mackey Keim, "Land Ownership and Women's Power in a Midwestern Farming Community," *Journal of Marriage and the Family* 41 (February 1979): 109–19; and Ernestine Friedl, "The Position of Women: Appearance and Reality," *Anthropological Quarterly* 40 (1967): 97–108. For a counterargument, see Barbara J. Cooper, "Farm Women: Some Contemporary Themes," *Labour/Le Travail* 24 (fall 1989): 167–80.

13. Kansas Board of Agriculture, Population Schedule, 1950, Kansas State Historical Society, Topeka; Beard, 112; Meade County Historical Society, 108; interview with Corny Z. Friesen, Meade City, Kans.: July 1992; Anna Z. Friesen Siemens, ed., *Genealogy and History of the J. R. Friesen Family, 1782–1990* (Meade City, Kans.: Privately published, 1990), n.p.

14. Beard, 152.

15. Kansas Board of Agriculture, Population Schedule, 1937, 1950, 1961, 1976.

16. *Meade Globe News,* 17 October 1963.

17. Kansas Board of Agriculture, Population Schedule, 1950, 1961, 1976.

18. Meade County Historical Society, 188.

19. Beard, 83.

20. Elda Plank, *'Twas Home on the Range: The Family History of Henry L. and Agnes Friesen* (Goshen, Ind.: [ca. 1976]), 40 and 44.

21. *Meade Globe News,* 17 July 1947.

22. *Meade Globe News,* 12 May 1960.

23. *Meade Globe News,* 4 March 1954.

24. Demographic surveys between 1935 and 1950 were not available for this study. A genealogical study of two extended Meade families—those of Abraham H. Friesen (1878–1927) and Cornelius J. Classen (1863–1931)—suggests falling birthrates in the 1930s and 1940s. Records of ten couples married between 1912

and 1928 reveal an average of 9.1 children; however, 27 of these children who married between 1935 and 1945 had only an average of 3.6 children themselves, while 31 of those who married between 1946 and 1956 had an average of 3.1 children. Plank, *'Twas Home*; Siemens.

25. Kansas Board of Agriculture, Population Schedule, 1953, 1961.

26. Donald H. Parkerson and Jo Ann Parkerson, "'Fewer Children of Greater Spiritual Quality': Religion and the Decline of Fertility in Nineteenth-Century America," *Social Science History* 12 (spring 1988): 49–70.

27. Emmanuel Mennonite Church Brotherhood minutes, 1944, Emmanuel Mennonite Church, Meade City, Kansas.

28. Ibid., 8 March 1955; *Emmanuel Mennonite Church Handbook* (Meade City, Kans.: Emmanuel Mennonite Church, [ca. 1970]).

29. *Meade Globe News*, 3 June 1948.

30. *Meade Globe News*, 10 June 1954. There were new definitions of the ideal mother. Obituaries in the 1930s had described a woman's relationship to children as a natural duty, over which she exercised little agency; when Katherina Ratzlaff Friesen died in December 1938 it was noted that "of [her first] marriage 10 children were born" and after her second marriage she "took on motherly duties of [an additional] six daughters and two sons." *Christlicher Familienfreund*, June 1939, 8. When Marie Classen Reimer died in 1959 there was a somewhat different cast: she was described "as mother of the home who gave herself unreservedly to seeing after the welfare of the home, physically and also spiritually, having the salvation of her children at heart." *Meade Globe News*, 6 August 1959.

31. *Christlicher Familienfreund*, June 1939, 8; *Meade Globe News*, 6 August 1959.

32. Thomas Walter Laqueur, *Making Sex: Body and Gender from the Greeks to Freud* (Cambridge: Harvard University Press, 1990).

33. *Meade Globe News*, 11 July 1957.

34. Neth.

35. Beard, 57 and 58.

36. *Meade Globe News*, 14 February 1957.

37. Beard, 57.

38. *Meade Globe News*, 14 February 1957.

39. *Emmanuel Mennonite Church Handbook*, ca. 1950, 11.

40. *Emmanuel Mennonite Church Yearbook* (Meade City, Kans.: Emmanuel Mennonite Church, 1965, 1966).

41. Letter to the author from Bertha Classen Johnson, August 1994.

42. Interview with Helen Loewen Reimer, Meade City, Kans.: July 1992. Other accounts trace this development: Margaret Isaac Friesen went to nurses' training against her mother's wishes, but later her mother was said to have been proud of her; Helen Reimer Bartel wanted to attend nurses' training, but her father said no, for which he later was sorry. Interviews, July 1992.

43. Walter S. Friesen, "History and Description of the Mennonite Community and Bible Academy at Meade, Kansas" (M.A. thesis, State Teachers College, Emporia, Kans., 1957), 51.

44. In April 1954 Agnes Classen was hired as fifth-grade teacher; Richard Enns was hired as sixth-grade teacher. *Meade Globe News,* 12 April 1954.

45. The 1956 poll, for example, revealed that nineteen students planned to become nurses and several more wanted to be teachers and missionaries, but only five wished to be secretaries and one each a chemist, a journalist, and a piano teacher. See Friesen, "Mennonite Community," 68.

46. Beard, 136.

47. Siemens.

48. Tilly and Scott, 229.

49. Shover, 158.

50. These figures may not reflect the rise in actual numbers of women working, since the number of male employees dropped from 2,012 in 1940 to 1,272 in 1970, reflecting a general trend of rural depopulation throughout the United States. The figures are almost identical to those for the central Kansas county of MacPherson, where 13.4 percent of the workforce was female in 1940 and 29.1 percent in 1960. U.S. Department of Commerce, U.S. Bureau of the Census, *Census of the United States* (Washington, D.C.: Government Printing Office, 1960, 1970), "Characteristics of the Population," Kansas, table 83, 18–244; 1970, table 121, 18–381.

51. Ibid., 1960, table 36, 18–167; 1970, table 121, 18–381.

52. Beard, 137.

53. Board of Agriculture statistics reveal that the average Mennonite farm in 1975 comprised 249.5 acres.

54. Interview, July 1992.

55. See Beard, 83, 97, 137, 143, and Siemens for experiences of other women on small farms; at least one exception to this patterns is Dan Loewen, who raised seven hundred acres of wheat in 1975, and whose wife Vesta began teaching about 1958. See Beard, 123.

56. Beard, 112, 137.

57. Ibid., 108, 139.

58. Ibid., 119.

59. This was derived by comparing the number of Mennonite families in Kansas Board of Agriculture, *Population Schedule*, 1961, with the number of Mennonite households listed as living in Meade City according to the Southwestern Bell telephone directory for Dodge City, Fowler, Meade, and Minneola. Meade County Historical Society, Meade City, Kansas.

60. Interview with Helen Reimer Bartel.

61. Beard, 136 and 138.

62. Tilly and Scott, 229.

13

Voices Within and Voices Without

QUAKER WOMEN'S AUTOBIOGRAPHY

Barbara Bolz

Mennonite women have often felt stifled by their tradition's emphasis on silence. By contrast, silence empowered Quaker women. Listening to God within led to public ministry and preaching in these autobiographies of eighteenth-century Americans. Active participation in silence is not the same as being silenced. Quaker women used silence and speaking to empower themselves to negotiate, through their lives and their writings, the conflicting ideologies of community and individuality.

The study of women's lives and writing often focuses on how women have spoken during the historical moments in which they lived. Speaking and silence are powerful metaphors for the historian who would understand how women have experienced those events. Feminist critics and Quaker autobiographers have interpreted the metaphors of women's silence and speaking in different ways. For feminist literary critics, silence restricts and oppresses women: a woman must struggle against the silencing force of patriarchy if she is

The London Quaker

71

This print of a Quaker woman from the *Les cris de Londres* (1799) is titled "The London Quaker." (Photograph courtesy of Friends Historical Library of Swarthmore College, Swarthmore, Pennsylvania.)

to make her voice heard. In fact this interpretation of the problem of "be-ing silenced" is a touchstone for many Mennonite women's experiences when described from a feminist perspective. Mennonite women tradi-tionally have "kept silent" according to scriptural direction. Quakers, on the other hand, have experienced silence as an expansive concept, freely chosen and empowering; a Quaker woman used a self-elected silence as a holy space intentionally created so that a "still, small voice" could be heard amid the din of daily life. To generalize the difference, Anabaptist women kept silent and remained in their domestic sphere, whereas Quaker women experienced silence and then left the domestic sphere to follow God's direction and speak publicly. Here I will discuss how Quaker women have used the concepts of silence and speaking to empower them-selves to negotiate, through their lives and their writings, the conflicting ideologies of community and individuality. I do not intend to create a point-by-point comparison between the experiences of Mennonite and Quaker women, though this pursuit is certainly worth undertaking.

Writing about silence, voices, and the experiences of Quaker women poses a difficult problem for me. As a woman of faith myself, I realize I am writing about my spiritual foremothers, who teach me with their words and to whom I wish to show respect and reverence. As a late twentieth-century scholar who has cut her academic teeth on feminist scholarship, however, I have been taught to think of these women's lives only in the light of latter-day ideologies about gender and power, which implicitly maintain that earlier eras were oppressive for women. Within this frame of reference Quaker women, who traveled and preached, become feminist "prototypes," subverting an unfair system, whereas Mennonite women, who remained constant embodiments of conservative religious values and the gender hierarchy that often accompanies those values, become merely "victims" of a cruel system. However, reading the women's jour-nals from the inside out, taking them at their word rather than always in-terpreting those words with a late twentieth-century mentality, compli-cates the issue considerably. When the subjects of this essay—Jane Hoskins, Elizabeth Collins, Susanna Morris, Elizabeth Ashbridge, Ann Moore, and Elizabeth Hudson—write about their lives and their min-istries, their words actively resist interpretations based in an ideology of subversion and oppression. The question of agency, which I take to mean the individual's ability to make meaningful decisions in life and to create change in her environment, becomes much more complex when one attempts to understand a woman's words from her own perspective.[1]

Many eighteenth-century Quaker women experienced agency by negotiating the conflicting personal, social, family, and religious ideologies in their lives. Often these negotiations would take the form of an internal struggle. In a typical Quaker narrative, a woman first argues with the "still, small voice" that leads her to preach, insisting that it is inappropriate for women to speak to mixed groups of men and women; then, true to the form of a conversion narrative, she becomes "convinced" that she must argue instead with her belief that she has nothing to say. She enters into this argument with the assurance that she has the will of God on her side, conveyed to her during the silence of worship. God's will wins out, and the woman goes forward to speak publicly. In short, the author's voice within leads her first to silence the voices without and then to make her physical voice heard in mixed public settings.

When Milton writes "He for God, she for God in him" and when William Penn writes "Sexes make no difference," each man speaks of the historical context within which the women featured in this chapter lived, a context primarily created by male religious thought. Milton's idea that men are closer to God than women demonstrates a traditional understanding of spiritual hierarchy.[2]

This understanding of a gendered hierarchy is the basis of Mennonite women's historical experience of being subordinate to Mennonite men. According to the descendants of the Anabaptists and most other religions of the eighteenth century, a woman was unable to have direct access to God's will and therefore experienced her religious life only through her relationship with the men who "ran" the church. As we will later see, this very act of subordination, though commonly interpreted as an enactment of patriarchal oppression, must be reconsidered within its own religious framework. For within a religion that values subordination to God as the primary manifestation of holiness, women, who practiced subordination to God and to men, were often considered "holier" than men. In addition, Anabaptist women, who maintained the sphere of the home and the family, have traditionally been "set apart" from the world more often than men, who have had to venture into the public realm to earn an income.

Women's cloistered existence, within the context of a religious culture that values sequestering from the "evils" of the world, again allows them to be "superior" Anabaptists.

Unlike Milton's statement, which demonstrates a commitment to a gendered spiritual hierarchy, the statement from Quaker William Penn presents a radical revision of this commonly accepted theology. With Quakerism, not only do women have direct access to the will of God, but their unmediated relationship with the divine often leads them to transcend what they understand to be social constructions of gendered behavior. The eighteenth-century American Quaker women who wrote journals about their experiences as missionaries and ministers followed a doctrine rooted in a theology of transcendence that dominated nearly every aspect of their lives.

The Carnal and the Divine

Quakers believed that everything carnal must be overcome, or transcended, so that a perfect, divine nature could be achieved. If anything in the seventeenth and eighteenth centuries determined how a Quaker woman would and could live, it was this theology of embracing the divine and rejecting the carnal. Of course a theology based on the differences between the flesh and the spirit is not unique to Quakerism, but the Quaker definitions for "carnal" and "divine" differ radically from those created by most other Christian religions. Early Quakers considered sinful all that was worldly, all that was fleshly, and all that was socially constructed. According to Quaker teachings, gender roles were part of a hierarchical order created not by God, but by the sinful nature of mankind. Quakers held that before the fall of the human race, Adam and Eve were "helpmeets" in the eyes of God. Only through sin, through a separation from God brought on by the desires of the flesh, was a hierarchy of gender behavior established, a hierarchy they believed was as detrimental to the soul as adultery, covetousness, or any other sin. And since members of the Society of Friends lived by a doctrine of perfectibility, they maintained that the Edenic quality of gender transcendence must always be held as a goal.[3]

Compare this understanding of transcendence with that of a typical Mennonite or Amish group, which holds that true spirituality is based not on equality in the eyes of God or on direct access to divine revelation, but on the careful submission inherent in a hierarchical system, which places God at the head, followed by Christ, man, woman, and then children. If submission is the greatest act of religious faith, then women have a natural spiritual advantage because of their daily submission to men, to Christ, and to God. In general, the more respected a person in the Amish faith is, the more likely that person is to remain silent. In one respect Mennonite experience with silence is similar to the Quaker experience, for Mennonite silence is not merely the absence of speech but the presence of something much more valuable than speech. With this vision of silence as a dynamic force, Amish women, who are more likely to embrace a doctrine of silence and thereby build the spiritual life of their community, are not oppressed by being "silenced" but rather are reinscribed into their religious circle. In contrast, for a Quaker woman to preach to a group of both men and women was not a secular act of rebellion against socially dictated gender roles but a manifestation of her increasing nearness to that perfect, genderless state of spirituality; her preaching was "proof" that she had embraced the Light to such an extent that she no longer had to adhere to constructed gender roles. She was not limited by her gender because she was always in the process of transcending it. When you are living in the Light, according to early Quaker theology, gender becomes irrelevant.[4] In addition to the Quaker rewriting of the definition of "carnal" to include culturally constructed social hierarchies, early Quakers also reformulated the meaning of "divine" to conform to the doctrine of the Light within. God, to early Quakers, was much more than a strict arbiter to those who would disobey his will as revealed in Scripture. Rather, God existed in the silent stillness in the minds and hearts of the faithful. Divine messages could be received in several ways: through Scripture, through a communal searching during meeting for worship, or through direct revelation.

The impact of these early teachings on carnality and divinity is clear in each of the journals I discuss in this chapter.[5] In fact, each of these autobiographies can be read as a narrative showing the progressive stripping away of the carnal self in order to embrace a divine nature. Fundamentally conversion narratives, these journals represent many journeys toward a single goal: "More of thee, less of me."

PATTERNS IN QUAKER WOMEN'S AUTOBIOGRAPHIES

The journals of eighteenth-century Quaker women usually follow a predictable pattern. The writer begins with a justification for writing, often given as a desire to instruct children and other members in the Society about religious matters. She includes an account of her spiritually idyllic childhood, followed by a remorseful discussion of her godless youth and a description of how she converted to the Religious Society of Friends. Though this convincement[6] is crucial to the autobiographer's view of herself, it is not as important as the second conversion she describes: the call to ministry. The remaining pages of a typical journal detail the author's life in the ministry: whom she visited, and for how long; how she ministered; and what she said during specific meetings for worship.[7]

Uniformity among these journals is not limited to structure: these texts share language patterns as well. The writers used similar metaphors for concepts such as self, sin, death, God, and Satan. Most of the eighteenth-century journals share language and structure patterns for at least three reasons. First, they were written in similar circumstances. Each author belonged to the Society of Friends, which in the eighteenth century was a well-defined, uniform religion.[8] Second, many Friends who wrote journals also read journals written by other Quakers. Though novels and other reading for pleasure were thought to be sinful, the Society of Friends has a long history of encouraging literacy and librarianship.[9] Most Friends of comfortable means had small libraries in their homes, libraries that usually included such works as *Pilgrim's Progress,* the Bible, the *Journal* of George Fox, and Robert Barclay's *Apology* as well as the journals of less well known Friends. Even Friends who were not affluent enough to own books had access to them through their meeting's library. If an individual monthly meeting could not collectively afford the books, members could borrow them from other Friends when they met at yearly meetings. Because these women read the same journals and inspirational literature, as well as each other's journals, their own journals assumed a uniformity.

Finally, and perhaps most important, these journals are similar because the women who wrote them belonged to a tightly woven community. These life stories are not the products of isolated individuals; rather, they are the products of a unified community. In any one of the journals, the names of the writers of many of the other journals figure prominently, primarily because these women knew each other and frequently interacted. Women who traveled to various Friends' communities always took along a companion,[10] and these pairs of ministers often met other pairs throughout their journeys. This active community building helped solidify their understanding of what it meant to be both ministers and women in the Society of Friends.

In addition, the Society itself helped standardize these journals after they were written by editing, revising, and publishing them. All but one of the six journals I discuss were published by the Society and were revised extensively by committees.[11] When an eighteenth-century Quaker had completed a journal, she submitted it to her yearly meeting for editing. Each yearly meeting had a committee called the Meeting for Sufferings, which was responsible for these editorial decisions and also for publishing and distributing a journal. Because women were not allowed membership in Meetings for Sufferings until the nineteenth century, the manuscripts written by the women who traveled and ministered in the Society of Friends were edited exclusively by men.[12] This was not entirely the case in England, where women in the eighteenth century could be appointed to the committee responsible for editing journals.[13] In addition to the eighteenth-century editorial process, Quaker journals went through another in the nineteenth century, when many of them were reprinted in one of two Quaker series. Both the Friends Library and the Friends Miscellany began in the 1830s as a direct result of the Hicksite-Orthodox separation.[14] Friends Library was the Orthodox series, published by William and Thomas Evans, and Friends Miscellany was the Hicksite series.[15] These two series became records of Quaker history as well as support for the diverging theological views on each side.[16]

Of course this conventionalizing of an original journal changes the way a twentieth-century critic might look at the text. These journals are more uniform, more indicative of what a community required, and less reflective of an individual's personality than most autobiographies written since then. But this does not remove their importance as historical references. In fact, in many ways the uniformity of these texts creates a lens through which we can see the individual. For early Quakers, individual personality was to be transcended. Because of this, the autobiographies that do not reflect a unique being do reflect the woman as she saw herself:

as a vessel whose only purpose was to forward the work of God within the framework of her religious society. From the journal writer's perspective, submitting her work to the editorial process of a yearly meeting was akin to submitting herself to the transforming touch of an all-powerful God. From the perspective of a twentieth-century scholar arguing that these women experienced some personal agency, this censorship may seem to challenge that notion. Yet by submitting to the dictates of her religious society, the eighteenth-century Quaker woman was able to move beyond the confines of an even more limiting general ideology that pervaded eighteenth-century America.

The Problem of the Individual

How do we approach an autobiography that is, by its very nature, deeply invested in stripping away the self, layer by layer? I choose to view these journals as writings of lives that are inextricably woven into the authors' religious community. It is through their connections with community that these women are able to resist the dominant social ideology of female passivity. The very structure of the journals, grounded in not one but two conversion narratives (first to the Society of Friends, then to their ministry), produces insights into the empowering religious values and ideologies these women embraced. Each of them recorded her life in ways that encapsulated her interior space by describing her intrinsic link with an exterior force: the religious society to which she belonged. In short, these texts do show the individual, but that individual—in the lived life and in the textual life—is inextricably linked to the community within which she lived and worked.

Many early feminist critics of autobiography theory maintained that this state of the individual enmeshed with the community is a fact of every woman's life story, whereas the story of a man's life can be separated from his connections to community.[17] In eighteenth-century Quaker autobiography, this connection to community is rooted more in religion than in gender. I do not wish to cast these women as either heroes or victims, two roles commonly assigned to those whose lives have been uncovered in the feminist quest to look at women's history. I see them instead as complex personalities complicit in a synergy of definition: they helped define the parameters of their religious community even as that community helped define whom they would become. It is within this synergistic relationship that Quaker autobiographers were able to articulate themselves and to enjoy some personal agency. Their relationship with their community, to use the words of autobiography theorist Paul John Eakin, was "mutually constituting."[18] According to the autobiographies these women wrote, if you took the community away from the woman, you would have but a shell of an individual. Equally important, though, if these women were removed from the Society of Friends, the remaining community would also become a shell, without substance or definition.

FROM EDEN TO SIN AND BACK AGAIN

A Quaker minister typically begins her journal by explaining why she is writing the story of her life and then recording her salvation narrative, which mirrors the biblical salvation story. She describes her godly up- bringing and a pure, Edenic childhood. This Eden is typically corrupted by the serpent's offer of forbidden fruit, almost always the youthful pursuit of singing and dancing. Like the children of Israel, a Quaker journal writer then wanders in a spiritual desert, searching for God. Once she finds the Society of Friends, she is saved from her youthful follies by a salvation that parallels the one brought by Christ in the Gospels. Finally, she trav- els and ministers to build up the church, activities that, ironically, parallel those of Paul in the New Testament.[19]

Typical of a Quaker autobiographer, Susanna Morris begins her jour- nal by justifying its existence:[20] "I have had it in my mind for to let my children or any other honest inquirer know how I have fared some parts of my life chiefly on the ever blessed Truth's account for I think I can speak and that truly from my youth upward the Living God helped me to love him and all good people."[21] These words, the very first she writes in her journal, justify her writing about the self even though she belongs to a religion that would have the self always subjected to the will of God.

As Daniel Shea has pointed out, the Quaker who would strip away the self for religious reasons is in an awkward position writing in a genre that by its very nature creates a centralized self.[22] To avoid this position, the Quaker autobiographer must explain from the very beginning of her nar- rative that God and others, rather than herself, are at the center of the en- deavor. Morris states that she is writing to instruct others about the "Liv- ing God"; by so doing she removes herself twice over from the center of the text. God is the subject, the first center of the text, and her children or other "honest inquirers" are the audience, the second center; the autobiographer becomes merely a third consideration, a necessary conduit to ensure that the message of God is brought to others. In effect, in the hands of these Quakers, autobiography extends their ministries of self-transcendence into the printed word.

After justifying their journals as extensions of their ministries, Quaker women typically turn to describing their childhood in terms of purity and godliness. A hundred years before Wordsworth wrote "Intimations of Immortality," these women were counting their youngest days as times when they were most connected to the God they would eventually remove themselves from, then ultimately seek out again. Often they portrayed their parents as pious, godly people, even if they were not Quakers. Jane Hoskins writes,[23] "I was born . . . of religious parents and by them strictly educated in the profession of the church of England, so called; who, according to the best of their understanding, endeavored to inculcate into my mind the knowledge of a Divine Being, and how necessary it was for all professing Christianity, to live in the fear of God."[24] Elizabeth Ashbridge describes her mother as "a good example to all about her, and Beloved by most that Knew her, Tho' not of the same perswasion [sic] I am now of."[25] She attributes her understanding of God to the education her mother gave her throughout her childhood: "She discharged her duty by endeavoring to instill in me, in my tender Age, the principles of virtue; for which I have since had Cause to be thankful to the Lord, & that he blessed me with such a parent, whose good Advice and Counsel to me has been as Bread cast on the Waters."[26] For Ashbridge, her upbringing firmly rooted her in the teachings of Christ and prepared her for the spiritual quest she would undertake on becoming an adult.

The description of a religious upbringing by godly parents is central to later configurations of the self. Because the mothers and fathers of these women raised them to be Christians, they have no "excuse" for the frivolity of youth described later in their narratives. They reason that the only explanation for why they strayed from a divine path to embrace a carnal nature must be that, by their very nature as human beings, they were unable to live upstanding lives without the direct help of God. This understanding that each person depends on God for her spiritual wholeness creates an inclination toward following God's voice wherever it may lead. Only within the context of salvation can the drastic choice of preaching, traveling, and leaving home and family be understood. By emphasizing her sinful youth, the Quaker autobiographer again displaces herself as the center of her narrative in order to exalt and emphasize the importance of God as savior in her life and in her life story.

Though early Quakers believed in the necessity of salvation, they did not emphasize the sinful nature of humans from their birth. Unlike the Puritans, who believed a child to be as sinful as any adult heathen, Quakers believed that children contained a seed of the Light.[27] Elizabeth Hudson[28] poetically portrays this sense of a childhood oneness with God as "those sweet influences of [God's] divine love . . . making me so far in love with him."[29] Elizabeth Ashbridge also depicts her childhood as one in communion with God. She says she was "sometimes guilty of faults incident to Children," but that she "always found something that made [her] sorry."[30] As a child, she had a consciousness that kept her from straying too far from what she would later determine as God's will in her life. She "had an awful regard for religion & a great love for religious people, particularly Ministers; and sometimes wept with Sorrow, that [she] was not a boy that [she] might have been one."[31] Here we see Ashbridge as a child lamenting her sex because it limited her service to God. During her childhood, as she longed to be what her socialization taught her she could not be, she experienced intimations of what she would later believe once she discovered what the Society of Friends held to be true: for God, "sexes make no difference."

After describing this idyllic stage of childhood, the journal writer describes a fall from that state of perfect divine communion and then relates a steady progression from carnal adolescence to spiritual maturity. This progress takes the form of movement away from the self and toward God. The text usually begins with a description of the most worldly self: youth or adolescent. Ashbridge says about the onset of this worldly self, "From my Infancy till fourteen years of age I was as innocent as most Children, about which time my Sorrows began."[32] For Ashbridge, as for most of the Quaker journal writers, the movement from idyllic early childhood into turbulent youth paralleled a burgeoning sexuality. As we will see later, relations with men often were presented as metaphors for the carnal life these ministers longed to leave behind.

Jane Hoskins also laments the follies of her youth. She declares that "a turn for music and singing" led her "into unprofitable company, all which had a tendency to lead [her] mind from God."[33] The touchstone of a sinful youth for many of these women was song and dance. When a women is singing and dancing, she is both indulging her own creative desires and encouraging the voyeuristic desires of an audience. In these activities, the female as she was viewed and appreciated by a male audience is anathema to Quaker belief, for worldly activity emphasizes the woman's physical being rather than her spiritual, higher being. To act as if one is merely flesh or to view another as merely flesh is to go against the implicit Quaker doctrine of the divine as superior to the carnal. For the Quaker who would eventually turn her life over to the service of a divine master, these pursuits that pleased a worldly audience ultimately became repulsive.

The moment Elizabeth Ashbridge officially gives up song and dance represents her movement from frivolous youth into sober, religious adulthood. Entering adulthood, for Ashbridge, is marked by refusing to dance and sing in order to please her husband and deciding instead to give service to God. In the following passage, one of the most emotional in her narrative, Ashbridge describes what happens after her husband takes her away from Pennsylvania to remove her from the influence of Quakers. She has begun to believe in Friends' teachings but has at this point not taken on the Quaker characteristics of simple clothing and plain language. While entertaining guests, Sullivan tries to get his wife to dance for them:

> These were my Concerns while he was Entertaining the Company with my Story, in which he told them that I had been a good Dancer, but now he Could get me neither to Dance nor Sing, upon which one of the Company stands up saying, "I'll go fetch my Fiddle, & we'll have a Dance," at which my husband was much pleased. The fiddle came, the sight of which put me in a sad Condition for fear if I Refused[,] my husband would be in a great Passion: however[,] I took up this resolution, not to Comply whatever be the Consequence. He comes to me, takes me by the hand saying, "come my Dear, shake off that Gloom, & let's have a civil Dance; you would now and then when you was a good Churchwoman, & that's better than a Stiff Quaker." I trembling desired to be Excused; but he Insisted on it, and knowing his Temper to be exceeding Cholerick, durst not say much, yet did not Consent. He then pluck'd me round the Room till Tears affected my Eyes, at Sight whereof the Musician Stopt and said, "I'll play no more, Let your wife alone," of which I was Glad.[34]

Here the tension between the two halves of her bifurcated life reaches its greatest level: Sullivan, representing all that is carnal and limiting for Ashbridge, insists she give in to his demands, arguing that she would do no less if she were still a "good churchwoman." He puts the blame for her grave personality on this new religion, which has made her a "stiff Quaker." Ashbridge, however, sees her refusal to dance as representing spiritual growth. No longer is she a youth who indulges in physical pleasure; now she has been called to be an adult, sober and diligent in her service to God. Sullivan understands her transformation as a regression. He insists this new religion has ruined the fine woman he married, a woman who understood there was a time for piety and a time for dance. Embarrassed and ashamed that his wife is taking on the characteristics of a despised group, Sullivan aggressively responds to this embarrassment by insisting she dance with him.

In this passage Sullivan represents an ideology that Ashbridge had previously embraced; he represents a time in her life that Ashbridge the narrator characterizes as "a time of sorrows." He is the embodiment of an ideology that held a younger Ashbridge captive. The act of forcing her to dance with him "till Tears affected [her] Eyes" functions as a controlling metaphor in this narrative. Sullivan may be able to force her to move from Pennsylvania and may be able to pull her onto the dance floor, but he is not able to coerce her into changing her beliefs.

For his part, Sullivan expects his wife to be just that: his wife. He wants her to perform so he can entertain his guests and perhaps show them he is in control of her behavior—that he is indeed the head of a well-run household, that his family complies to his wishes and is therefore well established within the socially accepted conventions of family.

Ashbridge briefly considers complying, fearful of her husband's rage. (At other points in the narrative we discover that Sullivan is capable of physical brutality. He ties her down to prevent her from attending meeting for worship and strikes her when she addresses him with "thee" and "thou.") But in the end Ashbridge does not comply with his request and instead chooses to remain still and quiet in the face of duress. She "took up this resolution, not to Comply whatever be the Consequence." Bolstered by the strength of her convictions about the wickedness of dance and song, Ashbridge is able to resist Sullivan's demands and stand up for what she understands to be right. This kind of negotiation of conflicting ideologies, this determining what is right and what is wrong by a set of values that are in direct conflict with more dominant social values, continues throughout Ashbridge's narrative and throughout the narratives written by her sisters in the faith.

Salvation rarely occurred in the same way for any two journal writers. For Elizabeth Ashbridge salvation came slowly. In several stages over the course of years, she sought out various religious communities, eventually finding and converting to Quakerism. For Jane Hoskins salvation came quickly, during an illness when she was sixteen years old. She describes her illness and her subsequent conversion as a gift from the hands of God:

> But he who had compassion on me from the days of my infancy, was pleased, in the sixteenth year of my age, to visit me with a sore fit of sickness, nigh unto death, which reduced me very low both in body and mind; for the terrors of the Almighty took hold of my soul; and then was brought into my remembrance all my sins and misspent time, as well as the good counsel my dear parents had tenderly given me, which I had unhappily disregarded. In this distressed condition I shed many tears, making my moan to Him who is the helper of his people in the needful time; and was ready to make covenant, that if he in mercy would be pleased to spare me a little longer, the remaining part of my days should be dedicated to his service; and it was as though it had been spoken to me, "if I restore thee, go to Pennsylvania."[35]

According to Hoskins, the delights of youthful passion were so treacherous that only being struck down by the hand of God could bring her into the Light. That she interpreted her illness as originating directly from the hand of God demonstrates her understanding of God as a powerful parental presence. According to Hoskins, only by being "reduced . . . very low both in body and mind" could the self be expunged in order to allow the work of God to occur. In Hoskins's mind, God struck her down so that he could lift her up in his service.

This notion of God as a parent going to extremes to ensure salvation for his children permeated every stage of Hoskins's life. After her deathbed salvation, she continued to do service to her divine parent, whom she described as giving "paternal care . . . carrying the lambs in his arms, lest they should be weary and faint."[36] Constructing God on the one hand as a parent who would strike his child down "for her own good" and on the other as one who would carry his weary and fainting child in his arms, she casts the divine as a stern yet nurturing parent, one to be both feared and loved. God, in effect, demanded everything from Hoskins and her sisters in the ministry, including complete loyalty, devotion, and fear.

Hoskins's ministry is a direct result of her deathbed experience at sixteen. After being saved in this fashion, she hears the voice of God say to her, "If I restore thee, go to Pennsylvania." Rarely do a conversion experience and a call to ministry occur at the same time in these Quaker journals, but from the moment of Hoskins's "salvation" she understood that she would serve the divine parent who changed the course of her life. Because Hoskins understood God as all powerful, all demanding, and all nurturing, her willingness to devote her life to his service was nearly compulsory.

Once a woman converted to Quakerism, once she left behind her frivolous youth and entered into the life she would live thereafter, she became transformed. The experience of convincement radically altered her life, whether she had been brought up as a Friend or not. For Elizabeth Ashbridge, as for others, it also meant a change in demeanor and dress. The change, which included donning plain clothing and using the plain language of "thee" and "thine" rather than "you" and your," was so extreme that others were quick to notice and respond. Elizabeth Hudson comments on how Elizabeth Ashbridge changed after her convincement. Hudson records that a group of people on Staten Island who knew Ashbridge before and after convincement were "surprised . . . exceedingly, to see such a change in her dress and deportment."[37]

QUAKER WOMEN CALLED TO THE MINISTRY

As convincement transformed a Quaker woman's outward appearance, the call to the ministry transformed her inward experience. When the voice of God calls these women away from singing and dancing, away from entertaining men, one could say that, metaphorically, the change "unsexes" them, leaving them unwilling and unable to interact with men in traditional ways as women. When the voice of God calls them to preach, it urges them to live a life that had previously been reserved exclusively for men. In effect, it redefines their gender in the image of men. These women were to preach to groups of men and women and travel throughout the colonies and even overseas, accompanied only by other women who had experienced a similar calling. This kind of life required women to abandon traditional women's roles and to embrace men's roles. For a late twentieth-century feminist, this reversal of gender roles might seem liberating and thrilling, but to an eighteenth-century woman it was daunting and quite possibly repugnant. From their words it is clear that God called them to give up what was precious—their roles as women, wives, and mothers—to do what seemed almost impossible: step down into a traditionally male world. That they followed this call is ultimate proof of the transformed condition that follows their salvation.

In many respects God's call reversed the conceptions of gender for both men and women. Men were called to be gentle and quiet; they were left with the household of children when their wives traveled for months at a time. In an age when a husband had the legal right to forbid his wife such freedom of movement, Quaker husbands encouraged their wives to go where the voice of God led them. Susanna Morris comments that God "helped my dear husband to give me up to the will of him who has called, by an high and holy calling to his service."[38] To make this service possible, husbands, with the support of their meetings, became caretakers for their children and helpmates for their wives. The Quaker message, for men and for women, was that God requires all of his servants to turn upside down what they might otherwise believe to be acceptable behavior for men and women.

The call to preach almost always came as a tremendous surprise to Quaker women. Unlike their male counterparts, rarely had they considered the ministry as a possibility in their lives. The following juxtaposed narratives, the first from Jane Hoskins and the second from her younger contemporary Rufus Hall, demonstrate the differences between typical male and female responses to God's call. First, a passage from Jane Hoskins:

> I concluded in my own mind, not knowing as yet what the Lord was preparing me for, nor that there was a further work allotted me, which I was a stranger to, till one time being in a meeting, and sitting very contented under my own vine and fig-tree, a call arose in my mind, "I have chosen thee a vessel from thy youth to serve me, and to preach the Gospel of salvation to many people: and if thou wilt be faithful, I will be with thee unto the end of time, and make thee an heir of my kingdom."[39]

And one from Rufus Hall:

> One thing often came into my mind, that seemed to be a mystery—it was this;
> how a minister of the gospel knew that he was rightly called to that weighty
> work; or how did he know when to stand up and what to say? It appeared to
> me he ought to be divinely inspired, and I could not see how it was brought
> about. Not thinking it would ever be my lot to be concerned that way, I en-
> deavored to get rid of these thoughts as matters that need not concern me.[40]

Hoskins's narrative is full of surprise and wonder. As a woman, even
one who had heard of other women in the ministry, she never considered
that she might be called. The words "I have chosen thee a vessel" shocked
her and revolutionized her life. Hall's narrative, on the other hand, carefully analyzes the possibility of a call. Though he never thought "it would
ever be [his] lot," he nevertheless imagined the various ways the call to
ministry might occur, and he had carefully considered that he might
someday become a minister. Even with the example of generations of
women traveling as ministers, eighteenth-century Quaker women rarely
considered this for themselves. Rather, they lived in conventional ways
until their second conversion experience occurred. For Quaker women
the call to preach was experienced with the same wonder and surprise
Saul experienced on the road to Damascus.

Whereas a Quaker man often saw himself as God's mouthpiece,
Quaker women viewed themselves as God's handmaidens, going on God's
errands. Elizabeth Collins spends most of her narrative describing how
she longed to be a more faithful handmaiden to the divine master.[41] She
writes, "I feel breathings of my soul, that I may be so attentive to the
pointings of Truth, and so obedient to my dear Lord and Master, as to answer this great end."[42] While a Quaker man might envision himself as an
extension of God, because a disembodied God needed a mouthpiece to fulfill his will on earth, women like Collins and Morris envisioned themselves as meek and humble servants of an all-powerful and all-loving
master.

When a Quaker woman received her call to preach, she often resisted
it for two reasons. First, like most Old Testament prophets, she felt un-
worthy to assume such responsibility. On receiving her call to the ministry, Elizabeth Hudson responded: "What bore . . . weight with me was

my unfitness for such an awful undertaking."[43] Jane Hoskins was even more distressed upon hearing her call: "Yet I must confess, this awful word of Divine command shocked me exceedingly, my soul and all within me trembled at the hearing of it; yea, my outward tabernacle shook, insomuch that many present observed the deep exercise I was under. I cried in spirit, 'Lord, I am weak and altogether incapable of such a task, I hope thou wilt spare me from such a mortification.'"[44] As a fallible human being, a Quaker woman typically felt herself unable to carry out the command to speak God's words. By viewing herself as unfit for divine service, she created a framework within which the only possible response to her call to ministry was resistance.

The second reason Quaker women resisted the call to preach was closely related to the first. If being human made her unfit to do God's bidding, being female made her even more so. Though members of a faith that allowed, even encouraged, women to take up the ministry, Quaker women themselves nevertheless often had personal reservations about women's preaching. Jane Hoskins asked God to spare her this particular fate because she had "spoken much against women appearing in that manner."[45] The call to preach required women to live a life, as women, they felt incapable of living. At this juncture their sense of appropriate behavior for women came in direct conflict with the requirements of divine service. Good women did not speak in public, but good Quakers did.

In the end these women felt God reminding them that if they did not preach, they would have their gifts taken from them. Hudson records that "a Dispensation of the Gospel was committed to me and woe was unto to me if I preached it not."[46] For Elizabeth Collins, God's response to her resistance was more direct: "This language was intelligibly spoken to my inward ear, 'If thou art not more faithful, thy gift shall be taken from thee.'"[47] A Quaker woman's resistance was perhaps a test to see if the call would persist, perhaps a validation process that would make her more acceptable to a potentially unaccepting public, or perhaps an honest response to the possibility of such a cataclysmic transformation. Once she resisted, she typically received more divine encouragement to enter the ministry. In effect, God did not merely request her service, he also threatened that if she failed to follow the call, her gifts, including the love and protection of a divine presence, would be taken from her.

In addition to feeling an internal resistance upon being called into the ministry, many Quaker women also had to face external forces that pressured them to remain unchanged. At every stage of moving toward the Quaker life, Elizabeth Ashbridge was confronted by her husband Sullivan, who wanted her to remain as she was when he married her. If anything infuriated Sullivan more than Ashbridge's assuming a Quaker manner and style, it was her becoming a minister. Upon seeing him after a long absence during which she had secretly converted to Quakerism, Ashbridge reports in her journal that she greeted him with, "'My Dear, I am glad to see thee,' at which he flew in a Passion of anger & said, 'the Divel thee thee, don't thee me.'"[48] The fury with which he responded to her Quaker use of "thee" was most likely based on a universal disdain for what he feared she might become: a Quaker minister. Ashbridge describes the societal disdain for women ministers, stating that "the Neighbors that were not friends began to revile me, calling me a Quaker, saying they supposed I intended to be a fool and turn Preacher."[49] Once Sullivan discovers that she has become a Quaker, he responds: "I'd rather heard She had been dead as well as I Love her, for if [she is a Quaker], all my comfort is gone."[50] He then goes to great lengths, including resorting to physical restraint and threatening violence, to keep her from attending meetings for worship. At every step of the way, Sullivan represents the social response to Quaker women ministers and thus represents the internalized responses the women themselves may have had to silence in themselves before responding to their call.

After they accepted a call to ministry, Quaker women did not go on one missionary trip and then resume a routine life. Rather, they spent the rest of their lives heeding many calls, going to different locations, leaving their children again and again to follow wherever they felt led to go. Often they felt pulled to travel to specific places. Ann Moore' recorded one such time: "I was so concerned to go to Albany that I could not rest day nor night, until I freely gave up to go, which I did."[51] Most of the ministers decided what direction their ministries would take based on similar mystical experiences. Elizabeth Hudson, perhaps more than any other, relied on the direct message of God to guide her through her ministry. She wrote that doing honor to God was not a matter of what one said or did but depended on "our obedience to the immediate direction or influence of the holy spirit."[52] Throughout her ministry she was so submissive to this influence that she refused to speak if she did not sense the spirit leading her to do so, even in meetings gathered specifically to hear her preach.

For many women, life in the ministry was grueling and demanding. They would often travel for months at a time, not knowing whether all of their family would be alive when they returned. For some, such as Hudson, life in the ministry also led them into states of serious depression. Hudson was so dependent on mystical insights and leadings that when they did not come, or when the people she preached to did not respond in a way she felt appropriate, she would become melancholic and listless. She called these periods of her life "suffering times" or "stripping times," and she often felt distant from the very God to whom she devoted her life. Though the lives these women led were filled with heartache and hardships, they also were filled with purpose and direction.

FACES OF PIOUS WOMANHOOD IN QUAKER AND MENNONITE WOMEN

If we return to the statements by Milton and Penn quoted earlier, we see that neither exactly represents the truth of the lives these women lived and wrote of in their journals. Certainly their ministries throw into question Milton's assessment that women served men and men served God. Their daily connection with a divine message free of any mediation demonstrated that, indeed, a woman needed no go-between to interpret her role as a servant of the divine. On the other hand, Penn's statement that sex does not matter since souls are sexless also does not represent the lives of Quaker women ministers, women who very much confronted the question of gendered identity when responding to their call to ministry. Never totally separate from the definitions of gender that permeated their daily lives, eighteenth-century Quaker women nevertheless were able, with the prompting of an insistent God, to exercise the freedoms of traveling with impunity and speaking with authority. Mennonite women, on the other hand, who traditionally embraced a more common form of gender identification, experienced God's call in more traditional ways, as mothers and wives and churchwomen. Though at first the historical Quakerism can appear to be more "freeing" for women than the Anabaptist faith, this "freedom" was construed by Quaker women themselves as a servitude, an extreme example of submission to God's authority. Even though Quaker women heard, within their worshipful silence, the voice of God calling them to travel and preach and speak in public, they followed those directions for precisely the same reason Mennonite women have traditionally stayed within the domestic sphere, keeping silent: to submit to the will of God and find there greater meaning than could be discovered by pursuing an individualistic course.

It is not surprising that Quaker women have "adjusted" to the modern age more easily than Mennonite women. In the nineteenth and twentieth centuries, Quaker women continued to thrive in the public sphere, spearheading almost every political social cause in America, while Mennonite women continued to care for the hearth and home. In the twentieth century, when American culture has increasingly devalued domestic work while placing emphasis only on success "in the real world," contemporary Mennonite women have come to resist what they understand to be a religious framework that is oppressive to women. Clearly, the traditional Mennonite roles for women and traditional Quaker roles for women have not really altered much in the past two hundred years, but the cultural responses to them have changed radically. Whereas eighteenth-century Quaker women faced a culture hostile to the ways they might be called to obey God's direction, a twentieth-century Mennonite woman—whether she wishes to remain in the private sphere or to "break out of" a silencing space—faces a culture hostile to, or at least dismissive of, everything that has traditionally been understood to belong to the realm of the feminine.

NOTES

1. My approach to these texts has been greatly influenced by Phyllis Mack, *Visionary Women: Ecstatic Prophecy in Seventeenth-Century England* (Berkeley: University of California Press, 1992). She interprets the lives and writings of seventeenth-century Quaker women within the framework they create.

2. Paul writing to the Corinthians would agree: "But I would have you know, that the head of every man is Christ; and the head of the woman is the man; and the head of Christ is God" (I Cor. 11:3). All biblical references are from the King James Version.

3. See Robert Barclay, *Barclay's "Apology" in Modern English* (Newberg, Ore.: Barclay Press, 1991), proposition 8, for a clear statement of the doctrine of perfectibility.

4. Though gender transcendence was the ideal held by most prominent Quakers, others continued to believe in gender as the natural state that came from the hand of God rather than from the fall of man; for these Quakers the fact of women preachers was disquieting. Gerardus Croese, *General History of the Quakers: Containing the Lives, Tenets, Sufferings, Tryals, Speeches, and Letters of All the Most Eminent Quakers, both Men and Women; from the First Rise of That Sect, Down to This Present Time* (London: John Dunton, 1696), wrote that Elizabeth Haddon, the first Quaker woman to become a minister, "was the first of her sex among the Quakers who attempted to imitate men, and preach" (37). After forty years of women ministering in the Society of Friends, not all Quakers believed that gender restraints should be transcended in the Light.

5. Quaker autobiographies have traditionally been called "journals" ever since George Fox detailed his spiritual journey in the late seventeenth century. I use the terms "autobiography" and "journal" interchangeably to refer to the writings of Quaker women. Though some autobiography theorists would create a clear delineation between autobiographies and journals, with autobiographies written retrospectively and journals written day by day, this distinction does not work with Quaker writing, because these texts for the most part fit the official definition of autobiography yet are called journals by both Quaker historians and the authors themselves.

6. Quakers have historically referred to conversion as "convincement." Convincement can occur in people who are new to the religion or in those who grew up as Quakers. The faithful are "convinced" when they decide to align their lives with the teachings of the Society.

7. For a useful description of a pattern in Quaker journals slightly different from the one I outline, see Howard H. Brinton, *Quaker Journals: Varieties of Religious Experience among Friends* (Wallingford, Pa.: Pendle Hill, 1972). Brinton has observed that Quaker journals, written by men and women, are usually divided into the following sections: divine revelations in childhood, youthful frivolity, the divided self, and following the Light.

8. In fact, the eighteenth century may be the only time the Religious Society of Friends could be considered even remotely monolithic. During the seventeenth century, as the Society was formed by a coalescence of several diverse groups of "seekers," the definition of "Quaker" remained in flux. Over the eighteenth century Quakerism developed a rather unified dogma, in part owing to the many ministers who traveled from meeting to meeting and from country to country

carrying news and spiritual messages. By the late eighteenth century, serious fractures began to develop in the Society, mostly because of disagreements about how God's will was revealed. These disagreements led to a major break in Quakerism in the early nineteenth century. Ever since, the Quaker faith has had no unifying theology. Today it consists of a wide range of theological viewpoints, from ultraconservative to radically liberal.

9. Elizabeth Hudson was so fond of reading that she felt compelled to relinquish it when she began heeding the voice of God. She describes herself as having a "lust [for] books . . . they being very engrossing both of our time and thoughts, and I finding this to be the effect of my studies, found it best to deny myself . . . them[,] which was no easy task." See "The Journal of Elizabeth Hudson," in *Wilt Thou Go on My Errand? Journals of Three Eighteenth-Century Quaker Women Ministers,* ed. Margaret Hope Bacon (Wallingford, Pa.: Pendle Hill, 1994), 114.

10. A traveling companion was always another women who had also heeded God's call to the ministry. Rarely were male companions welcome on these journeys; in this way the women would remain free from any appearance of impropriety.

11. For more information about Quaker publishing practices in America, see Christopher Densmore, "Quaker Publishing in New York State, 1784–1860," *Quaker History* 74 (1985): 39–57, and Joan M. Hoy, "The Publication and Distribution of Books among New England Quakers, 1775–1836" (Ph.D. diss., Boston University, 1989). For a more general understanding of early American publishing and printing practices, see George J. Willauer Jr., "Editorial Practices in Eighteenth-Century Philadelphia: The Manuscript Journal of Thomas Chalkley in Manuscript and Print," *Pennsylvania Magazine of History and Biography* 107 (April 1983): 218–34.

12. The exclusion of women from high offices in yearly meetings shows that what is presented as a spiritual truth ("women and men are equal in spiritual matters") does not always affect the day-to-day reality of Quaker process.

13. In addition, one of the important English Quaker printers of the eighteenth century, Tacy Sowle, was a woman.

14. The Hicksite-Orthodox split occurred in 1827 over the teaching of Elias Hicks, who preached about the continuing revelation of God's will. Hicksites tended to be theologically more liberal than Orthodox Quakers. For a thorough history of the split and its influence on nineteenth-century Quakerism, see

Thomas D. Hamm, *The Transformation of American Quakerism: Orthodox Friends, 1800–1907* (Bloomington: Indiana University Press, 1988). In addition, H. Larry Ingle, *Quakers in Conflict: The Hicksite Reformation* (Knoxville: University of Tennessee Press, 1986), has thoroughly investigated the many layers of conflict embedded in this important schism in the Quaker faith. He looks closely at the personalities and problems of Quakerism's first split, always carefully considering the cultural and emotional context of the divisions.

15. In many instances these editors changed original texts considerably. Historian Christopher Densmore has compared the original manuscript of *The Journal of William Story* with the versions appearing in the Friends Library and found many important details omitted.

16. Briefly, the publishing history of the six journals covered in this chapter is as follows: Elizabeth Hudson's journal remained in unpublished manuscript form until 1994, when it was included in Bacon, *Wilt Thou Go on My Errand?* Elizabeth Ashbridge's journal was reviewed and edited by the morning meeting of London yearly meeting, even though she was American. Most likely Jane Hoskins's and Elizabeth Collins's journals went through the Meeting for Sufferings of Philadelphia yearly meeting. Ann Moore's and Susanna Morris's journals appear to have remained in manuscript form until they were published as part of John and Isaac Comly's Friends Miscellany in the 1830s.

17. See Estelle C. Jelinek, ed., *Women's Autobiography: Essays in Criticism* (Bloomington: Indiana University Press, 1980), for a collection of essays about gender and autobiography. Many feminist scholars at the time maintained that women's lives are communal and men's lives are autonomous.

18. See Paul John Eakin, *Fictions in Autobiography: Studies in the Art of Self-Invention* (Princeton: Princeton University Press, 1985), and his *Touching the World: Reference in Autobiography* (Princeton: Princeton University Press, 1992) for further discussion of the relation between the self and society.

19. Ironically because Paul commanded: "Let your women keep silence in the churches: for it is not permitted unto them to speak; but they are commanded to be under obedience" (I Cor. 14:34).

20. Susanna Morris (1682–1755) was born in England to Quaker parents. Her family migrated to Pennsylvania in 1701. She married Morris Morris in 1703, when she was twenty-one years old. She had a child every two years or so for twenty-one years, eventually bearing thirteen children. Her first child, David, was born soon after she returned from her first trip in the ministry. Only nine of her children survived to adulthood. She traveled throughout the colonies, as well

as in England and Scotland, often leaving her children behind as she ventured out. At sixty-six years old she became Elizabeth Ashbridge's traveling companion. She continued traveling in the ministry into her early seventies. See "The Journal of Susanna Morris," in Bacon, *Wilt Thou Go on My Errand?*

21. Ibid., 31.

22. Daniel Shea, *Spiritual Autobiography in Early America* (Princeton: Princeton University Press, 1908; reprint Madison: University of Wisconsin Press, 1988).

23. Jane Hoskins (1694–ca. 1765) was born Jane Fenn and came to the colonies as an indentured servant in 1712. When she was sixteen years old she became very ill, which she interpreted as God's way of removing her from a life of singing and music so she could turn her attention to religious matters. She traveled throughout the colonies as well as in Barbados, Ireland, and England. In 1738 she married. Though her name is spelled "Hoskens" in her journal, this is an editorial error. See Jane Hoskins, *The Life of That Faithful Servant of Christ, Jane Hoskens, a Minister of the Gospel, among the People Called Quakers* (Philadelphia: Friends Library, 1837).

24. Hoskins, 3.

25. Elizabeth Ashbridge (1713–55) was born in England to a strict father and a "strictly religious" mother. Her father disowned her because of her poor marriage choice; she lost her husband, traveled to America to work as an indentured servant, and married a man named Sullivan who abused her and tried to keep her from her spiritual calling; ultimately she became a traveling minister in the Society of Friends. Her journal has received more scholarly recognition than any other, in part because it is a narrative that ends just as the central conflicts in her life have been mostly resolved, the kind of narrative twentieth-century audiences have been trained to appreciate. See Elizabeth Ashbridge, "Some Account of the Fore Part of the Life of Elizabeth Ashbridge," in *Journeys in New Worlds: Early American Women's Narratives,* ed. William L. Andrews (Madison: University of Wisconsin Press, 1990), 147–80.

26. Ibid., 147.

27. For a more detailed explanation of the differences between Quaker and Puritan treatment of children, see the second chapter of Brinton, *Quaker Journals.*

28. Elizabeth Hudson (1721–83) was born into a comfortable Philadelphia Quaker family. She traveled extensively in the colonies and in Europe. Her traveling companion for many years, Jane Hoskins, became very dear to her, and

when difficulties arose between them Hudson entered one of her many depressed states. She married Anthony Morris, sixteen years older than herself, when she was thirty-one years old. They had three sons, though the third died in infancy. See Elizabeth Hudson, "The Journal of Elizabeth Hudson," in Bacon, *Wilt Thou Go on My Errand?*

29. Hudson, 10.

30. Ashbridge, 148.

31. Ibid.

32. Ibid.

33. Hoskins, 3.

34. Ashbridge, 162.

35. Hoskins, 3–4 (emphasis hers).

36. Hoskins, 8.

37. Hudson, 117–18.

38. Morris, 70.

39. Hoskins, 10–11.

40. Rufus Hall, *A Journal of the Life, Religious Exercises, and Travels in the Work of the Ministry, of Rufus Hall, Late of Northampton, Montgomery County, in the State of New York* (Philadelphia: John and Isaac Comly, 1840), 7.

41. Elizabeth Collins (1755–1831) was a traveling minister in the Society of Friends for fifty-two years and a birthright Quaker. When she was eighteen she married John Mason, who died four years later, leaving her to care for two children. In 1778 she married Job Collins. When she was twenty-four she began her ministry. Her life was punctuated by periods of ministry followed by periods of child rearing and sickness. See Elizabeth Collins, *Memoirs of Elizabeth Collins, of Upper Evesham, New Jersey, a Minister of the Gospel of Christ, in the Society of Friends* (Philadelphia.: Wm. H. Pile's Sons, 1894).

42. Collins, 24.

43. Hudson, 111.

44. Hoskins, 11. Compare this and Hudson's response with the response from Moses: "And Moses said unto God, Who am I, that I should go unto Pharaoh, and that I should bring forth the children of Israel out of Egypt?" (Exod. 3:11) and Jeremiah's: "Then said I, Ah, Lord God! behold, I cannot speak: for I am a child" (Jer. 1:6).

45. Ibid.

46. Hudson, 113.

47. Collins, 28.

48. Ashbridge, 161.

49. Ashbridge, 160.

50. Ashbridge, 161.

51. Ann Moore, "The Journal of Ann Moore," in Bacon, *Wilt Thou Go on My Errand?* 269.

52. Hudson, 187.

14

"We Weren't Always Plain"

Poetry by Women of

Mennonite Backgrounds

Julia Kasdorf

Traditions are not always traditional. Mennonite women poets interrogate their own communities and family memories to uncover and recover oral traditions, leading to a certain suspicion that the past was not precisely as they had been told. By reconstructing tradition and actively mourning dislocation and discontinuity, poets work beside scholars in revealing the emotional and actual realities of women's experience.

One afternoon my maternal grandmother's sister, Sara (Hartzler) Hartzler, whom the family calls "Toot," invited me into the den of her cottage at a Mennonite retirement village in Mifflin County, Pennsylvania. She lifted the lid of her most treasured object, an old wooden salt box painted by nineteenth-century Amish schoolteacher and folk artist Samuel L. Plank, her great-grandfather. "Here," she said, pulling a small pasteboard cube from the box, "This is for you. It belonged to my grandmother, Sara Plank, your great-great-grandmother." Inside glinted a wide pinkish gold band engraved with daisies framed by ornate rectangles. I was baffled, unable to imagine any of my Amish ancestors owning such a thing. "We weren't always plain," she explained. "And now you can finally wear this in public again."

Sara Demaris Plank (1860–1937), daughter of the painter Samuel, must have put the ring away in about 1887, when she married her Amish beau, Levi Hartzler. For more than a century, as Mifflin County Amish and Amish-Mennonite congregations fractured and cycled through periods of intense concern about plain dress and cultural assimilation, the forbidden ring lay in its original box. Evidence that times had not always been so severe, it offered hope to Sara's namesake, Toot, who has always liked fancy things. Growing up in an "old Mennonite" (Mennonite Church) family during the 1970s, I knew I was witnessing events of great consequence when my mother cut her hair for the first time and later left her head covering home on the dresser one Sunday morning. During that era of disorienting change in society and our religious community, I internalized the myth that Mennonite history follows a continuous path from plain to fancy, from pure to corrupt. And following that path, dress restrictions for women gradually grow more lenient.

That assumption was surely unsettled by Sara's ring, more than a hundred years old yet showing no sign of wear. To my questions, Toot offered little more than material evidence: photographs of ancestors in elegant Victorian attire and a pair of gold earrings. She could not explain why rules were so lax back then, before plain dress came to became a necessary sign of members' commitment to remain nonconformed to the world.[1] I doubt Toot saw the value of the information she was passing on. She would not think of herself as a historical revisionist or admit that once you see that your religious tradition has been inconsistent, its absolutes appear relative and their authority starts to erode. (A recognition of this truth was expressed in the old maxim about removing the ribbons attached to Mennonite women's head coverings: "When the strings go, everything goes.")[2] Toot would never compare her revelations with the troublesome poems I write from family stories. Nor would she see that in giving me Sara's ring she was opening for me a new entrance into that Amish settlement established in the 1790s that eventually fractured into more than a dozen distinct groups.[3]

On another visit, the same great-aunt and I sat side by side on the sofa, a dress box full of old photographs balanced on our knees. As we sorted

This austere photograph shows the author's aunt in a prayer covering and cape dress—ready for Sunday church services. (Photograph courtesy of Julia Kasdorf.)

through the images I paused, holding up two black-and-white snapshots. "Look at this," I said. "Look at you." She looked, then realizing what I must see, laughed a bit. "Oh, that was me on Sunday, and that was me the rest of the week." In the first photo, a stern-faced girl of sixteen or seventeen wears a pale cape dress and stares blandly at the camera. Her dark hair is plastered against her skull, and the strings of her head covering drape back over her shoulders. Her arms hang loosely at her sides, and long sleeves cover her wrists. Black high-throated shoes make her legs look like stumps. A white picket fence forms a corner several yards behind her back.

"Aunt Toot" wearing "modern" clothing and high-heeled shoes. The sparkle of her wristwatch matches her smile. (Photograph courtesy of Julia Kasdorf.)

In the other photograph the girl, who may be slightly older, grins from the lawn in front of a bed of cannas; their wide tropical leaves flare wildly behind one shoulder. Her short-sleeved shirtwaist dress has contrasting handkerchiefs tucked into the breast pockets and a row of six dark buttons. She leans on one hand and drapes the other arm across her lap, displaying a dainty wristwatch. One black pump with a cutout toe and scallopy white stitching juts out from under her skirt. No head covering is visible. Her hair is drawn back in a bun, but waves crest at the corners of her forehead. Behind her the picket fence angles off at an odd slant. "Oh, I remember that dress," she murmured. "I loved that dress."

Knowing how much I treasure scraps of the past, Toot told me to take the photographs with me when I left. What was she trying to show me? What will I learn despite her intentions? Little is ever entirely clear in the objects and stories she gives me. Both photographs are evidence. Both are true. Shall I view her as a woman who was divided by a culture that supplies too few possibilities for a life: only the submissive acceptable self or the grinning real self? Yet a conservative Mennonite woman could live her whole life within the tight frame of that picket fence and also grow cannas, huge scarlet-flowering plants so exotic that their roots cannot bear Pennsylvania winters and have to be dug up and stored in the cellar. A Mennonite woman could wear a cape dress as well as those shoes, which I am certain I have seen on sweethearts in World War II movies. She is more complex than the plain/fancy duality that divided her life into Sunday and "the rest of the week" and repeatedly caused disputes that split congregations in her community. She wants me to see both parts; she wants to be constructed as one whole person in my memory. Or not. And all of this is just what can be deduced by the young niece bound to Toot by blood but living and thinking outside traditional constructs. It takes talk with her, then writing these images, for me to begin see in meaningful ways the things that have lain before my eyes all my life.

RE-VISION FROM THE MOTHER TONGUE

Among the primary intentions of American and Canadian female poets, Alicia Suskin Ostriker finds two that seem useful in considering Mennonite women's poetry: the need to integrate polarities and dissolve boundaries and the desire to make communal transactions rather than static art objects. She identifies these intentions in a study of poems published between 1960 and 1980, when American women's literature came into its own, often in conversation with the civil rights and women's liberation movements.[4] For Mennonite poets, a will to integrate polarities is apparent in works that seek to express dissonant parts of the female self—parts that have been separated, repressed, or denied. This desire is especially powerful when it intersects with the need to incorporate parts of community experience that have been ignored or forgotten. As women shaped by traditional Mennonite cultures uncover our hair, elbows, and knees, publicly exposing our bodies and voices, we also seek to incorporate those individuals and aspects of the Mennonite experience that have been suppressed in official memory but often preserved through the transactions of oral tradition. For less than two decades—in Canada and in the United States—this quest has produced narrative, autobiographical, and lyric poems that enlarge, complicate, and even challenge the conventional Anabaptist story.

The first books of poetry written by women of Mennonite backgrounds invariably include work drawn from community memory. Engagement with family and community stories seems to be both a means of articulation and an act of appropriation. Imaginative writing by Mennonite men often draws on historical sources as well. The first literary Mennonite novel written in English was Rudy Wiebe's 1962 *Peace Shall Destroy Many,* which exposes the moral complexities of a Mennonite refugee settlement in Canada, and Jeff Gundy's recent work of creative nonfiction, *A Community of Memory,* portrays his family's American migrations. History is a rich source for Mennonite writers because our group has consistently relied on historical narratives to sustain a sectarian cultural and religious identity—from oral stories about rotten tomatoes thrown at Mennonite merchants during World War II to *Martyrs' Mirror,* the great seventeenth-century work of resistance writing that is a compilation of personal narratives, court records, and other texts recounting Anabaptist persecution. More than theological writings or church doctrine, community and family stories have shaped a sense of Mennonite identity in North America.[5]

Given the importance of history, it is understandable that women must address and even revise narratives from the past if we are to clear a public space for our own stories. We must engage in "re-vision," defined by Adrienne Rich in her classic work of feminist poetics as "the act of looking back, of entering an old text from a new critical direction." The old texts include the received scripts for a woman's life, stories of lives that came before hers, and the narratives that structure the reality of an entire community. Sometimes these texts come by way of scholarly research, but more often they are retrieved from conversation and the author's memory. The desire to revise these stories is not fueled by mere academic interest, Rich reminds us: "more than a chapter in cultural history: it is an act of survival."[6] Begun as an individual's task, the work of re-vision saves the lives of both author and community, because it increases the possible strategies for living and interpreting experience—although for exactly these reasons such work can be unsettling to the common order and may be perceived as a threat to family and community values.

In order to write some women, perhaps intuitively, distance themselves from the enmeshing and often silencing culture of childhood. Traditional Mennonite life has been silencing for women because, although we have been essential and sometimes quite powerful in the domestic sphere, we have been marginal in social and religious structures.[7] In the past, most Mennonite men may have also been denied opportunities to pursue artistic and personal expression, but they were always permitted a public voice in church, and husbands and fathers held sanctified authority in the home. Jean Janzen and Sarah Klassen, two poets considered in this chapter, are members of a Mennonite group that still will not ordain women. In the face of this biased power structure, many wives, mothers, and daughters remained silent and passive—or passive-aggressive—at least in public. For some like Di Brandt, Sheri Hostetler, and me, higher education and moves to urban areas afforded enough distance from traditional inhibitions so that we could break into print.

Nevertheless, despite being an award-winning author of four volumes of poetry and two book-length prose works, Brandt has said that she could not imagine publishing *Questions I Asked My Mother* until well after the death of her authoritarian father in 1979. This may not be news to those familiar with her first collection, charged with rage against punishing male patriarchs and a rural Mennonite community influenced by evangelical fundamentalism. Those who know Canadian poet Sarah Klassen's writing may be surprised to learn that she had a similar experience, though she shares little else with Brandt. No longer officially affiliated with a Mennonite church, Brandt is infamous for the rebellious tone of her early work and her incisive feminist critiques of Mennonite culture, whereas Klassen is an active member of the Mennonite Brethren church, editor of a denominational newsletter for women, and author of several books of poetry that pay tribute to her faith and heritage. Yet Klassen could not even consider trying to write until her father was dead. "I think that's all for the good," she reflected in her typically soft-spoken manner; "I'm not sure he would have been thrilled."

Despite the prohibitions of a patriarchal culture and father, Klassen traces her literary instincts home to a storytelling mother. Her first collection, *Journey to Yalta*, was inspired by reveries of Barvenkovo and Vassilyevka, Mennonite villages in the former Soviet Union. "Da war's am schoensten" (that was the most beautiful place), her mother said not long before her death, remembering her birthplace at Kronberg. Unable to find a village with that name on any map, Klassen remains intrigued by the life her parents were forced to abandon in 1926, when they migrated to western Canada. From her mother's memory and her own desire, she writes poetry to recover history. She admits that her efforts reconstruct an imaginary homeland "both idyllic and ideal," down to its picket fences and pear orchards. Even in Klassen's later work, dislocation and home, safety and danger, real and imagined homelands, and her own mother remain among her central subjects.

Mothers and mothers' stories emerged as a powerful theme in prepared statements presented at the panel discussion "Mennonite Women Writing Home" at the "Quiet in the Land?" conference, although the panel included women ranging in age from their early thirties to their seventies, drawn from various Mennonite backgrounds. Mothers who speak are bound by talk to their writing daughters, and the spoken word serves both as a source of knowledge and as a model for literary style among this first generation of poets. Whether our mothers spoke a dialect of German or New World English, the Mennonite mother tongue is gossip, idle chat, those stories exchanged over quilt frames or enamel basins of shell peas. Talk links generations and sustains a rich historical and literary imagination, even within an aesthetically meager ethos. Writerly voices do not erupt from silence by sheer force of will or individual genius; there were always voices before ours, talking. And we write with our ears open—even when much of the story remains unspoken.

By now the connection between oral tradition and literature written by women who come from distinct ethnic backgrounds has been observed so often that it is almost a cliché. In the era of multicultural studies, much was made of the rich social sources of language and story. Novels enacted the process, as modern characters found in oral tradition clues to their own identities; this quest figures prominently in the plots of works by Chinese American authors Amy Tan (*The Joy Luck Club*) and Maxine Hong Kingston (*Woman Warrior*), Native American author Leslie Marmon Silko (*Ceremony*), and African American author Toni Morrison (*Song of*

Solomon). In her famous essay tracing the emergence of African American women's writing, Alice Walker named her debt to mother's stories: "Yet so many of the stories that I write, that we all write, are my mother's stories. Only recently did I fully realize this: that through years of listening to my mother's stories of her life, I have absorbed not only the stories themselves, but something of the manner in which she spoke, something of the urgency that involves the knowledge that her stories—like her life—must be recorded."[8] Canadian critic Hildi Froese Tiessen noted a similar maternal presence and urgency in fiction and poetry by female Mennonite writers: "Always prominent at the heart of their work are the voices of women, often projections of the authors' foremothers who suffered an enforced silence throughout the official histories of their people."[9]

Di Brandt traced her powerful and urgent voice to oral stories told by the Mennonite women of the farm village in Rheinland, Manitoba, where she grew up. She recalled first writing verse that was "really really tight . . . words together like beads on a string, tight tight tight, laced with poison," but she later abandoned conventional (literate) punctuation, rejected patriarchal figures and texts, and found her own voice, which is characterized by immediacy, irreverence, and humor. At the Millersville conference, Brandt described how this voice finally emerged from listening to the talk of women in her family:

Bang! The poems shifted, from being these large unwieldy constructions in my head, to much simpler, smaller pieces, bubbling up from my belly, breathless outbursts in a child's voice, daring to speak the forbidden, pushing back against the overwhelming weight of the culture, beginning to name her own fragmented desire. I found that without punctuation you can't use discursive language, no howevers and therefores and thuses, just this and this, or and then and then. This put me back in touch not only with the child's voice but also the fundamental orality of Mennonite culture, which I'd forgotten about with all my book learning and obsession with text, my fight with Menno Simons and my dead dad and the Bible. I started realizing that our Mennonite village, despite the violent and lasting impact of Christianity and the Reformation, was in some ways more like traditional Aboriginal culture than like twentieth-century postindustrial culture. I started remembering the marvelous storytelling of the women in my family, recounting the family stories, over and over, with great drama and suspense and much laughter.[10]

Through conversation, members of the panel further identified a dynamic between mother, writer, and a reading audience common to some of our experiences. Di Brandt, Sheri Hostetler, and I all moved away from the communities of childhood and published more-or-less controversial texts while our mothers were still alive, so our mothers were left to explain, defend, and apologize to members of paternalistic Mennonite communities who hold parents responsible for the actions of their adult children. Although they may not have always approved of the writing, our mothers became our allies, functioning like the figure of Janus, the ancient Roman god of doorways and fortunate beginnings. In his main temple at Rome, a great statue with two faces, old and young, looking toward past and future, was situated between doors facing east and west. These doors were closed only in peacetime, which was infrequent during the conquests of the empire. "Janus," which names the first month of our calendar as well as the work of janitor, is also related to *ianua*, the principal door to a house—the opener and fastener of all things—portal between here and there, home and the world. The figure who stands there is bound to experience conflict. I used to think Janus symbolized the position of the Mennonite writer, but now I realize that we often write from memory and imagination, in relative safety on the margins of the ethnic and religious empire. Our mothers remain at the doorways, forced to clean up—employing womanly arts of mediation and conversation to restore the relational damage done by their author daughters.

I turn to some poems to briefly demonstrate ways female poets enlarge understandings of Anabaptist history by exposing previously hidden aspects of Mennonite experience. I must stress that this work is motivated by urgent personal quests for re-vision and meaning, although the resulting poems contain knowledge that can be of use to the community and that frequently travels well beyond the community's boundaries.

JEAN JANZEN: "LIFE IS OF ONE PIECE"

In 1980 at the age of forty-six, Jean Janzen returned to poetry and to an education disrupted several times by mothering four children and homemaking for a busy physician. Identifying with Emily Dickinson's famous declaration to her editor, "Shortness to live has made me bold," Jean extricated herself from some church and family obligations and returned to school. Early in graduate studies at Fresno State University, she discovered a family secret—her paternal grandmother's suicide in the former Soviet Union—which became the impetus for her most important early poem and charted the direction of later work. It is no coincidence that her poetic voice developed simultaneously with a quest to tell a long-suppressed family story. *Words for the Silence* establishes the connection between articulation and the writer's redemptive intent. That it was published by the Mennonite Brethren Historical Center suggests that her poetry was recognized as a useful work of community memory.

> *These Words Are for You, Grandmother*
> i
> I imagine you sitting on the doorstep,
> your dark braid undone and rippling
> down your back. You are plucking
> melodies from the guitar which
> he made for you, and he is there
> singing along, his arm soft around you
> in the Ukrainian dusk. And now it seems
> that we are both entering the darkening
> house to the pale bed, this bed
> of beginnings and endings, or arms
> encircling and then letting go,
> this bed which you have given me
> by your womb.
>
> ii
> The crude violin, the little organ
> he made of wood scraps and animal bones,
> and your guitar are all silent in the room,
> the strings untouched. His long hand
> slipped from yours after the last embrace,
> after his last gathering of the nine
> young faces around the terrible bed.
> And then the cold light in the room
> and the silence, and heaven so far away.

The ministers brought shoes for the children,
flour for your bin. But you were silent,
your eyes empty, your mouth still.

The photograph tells me that I
have eyes and hands like yours
and a mouth with a heavy lower lip.
Look, I am shaping it for words,
making sounds for you. I am speaking
the syllables you couldn't say.
See my breath is pushing away the cold.

iii
After you hanged yourself
they buried you outside the gate
without songs, just a prayer
in the harsh light. My father,
ten years old, had found you
in the barn, your body
a still dark strip, your face
swollen and purple. And by the grave
he could not sing for you;
he did not speak of you.
He sealed his mouth with a heavy stone
and walked away.
And when he held me in his arms
he spoke of rivers
and a black crow against the sky.

Helen of darkness,
I sing you a song.
It is like water from a clear stream,
like a white linen dress.
I take you down, wash you
and comb your hair.
I lay you down beside the man you loved.

iv

The small, abandoned graveyard
lies in tall autumn grass, the markers
tumbled and covered. Last grasshoppers
have gone from the nearby stubbled fields
and a light frost whitens the feathery heads of foxtail.
I have come down the long narrow road. I have come
with my passport, my photograph
and my name to stand on the unmarked dust
of your body, and there is no sound
but the dry leaves stirring in the alders,
the groaning of roots, and these words
breathing on a page.

In keeping with religious tradition, the suicide's body is buried outside sanctified ground, but Janzen's voice, like baptismal waters, redeems and resurrects this grandmother of "darkness," saving her spirit by returning her body to the body of the man she loved in life. In this poem, boundaries blur between sacred and profane, spirit and flesh, divine and human love, silence and singing as a distinction between the past grandmother and the present speaker slips away. The telling paradox of this poem is that Janzen learned the story of her grandmother's suicide only as her father was dying, after he had carried it in shameful silence most of his life. Through her writing, the secret now endures in public, in permanent and inanimate form, yet "breathing on a page" as it is resurrected by each person who reads it.

Refusing to suppress this one tragic story, Janzen's vision also refuses the oppressive denials common to most patriarchal expressions of Christianity—denials of the female body and sexuality (associated with Eve) and death (associated with evil). In her presentation at the "Quiet in the Land?" conference, Janzen boldly admitted a curious connection between her search for a lost history and her ongoing quest for a fuller, more embodied and satisfying spirituality. She reflected on the fruits of that search:

What did I find? My own father's unwritten stories about his boyhood in the Ukraine, about my grandmother's suicide, a story silenced by him and all the family. I found my lost first cousins in central Asiatic USSR where they had been exiled as children during World War II, visited with them, and wrote about it. I said that life is of one piece, that the physical and spiritual cannot be separated, that I know who God is through my body, by longing for another, by having sex, by giving birth, by mothering and wifing, by watching my parents and my brother die.

The yearning that compelled her to recover family secrets and search for displaced relatives—those hidden and lost parts—helped Janzen to recognize that "life is of one piece." Nothing should be devalued or repressed, and thus she found a way to heal the ancient wound that severed flesh from spirit. Her triumph is the recognition that spiritual knowledge is also carnal knowledge.

SHERI HOSTETLER: "TO CELEBRATE ALL"

The link between what is suppressed in the individual body and what is excluded from the religious community—biblically and traditionally conceived as a body—is strongly articulated by Sheri Hostetler, Mennonite pastor, poet, and founding editor of *Mennonot*, an alternative newsletter for "Mennos on the Margins." Hostetler shares Janzen's vision that "life is of one piece" and aims to celebrate all its parts. She reflected:

> For many of us who grew up Mennonite, there were large parts of ourselves that couldn't be known, that we had to keep hidden because we feared the community wouldn't honor them. As in most communities with rigid boundaries between who is in and who is out, certain thoughts, behaviors, and feelings are off limits to "respectable" members of that community. . . . Both *Mennonot* and my poetry then are a way to celebrate all of who I am, who we are. . . . I founded *Mennonot* because I wanted there to be at least one forum within the Mennonite community where we could be all of who we are, where we didn't have to hide parts of ourselves. I wanted to pierce that polite veneer of dishonesty that hides our ugliness as well as our beauty.

As parts of the woman's body were once hidden by sectarian garb, so unacceptable parts of a person's life must be kept hidden from the judgment of the religious community. Through her work with *Mennonot*, Hostetler has provided a public forum for marginal Mennonites, including gays and lesbians. She recognizes that the fragmentation of self and the fragmentation of community for righteousness' sake are the most brutal kinds of violence Anabaptist pacifists can practice. Her poetry, which is often overtly political, seeks to render whole and more complex images of the individual and community, thereby helping to heal wounds inflicted by that violence. In the spirit of early Anabaptist fathers and mothers who made a biblical case for pacifism even as Turks were sacking European villages, she seeks to make peace.

Hostetler recognizes that the fragmentation caused by repression *within the community* is somehow related to the community's separation from others *outside* itself. The latter impulse is expressed in the sectarian emphasis on maintaining separation from culture and "the world"—a value that is particularly strong in her Swiss–South German "old" Mennonite background. This sectarian habit of mind sorts light from dark and acceptable from unacceptable, striving to maintain boundaries that protect the religious community from external influence. In publishing poems about growing up in the farm village of Berlin, Ohio, Hostetler acknowledges her desire to transport those stories out of their local context, breaking the boundaries that separated her religious community from society so that it may positively influence broader culture. She says, "My poetry, then, is about generosity, about giving this gift of my home culture to the world." For her, publication is construed not in terms of betrayal or telling tribal secrets, but as sharing the goodness of a community that she regards as redemptive and humane, in contrast to so much of homogenized mainstream American culture. She seeks "to witness" or "share the good news," in the terminology of her religious background.

A Bible verse traditionally used to express the values of religious sectarianism encourages the faithful to be "in the world but not of it." One of Hostetler's poems borrows its title from this verse and explores ways this value fosters judgmental attitudes toward others and a sense of self that is divided. Here the speaker articulates a dilemma commonly found in the relationship between Mennonites and the American mainstream: she is both alien other on the margins and the religiously pure one—outsider and insider, culturally inferior but spiritually superior.

Not of This World
I am like none of you. You must recognize
deep in me how different I am. You're all
Wonder bread and drive-ins. I am fertile
fields, head coverings, memories of martyrdom
like yesterday, hymns without organ. The
Bible whispers in my ear at night, it will
not keep still.
But my people do. *Die Stille im Lande.* We
never talk. Quietly we move, quietly the
field is plowed, in quiet are the dishes
washed, the sheets pulled taut, silently the
hay flung high atop the wagon. Our horses
clip clop in a virtual vacuum. All around
us pins drop, and still, we are still.

Nature loves our vacuum, blesses us with a
bounty you cannot imagine. Look at our barns,
they are filled with sweet hay, hay without
end, stacked fragrant, stacked sweet. We
do not talk but we smell the sweetness of
hay every day, oh stranger, you know not what
you are not.

I am not like you. I talk to you, laugh
with you, make love with you, break bread
with you, I will even die with you. And my soul
will rest atop a haymow on Weaver Ridge while yours
goes to heaven.

    The final image suggests that despite her best efforts to connect with "the world" and this stranger, the speaker will never completely break free of the community's embrace. She knows that to divide herself from her past, which constructs who she is now, would be as painful and limiting as attempts at sectarian purity. Whatever critique it may offer, the poem also self-consciously proclaims Mennonite difference and asserts its value. Now living in the San Francisco Bay area, Hostetler says she writes and lives "on a fault line between two cultures, two worlds that often grate against each other"—refusing to exclude either one.

This dualistic reality is well expressed in her poem by an untranslated phrase of German in the otherwise English text. The familiar phrase that names Mennonites, *Die Stille im Lande* (the quiet in the land), persists in her memory like a memorized Bible verse, but she playfully puns on the word *Stille,* hearing in it the English word "still." Obviously, these busy farmers and housewives are not "still," although they are traditional— still doing it the old way—or, in Pennsylvania German-influenced English, "Doing it that way, still." This pun, like the whispering Bible verse, depends on spoken language. Talk is essential to understanding. As in Janzen's "These Words Are for You Grandmother," Hostetler's conversation with the stranger stands in stark contrast to the silence of the community. It is this "talk"—the poetic voice construed in oral terms— that both articulates tradition and breaks traditional silence, placing Janzen in relation to her dead grandmother and Hostetler in relation to a stranger.

JULIA KASDORF: "I HAVE NOT TOLD IT AS SHE WOULD"

The use of talk and traditional stories in poetry can keep conversational transactions going even after poems are fixed on the page. I discovered this at a reading during a Sunday service at my brother's Mennonite church, shortly after *Sleeping Preacher* appeared. In the discussion period afterward, a younger woman in the congregation said she was saddened by my poems because they reminded her of the stories, especially women's stories, that have been lost in our culture. With this remark, my mother's hand shot up from the audience. "First," she said, "I'd like to say that I would not have told these stories as Julia has. Also—women's stories have not been lost. My mother told them to me, and I told them to Julia, and she wrote them down!"

I love this reply because in it my mother acknowledges that there are multiple authors of the text. Furthermore, the poems are part of a conversation that does not cease with their publication, so she must scramble to distance herself from them. Although a poem like *Vesta's Father* attributes the story's source to my mother, she knows I have not told it as she would.

Vesta's Father
Mom's in the kitchen telling stories
from before she was born, how Vesta figured
if her father quit smoking, he'd save enough
to buy new winter coats that she and her sisters
would not be ashamed to hang in the anteroom
of Locust Grove Mennonite Church
where the ladies couldn't help but smell smoke
when the girls pressed around the mirror
to jab pins in their buns and straighten prayer coverings.
He drank, too. Deer season each year
when he went with the Hoot Owls to their camp
on Back Mountain, someone always brought him home, drunk,
to his wife who had spells when she couldn't stop crying.
The bishop found out he wore a baseball cap
and made him confess that worldliness
to the whole congregation. And when he died,
with whiskey on his nightstand,
he was buried by the Lutherans.

Tears gleam on Mother's cheeks
as she traces the grain in the table boards,
but I am not weeping like his wife or daughters.
The sins of the fathers won't be visited
on my generation. I say there is no shame
in lying among Lutherans where folks are allowed
to put flowers on graves, his plot in plain view
of those mountains that rise dark and silent
as old Mennonites standing in pews—
black-stockinged women on one side,
black-suited men on the other—
those mountains so high they slow the sunrise
and hurry the night.

Viewing this poem as a transcription of oral tradition, my mother finds
it seriously flawed and probably hopes that neither of us will be held responsible for my mistakes. My maternal great-grandfather Hartzler was

not buried in the Lutheran cemetery as I had written; he was buried in a Mennonite cemetery after the Lutherans performed the funeral service. Yet I had remembered the story with him ending up with the Lutherans—a detail that seemed to convey more truth than fact—so I chose not to correct this mistake. Although she understood this decision, she had hoped I would change the details to match reality. I do not know what concerned her more: that I would willfully publish a lie or that it would be discovered by members of the community who know where Ezra Hartzler is buried and who believe that writers should stick to the facts.

In another sense, I have not *told* the stories as she would, since she would have spoken them, and they would have remained contained within the family and community for whom the interpretation of each story is as scripted and canonical as the details of the oral text. The force that originally propelled this story into a poem probably came from a tension between what the story seemed to mean in its traditional, oral context and the possibilities I saw for alternative interpretations. Here the Mennonite community appears to be punishing and cruel, although traditional versions of the story stress the suffering caused by Ezra's alcoholism. Emphasis on a family's suffering makes the story a cautionary tale about temperance, yet in the details that persisted in each retelling, Ezra's daughter, Toot—and even his granddaughter, my mother—preserved every feature necessary to read (and tell) the story as a strong indictment of a graceless community. Embedded in the structure and details of the oral text were the elements necessary to subvert it. Dissonance between the stories' public meaning and their complicated private feelings may be what kept Ezra's daughters repeating it more than fifty years after the events had occurred—so that I would eventually hear its ambiguous intent.

DI BRANDT: "THE RAGE OF FOUR CENTURIES"

Much like stories retained in family and community tradition, the language of religion appears to be material that is previously constructed and owned by the community. The language of hymnal and Scripture is borrowed, but in the hands of Di Brandt, these familiar figures of speech become strange and even shocking. Probably the most controversial poems in her first book, the "missionary position" sequence playfully appropriates and exposes traditional metaphors used to characterize God, Jesus, and the relationship between the deity and humanity.[11] The erotic and sexual tenants of these familiar figures—like much forbidden experience—generally linger in the dim corners of the Mennonite mind or are denied altogether, but Brandt restores those dead metaphors to their lively, explicit meanings.

> *Missionary Position (1)*
> let me tell you what it's like
> having God for a father & jesus
> for a lover on this old mother
> earth you who no longer know
> the old story the part about the
> Virgin being of course a myth
> made up by Catholics for an easy
> way out it's not that easy i can
> tell you right off the old man
> in his room demands bloody hard
> work he with his rod & his hard
> crooked staff well jesus he's
> different he's a good enough lay
> it's just that he prefers miracles
> to fishing & sometimes i get tired
> waiting all day for his bit of
> magic though late at night i burn
> with his fire & the old mother
> shudders & quakes under us when
> God's not looking

Here Brandt revises the old myths and figures of speech to suit her own subversive purposes. Ostriker identifies this transformational habit common in contemporary women's poetry, describing it in biblical language as "the old vessel filled with new wine, initially satisfying the thirst of the individual but ultimately making cultural change possible."[12] There is both safety and mischief in revising sacred material created and interpreted by the group. When they come to blame her, the poet can simply shrug her shoulders and coyly reply, "But you've said it yourself." The critique cuts deeper because it surprises readers with their own language, and this poem goes a long way toward injecting female experience and perspectives into the trinitarian family drama of Christian tradition.

Concerning the composition of this particular piece in the six-part "missionary position" sequence, Brandt reflected at the panel:

> I sat at my desk in my study and looked up at the ceiling and thought, this is it, now I will be struck by lightning and that will be that. I have done the ultimate, I have offended God. And nothing happened. The sound of God's voice was a deafening silence. He doesn't even bloody care, I thought, He doesn't give a shit whether I write blasphemous poems or not. It was all a plot made up by our fathers to keep us submissive and passive. And I began to feel this huge rage inside me, the rage of four centuries of women frightened and bullied into obedience and silence.

In these comments we see Brandt's defiance of polarities and her instinct for mythic revision. Here God is not silent because God is absent or nonexistent; God simply turns out to be not what we expected. This God is so much larger in heart than the petty and mean Daddy projected in the sky by "our fathers," so this God does not act like the men who created him in their own image. In fact, by keeping a "deafening silence," this God resembles certain Mennonite women, "frightened and bullied into obedience and silence"! And Di Brandt is an author powerful enough to effectively revise the deity.

SARAH KLASSEN: "TRAVEL THE WHOLE BLOODY WAY"

Mennonites who write from communal stories must reckon with local and biblical memory as well as the identity-forming tales of sixteenth-century Anabaptist persecution. Specters from the age of martyrdom haunt contemporary literary imaginations and frequently appear in poems by current women writers.[13] For Sarah Klassen, whose family survived the systematic violence and famine of the Soviet holocaust of 1917–32, Anabaptist martyrdom is imaginatively conflated with memories from that time.

A bus tour in search of her parents' lost homeland becomes an opportunity to examine the Mennonite obsession with martyrdom and persecution. This poem, like many written by Mennonite women, begins with the unspeakable—something *hard to say*—but it also gathers knowledge through conversation. Klassen deftly evades the authoritative voices of both history professor and minister to articulate connections between the Anabaptist exterminations of sixteenth-century western Europe and those losses in her own family's past.

> *Origins*
> Hard to say
> how we got talking
> on the bus from Sebastopol
> past shivering wheatfields
> cradled like white lakes
> in the folds of Crimean hills
> about Felix Manz.
>
> Was it the history professor
> or the pastor from Altona
> started us rehearsing
> who we are. Mennonites
>
> having come a long way
> like to return
> in herds like lemmings
> to places of death.
>
> Frozen forests declared out of bounds
> we surround the old oak tree we owned
> once. We stretched warm limbs
> along its rough-ridged branches, its roots
> loved the same rivers we loved. We believed
> it would be always summer
>
> always Sunday. On Khortiza Island
> we fall to our knees
> searching reluctant undergrowth
> for evidence of our having been here.
> Our fingers trace names

once chiselled deep
in weathered stone.

Hildebrand Friesen Regehr
Rare for us to travel
the whole bloody way
back to the cold Limmat River.
Felix Manz in the small boat
bound hand and foot, his heart breaking
free
to watch sunlight dancing
on radiant peaks of ice-topped mountains.

It's where we were born.

Here Klassen's imagination resists the "lemming" and "herd" mentality of Mennonite tour groups that love too much their history of extinction and loss. Her search for a physical and spiritual heritage, "evidence of our having been there," leads her to trace Mennonite names on gravestones and refer to "frozen forests," the gulags where Mennonite exiles chopped wood during the Stalinist era. But those forests are still off-limits, and Klassen's quest finally leads to an ancient tree that "we once owned." Here mourning finds comfort in nature as human arms embrace tree limbs, and the speaker realizes that this tree's roots "loved the same rivers" that her ancestors loved—the Dnieper River. This leads her to another river, the Limmat in Zurich, Switzerland, where Felix Manz was drowned in 1527. Mennonites trace their beginnings to Manz, the first Anabaptist martyr, so he represents the inception of new life in this poem. His ecstatic, wet martyrdom becomes as a metaphor for "the whole bloody way" of birth. Water is the elemental source of transformation in this myth of origins, which actually follows orthodox Christian symbolism and understandings. The place of death is a place of birth; the place of sacrificial remembrance is the place of re-vision.

LAST THOUGHTS

Since antiquity, a connection between memory and imagination has been clear: Mnemosyne, the Greek goddess of memory, is also the mother of the Muses. In recent years, scientific and theoretical studies increasingly confirm that remembrance is a made thing, built and shaped by present understandings and desires. Poems spring from memories lodged in objects, gestures, figures of speech, sensations—all things tending toward the particular. History, by contrast, carefully traces through time relationships, progressions, and broad narratives tending toward the general. As poet Robert Penn Warren put it, poetry is the little myth; history is the big myth. In current poetry by women from Mennonite backgrounds, these myths meet and mingle. Indian-born author Salman Rushdie has observed from his temporary home in England that for all of us the past is a lost homeland. The displaced writer who imagines that land views it through "broken mirrors" that are especially charged with feelings of longing, anger, and regret. Yet precisely because they are remains, he argues, these fragments may offer insights more valuable than the view from close up.[14] Elsewhere Rushdie dismisses his mother's claim that his stories are inaccurate: "My bad memory—what my mother would call a forgettery—is probably just as well. I remember what matters."[15]

What matters for women of Mennonite backgrounds, at least in some of their first poems? *Writing Like a Woman,* the title of one of Alicia Ostriker's other critical works, prompts me to guess that "writing like a Mennonite" means being obsessed with the past. At the same time, I have grown increasingly suspicious of the tendencies Ostriker assigns to women's work. It could reasonably be argued that the writing of Mennonite males is also motivated by those purposes. With our emphasis on pacifism and peacemaking, couldn't all Mennonites be seen as a people who strive to break boundaries and dissolve polarities? Rooted as we are in an ethic of community, wouldn't our ideal aesthetic be a communal transaction? This is not to suggest that gender does not figure strongly in the construction of Mennonite women's writing; I mean only that the nexus of gender and culture is complex. It is impossible to see how these factors independently inspire artistic expression. For years I understood my primary identity to be Mennonite and only later came to consider the profound ways gender has shaped my life and writing. A few years ago I was surprised to learn that *Sleeping Preacher,* which I regarded as a "Mennonite book," was regarded by many as a "woman's book."

Both are true. Which, of course, is the lesson I must learn from the snapshots of a teenaged Aunt Toot. She may not be able to tell it as clearly or "plain" as I do, but that does not mean she has not hoarded contradictory questions and desires as secretly as she hoarded that gold ring all those years. It is now my pleasure to wear Sara's ring in public again, as it is my privilege to try to write meaning from memories and objects. After thirteen lucky years in New York City, I moved to an older house in central Pennsylvania. While working on this essay one spring, I cleaned out some planters that had been left in the basement by previous owners. Knocking soil from the clay pots, I came across several mysterious tubers, which I stuck in the side yard on a lark. After a soaking rain and some warm days, bright green swirls appeared in the earth, and by August my suspicion was confirmed. Scarlet cannas, just outside the kitchen door.

NOTES

I am grateful to Di Brandt, Sheri Hostetler, Jean Janzen, and Sarah Klassen for their willingness to read their own work at the "Quiet in the Land?" conference and for their permission to use for this chapter written versions of statements they presented during a panel discussion at the conference. The poems reprinted here by permission are drawn from the authors' first books. These collections include Brandt, *Questions I Asked My Mother* (Winnipeg, Man.: Turnstone Press, 1987); Janzen, *Words for the Silence* (Fresno, Calif.: Center for Mennonite Brethren Studies, 1984; reprinted by permission from *Three Mennonite Poets* © Good Books, 1986. All rights reserved); Kasdorf, *Sleeping Preacher* (Pittsburgh: University of Pittsburgh Press, 1992); and Klassen, *Journey to Yalta* (Winnipeg, Man.: Turnstone Press, 1988). Sheri Hostetler's poems have appeared in magazines but are not yet collected in a single volume. I regret that the scope of this project made it impossible to include poems by Juanita Brunk, Raylene Hinz-Penner, Audrey Poetker, Shari Wagner, Cynthia Yoder, and others whose work is also informed by Mennonite experience.

1. Elsewhere in this collection, plain dress as a means of resisting cultural assimilation and maintaining social order is discussed in the introduction and in the chapter by Kimberly D. Schmidt and further explored in a contemporary Pennsylvania setting by Beth E. Graybill.

2. Laura H. Weaver discusses this adage in her reflection on an academic career and its relation to wearing a head covering, "Beyond Cap and No Cap: Reentry into Life and Scholarship," in *The Road Retaken: Women Reenter the Academy,* ed. Irene Thompson and Audrey Roberts (New York: Modern Language Association, 1985), 48.

3. The history of these divisions is traced in S. Duane Kauffman, *Mifflin County Amish and Mennonite Story, 1791–1991* (Belleville, Pa.: Mifflin County Mennonite Historical Society, 1991). A chart of concentric circles concisely representing the degree of cultural assimilation for each group along with a brief narrative of their history also appears in John A. Hostetler's *Amish Society*, 4th ed. (Baltimore: Johns Hopkins University Press, 1993), 290–99. Paton Yoder attributes the major nineteenth-century schism that established the Old Order—and prefigured some later congregational divisions—to community stresses caused by disputes about how to respond to innovations of the Industrial Revolution and other aspects of modern life. See Paton Yoder, *Tradition and Transition: Amish Mennonites and Old Order Amish, 1800–1900* (Scottdale, Pa.: Herald Press, 1991).

4. See Alicia Suskin Ostriker, *Stealing the Language: The Emergence of Women's Poetry in America* (Boston: Beacon Press, 1986). In a general way I am indebted to Ostriker's study, since it supported many of my hunches about the sources and intentions of contemporary Mennonite women's poetry and offered a lens through which to view this work.

5. John Ruth has argued that the shift from German dialect to English curtailed the transmission of identity-forming oral stories among Pennsylvania Mennonites during the past century and he passionately pleaded for the creation of a Mennonite literary tradition to serve this function. See *Mennonite Identity and Literary Art* (Scottdale, Pa.: Herald Press, 1978), 39.

6. See Adrienne Rich, "When We Dead Awaken: Writing as Re-vision," in *Adrienne Rich's Poetry*, ed. Barbara Charlesworth Gelpi and Albert Gelpi (New York: Norton, 1975), 90.

7. A revision of the statement of Mennonite belief, "Confession of Faith in a Mennonite Perspective," adopted at the 1995 General Assembly of the Mennonite Church, reflects official changes in this position.

8. Alice Walker, "In Search of Our Mothers' Gardens," in her *In Search of Our Mothers' Gardens: Womanist Prose* (New York: Harcourt Brace, 1983), 240.

9. See Hildi Froese Tiessen, Introduction to "Mennonite(s) Writing in Canada," *New Quarterly* 10 (spring–summer 1990): 12.

10. An adaptation of this panel presentation titled "Because Because Because" is included in Brandt's new collection of essays reflecting on ethnicity, gender, and poetics. See *Dancing Naked: Narrative Strategies for Writing across Centuries* (Stratford, Ont.: Mercury Press, 1996).

11. For a reading of these poems with a slightly different emphasis see Al

Reimer, *Mennonite Literary Voices Past and Present* (North Newton, Kans.: Bethel College, 1994), 43–44.

12. Ostriker, 213.

13. Canadian Audrey Poetker-Thiessen devoted nearly all of her most recent collection to a consideration of this subject; see *Standing All the Night Through* (Winnipeg, Man.: Turnstone Press, 1995). References to Anabaptist martyrdom also appear in my work and that of Jean Janzen, Sarah Klassen, and others. Di Brandt associates a visceral connection to Anabaptist suffering and sacrifice with domestic violence and the subordination of women in some contemporary Mennonite communities. See "Pornography and Silence and Mennonites and Women," in *Dancing Naked*, 50. Critic and imaginative writer Maggie Redekop has also noted an affinity between the current wave of Mennonite writers and the Reformation martyrs, since both groups boldly challenge common religions conceptions (quoted in Hildi Froese Tiessen's introduction to a new "Mennonite Writing," *Prairie Fire* 2 (summer 1990): 8.

14. Salman Rushdie, *Imaginary Homelands* (New York: Penguin, 1992), 11–12.

15. Salman Rushdie, *The Wizard of Oz* (London: British Film Institute, 1992), 9.

"She May Be Amish Now, but She Won't Be Amish Long"

ANABAPTIST WOMEN

AND ANTIMODERNISM

Jane Marie Pederson

Nonconformity to the world is one of the core tropes of Mennonite history. But resistance to "worldliness" has fallen unequally on men and women. Pederson relates the Mennonite experience to the general clash of traditional communities with modernity and postmodernity and discovers that female subordination is one of the few locations of antimodernity that remain active.

At the conference "The Quiet in the Land? Women of Anabaptist Traditions in Historical Perspective," a woman in the audience of a session on Old Order Amish dress related the following experience. As a resident in a community that included a notable Amish presence, she frequently encountered Amish women. After briefly observing one local young woman, she commented to her companions, "She is Amish, isn't she?" All agreed, noting the clearly identifiable cap and dress design. But something in her demeanor and in the way she moved prompted a prediction: "Well, she may be Amish now, but she won't be Amish long." Indeed, a short time thereafter the young woman married a distinctly non-Amish man, the owner of a local pizza parlor.[1]

This account hints at the complex past and present of women rooted in American Anabaptist traditions. Though we do not know the context of her choices or her relationship to her family and community, this young woman conspicuously resisted and rejected her culture's expectations and definitions of womanhood and made a choice to transform her own life. Other women struggle to remain within the cultural and religious boundaries of their communities. In myriad ways, women from the American Anabaptist traditions encapsulate in their lives and thought two centuries of transformation. Because Anabaptists, especially the Old Order Amish, self-consciously chose to resist many of the cultural and economic changes of the dominant society, they now stand on unique ground. In a single generation these women sometimes move from a premodern social order not unlike that described by Laurel Thatcher Ulrich in *A Midwife's Tale: The Life of Martha Ballard Based on Her Diary, 1785–1812* to the postmodern context of an urban woman.[2] Recent scholarship on Anabaptist women raises important questions that tangle with the complexities of religious ideology, gender constructions, and modernity.

ANTIMODERNISM

A definitive theme in the history and identity of Anabaptists is resistance to "worldliness" and its progeny—modernity. Self-chosen and determined "outsiders," originally these pious German sectarians came to the United States with the conservative cause of creating religious communities that would guard a traditional way of life from the teeming temptations and corruption of the world. At the heart of their culture was a religious community relying on an agrarian economic base.

The essentials of Anabaptist identity stressed community, family, and separation from a "worldly society." Anabaptist resistance has taken many forms, has changed over time, and has generated a host of schisms. Today Anabaptists include a broad range of theological and lifestyle positions that define their resistance to dominant cultural trends and act as

Old Order Mennonite girls in Lancaster County bicycling home from Sunday morning worship services. (Photograph courtesy of Dennis L. Hughes.)

markers of group and individual identity. For over a century, American Anabaptists of one persuasion or another have chosen to resist almost every major intellectual and cultural trend of the dominant society. The locale of most sustained resistance to "worldliness" or modernity centered on revitalizing and sustaining traditional communities' centers of power: church, family, rural economy, and community.[3]

Discomfort with the modern world is hardly unique to Anabaptists. Cultural historian T. Jackson Lears's archaeology of elite antimodernists in *No Place of Grace: Antimodernism and the Transformation of American Culture, 1880–1920* suggests the historical conjuncture of their concerns with those of German American Anabaptists. As Lears noted, "Along with scientific and technological advances, modernizers have always brought cultural strain, moral confusion, and anomie."[4] Antimodernists' anxiety reflected the fear that the modern gods of science and technology dissolved the structure of meaning and morality of religious traditions, that individualism threatened cooperative collective traditions, and that industrial production and consumerism undermined earlier craft traditions, the work ethic, and human authenticity.

Underlying the alienation of the iron cage of modernity is the ever expansive process of bureaucratic "rationalization": "the systematic organization of economic life for maximum productivity and of individual life for maximum personal achievement; the drive for efficient control of nature under the banner of improving human welfare; the reduction of the world to a disenchanted object to be manipulated by rational technique." Both social organizations and the human psyche are subject to progressive penetration by the rationalization of human existence.[5]

Lears's analysis of the antimodernist impulse is useful when considering the Anabaptist response. It will not suffice to simply dismiss protest as "backward looking." Antimodernists contended with serious issues, which haunt us today. Lears vividly explained his own interest in antimodernists: "I shared their discontent with modern culture: its crackpot obsession with efficiency, its humanist hubris, its complacent creed of progress. . . . I concluded that the most powerful critics of capitalism have often looked backward rather than forward, directing their fire at the bureaucratic 'rationality' common to corporate systems, indicting capitalist progress for its corrosive impact on family, craft, community, or faith."[6] Defending family, craft, community, and faith from the acids of modernity has been precisely the Anabaptist agenda. At its most radical, Anabaptist antimodernism challenged the essentials of industrial capitalism, including economic injustice, a complacent confidence in progress and technology, the secularization of knowledge, and the commodification of nature and self.[7]

To an outsider, Anabaptist antimodernism inspires a messy mix of ambivalence and admiration. Like other antimodernists, Anabaptists looked to their past for guidance, though elite resistance to modernity pales in comparison with that of some Anabaptist religious communities. Unapologetic agrarians, they looked to the land as a means of sustaining a godly way of life. Today some still rely exclusively on horsepower and human skills for household and market production. One cannot but admire the beautiful quilts, designed and hand-stitched by women, and the communal and craft traditions that make barn raising and quilting bees a reality. As such, their culture of protest potentially avoided many of the excesses of modernity—individualism preoccupied with self-fulfillment that rots into narcissism, gluttonous consumerism, a rapacious capitalism, and technologies that are creating an ecological and human nightmare.[8]

Anabaptists often view with skepticism faith in material progress through new technologies. Among some Old Order adherents, many twentieth-century technologies remain suspect, as is indicated by the persistence of the Amish reliance on horses and their distinctive plain black buggies for transport. While liberal ideology promoted science as the source of knowledge, Anabaptists remained deeply committed to nonsecular, religious ways of knowing.[9] Intellectually, religion and theology grounded their historical stance. Unlike nineteenth-century liberals, they were not inclined to equate material improvements and physical and emotional comfort with moral progress. As corporate capitalism dominated an urban industrial economy, many Anabaptists remained committed to life on the land in rural communities characterized by community cooperation and interdependence. Despite their rejection of modern mechanization and technology, the Amish and Mennonites historically have been skilled and successful farmers. However, the commitment to agriculture as a profit-making endeavor was subordinated to farming as a basis of family and community and as a way of holding the world at bay.[10]

Lears has argued that for antimodernists "commitments outside the self . . . [were] their key resource for resistance." Such commitments have long typified Anabaptists. Unlike the modern self, represented by the autonomous individual, the hubristic self-made man—a lord of creation—whose only moral master was the self, Anabaptists grounded their identities in commitments beyond the self. They elevated self-denial and submission as moral principles and called for subordination to God, family, and community. This vision of individual subordination to the public good found support in their religion, community, and family organization.[11]

Whereas militarism and jingoism represented a common response to the modern male's crisis of meaning, Anabaptists often clung tenaciously to traditions of pacifism. During all the wars of this century, a portion of Anabaptists responded as conscientious objectors.[12] While the therapeutic ethos and a leisure culture took shape, Anabaptist women and men elevated the work ethic grounded in Protestant ethos and German culture. Always to be "doing something" useful is a firmly entrenched cultural maxim for both women and men.[13] Conspicuous consumption and conspicuous display were aggressively rejected in favor of "plain dress," modesty, and humility.[14] Nineteenth-century bourgeois culture divided the world into separate spheres for men and women and cultivated a domestic ideology to rationalize both market capitalism and gender hierarchy. Anabaptists who remained on the land, such as the Mennonites and Old Order Amish, continued the partnership relations typical of family farm organization. While corporate America placed the business of the world in the hands of men, Mennonite farm communities persisted in dividing their estates equally between daughters and sons, which notably empowered women within the rural household.[15]

Whatever the original theology and cultural stance, today Anabaptists are highly diverse. As individuals, families, communities, and churches they are constantly adapting and changing. Like other rural Americans since World War II, they have been less able to rely on an agrarian economic base and have been buffeted by the same cultural and economic pressures. In this context accommodation has occurred on various levels. Some groups like the Mennonites selectively adapted and adopted new technologies. Moving into urban occupational environments, some called for more "progressive" attitudes. Such adjustments triggered debates, division, and church schisms. Many would ultimately abandon ethnic and religious norms and be excommunicated, but others successfully negotiated change. By World War II, pacifist traditions had begun to weaken.[16]

ANTIMODERNISM AND GENDER

Interwoven with the story of resistance and accommodation to modernity is the discourse on gender. Several questions come to mind: What has the protest against "worldliness" meant for women? How have women shaped Anabaptist antimodernist protest, attitudes, and culture? What have been their choices, actions, ideas, and options? Any discussion of premodern culture raises the specter of historical patriarchy. Did the "worldliness" of the modern world loosen the bonds for women, or did it contrive a gendered gilded cage? According to Steven D. Reschly, despite a long history of social radicalism, Anabaptists did nothing to challenge family patriarchy; within the Amish communities affirming paternal authority was a "virtually instinctive" response to social crisis among male leaders.[17] The ideal of women's submission and subordination is uniformly recognized as central to the gender constructions of Anabaptists.

Nevertheless historical constructions and assumptions about patriarchy and modernity are complex. Research by linguists and historians studying Amish and Mennonites developed a provocative thesis. Among the Amish, such as the Beachy Amish, who embrace "higher church" or "liberal" traditions and modern technologies, women experienced a decline in equality and authority, losing their voice in the church and in economic decisions. For Anabaptists, gender roles are scripturally prescribed. However, scholars have found that the meanings of those scriptural definitions varied dramatically as new technologies and lifestyles were introduced.[18]

Subjection did not necessarily mean subordination in a world of traditional production on the farms of Old Order Amish. In the household economy, where domestic work meant primarily productive work rather than consumerism, women may not have had access to formal power in important "public institutions" such as the church, but they nonetheless wielded a great deal of informal power in personal relations. In that context women shared responsibility for maintaining the local religious communities' *Ordnung*— prescriptions for dress, decorum, and behavior. Women organized kin and community life, and everyone placed a high valuation on their domestic craft tradition. Regard for women's skills and productive and reproductive labor meant the home provided the power base for their autonomy and identity. Men and women generally did different work, but partnership relations in the farming household created an equality of separate spheres. Women and men submitted themselves to the church *Ordnung*—but women were not notably submissive to their husbands. Old Order Amish upheld humility and subordination as appropriate values for both women and men. This analysis parallels the findings of Royden K. Loewen among Mennonite women on farms in Meade County, Kansas, in the 1940s and that of several historians of rural women. The unique demands and organization of work on farms often create relatively egalitarian relationships between women and men.[19]

On the other hand, the more modern or "liberal" the Amish become and the greater their acceptance of technology and urban work and lifestyles, the greater the gender inequality. Unlike the Old Order Amish,

Beachy Amish women were "submissive and subordinate." As men claimed more modern identities and work, they also embraced an evangelical and missionary spirit and a new stress on male "headship." Because "worldliness" had earlier been devalued, venturesome activities in the market and political arena did not command high esteem. Everything outside the local religious community was equated with evil and sinfulness. The more "liberal" increasingly saw "worldliness" as something that primarily women must be protected from. Women's voice and role in the construction and maintenance of the church *Ordnung* was muted. Other "liberal" Anabaptists appear to have evolved in similar ways. As men increasingly valued their contact with the world as evangelicals and in the marketplace, women were pressured to accept more restricted positions. A twentieth-century revival of "preservationist patriarchy" shaped the response to social change and crisis. Male dominance thus became a reality as women grew more dependent and were denied access to "worldly roles." Work outside the home for women threatened male identity and led men to intensify their demands and to need assurance of women's subordination.[20]

From the beginning industrial capitalism had the potential to break down the distinctions between women's and men's work and to strengthen women's bid for autonomy and for economic independence from husbands and fathers. Religious and secular ideologies have played a powerful role in sustaining gender hierarchy as its economic base was progressively undermined. A high priority for many confronting the transitions that some Anabaptists face today has been to prevent women from claiming the status of autonomous individuals, "masterless women" subject to no moral authority but the self, men's equals in the pursuit of self-fulfillment. Women and men in the Anabaptist and other traditions were and are often profoundly disturbed at the idea of women's laying claim to the modern male ethic of individualism.

Religious groups and women's culture more broadly converge in their resistance to and discomfort with possessive individualism's consequences for human relationships. The nineteenth-century bourgeois solution to this threat was the ideology and culture of domesticity. As Americans left behind the household economies of rural America and as men pursued nonfarming occupations in the industrial city, they abandoned earlier religious and republican ideals to women and the home, thereby freeing themselves for the competitive and acquisitive demands of the marketplace. Nineteenth-century Protestantism negotiated the same deal that the Anabaptists have made and more broadly the same one the religious right has proposed for the present. The challenges of the transition from an agrarian life to an urban market-driven economy prompted many men to a "lord of creation" mentality, or "preservation-ist patriarchy" as Reschly has described it. Male headship becomes a different reality as women become more economically dependent and are denied access to "worldly" roles.[21]

Margaret C. Reynolds detailed the ideological construction of women's status decline among the relatively "liberal" Old Order River Brethren, providing a paradigm of the changes. As one woman described their orientation, "Oh, we're modern; we just dress plain." These Pennsylvania German farmers adopted modern technologies and lifestyles rejected by many Old Order Mennonites or Amish, but they articulate an explicit ideology of fundamentalist gender control. The only distinct markers of group identity and distance from the dominant culture are rooted in a highly self-conscious commitment to maintaining a traditional gender asymmetry. Unlike men, women must wear folk dress and cooperate in rituals of submission. Folk dress and ritual set cultural boundaries and establish identity and distinguish this group from the mainstream. Only the rejection of contemporary fashions for women sets them apart. For this group, resistance to modernity has narrowed to gender prescriptions for women. Scripturally based gender inequality and women's subjection are all that remain of their antimodernism.[22]

No doubt, as the basis of resistance to the dominant culture was pared down simply to gender prescription, preoccupation with headship and women's subjection intensified. Religious leaders become painfully conscious that the meaning of manhood, and headship depended on women's compliance. If women do not obey, men cannot be heads—their entire cultural and religious identity depends on women's submission. The focus of the church *Ordnung* narrowed to the regulation of women's dress and other forms of self-expression. This preoccupation with dress codes including prayer coverings for the hair, aprons, and long skirts bespoke men's anxiety about sexuality and their own compromised relationship to modernity. A woman's refusal to accept plain dress symbolized for them the refusal of women's subjection to men and the church. Apparently the only aspect of modernity that continues to terrify Old Order River Brethren is the threat it represents to gender hierarchy.[23]

Today the male religious leadership of many "liberal" Anabaptists articulates a variation on the ideology of domesticity that typified bourgeois culture in the nineteenth century. Both ideologies insist that women are responsible for the moral and cultural survival of the group. Women's domesticity, piety, and submission to men are the foundation of moral order and male identity. Women's silence and self-denial are the basis of their virtue. Women's sexuality and women's voice must be denied in the interest of the traditional social order. As men entered the marketplace, they insisted that women bear the burden of the contradictory demands of tradition.

It is apparent that the Anabaptists' stress on women's subordination has ceased to represent resistance and really become a fairly ordinary form of accommodation to the dominant culture. The hard edge of meaningful protest against the modern social system has collapsed. One of most common forms of accommodation to the modern crisis of meaning and values was and is an aggressive rearguard effort to sustain some vision of "traditional" gender prescriptions that in fact often imposes new restrictions and demands on women. Historians of women and of antimodernism note that by romanticizing domesticity the nineteenth-century bourgeoisie legitimized modern market capitalism and contributed to the creation of American consumer culture. Contemporary Anabaptists' domestic ideals similarly may represent a strategy of evasion and compromise.[24]

Ironically, even though resistance to the modern has been the hallmark of Anabaptist traditions, historians long were hard pressed to acknowledge resistance by women to patriarchy within the Anabaptists' world. Scholars who study Anabaptist culture and history often focus on resistance to the outside world but neglect resistance to patriarchy within. Historians of women are well aware that family and community interests are fraught with divisions and multiple positions of power and resistance. Women may share the deep commitment to community and family and to resisting the dominant culture at the same time that they resist patriarchal power.

A key issue is the extent of women's agency in the articulation of Anabaptist gender structures. Some scholars suggest that women in agrarian communities negotiated relations of partnership and mutuality that empowered them. But as is true everywhere, gender is an arena of continuous contestation. Loewen identified a dialectic of gender among the Mennonites in Kansas in which "each group of women found new ways to assert lives that they found autonomous and meaningful within societies that continued to produce new expressions of male dominance."[25] Among Quaker women of the eighteenth and nineteenth centuries silence served as a potent strategy for self-definition, leading at least some women into public speaking and activism. Self-denial, submission, "stripping away the self," paradoxically nurtured autonomy and independence from restrictive gender codes. Nineteenth-century Mennonite women publicly protested their dissatisfaction by refusing to participate in community religious rituals of Communion.[26]

Some scholars conclude that conformity and compliance came easier than resistance. Reynolds found a willing collaboration by women in support of gender hierarchy in the recently created ritual of breadmaking. Presumably women collaborate in exchange for security, community, and cultural identity. Compliance yields the security of conformity. As collaborators in gender hierarchy, women supported an ideology of submission and domesticity. Reynolds documented a distinct breadmaking ritual that symbolically and publicly identified the importance of such "female submission" and domesticity. The recent creation of this ritual affirmed their orthodoxy, their ethnic identity, and their protest against modernity and feminism. She notes, "It is significant that men . . . sustain a religious ritual exclusively for women" and that "men give women considerable religious authority. . . . Women's silence during ritual is an accepted religious and social restraint, a trade-off for women's religious authority granted in breadmaking."[27] This raises the question of women's agency in the creation and continuation of such rituals. The breadmaking ritual is enacted today as a symbol of women's submission. Women are silenced, while only the male leadership articulates spiritual and public meanings.

Though words, rituals, and other symbols change meaning across time, the emphasis on women's submission and the invention of new rituals to affirm their subordinate status may be a transitional reflection of the present preoccupation with a fragile male "headship." Breadmaking bespeaks women's traditional work, skills, and status but is ritualized at a historical moment when baking bread is no longer an important activity for women. Women and men obviously invested different meanings in words and ritual. Although Reynolds concluded that this ritual enhances women's status, one wonders if a ritual of submission can ever really elevate. Rituals of submission could also humiliate—depending on one's viewpoint.[28]

CAPS, CAPE DRESSES, COLLABORATION, AND RESISTANCE

Research on Anabaptist women raises one of the conundrums of women's history. Why do women become collaborators in patriarchy? Researchers have often noted that woman informally but actively police each other to maintain the *Ordnung*. To what extent did women cooperate in shaping local standards that men formalized in the church *Ordnung*, and to what extent does the *Ordnung* reflect the concerns of men? The distinctive dress assigned to women is a particularly rich issue related to this question.

Dress raises questions of women's agency in relation to both internal patriarchy and the dominant culture. Among the more "liberal," only women's dress and prayer caps set them apart from the mainstream. It is curious that Old Order River Brethren express two contradictory views of women's plain dress: that it is a symbol of submission and that it is liberating for women. Perhaps the former view typifies the male religious leadership, but women themselves may construct their own interpretation.[29]

Although many historians of this topic agree that Anabaptist men "regulate women's expressive culture," the important question is, To what extent has women's agency shaped ideals and standards of plain dress? According to several scholars, plain dress represented many, often contradictory ideas, including an "antifashion" and antimodern statement of opposition, a sacred symbol, markers of gender and ethnic identity, and a form of self- and class discipline.[30] Linda Boynton Arthur found that women monitored each other's dress based on status and class. High-status women could criticize low-status women, and claiming the role of critic could enhance status. Violations of dress codes could lead to "church trouble," most seriously excommunication by male religious authorities. That male power was invoked only after women's networks failed demonstrates women's construction of social hierarchy within women's culture. Some women believe that plain dress shifted the focus to the "inner person" and allows the River Brethren to transcend the worldly emphasis on physical appearances. For some women dress is a way of "knowing their own" and of sustaining a valued and distinctive female culture.[31]

Though Old Order women often offer an "unquestioning defense" of dress codes as a standard of group membership, refusal to conform readily signifies their discontent. Whether in rebellion or in conformity, women seemingly have been actively engaged in constructing their own cultural identity. Beth Graybill and Pamela Klassen conclude that the prayer coverings of Mennonite women acted as a banner of women's religiosity, though they do not indicate how its meaning may have changed over time. A symbol of status at one historical moment can become a symbol of oppression at another. Linda Boynton Arthur interviewed a woman for whom the idea of a head covering brought nightmares years after her expulsion from the church. For such a woman, exclusion from the church and the rejection of traditional garb represented freedom.[32]

Plain dress raises another question: Is it an indication of "men limiting women's expressive culture," or is it an effort by some women to protect craft traditions they value?[33] For many women, crafts such as sewing and quilting are highly meaningful forms of self-expression. Artistic and craft traditions stimulate creativity within defined boundaries. While much of the drudgery of textile production has been relinquished to the market, the more creative and communal aspects of it, such as quilting, are preserved. Plain dress and resistance to consumerism are linked to sustaining a distinct expressive culture. While preventing the destruction of a craft tradition, these women also aggressively rejected the stigmatizing of the homemade that became common in consumer-oriented post–World War II America. Kimberly D. Schmidt's analysis of a schism among Amish Mennonites during the Great Depression illustrates that when women really want changes in the dress codes, change occurs.[34]

For many Anabaptists, modern fashions symbolize godlessness and the perversion of God's natural order. It is often hard not to sympathize with such a point of view. Frustration with and ambivalence toward the fashion and cosmetic industries runs deep, but real resistance is exceptional. Ideologues of all kinds, from the Puritans of the seventeenth century to many Marxists and feminists in the twentieth, have heralded the virtues of plain dress and decried the corruption of consumerism, but Old Order women are among the very few who have achieved sustained and meaningful resistance to the beauty industry. This is not trivial. As any feminist or fashion editor can tell you, dress has highly symbolic and often political purposes. Fashion is a surprisingly sensitive barometer of shifting meanings of gender. Naomi Wolf's *The Beauty Myth* and Susan Faludi's *Backlash* are only two recent critiques of the nasty politics and crippling consequences of the commodification of women through the fashion industry.[35]

Although the engendering of consumerism is a topic of debate, it is not difficult to think of reasons why plain dress is a wonderful idea.[36] Modest dress does represent a serious protest against modern consumer culture and in particular the commodification of women's bodies. An advantage noted by women themselves is that plain dress promises security and freedom from sexual objectification and discourages sexual harassment.[37] Though women in bourgeois culture are encouraged to think of consumerism as self-expression, the choice of plain dress clearly defies this logic. Success in subverting the manipulations of the fashion and cosmetics industry is no small achievement. Any parent returning from a trip to the mall with a junior-high daughter can appreciate the profundity and economy of this protest in the face of entrepreneurial promotion of consumerism and precocious sexuality among adolescents.[38]

The dress codes and head coverings are a late nineteenth- and early twentieth-century development. They appear almost precisely at the historical moment when advertising and the widespread marketing of ready-made clothes for women began—at the time when fashion was mass marketed rather than being the expression of an elite leisure culture. Prayer coverings for women were mandated at about the same time the beauty shop became a ubiquitous neighborhood institution. When Anabaptist women chose to "hide their glory," most women were encouraged to expose theirs in ever more costly and provocative ways. One could argue that Anabaptist women made choices parallel to men's. In Western culture as a whole, nineteenth-century men embraced a fairly uniform code of dress—the dark suit and tie. Like the suit, dress codes created uniform styles that allowed some creativity, but within very clear constraints.[39] Like men in suits, Anabaptist women do not become objects of conspicuous display and conspicuous consumption. This "inconspicuous consumption" is a bold stand, providing women with a clear basis of identity and expressing meaningful resistance to the dominant culture's consumerism and gender ideals.[40]

Male leaders of the Old Order River Brethren, like the nineteenth-century ideologues of domesticity, held women responsible for restraining male sexuality. "Big hair," as Dolly Parton and many Anabaptists agree, is a symbol of sexuality. Women's prayer caps and tightly bunned hair reflect the expectation that they should "hide their glory" and not provoke the passions of men. Lears noted, "Men who worshipped at the domestic shrine created an image of serene womanhood, free from the erotic and aggressive impulses they distrusted in themselves."[41] However, nineteenth-century women and twentieth-century Anabaptist women had powerful reasons for discouraging the "erotic and aggressive impulses" of men. In both contexts women were prohibited from using birth control or had very limited access to it. In such a situation, exciting male passion may have been the last thing a mature woman wanted to do. Twentieth-century Old Order women push the limits of human fertility—among the Amish the average woman has seven children. These extraordinarily high fertility rates mirror those of American women at the beginning of the nineteenth century, when women were averaging almost eight children.[42]

One wonders if prayer coverings were first required owing to men's fear of women's sexuality or because of women's desire to restrain male sexuality and limit fertility. Or were both concerns significant? In rural communities where the birthrate often remained at eighteenth-century levels and where religious prohibitions against birth control prevailed, women may have had powerful reasons for "hiding their glory." In this context plain dress and prayer caps may represent resistance to the dominant culture and may be a means of self-protection within their community as well. Klassen noted that Mennonite men sometimes need to be persuaded that they should desire covered women.[43]

Hair and clothes are often associated with women's freedom of expression and identity, but freedom can mean different things in different times and places. In the Victorian era of gilded excess, plain dress could well have been a religious statement protesting worldliness. In addition, it may have symbolized genuine freedom when many women wore corsets. In an era of jeans, T-shirts, and spandex, plain dress may seem rather different. It could also indicate a class issue, a creative inclination to make a virtue of necessity: rural women have long prided themselves on "making do," disdaining frivolous consumption and stretching limited resources during hard times.[44] Limiting consumption by home production remains a priority and a source of pride to Old Order women.[45] Thus what plain dress looks and feels like varies with the historical context and the individual.

Antimodernism and plain dress have set Anabaptist women apart from the mainstream, but how does their story fit into the larger American experience? There is much that is unique, and there is much that they share with others. In many ways they encounter the same dilemmas faced by other American women. As Julia Kasdorf noted about her work, "I was surprised to learn that [what] . . . I regarded as a 'Mennonite book,' was regarded by many as a 'woman's book.'"[46] Family, community, religion, and work arrangements reflect a common rural and German American ethnic experience. In immigrant communities, antimodernism, preserving ethnic and gender identities, and resistance to assimilation are inextricably interwoven. For many rural Americans, modernity was the "resisted revolution." Many immigrant and ethnic groups viewed with suspicion the dominant culture's gender system.[47]

Nonetheless, in the United States seemingly marginal groups have a subversive talent for shaping the mainstream on the right and left of the political spectrum. The analysis of Anabaptist women's experience does offer insight into the historical and contemporary politics of gender. It suggests the social and cultural origins of the gender ideologies of the new religious right and its family values stance. The church and family, once the basis of community building and the locale of separation from and resistance to the worldly, function in a quite different way as those communities lose their agrarian base. As cultural localism and separation structurally break down, an evangelical response follows: an aggressive effort to carry "the essence" or core values and ideals of their ethnic and religious culture into the mainstream. For the "modern" Anabaptists, "the essence" of life is grounded in their gender system. The evangelical effort eases the inevitable sense of loss of control, of ambivalence, and of the conflict of values.[48]

The *Ordnung,* which concentrates on control of women, no longer represents resistance but acts as a vehicle for accommodation to the mainstream culture. It promises the salvation of culture, community, and mas-

culine identities through self-denial by women. It tolerates possessive individualism for men but draws the line by refusing to extend the new
ethos to women. Not only do Anabaptists abandon meaningful protest,
but this pale ghost of protest facilitates the contemporary unholy alliance
of the religious right with corporate America. In the politics of the marketplace, economic man must abandon communal and religious ideals of
service, community, and self-denial. Although the gender constructs are
a reaction against secularization, they in fact permit accommodation to
secular cultural modes. Women's subordination allows accommodation to
modern structures of domination and disguises the compromises with a
postmodern world. The gender ideologies of contemporary Anabaptists
have much in common with the moral philosophers of the Gilded Age analyzed by T. Jackson Lears: "They were sincere moralists who were desperately trying to reconcile traditional Christian ethics with the corrosive
individualism of the expanding market economy." The domestic ideal became one of essential components of nineteenth-century liberals' legit-
imization of the "irresponsible accumulations of wealth and a corrosive
doctrine of possessive individualism."[49]

Perhaps modernization, like immigration, is a "theologizing experience," as Timothy L. Smith once suggested.[50] Like immigration, modern
bourgeois culture threatened belief systems, creating a disorienting sense
that "all that is solid melts into air, all that is sacred is profaned."[51] In a
context of crisis of meaning, a frantic effort to shore up masculine identity and male authority is common. But to say the least, women's subordination is a fragile base for identity and cultural salvation. Male identity
is held hostage to women's choosing or being coerced into silence and submission. This combination of ideas and circumstances often contributes to
family violence and the physical and emotional abuse of women. It is no
secret that the modern family has manufactured much mayhem. Historically, patriarchy has relied on varying levels of coercion, from denying
women access to resources and status to physical force.

What happens when a young girl or a wife resists, as surely many do?[52]
It is possible that the historical commitment to pacifism protected women
in Anabaptist communities from patriarchal excesses? Pacifism sometimes is associated with a commitment to nonviolence; therefore it is important to know the internal meaning of nonresistance and pacifism. Unfortunately, personal accounts by Anabaptist women expressed in poetry,

fiction, autobiography, and scholarly work suggest that the Anabaptists' capacity for psychic and physical violence and emotional coercion is as compelling as any. Although in Anabaptist men's relationship to the state pacifism is frequently a key principle, nonviolence in family and social relationships is not.[53]

This raises embarrassing questions about the real meanings of pacifism and manhood among Anabaptists. Although they proclaim their gender system as the source of their identity and resistance to modernity, have they not perhaps already succumbed to the egoistic individualism of modern culture, claiming the status not only of masterless men but also of unjust and self-absorbed lords of creation in relation to women? Pacifism is declining among Anabaptists, and this could be related to the changing gender system.[54]

For noncompliance, women and men face social and family ostracism, excommunication, and more. Religious, family, and community expectations can deny women voice, self, even life itself. Closed cultures, such as the Anabaptists often aspired to be, can marshal powerful strategies of emotional manipulation and both physical and emotional violence to maintain their *Ordnung*. To some extent Anabaptist women face the perils and vulnerabilities of all women, but they also wrestle with community and religious traditions that inspire deep commitment, passion, fear, and dependence.[55]

In a context of increased risks and responsibilities, to what extent will women be inclined to remain attached to transcendent values and nurture meaningful resistance? This raises questions about what, if any, may be the consequences of overloading women as the bearers of culture and morality. Will the self-sacrificing Anabaptist true woman give birth to a feminist daughter, as did the nineteenth-century true woman of the culture of domesticity? Loewen identified a "maternal feminism" among Mennonite women as early as the 1950s.[56] The contradictions of bourgeois culture and its ideology of domesticity nurtured among women a culture of protest, which articulated an incisive critique of the dominant culture. Women launched a reform drive, which gave birth to dozens of movements, from antislavery to the temperance crusade, ultimately helping to ignite the Civil War. Their movements helped lead to the creation of the welfare state in the 1930s. Among the voices of protest beginning to appear among Anabaptist women, could there be a Harriet Beecher

Stowe, a woman whose extravagant confidence in the worth of women and in her religious faith inspired *Uncle Tom's Cabin?* This brilliant polemic indicted both the "lords of the loom and the lords of the lash," the capitalist market mentality of the North and the slave owners of the South.[57]

One woman who aspires to scholarship and remains true to her faith asked a telling question: "How do I distinguish between the 'traditions of men' that would enslave me and the voice of God which frees me?"[58] When deeply religious women ask such questions, will a new radicalism not soon follow? That women create a culture and identity for themselves on the horns of the patriarchal dilemma, I do not doubt. It is possible a new woman's culture of protest could result? The poetry of Jean Janzen, Di Brandt, and Sheri Hostetler certainly suggests the possibility.[59] When confronted by crisis and unavoidable change, conservative Anabaptist traditions have creatively recast gender constructions to sustain male authority; but women have been equally creative in cultivating their own opportunities for self-definition, autonomy, and resistance. Anabaptist women, like women's culture as a whole, remain capable of and willing to make commitments essential to meaningful and sustained resistance and protest. If the postmodern Anabaptist woman nurtures a moral and religious authority capable of critiquing both her husband and American culture, then "she may be Amish now, but she won't be Amish long."

NOTES

1. This comment was made by an unidentified woman at the session titled "The Symbolism of Gendered Clothing," at the conference "The Quiet in the Land? Women of Anabaptist Traditions in Historical Perspective," Millersville, Pa., June 1995.

2. Laurel Thatcher Ulrich, *A Midwife's Tale: The Life of Martha Ballard Based on Her Diary, 1785–1812* (New York: Knopf, 1990).

3. Donald B. Kraybill, "The Amish Encounter with Modernity," in *The Amish Struggle with Modernity,* ed. Donald B. Kraybill and Marc A. Olshan (Hanover, N.H.: University Press of New England, 1994), 21–34; Royden K. Loewen, *Family, Church, and Market: A Mennonite Community in the Old and the New Worlds, 1850–1930* (Urbana: University of Illinois Press, 1993), 53–58; and Richard K. MacMaster, *Land, Piety, Peoplehood: The Establishment of Mennonite Communities in America, 1683–1790* (Scottdale, Pa.: Herald Press, 1985).

4. T. Jackson Lears, *No Place of Grace: Antimodernism and the Transformation of American Culture, 1880–1920* (New York: Pantheon, 1981), xix.

5. Ibid., 7.

6. Ibid., xx.

7. See Kraybill, "Amish Encounter with Modernity," 25–32; Loewen, *Family, Church, and Market*; Steven D. Reschly and Katherine Jellison, "Production Patterns, Consumption Strategies, and Gender Relations in Amish and Non-Amish Households in Lancaster County Pennsylvania, 1935–1936," *Agricultural History* 67 (spring 1993): 134–62; and Steven M. Nolt, *A History of the Amish* (Intercourse, Pa.: Good Books, 1992).

8. For a discussion of Amish resistance and accommodation to modern technologies and consumers, see Donald B. Kraybill, "Plotting Social Change across Four Affiliations," in *The Amish Struggle with Modernity*, ed. Donald B. Kraybill and Marc A. Olshan (Hanover, N.H.: University Press of New England, 1994), 53–74.

9. Limiting public schooling to the eighth grade and retaining control over the education of children has been a high priority among the Amish. For a discussion of Amish resistance to public education see Gertrude Enders Huntington, "Persistence and Change in Amish Education," in *The Amish Struggle with Modernity*, ed. Donald B. Kraybill and Marc A. Olshan (Hanover, N.H.: University Press of New England, 1994), 77–95.

10. Kraybill, "Plotting Social Change"; Reschly and Jellison, 138–39.

11. Lears, xx; for a discussion of Amish views, see Donald B. Kraybill, "Introduction: The Struggle to be Separate," in *The Amish Struggle with Modernity*, ed. Donald B. Kraybill and Marc A. Olshan (Hanover, N.H.: University Press of New England, 1994), 6–8.

12. Mary Jane Heisey, "They Also Served; Brethren in Christ, Women and Civilian Public Service," paper presented at "The Quiet in the Land? Women of Anabaptist Traditions in Historical Perspective," Millersville, Pa., June 1995; for a discussion of antimodernism and militarism see Lears, 97–139.

13. Laura Weaver, "Independence and Community in Mennonite Women's Work," paper presented at "The Quiet in the Land? Women of Anabaptist Traditions in Historical Perspective," Millersville, Pa., June 1995. On the therapeutic ethos, see Lears, 47–58, and Christopher Lasch, *Haven in a Heartless World: The Family Besieged* (New York: Basic Books, 1977).

14. Kraybill, "Amish Encounter with Modernity," 30; Margaret C. Reynolds, "Controlling Women, Preserving Orthodoxy: Gender Asymmetry as a Joint

Strategy for Keeping 'Order' in Old Order Culture," paper presented at "The Quiet in the Land? Women of Anabaptist Traditions in Historical Perspective," Millersville, Pa., June 1995.

15. Marc A. Olshan and Kimberly D. Schmidt, "Amish Women and the Feminist Conundrum," in *The Amish Struggle with Modernity*, ed. Donald B. Kraybill and Marc A. Olshan (Hanover, N.H.: University Press of New England, 1994), 221–23; Loewen, 219; Reschly and Jellison, 156–62; Karen M. Johnson-Weiner, "The Brethren and Their Sisters: The Role of Women in Old Order, Beachy Amish and Fellowship Churches," paper presented at "The Quiet in the Land? Women of Anabaptist Traditions in Historical Perspective," Millersville, Pa., June 1995.

For recent studies on rural gender relations see Mary Neth, *Preserving the Family Farm: Women, Community and the Foundations of Modern Agribusiness, 1900–1940* (Baltimore: Johns Hopkins University Press, 1995); Nancy Grey Osterud, *Bonds of Community: The Lives of Farm Women in Nineteenth-Century New York* (Ithaca: Cornell University Press, 1991); Katherine Jellison, *Entitled to Power: Farm Women and Technology, 1913–1963* (Chapel Hill: University of North Carolina Press, 1993); and Marilyn P. Watkins, *Rural Democracy: Family Farmers and Politics in Western Washington, 1890–1925* (Ithaca: Cornell University Press, 1995).

16. Donald B. Kraybill, "War against Progress: Coping with Social Change," in *The Amish Struggle with Modernity*, ed. Donald B. Kraybill and Marc A. Olshan (Hanover, N.H.: University Press of New England, 1994), 35–50; Kraybill, "Plotting Social Change"; Reynolds, "Controlling Women"; Royden K. Loewen, "Coffee Klatches and Household Hearth: Mennonite Farm Women of Kansas, Manitoba, and Belize in the 1950s," paper presented at "The Quiet in the Land? Women of Anabaptist Traditions in Historical Perspective," Millersville, Pa., June 1995.

17. See Steven D. Reschly's chapter in this volume.

18. See Johnson-Weiner. Other scholars have identified similar trends, though some indicate three positions or stages that include a final more "progressive" orientation in which a more egalitarian gender system resurfaces. See Reschly and Jellison, 160–62, and Loewen, "Coffee Klatches."

19. See Johnson-Wiener.

20. See Johnson-Wiener and also Reynolds, "Controlling Women."

21. The nineteenth-century ideology of domesticity has been addressed by numerous historians. See Lears, 12–19; Barbara Welter, "The Cult of True Wom-

anhood: 1820–1860," *American Quarterly* 18 (summer 1966): 151–74; Kathryn Kish Sklar, *Catharine Beecher: A Study in American Domesticity* (New Haven: Yale University Press, 1973); and Nancy F. Cott, *The Bonds of Womanhood: "Women's Sphere" in New England, 1780–1835* (New Haven: Yale University Press, 1977). For the best overview and synthesis of the literature domesticity see Glenna Matthews, *Just a Housewife: The Rise and Fall of Domesticity in America* (New York: Oxford University Press, 1987).

22. Reynolds, "Controlling Women."

23. Ibid.

24. Lears, 17.

25. Loewen, "Coffee Klatsch," 25.

26. See Barbara Bolz's and Steven D. Reschly's chapters in this volume.

27. Reynolds, "Controlling Women."

28. Ibid. For a recent analysis of the psychological costs of silencing and humiliation, see Patricia Evans, *The Verbally Abusive Relationship* (Holbrook, Mass.: Adams Media, 1996).

29. Evans; Kraybill, "War against Progress."

30. See Beth E. Graybill's and Kimberly D. Schmidt's chapters in this volume.

31. Ibid.; Linda Boynton Arthur, "Clothing Is a Window to the Soul: The Social Control of Women in a Holdeman Mennonite Community," *Journal of Mennonite Studies* 15 (1997): 11–30.

32. Reynolds, "Controlling Women"; Arthur; and Pamela Klassen, "Women's Heads: Coverings in Religious and Anthropological Perspective," paper presented at "The Quiet in the Land? Women of Anabaptist Traditions in Historical Perspective," Millersville, Pa., June 1995.

33. Reynolds, "Controlling Women."

34. Schmidt, this volume; that women's priorities determine the forms of accommodation is clearly revealed in adaptation of household technologies. Even the most conservative Amish, who reject everything from indoor plumbing to refrigerators and linoleum, nonetheless used washing machines, according to Kraybill, "Plotting Social Change," 63. For a discussion of devaluation of women's craft traditions see Matthews, 145–71; Jane Marie Pederson, *Between Memory and Reality: Family and Community in Rural Wisconsin, 1870–1970* (Madison: University of Wisconsin Press, 1992), 177–85.

35. Naomi Wolf, *The Beauty Myth: How Images of Beauty Are Used against Women* (New York: Morrow, 1991), and Susan Faludi, *Backlash: The Undeclared War against American Women* (New York: Crown, 1991).

36. For a review of recent historical literature on gender and consumerism see Mary Louise Roberts, "Review Essay: Gender, Consumption, and Commodity Culture," *American Historical Review* 103 (June 1998): 817–44.

37. Graybill, this volume; Reynolds, "Controlling Women."

38. For a history of adolescent sexuality see Joan Jacobs Brumberg, *The Body Project: An Intimate History of American Girls* (New York: Vintage Books, 1997).

39. See Julia Kasdorf's chapter in this volume. Kasdorf notes the Victorian dress of family photographs. According to Loewen, *Family, Church and Market*, 34, prescriptions for women's dress began to appear among Mennonites as early as 1846. For discussions of the beauty industry, see Lois Banner, *American Beauty* (Chicago: University of Chicago Press, 1983), and Kathy Peiss, "Making Faces: The Cosmetics Industry and the Cultural Construction of Gender, 1890–1930," *Genders* 7 (spring 1990); 143–69.

40. Roberts, 824.

41. Lears, 16.

42. See Diane Zimmerman Umble's chapter in this volume and also Reynolds, "Controlling Women." Attitudes toward sexuality have been examined by several historians, including Daniel Scott Smith, "Family Limitation, Sexual Control and Domestic Feminism in Victorian America," in *Clio's Consiousness Raised: New Perspectives on the History of Women*, ed. Mary Hartman and Lois W. Banner (New York: Harper and Row, 1974), 119–36, and John D'Emilio and Estelle B. Freedman, *Intimate Matters: A History of Sexuality in America* (New York: Harper and Row, 1988), 55–84.

43. Klassen.

44. Neth, 187–213.

45. Olshan and Schmidt, 221.

46. Kasdorf, this volume.

47. On German American ethnicity and gender, see Linda Schelbitzki Pickle, *Contented among Strangers: Rural German-Speaking Women and Their Families in the Nineteenth-Century Midwest* (Urbana: University of Illinois Press, 1996); Carol K. Coburn, *Life at Four Corners: Religion, Gender, and Education in a German-Lutheran Community, 1868–1945* (Lawrence: University of Kansas Press, 1992); and Walter D. Kamphoefner, *The Westfalians: From Germany to Missouri* (Princeton: Princeton University Press, 1987).

48. Gary Y. Okihiro, *Margins and Mainstreams: Asians in American History and Culture* (Seattle: University of Washington Press, 1994); Okihiro argues that "core values and ideals of the nation emanate not from the mainstream but from

the margins" (ix). Although he stresses the preservation of democratic ideals in marginal groups like blacks, Asian Americans, and Latino women, adding gender to the analysis complicates the discussions of democracy and equality.

49. Lears, 18–20.

50. Timothy L. Smith, "Religion and Ethnicity in America," *American Historical Review* 83 (1978): 1161.

51. Karl Marx as quoted by Lears, 41.

52. For an analysis of issues of family violence in Germany in the nineteenth century, where ideas of headship or *Herrschaft* prevailed, see Lynn Abrams, "Companionship and Conflict: The Negotiation of Marriage Relations in the Nineteenth Century," in *Gender Relations in German History: Power, Agency and Experience from the Sixteenth to the Twentieth Century,* ed. Lynn Abrams and Elizabeth Harvey (Durham, N.C.: Duke University Press, 1997), 101–20.

53. Kasdorf, this volume; Joel Hartman, "Traditional Authority vs. Right to Life Claims: A Case Study of Community Response to HIV/AIDS," paper presented at "The Quiet in the Land? Women of Anabaptist Traditions in Historical Perspective," Millersville, Pa., June 1995. The theme of physical and emotional abuse in Anabaptist families was revealed in "Prayers for Girls: A Meditation on Red and Blue," written and performed by Johnna Schmidt, and "Quietly Landed?" a musical and dramatic piece based on writings of Mennonite-background women, compiled by Carol Ann Weaver, Carol Penner, and Cheryl Nafziger-Leis with music composed by Carol Ann Weaver, performed at the same conference.

54. Heisey.

55. Kasdorf, this volume; Reynolds, "Controlling Women"; Arthur.

56. Loewen, "Coffee Klatch."

57. There is an extensive literature on women and reform. Some helpful overviews include Robyn Muncy, *Creating a Female Dominion in American Reform, 1890–1935* (New York: Oxford University Press, 1991); Genna Matthews, *The Rise of Public Woman: Woman's Power and Woman's Place in the United States, 1630–1970* (New York: Oxford University Press, 1992); Mary P. Ryan, *Women in Public: Between Banners and Ballots, 1825–1880* (Baltimore: Johns Hopkins University Press, 1990); and Paula Baker, "The Domestication of Politics: Women and American Political Society," *American Historical Review* 89 (June 1984): 620–47. For an analysis of Harriet Beecher Stowe's *Uncle Tom's Cabin* in relation to the culture of domesticity, see Matthews, *Just a Housewife,* 49–57.

58. Phyliss Brien Hammerstrom, "Keepers at Home: Contemporary Baptist Women and Work outside the Home," paper presented at "The Quiet in the Land? Women of Anabaptist Traditions in Historical Perspective," Millersville, Pa., June 1995.

59. Kasdorf, this volume.

Works Cited

Abrams, Lynn. "Companionship and Conflict: The Negotiation of Marriage Relations in the Nineteenth Century." In *Gender Relations in German History: Power, Agency and Experience from the Sixteenth to the Twentieth Century,* ed. Lynn Abrams and Elizabeth Harvey, 101–20. Durham, N.C.: Duke University Press, 1997.

Adams, Jane H. "The Decoupling of Farm and Household: Differential Consequences of Capitalist Development on Southern Illinois and Third World Family Farms." *Comparative Studies in Society and History* 30 (July 1988): 453–82.

Adler, Patricia, and Peter Adler. *Membership Roles in Field Research.* Newbury Park, Calif.: Sage, 1987.

Adrian, Marlin Wayne. "Mennonites, Missionaries, and Native Americans: Religious Paradigms and Cultural Encounters." Ph.D. diss., University of Virginia, 1989.

Alcoff, Linda. "Cultural Feminism versus Post-structuralism: The Identity Crisis in Feminist Theory." *Signs* 13 (spring 1988): 405–36.

Anderson, Bonnie S., and Judith P. Zinsser. *A History of Their Own: Women in Europe from Prehistory to the Present.* Vol. 1. New York: Harper and Row, 1988.

Arthur, Linda Boynton. "'Clothing Is a Window to the Soul': The Social Control of Women in a Holdeman Mennonite Community." *Journal of Mennonite Studies* 15 (1997): 11–30.

Ashbridge, Elizabeth. "Some Account of the Fore Part of the Life of Elizabeth Ashbridge." In *Journeys in New Worlds: Early American Women's Narratives,* ed. William L. Andrews, 147–80. Madison: University of Wisconsin Press, 1990.

Bacon, Margaret Hope. *Mothers of Feminism: The Story of Quaker Women in America.* San Francisco: Harper and Row, 1986.

———, ed. *Wilt Thou Go on My Errand? Journals of Three Eighteenth-Century Quaker Women Ministers.* Wallingford, Pa.: Pendle Hill, 1994.

Bainton, Roland H. *Women of the Reformation in Germany and Italy.* Minneapolis: Augsburg, 1971.

Baker, Paula. "The Domestication of Politics: Women and American Political Society." *American Historical Review* 89 (June 1984): 620–47.

Bancroft, H. H. *Arizona and New Mexico, 1530–1888.* Vol. 17 of *The Works of Hubert Howe Bancroft.* San Francisco: History Company, 1889.

Banner, Lois W. *American Beauty.* Chicago: University of Chicago Press, 1983.

Barclay, Robert. *Barclay's "Apology" in Modern English.* Newberg, Ore.: Barclay Press, 1991.

Barnes, Ruth, and Joanne B. Eicher, eds. *Dress and Gender: Making and Meaning in Cultural Contexts.* New York: St. Martin's Press, 1992.

Barrett, Lois. "Women in the Anabaptist Movement." In *Women in the Bible and Early Anabaptism,* ed. Herta Funk, 1:33–38. Newton, Kans.: Faith and Life Press, 1975.

———. Barrett, Lois. "Wreath of Glory: Ursula Jost's Prophetic Visions in the Context of Reformation and Revolt in Southwestern Germany, 1524–1530." Ph.D. diss., Union Institute, 1992.

Bartel, Daniel J. *The Emmanuel Mennonite Church of Meade, Kansas.* Meade, Kans., 1975.

Bauman, Richard. *Folklore, Cultural Performances, and Popular Entertainments: A Communications-Centered Handbook.* New York: Oxford University Press, 1992.

Beard, Larry, ed. *Centennial History of Meade, Kansas.* Meade, Kans.: Meade County Historical Society, 1985.

Behar, Ruth. *Translated Woman: Crossing the Border with Esperanza's Story.* Boston: Beacon Press, 1993.

Beiler, Joseph F. "Revolutionary War Records." *Diary* 7 (March 1975): 71.

Bender, Harold S. "An Amish Church Discipline of 1779." *Mennonite Quarterly Review* 11 (April 1937): 163–68.

———. *Conrad Grebel, c. 1498–1526: The Founder of the Swiss Brethren.* Goshen, Ind.: Mennonite Historical Society, 1950.

———. "The Discipline Adopted by the Strasburg Conference of 1568." *Mennonite Quarterly Review* 1 (January 1927): 57–66.

———, trans. and ed. "An Amish Bishop's Conference Epistle of 1865." *Mennonite Quarterly Review* 20 (July 1946): 222–29.

———, trans. and ed. "Some Early American Amish Mennonite Disciplines." *Mennonite Quarterly Review* 8 (April 1934): 90–98.

Berg, Ella. "My Visit to the Chaco's New Colony." *MCC Services Bulletin* 2 (June 1948): 2, 6.

Bergland, Betty. "Immigrant History and the Gendered Subject: A Review Essay." *Ethnic Forum* 8 (1988): 24–39.

Blanke, Fritz. *Brothers in Christ: The History of the Oldest Anabaptist Congregation, Zollikon, Near Zürich, Switzerland.* Scottdale, Pa.: Herald Press, 1961.

Blickle, Peter. *The Revolution of 1525: The German Peasants' War from a New Perspective.* Trans. Thomas A. Brady Jr. and H. C. Erik Midelfort. Baltimore: Johns Hopkins University Press, 1981.

Boserup, Ester. *Women's Role in Economic Development.* London: Allen and Urwin, 1970.

Boulding, Elise. *The Underside of History: A View of Women through Time.* Boulder, Colo.: Westview Press, 1976.

Brandt, Di. *Dancing Naked: Narrative Strategies for Writing across Centuries.* Stratford, Ont.: Mercury Press, 1996.

———. *Questions I Asked My Mother.* Winnipeg, Man.: Turnstone Press, 1987.

Brettell, Caroline B., and Rita James Simon. "Immigrant Women: An Introduction." In *International Migration: The Female Experience,* ed. Rita James Simon and Caroline B. Brettell, 3–20. Totowa, N.J.: Rowman and Allanheld, 1986.

Briggs, Charles L. *Learning How to Ask: A Sociolinguistic Appraisal of the Role of the Interview in Social Science Research.* New York: Cambridge University Press, 1986.

Brinton, Howard H. *Quaker Journals: Varieties of Religious Experience among Friends.* Wallingford, Pa.: Pendle Hill, 1972.

Brown, Kathleen M. "Brave New Worlds: Women's and Gender History." *William and Mary Quarterly,* 3d ser., 50 (April 1993): 311–28.

Brumberg, Joan Jacobs. *The Body Project: An Intimate History of American Girls.* New York: Vintage Books, 1997.

Building Christian Homes: A Manual of Bible Principles and Practical Instructions. Litiz, Pa.: Eastern Mennonite Publications, 1991.

Cagidemetro, Alide. "A Plea for Fictional Historic and Old-Time 'Jewesses.'" In *The Invention of Ethnicity,* ed. Werner Sollors, 14–43. New York: Oxford University Press, 1989.

Caughey, John. "Epilogue: On the Anthropology of America." In *Symbolizing America,* ed. Hervé Varenne, 229–50. Lincoln: University of Nebraska Press, 1986.

Chandler, Joan. *Women without Husbands: An Exploration of the Margins of Marriage.* New York: St. Martin's Press, 1991.

Chodorow, Nancy. *The Reproduction of Mothering: Psychoanalysis and the Sociology of Gender.* Berkeley: University of California Press, 1978.

Chrisman, Miriam Usher. "Women and the Reformation in Strasbourg, 1490–1530." *Archive for Reformation History* 63 (1972): 143–68.

The Chronicle of the Hutterian Brethren. Vol. 1. Trans. and ed. Hutterian Brethren. Rifton, N.Y.: Plough, 1987.

Clasen, Claus-Peter. *Anabaptism: A Social History, 1525–1618.* Ithaca: Cornell University Press, 1972.

———. "The Anabaptist Leaders: Their Number and Background, Switzerland, Austria, South and Central Germany, 1525–1618." *Mennonite Quarterly Review* 69 (April 1975): 122–54.

Clemmer, Richard O. *Roads in the Sky: The Hopi Indians in a Century of Change.* Boulder, Colo.: Westview Press, 1995.

Coburn, Carol. *Life at Four Corners: Religion, Gender and Education in a German-*

Lutheran Community, 1868–1945. Lawrence: University of Kansas Press, 1992.

Cole, Ellen, Olivia M. Espin, and Esther D. Rothblum, eds. *Refugee Women and Their Mental Health: Shattered Societies, Shattered Lives.* New York: Haworth Press, 1992.

Collins, Elizabeth. *Memoirs of Elizabeth Collins, of Upper Evesham, New Jersey, a Minister of the Gospel of Christ, in the Society of Friends.* Philadelphia, Pa.: Wm. H. Pile's Sons, 1894.

Collins, Patricia Hill. "Learning from the Outsider Within: The Sociological Significance of Black Feminist Thought." *Social Problems* 33 (December 1986): 14–32.

Conzen, Kathleen Neils, et al. "The Invention of Ethnicity: A Perspective from the USA." *Journal of American Ethnic History* 12 (fall 1992): 3–41.

Cooper, Barbara J. "Farm Women: Some Contemporary Themes." *Labour/Le Travail* 24 (fall 1989): 167–80.

Cott, Nancy F. *The Bonds of Womanhood: "Women's Sphere" in New England, 1780–1835.* New Haven: Yale University Press, 1977.

Cotterill, Pamela. "Interviewing Women: Issues of Friendship, Vulnerability, and Power." *Women's Studies International Forum* 15, nos. 5–6 (1992): 593–606.

"Courtship: The Ideal Young Man and the Ideal Young Woman." *Eastern Mennonite Testimony* 2 (March 1970): 8–9.

Croese, Gerardus. *General History of the Quakers: Containing the Lives, Tenets, Sufferings, Tryals, Speeches, and Letters of All the Most Eminent Quakers, both Men and Women; from the First Rise of That Sect, Down to This Present Time.* London: John Dunton, 1696.

Cummings, Mary Lou. *Full Circle: Stories of Mennonite Women.* Newton, Kans.: Faith and Life Press, 1978.

Cunningham, Patricia A., and Susan Voso Lab, eds. *Dress in American Culture.* Bowling Green, Ohio: Bowling Green State University Popular Press, 1993.

Davidman, Lynn. "Women's Search for Family and Roots: A Jewish Religious Solution to a Modern Dilemma." In *In Gods We Trust: New Patterns of Religious Pluralism in America,* 2d ed., ed. Thomas Robbins and Dick Anthony, 385–407. New Brunswick, N.J.: Transaction Books, 1990.

Davis, Fred. *Fashion, Culture, and Identity.* Chicago: University of Chicago Press, 1992.

Davis, Natalie Zemon. "City Women and Religious Change." In *Society and Culture in Early Modern France: Eight Essays,* 65–95. Stanford: Stanford University Press, 1975.

DeFehr, C. A. "Our Visit to Colony Volendam." *MCC Services Bulletin* 1 (December 1947): 2.

D'Emilio, John, and Estelle B. Freedman. *Intimate Matters: A History of Sexuality in America.* New York: Harper and Row, 1988.

Denlinger, A. Martha. *Real People: Amish and Mennonites in Lancaster County, Pennsylvania.* Intercourse, Pa.: Good Books, 1985.

Densmore, Christopher. "Quaker Publishing in New York State, 1784–1860." *Quaker History* 74 (1985): 39–57.

Di Leonardo, Micaela. *The Varieties of Ethnic Experience: Kinship, Class, and Gender among California Italian-Americans.* Ithaca: Cornell University Press, 1984.

Dilworth, Leah. *Imagining Indians in the Southwest: Persistent Visions of a Primitive Past.* Washington, D.C.: Smithsonian Institution Press, 1996.

Diner, Hasia R. *Erin's Daughters in America: Irish Immigrant Women in the Nineteenth Century.* Baltimore: Johns Hopkins University Press, 1983.

———. *In the Almost Promised Land: American Jews and Blacks, 1915–1935.* Westport, Conn.: Greenwood Press, 1977. Reprint, Baltimore: Johns Hopkins University Press, 1995.

———. *A Time for Gathering: The Second Migration, 1820–1880.* Vol. 2 of *The Jewish People in America,* ed. Henry L. Feingold. Baltimore: Johns Hopkins University Press, 1992.

Directory of the Eastern Pennsylvania Mennonite Church and Related Areas. Ephrata, Pa.: Publication Board of the Eastern Pennsylvania Mennonite Church, 2001.

Doerksen, Victor G. "Survival and Identity in the Soviet Era." In *Mennonites in Russia, 1788–1988: Essays in Honour of Gerhard Lohrenz,* ed. John Friesen, 289–98. Winnipeg, Man.: CMBC, 1989.

Douglas, Mary Tew. *Purity and Danger: An Analysis of Concepts of Pollution and Taboo.* London: Routledge and Kegan Paul, 1966.

Dublin, Thomas. *Women at Work: The Transformation of Work and Community in Lowell, Massachusetts, 1820–1860.* New York: Columbia University Press, 1979.

Dyck, Cornelius J., ed. *An Introduction to Mennonite History: A Popular History of the Anabaptists and Mennonites.* 3d ed. Scottdale, Pa.: Herald Press, 1993.

Dyck, Peter, and Elfrieda Dyck. *Up from the Rubble: The Epic Rescue of Thousands of War-Ravaged Mennonite Refugees.* Scottdale, Pa.: Herald Press, 1991.

Eakin, Paul John. *Fictions in Autobiography: Studies in the Art of Self-Invention.* Princeton: Princeton University Press, 1985.

———. *Touching the World: Reference in Autobiography.* Princeton: Princeton University Press, 1992.

Eggan, Fred. *Social Organization of the Western Pueblos.* Chicago: University of Chicago Press, 1950.

Eicher, Joanne B., and Mary Ellen Roach-Higgins. "Definition and Classification of Dress." In *Dress and Gender: Making and Meaning in Cultural Contexts,* ed. Ruth Barnes and Joanne B. Eicher, 8–28. New York: St. Martin's Press, 1992.

Enns-Rempel, Kevin. "The Fellowship of Evangelical Bible Churches and the Quest for Religious Identity." *Mennonite Quarterly Review* 63 (July 1989): 247–64.

Epp, Frank H. *Mennonite Exodus: The Rescue and Resettlement of the Russian Men nonites since the Communist Revolution.* Altona, Man.: Friesen, 1962.

————, ed. *Partners in Service: The Story of Mennonite Central Committee Canada.* Winnipeg, Man.: Mennonite Central Committee Canada, 1983.

Epp, George K. "Mennonite Immigration to Canada after World War II." *Journal of Mennonite Studies* 5 (1987): 108–19.

Epp, Marlene. "Carrying the Banner of Nonconformity: Ontario Mennonite Women and the Dress Question." *Conrad Grebel Review* 8 (fall 1990): 237–57.

————. "The Memory of Violence: Soviet and East European Mennonite Refugees and Rape in World War II." *Journal of Women's History* 9 (spring 1997): 58–87.

————. "Women in Canadian Mennonite History: Uncovering the 'Underside.'" *Journal of Mennonite Studies* 5 (1987): 90–107.

————. *Women without Men: Mennonite Refugees of the Second World War.* Toronto: University of Toronto Press, 2000.

Evans, Patricia. *The Verbally Abusive Relationship.* Holbrook, Mass.: Adams Media, 1996.

Faludi, Susan. *Backlash: The Undeclared War against American Women.* New York: Crown, 1991.

Fast, Henry L. "The Kleine Gemeinde in the United States of America," *Profile of the Kleine Gemeinde, 1874,* ed. Delbert F. Plett, 87–140. Steinbach, Man.: DFP, 1987.

Fink, Deborah. *Agrarian Women: Wives and Mothers in Rural Nebraska, 1880–1940.* Chapel Hill: University of North Carolina Press, 1992.

Fitzpatrick, Sheila. *Stalin's Peasants: Resistance and Survival in the Russian Village after Collectivization.* New York: Oxford University Press, 1994.

Fleischhauer, Ingeborg, and Benjamin Pinkus. *The Soviet Germans: Past and Present.* London: Hurst, 1986.

Fretz, J. Winfield. "Paraguay—Where Women Carry the Heavy End of the Load." *Canadian Mennonite,* 18 December 1958, 4–5.

————. *Pilgrims in Paraguay.* Scottdale, Pa.: Herald Press, 1953.

Friedl, Ernestine. "The Position of Women: Appearance and Reality." *Anthropological Quarterly* 40 (1967): 97–108.

Friesen, Walter S. "History and Description of the Mennonite Community and Bible Academy at Meade, Kansas." M.A. thesis, State Teachers College, Emporia, Kans., 1957.

Gabaccia, Donna. *From the Other Side: Women, Gender, and Immigrant Life in the U.S., 1820–1990.* Bloomington: Indiana University Press, 1994.

————. "Immigrant Women: Nowhere at Home?" *Journal of American Ethnic History* 10 (summer 1991): 61–87.

Geertz, Clifford. *The Interpretation of Cultures.* New York: Basic Books, 1973.

————. *Local Knowledge: Further Essays in Interpretive Anthropology.* New York: Basic Books, 1983.

———. "Religion as a Cultural Symbol." In *Anthropological Approaches to the Study of Religion,* ed. Michael Banton, 1–46. London: Tavistock, 1966.

Gingerich, James Nelson. "Ordinance or Ordering: *Ordnung* and the Amish Ministers' Meeting, 1862–1878." *Mennonite Quarterly Review* 60 (April 1986): 180–99.

Gingerich, Melvin. *Mennonite Attire through Four Centuries.* Breinigsville, Pa.: Pennsylvania German Society, 1970.

———. *The Mennonites in Iowa, Marking the One Hundredth Anniversary of the Coming of the Mennonites to Iowa.* Iowa City: State Historical Society of Iowa, 1939.

Glenn, Evelyn Nakano. "From Servitude to Service Work: Historical Continuities in the Racial Division of Paid Reproductive Labor." *Signs* 18 (autumn 1992): 1–43.

Glenn, Susan. *Daughters of the Shtetl: Life and Labor in the Immigrant Generation.* Ithaca: Cornell University Press, 1990.

Goossen, Rachel Waltner. *Women against the Good War: Conscientious Objection and Gender on the American Home Front, 1941–1947.* Chapel Hill: University of North Carolina Press, 1997.

Gordon, Linda. *U.S. Women's History.* Rev. ed. Washington, D.C.: American Historical Association, 1997.

Graber, Robert B. "An Amiable Mennonite Schism: The Origin of the Eastern Pennsylvania Mennonite Church," *Pennsylvania Mennonite Heritage* 7 (October 1984): 2–10.

Graybill, Beth E. "Gendered Interpretations: Toward a Feminist Reading of Mennonite Traditions." Paper presented at the National Women's Studies Association conference, Washington, D.C., 17 June 1993.

———. "Mennonite Women and Their Bishops in the Founding of the Eastern Pennsylvania Mennonite Church." *Mennonite Quarterly Review* 72 (April 1998): 251–74.

Gregory, Brad. "Soetken van den Houte of Oudenaarde." In *Profiles of Anabaptist Women: Sixteenth-Century Reforming Pioneers,* ed. C. Arnold Snyder and Linda A. Huebert Hecht, 365–77. Waterloo, Ont.: Wilfrid Laurier University Press, 1996.

Griffith, R. Marie. *God's Daughters: Evangelical Women and the Power of Submission.* Berkeley: University of California Press, 1997.

Gross, Leonard. *The Golden Years of the Hutterites: The Witness and Thought of the Communal Moravian Anabaptists during the Walpot Era, 1565–1578.* Kitchener, Ont.: Pandora Press, 1980. Reprint, Scottdale, Pa.: Herald Press, 1988.

Hagen, William T. *The Indian Rights Association: The Herbert Welsh Years, 1882–1904.* Tucson: University of Arizona Press, 1985.

Hall, Rufus. *A Journal of the Life, Religious Exercises, and Travels in the Work of the Ministry, of Rufus Hall, Late of Northampton, Montgomery County, in the State of New York.* Philadelphia: John and Isaac Comly, 1840.

Hamm, Thomas D. *The Transformation of American Quakerism: Orthodox Friends, 1800–1907.* Bloomington: Indiana University Press, 1988.

Hammerstrom, Phyliss Brien. "Keepers at Home: Contemporary Baptist Women and Work outside the Home." Paper presented at "The Quiet in the Land? Women of Anabaptist Traditions in Historical Perspective," Millersville, Pa., June 1995.

Handbook of the Numidia Mennonite Bible School. Ephrata, Pa.: Eastern Mennonite Publications, 1994).

Haraway, Donna J. *Simians, Cyborgs, and Women: The Reinvention of Nature.* New York: Routledge, 1991.

Handbook of the Numidia Mennonite Bible School. Ephrata, Pa.: Eastern Mennonite Publications, 1994.

Harder, Leland. *The Sources of Swiss Anabaptism: The Grebel Letters and Related Documents.* Scottdale, Pa.: Herald Press, 1985.

Harrison, Wes. "The Role of Women in Anabaptist Thought and Practice: The Hutterite Experience of the Sixteenth and Seventeenth Centuries." *Sixteenth Century Journal* 23 (spring 1992): 49–71.

Hartman, Joel. "Traditional Authority vs. Right to Life Claims: A Case Study of Community Response to HIV/AIDS." Paper presented at "The Quiet in the Land? Women of Anabaptist Traditions in Historical Perspective," Millersville, Pa., June 1995.

Hege, Christian. "Augsburg and the Early Anabaptists." In *The Mennonite Encyclopedia: A Comprehensive Reference Work on the Anabaptist and Mennonite Movement,* 182–85. 4th ed. Scottdale, Pa.: Mennonite Publishing House, 1982.

Heilman, Samuel C. *Synagogue Life: A Study in Symbolic Interaction.* Chicago: University of Chicago Press, 1976.

Heisey, Mary Jane. "They Also Served: Brethren in Christ Women and Civilian Public Service." Paper presented at "The Quiet in the Land? Women of Anabaptist Traditions in Historical Perspective," Millersville, Pa., June 1995.

Hermansen, Marcia K. "Two-Way Acculturation: Muslim Women in America between Individual Choice (Liminality) and Community Affiliation (Communitas)." In *The Muslims of America,* ed. Yvonne Yazbeck Haddad, 188–201. New York: Oxford University Press, 1991.

Hewitt, Nancy. "Beyond the Search for Sisterhood: American Women's History in the 1980s." *Social History* 10 (October 1985): 299–321.

Hinsley, Curtis M. *Savages and Scientists: The Smithsonian Institution and the Development of American Anthropology, 1846–1910.* Washington, D.C.: Smithsonian Institution Press, 1981.

Hollander, Anne. *Sex and Suits: The Evolution of Modern Dress.* New York: Knopf, 1994.

Hoskins, Jane. *The Life of That Faithful Servant of Christ, Jane Hoskens, a Minister of the Gospel, among the People Called Quakers.* Philadelphia, Pa.: Friends Library, 1837.

Hostetler, Beulah S. "An Old Order River Brethren Love Feast." *Pennsylvania Folklife* 24 (winter 1974–75): 8–20.

Hostetler, John A. *Amish Society.* 4th ed. Baltimore: Johns Hopkins University Press, 1993.

———. *Hutterite Society.* Baltimore: Johns Hopkins University Press, 1974.

Hoy, Joan M. "The Publication and Distribution of Books among New England Quakers, 1775–1836." Ph.D. diss., Boston University, 1989.

Huebert Hecht, Linda A. "Anna Gasser of Lüsen." In *Profiles of Anabaptist Women: Sixteenth-Century Reforming Pioneers,* ed. C. Arnold Snyder and Linda A. Huebert Hecht, 140–55. Waterloo, Ont.: Wilfrid Laurier University Press, 1996.

———. "A Brief Moment in Time: Informal Leadership and Shared Authority among Sixteenth Century Anabaptist Women." *Journal of Mennonite Studies* 17 (1999); 52–74.

———. "An Extraordinary Lay Leader: The Life and Work of Helene of Freyberg, Sixteenth Century Noblewoman and Anabaptist from the Tirol." *Mennonite Quarterly Review* 66 (July 1992): 312–41.

———. "Faith and Action: The Role of Women in the Anabaptist Movement of the Tirol, 1527–1529." Cognate essay, M.A., history, University of Waterloo, 1990.

———. "Women and Religious Change: The Significance of Anabaptist Women in the Tirol, 1527–29." *Studies in Religion: A Canadian Journal* 21, no. 1 (1992): 57–66.

Huntington, Gertrude Enders. "Dove at the Window: A Study of an Old Order Amish Community in Ohio." Ph.D. diss., Yale University, 1956.

———. "Persistence and Change in Amish Education." In *The Amish Struggle with Modernity,* ed. Donald B. Kraybill and Marc Olshan, 77–95. Hanover, N.H.: University Press of New England, 1994.

Iacovetta, Franca. "Manly Militants, Cohesive Communities, and Defiant Domestics: Writing about Immigrants in Canadian Historical Scholarship." *Labour/Le Travail* 36 (fall 1995): 217–52.

Ingle, H. Larry. *Quakers in Conflict: The Hicksite Reformation.* Knoxville: University of Tennessee Press, 1986.

Irwin, Joyce L. *Womanhood in Radical Protestantism, 1525–1675.* New York: Edwin Mellen, 1979.

Isaak, Jakob. "The Settlement in Paraguay from the Point of View of the Colonist." *Proceedings of the Fourth Mennonite World Conference,* 1948, 192–93.

Isenberg, Nancy. "The Personal Is Political: Gender, Feminism, and the Politics of Discourse Theory." *American Quarterly* 44 (September 1992): 449–59.

Jack, Dana Crowley. *Silencing the Self.* New York: Routledge, 1992.

Jacobs, Jane Liebman. *Divine Disenchantment: Deconverting from New Religions.* Bloomington: Indiana University Press, 1989.

Janzen, Jean. *Words for the Silence.* Fresno, Calif.: Center for Mennonite Brethren Studies, 1984.

Jelinek, Estelle C., ed. *Women's Autobiography: Essays in Criticism.* Bloomington: Indiana University Press, 1980.

Jellison, Katherine. *Entitled to Power: Farm Women and Technology, 1913–1963.* Chapel Hill: University of North Carolina Press, 1993.

Jensen, Joan M. *Loosening the Bonds: Mid-Atlantic Farm Women, 1750–1850.* New Haven: Yale University Press, 1986.

Johnson, Paul E., and Sean Wilentz. *The Kingdom of Matthias: A Story of Sex and Salvation in Nineteenth-Century America.* New York: Oxford University Press, 1994.

Johnson-Weiner, Karen M. "The Brethren and Their Sisters: The Role of Women in Old Order, Beachy Amish and Fellowship Churches." Paper presented at "The Quiet in the Land? Women of Anabaptist Traditions in Historical Perspective," Millersville, Pa., June 1995.

Joseph, Nathan. *Uniforms and Nonuniforms: Communication through Clothing.* New York: Greenwood Press, 1986.

Juhnke, James C. *A People of Mission: A History of General Conference Mennonite Overseas Missions.* Newton, Kans.: Faith and Life Press, 1979.

Kaiser, Susan B. *The Social Psychology of Clothing: Symbolic Appearances in Context.* 2d ed. New York: Macmillan, 1990.

Kamphoefner, Walter D. *The Westfalians: From Germany to Missouri.* Princeton: Princeton University Press, 1987.

Karant-Nunn, Susan C. "Continuity and Change: Some Effects of the Reformation on the Women of Zwickau." *Sixteenth Century Journal* 13 (summer 1982): 17–42.

———. "The Transmission of Luther's Teachings on Women and Matrimony: The Case of Zwickau." *Archive for Reformation History* 77 (1986): 31–46.

Karttunen, Frances. *Between Worlds: Interpreters, Guides and Survivors.* Piscataway, N.J.: Rutgers University Press, 1994.

Kasdorf, Julia. *Eve's Striptease.* Pittsburgh: University of Pittsburgh Press, 1998.

———. *Sleeping Preacher.* Pittsburgh: University of Pittsburgh Press, 1992.

Kauffman, Bette J. "Feminist Facts: Interview Strategies and Political Subjects in Ethnography." *Communication Theory* 2 (August 1992): 187–206.

Kauffman, S. Duane. *Mifflin County Amish and Mennonite Story, 1791–1991.* Belleville, Pa.: Mifflin County Mennonite Historical Society, 1991.

Kerber, Linda K. "Separate Spheres, Female Worlds, Women's Place: The Rhetoric of Women's History." *Journal of American History* 75 (June 1988): 9–39.

———. *Women of the Republic: Intellect and Ideology in Revolutionary America.* Chapel Hill: University of North Carolina Press, 1980.

Kessler-Harris, Alice. *Out to Work: A History of Wage-Earning Women in the United States.* Oxford: Oxford University Press, 1982.

Kirkendall, Richard. *Social Scientists and Farm Politics in the Age of Roosevelt.* Columbia: University of Missouri Press, 1966.

Klaassen, Walter. *Michael Gaismair, Revolutionary and Reformer.* Leiden: Brill, 1978.

Klassen, Pamela E. *Going by the Moon and Stars: Stories of Two Russian Mennonite Women.* Waterloo, Ont.: Wilfrid Laurier University Press, 1994.

———. "Practicing Conflict: Weddings as Sites of Contest and Compromise." *Mennonite Quarterly Review* 72 (April 1998): 225–42.

———. "What's Bre(a)d in the Bone: The Bodily Heritage of Mennonite Women." *Mennonite Quarterly Review* 68 (April 1994): 229–47.

———. "Women's Heads: Coverings in Religious and Anthropological Perspective." Paper presented at "The Quiet in the Land? Women of Anabaptist Traditions in Historical Perspective," Millersville, Pa., June 1995.

Klassen, Peter P. *Die Mennoniten in Paraguay: Reich Gottes und Reich dieser Welt.* Bolanden-Weierhof, Germany: Mennonitischer Geschichtsverein, 1988.

Klassen, Sarah. *Journey to Yalta.* Winnipeg, Man.: Turnstone Press, 1988.

Klingenstein, Susanne. *Jews in the American Academy, 1900–1940: The Dynamics of Intellectual Assimilation.* New Haven: Yale University Press, 1991.

Klötzer, Ralf. *Die Täuferherrschaft von Münster: Stadtreformation und Welterneuerung.* Münster, Germany: Aschendorff, 1992.

Kobelt-Groch, Marion. *Aufsässige Töchter Gottes: Frauen im Bauernkrieg und in den Täuferbewegungen.* New York: Campus Verlag, 1993.

———. "Divara of Haarlem." In *Profiles of Anabaptist Women: Sixteenth-Century Reforming Pioneers,* ed. C. Arnold Snyder and Linda A. Huebert Hecht, 298–304. Waterloo, Ont.: Wilfrid Laurier University Press, 1996.

———. "Von 'Armen Frowen' und 'Boesen Wibern': Frauen im Bauernkrieg zwischen Anpassung und Auflehnung." *Archive for Reformation History* 79 (1988): 103–37.

Kollmorgen, Walter M. *Culture of a Contemporary Rural Community: The Old Order Amish of Lancaster County, Pennsylvania.* Rural Life Studies, vol. 4. Washington, D.C.: Government Printing Office, 1942.

———. "Kollmorgen as a Bureaucrat." *Annals of the Association of American Geographers* 69 (March 1979): 77–89.

Kraybill, Donald B. "The Amish Encounter with Modernity." In *The Amish Struggle with Modernity,* ed. Donald B. Kraybill and Marc Olshan, 21–34. Hanover, N.H.: University Press of New England, 1994.

———. "Introduction: The Struggle to Be Separate." In *The Amish Struggle with Modernity,* ed. Donald B. Kraybill and Marc Olshan, 1–17. Hanover, N.H.: University Press of New England, 1994.

———. "Mennonite Women's Veiling: The Rise and Fall of a Sacred Symbol." *Mennonite Quarterly Review* 61 (June 1987): 298–320.

———. "Plotting Social Change across Four Affiliations." In *The Amish Struggle with Modernity,* ed. Donald B. Kraybill and Marc Olshan, 53–74. Hanover, N.H.: University Press of New England, 1994.

———. *The Riddle of Amish Culture.* Baltimore: Johns Hopkins University Press, 1989.

———. "War against Progress: Coping with Social Change." In *The Amish Struggle with Modernity,* ed. Donald B. Kraybill and Marc Olshan, 35–50. Hanover, N.H.: University Press of New England, 1994.

Kraybill, Donald B., and Marc Olshan, eds. *The Amish Struggle with Modernity.* Hanover, N.H.: University Press of New England, 1994.

Kreider, Robert. *Interviews with Peter J. Dyck and Elfrieda Klassen Dyck: Experiences in Mennonite Central Committee Service in Europe, 1941–1949.* Akron, Pa.: MCC, 1988.

Laqueur, Thomas Walter. *Making Sex: Body and Gender from the Greeks to Freud.* Cambridge: Harvard University Press, 1990.

Lasch, Christopher. *Haven in a Heartless World: The Family Besieged.* New York: Basic Books, 1977.

Lawless, Elaine J. *Handmaidens of the Lord: Pentecostal Women Preachers and Traditional Religion.* Philadelphia: University of Pennsylvania Press, 1988.

Lears, T. Jackson. *No Place of Grace: Antimodernism and the Transformation of American Culture, 1880–1920.* New York: Pantheon, 1981.

Lerner, Gerda. "Placing Women in History: Definitions and Challenges." *Feminist Studies* 3 (fall 1975): 5–14. Reprinted in Gerda Lerner, *The Majority Finds Its Past: Placing Women in History,* 145–59. New York: Oxford University Press, 1979.

———. "Reconceptualizing Differences among Women." *Journal of Women's History* 1 (winter 1990): 106–22.

Loewen, Royden K. "'The Children, the Cows, and My Dear Man': The Transplanted Lives of Mennonite Farm Women, 1874–1900." *Canadian Historical Review* 73 (September 1993): 344–73.

———. "Coffee Klatches and Household Hearth: Mennonite Farm Women of Kansas, Manitoba, and Belize in the 1950s." Paper presented at "The Quiet in the Land? Women of Anabaptist Traditions in Historical Perspective," Millersville, Pa., June 1995.

———. *Family, Church and Market: A Mennonite Community in the Old and the New Worlds, 1850–1930.* Urbana: University of Illinois Press, 1993.

Lowenthal, David. *The Past Is a Foreign Country.* Cambridge: Cambridge University Press, 1985.

Mack, Phyllis. *Visionary Women: Ecstatic Prophecy in Seventeenth-Century England.* Berkeley: University of California Press, 1992.

MacMaster, Richard K. *Land, Piety, Peoplehood: The Establishment of Mennonite Communities in America, 1683–1790.* Scottdale, Pa.: Herald Press, 1985.

Manning, Christel. *God Gave Us the Right: Conservative Catholic, Evangelical Protestant, and Orthodox Jewish Women Grapple with Feminism.* New Brunswick, N.J.: Rutgers University Press, 1999.

Marr, M. Lucille. "Anabaptist Women of the North: Peers in the Faith, Subordinates in Marriage." *Mennonite Quarterly Review* 61 (October 1987): 347–62.

Marshall, Sherrin, ed. *Women in Reformation and Counter-Reformation Europe: Public and Private Worlds.* Bloomington: Indiana University Press, 1989.

Masayesva, Victor, and Erin Younger. *Hopi Photographers, Hopi Images.* Tucson: Sun Tracks and University of Arizona Press, 1984.

Matthews, Glenna. *Just a Housewife: The Rise and Fall of Domesticity in America.* New York: Oxford University Press, 1987.

———. *The Rise of Public Woman: Woman's Power and Woman's Place in the United States, 1630–1970.* New York: Oxford University Press, 1992.

McCracken, Grant. "Clothing as Language: An Object Lesson in the Study of the Expressive Properties of Material Culture." In *Culture and Consumption,* by Grant McCracken, 57–70. Bloomington: Indiana University Press, 1988.

———. *Culture and Consumption.* Bloomington: Indiana University Press, 1988.

McMurry, Sally. *Transforming Rural Life: Dairying Families and Agricultural Change, 1820–1885.* Baltimore: Johns Hopkins University Press, 1995.

Meade County Historical Society. *Pioneer Stories of Meade County.* Meade, Kans.: Meade County Historical Society, 1985.

Mecenseffy, Grete. "Anabaptists in Kitzbühel." *Mennonite Quarterly Review* 46 (April 1972): 99–112.

———, ed. *Quellen zur Geschichte der Täufer.* Vol. 11, *Österreich,* part 1. Gütersloh, Germany: Gerd Mohn, 1964.

———, ed. *Quellen zur Geschichte der Täufer,* Vol. 13, *Österreich,* part 2. Gütersloh, Germany: Gerd Mohn, 1972.

Mecenseffy, Grete, assisted by Matthias Schmelzer, eds. *Quellen zur Geschichte der Täufer.* Vol. 14. *Österreich,* part 3. Gütersloh, Germany: Gerd Mohn, 1983.

"Mennonite Central Committee, 1920–1970." Special issue of *Mennonite Quarterly Review* 44 (July 1970).

"Mennonites and the Soviet Inferno." Special issue of *Journal of Mennonite Studies* 16 (1998).

Mernissi, Fatima. *Beyond the Veil: Male-Female Dynamics in a Modern Muslim Society.* New York: Schenkman, 1975.

Meyers, Thomas J. "The Old Order Amish: To Remain in the Faith or to Leave." *Mennonite Quarterly Review* 68 (July 1994): 378–95.

Miller, Ivan J. "Conservative Amish Mennonite Conference." In *The Mennonite Encyclopedia: A Comprehensive Reference Work on the Anabaptist and Mennonite Movement,* 1:700–702. 4th ed. Scottdale, Pa.: Mennonite Publishing House, 1982.

Muncy, Robyn. *Creating a Female Dominion in American Reform, 1890–1935.* New York: Oxford University Press, 1991.

Neth, Mary. *Preserving the Family Farm: Women, Community and the Foundations of Agribusiness in the Midwest, 1900–1940.* Baltimore: Johns Hopkins University Press, 1995.

Neuschwander, Vernon. "Mennonite Settlement in the Chaco." *MCC Services Bulletin* 1 (November 1947): 2.

New Catholic Encyclopedia. New York: McGraw-Hill, 1967–96.

Newman, Louise M. "Critical Theory and the History of Women: What's at Stake in

Deconstructing Women's History." *Journal of Women's History* 2 (winter 1991): 58–68.

Nolt, Steven M. *A History of the Amish*. Intercourse, Pa.: Good Books, 1992.

———. "The Mennonite Eclipse." *Festival Quarterly* 19 (summer 1992): 8–12.

Norton, Mary Beth. *Liberty's Daughters: The Revolutionary Experience of American Women, 1750–1800*. Boston: Little, Brown, 1980.

Novick, Peter. *That Noble Dream: The "Objectivity Question" and the American Historical Profession*. Cambridge: Cambridge University Press, 1988.

Oakley, Ann. "Interviewing Women: A Contradiction in Terms." In *Doing Feminist Research*, ed. Helen Roberts, 30–61. New York: Routledge, 1981.

Okihiro, Gary Y. *Margins and Mainstreams: Asians in American History and Culture*. Seattle: University of Washington Press, 1994.

Olshan Marc A., and Kimberly D. Schmidt. "Amish Women and the Feminist Conundrum." In *The Amish Struggle with Modernity*, ed. Donald B. Kraybill and Marc A. Olshan, 215–30. Hanover, N.H.: University Press of New England, 1994.

Orsi, Robert A. *The Madonna of 115th Street: Faith and Community in Italian Harlem*. New Haven: Yale University Press, 1985.

Ortner, Sherry B., and Harriet Whitehead. "Introduction: Accounting for Sexual Meanings." In *Sexual Meanings: The Cultural Construction of Gender and Sexuality*, 1–27. New York: Cambridge University Press, 1981.

Osterud, Nancy Grey. *Bonds of Community: The Lives of Farm Women in Nineteenth-Century New York*. Ithaca: Cornell University Press, 1991.

Ostriker, Alicia Suskin. *Stealing the Language: The Emergence of Women's Poetry in America*. Boston: Beacon Press, 1986.

Oyer, John S. "Anabaptism in Central Germany: 2. Faith and Life." *Mennonite Quarterly Review* 35 (January 1961): 5–37.

———. "Anabaptist Women Leaders in Augsburg: August 1527 to April 1528." In *Profiles of Anabaptist Women: Sixteenth-Century Reforming Pioneers*, ed. C. Arnold Snyder and Linda A. Huebert Hecht, 82–105. Waterloo, Ont.: Wilfrid Laurier University Press, 1996.

Packull, Werner O. *Hutterite Beginnings: Communitarian Experiments during the Reformation*. Baltimore: Johns Hopkins University Press, 1995.

———. "'We Are Born to Work Like the Birds to Fly': The Anabaptist-Hutterite Ideal Woman." *Mennonite Quarterly Review* 73 (January 1999): 75–86.

Parkerson, Donald H., and Jo Ann Parkerson. "'Fewer Children of Greater Spiritual Quality': Religion and the Decline of Fertility in Nineteenth-Century America." *Social Science History* 12 (spring 1988): 49–70.

Parvanta, Sultana. "The Balancing Act: Plight of Afghan Women Refugees." In *Refugee Women and Their Mental Health: Shattered Societies, Shattered Lives*, ed. Ellen Cole, Oliva M. Espin, and Esther D. Rothblum, 113–28. New York: Haworth Press, 1992.

Peachey, Paul. *Die soziale Herkunft der Schweizer Täufer in der Reformationzeit: Ein religionssoziologische Untersuchung.* Karlsruhe, Germany: Schneider, 1954.

Pederson, Jane Marie. *Between Memory and Reality: Family and Community in Rural Wisconsin, 1870–1970.* Madison: University of Wisconsin Press, 1992.

Peiss, Kathy. "Making Faces: The Cosmetics Industry and the Cultural Construction of Gender, 1890–1930." *Genders* 7 (spring 1990): 143–69.

Penner, Carol. "Mennonite Women's History: A Survey." *Journal of Mennonite Studies* 9 (1991): 122–35.

Pickle, Linda Schelbitzki. *Contented among Strangers: Rural German-Speaking Women and Their Families in the Nineteenth-Century Midwest.* Urbana: University of Illinois Press, 1996.

Plank, Elda. *'Twas Home on the Range: The Family History of Henry L. and Agnes Friesen.* Goshen, Ind., [ca. 1976].

Plett, Delbert F. *The Golden Years: The Mennonite Kleine Gemeinde in Russia, 1812–1849.* Steinbach, Man.: DFP, 1985.

———. *Storm and Triumph: The Mennonite Kleine Gemeinde, 1850–1875.* Steinbach, Man.: DFP. 1986.

Poetker-Thiessen, Audrey. *Standing All the Night Through.* Winnipeg, Man.: Turnstone Press, 1995.

Prucha, Francis Paul. *Documents of United States Indian Policy.* Lincoln: University of Nebraska Press, 1975.

———. *The Great Father: The United States Government and the American Indians.* Lincoln: University of Nebraska Press, 1986.

Rakow, Lana Fay. *Gender on the Line: Women, the Telephone, and Community Life.* Urbana: University of Illinois Press, 1992.

Redekop, Calvin W. *Mennonite Society.* Baltimore: Johns Hopkins University Press, 1989.

———. *The Old Colony Mennonites: Dilemmas of Ethnic Minority Life.* Baltimore: Johns Hopkins University Press, 1969.

Reimer, Al. *Mennonite Literary Voices Past and Present.* North Newton, Kans.: Bethel College, 1994.

———. "Where Was/Is the Women's Voice? The Re-membering of the Mennonite Women." *Mennonite Life* 47 (1992): 20–25.

Rempel, G. S., ed. *A Historical Sketch of the Churches of the Evangelical Mennonite Brethren.* Rosthern, Sask.: D. H. Epp, 1939.

Reschly, Steven, D. *The Amish on the Iowa Prairie, 1840–1910.* Baltimore: Johns Hopkins University Press, 2000.

Reschly, Steven D., and Katherine Jellison. "Production Patterns, Consumption Strategies, and Gender Relations in Amish and Non-Amish Farm Households in Lancaster County, Pennsylvania, 1935–1936." *Agricultural History* 67 (spring 1993): 134–62.

Reynolds, Margaret C. "Controlling Women, Preserving Orthodoxy: Gender Asymmetry as a Joint Strategy for Keeping 'Order' in Old Order Culture." Paper presented at "The Quiet in the Land? Women of Anabaptist Traditions in Historical Perspective," Millersville, Pa., June 1995.

———. "Transmission of Tradition in the Old Order River Brethren: Gender Roles and Symbolic Behavior in a Plain Sect." Ph.D. diss., Pennsylvania State University, 1996.

Rich, Adrienne. "When We Dead Awaken: Writing as Re-vision." In *Adrienne Rich's Poetry*, ed. Barbara Charlesworth and Albert Gelphi, 90–98. New York: Norton, 1975.

Rich, Elaine Sommers. *Mennonite Women: A Story of God's Faithfulness, 1683–1983*. Scottdale, Pa.: Herald Press, 1983.

Richardson, Laurel. "Trash on the Corner." *Journal of Contemporary Ethnography* 21 (April 1992): 107–19.

Rimland, Ingrid. *The Wanderers: The Saga of Three Women Who Survived*. St. Louis, Mo.: Concordia, 1977.

Riney-Kehrberg, Pamela. *Rooted in Dust: Surviving Drought and Depression in Southwestern Kansas*. Lawrence: University Press of Kansas, 1994.

Ritterband, Paul, and Harold S. Wechsler. *Jewish Learning in American Universities: The First Century*. Bloomington: Indiana University Press, 1994.

Roberts, Mary Louise. "Review Essay: Gender, Consumption, and Commodity Culture." *American Historical Review* 103 (June 1998): 817–44.

Roe, Michael. "Displaced Women in Settings of Continuing Armed Conflict." In *Refugee Women and Their Mental Health: Shattered Societies, Shattered Lives*, ed. Ellen Cole, Oliva M. Espin, and Esther D. Rothblum, 89–104. New York: Haworth Press, 1992.

Roper, Lyndal. *The Holy Household: Women and Morals in Reformation Augsburg*. New York: Oxford University Press, 1989.

Rosaldo, Michelle Zimbalist. "The Use and Abuse of Anthropology: Reflections on Feminist and Cross-Cultural Understanding." *Signs* 5 (spring 1980): 389–417.

Roth, Friedrich. "Zur Geschichte der Wiedertäufer in Oberschwaben: 3. Der Höhepunkt der wiedertäuferischen Bewegung in Augsburg und ihr Niedergang in Jahre 1528." *Zeitschrift des Historischen Vereins für Schwaben und Neuburg* (Augsburg) 28 (1901): 1–154.

Roth, John D., trans. and ed. *Letters of the Amish Division: A Sourcebook*. Goshen, Ind.: Mennonite Historical Society, 1993.

Rozen, Frieda Shoenberg. "The Permanent First Floor Tenant: Women and Gemeinschaft." *Mennonite Quarterly Review* 51 (October 1977): 319–28.

Rushdie, Salman. *Imaginary Homelands*. New York: Penguin, 1992.

———. *The Wizard of Oz*. London: British Film Institute, 1992.

Rushforth, Scott, and Steadman Upham. *A Hopi Social History: Anthropological Perspectives on Sociocultural Persistence and Change*. Austin: University of Texas Press, 1992.

Ruth, John. *Mennonite Identity and Literary Art*. Scottdale, Pa.: Herald Press, 1978.

Ryan, Mary P. *Women in Public: Between Banners and Ballots, 1825–1880.* Baltimore: Johns Hopkins University Press, 1990.

Salamon, Sonya, and Ann Mackey Keim. "Land Ownership and Women's Power in a Midwestern Farming Community." *Journal of Marriage and the Family* 41 (February 1979): 109–19.

———. *Prairie Patrimony: Family, Farming and Community in the Midwest.* Chapel Hill: University of North Carolina Press, 1992.

Schaufele, Wolfgang. "The Missionary Vision and Activity of the Anabaptist Laity." In *Anabaptism and Mission,* ed. Wilbert R. Shenk. Scottdale, Pa.: Herald Press, 1984.

Schmelzer, Matthias. "Jakob Huters Wirken im Lichte von Bekenntnissen gefangener Täufer." *Der Schlern: Monatszeitschrift für Südtiroler Landeskunde* 63 (November 1989): 596–618.

Schmidt, Johnna. "Prayers for Girls: A Meditation on Red and Blue." Drama performed at "The Quiet in the Land? Women of Anabaptist Traditions in Historical Perspective," Millersville, Pa., June 1995.

Schmidt, Kimberly D. "Transforming Tradition: Women's Work and the Effects of Religion and Economics in Two Rural Mennonite Communities, 1930–1990." Ph.D. diss., Binghamton University, 1995.

Schmidt, Kimberly D., and Steven D. Reschly. "A Women's History for Anabaptist Traditions: A Framework of Possibilities, Possibly Changing the Framework." *Journal of Mennonite Studies* 18 (2000): 29–46.

Schwab, Paul J. "Augsburg and the Early Anabaptists." In *Reformation Studies: Essays in Honor of Roland H. Bainton,* ed. Franklin H. Littell, 212–28. Richmond, Va.: John Knox Press, 1962.

Scott, Joan W. "Gender: A Useful Category of Historical Analysis." *American Historical Review* 91 (December 1986): 1053–75. Reprinted in Joan Wallach Scott, *Gender and the Politics of History,* 28–50. New York: Columbia University Press, 1988.

Scott, Stephen E. "The Old Order River Brethren." *Pennsylvania Mennonite Heritage* 1 (July 1978): 13–22.

———. "The Old Order River Brethren." Lecture delivered as part of lecture series "Minority Voices: Old Order Anabaptists in North America," Young Center for the Study of Anabaptist and Pietist Groups, Elizabethtown College, Elizabethtown, Pa., 17 March 1993.

Seaman, David P. *Born a Chief: The Nineteenth Century Hopi Boyhood of Edmund Nequaptewa as Told to Alfred F. Whiting.* Tucson: University of Arizona Press, 1993.

Segalen, Martine. *Love and Power in the Peasant Family: Rural France in the Nineteenth Century.* Trans. Sarah Matthews. Chicago: University of Chicago Press, 1983.

Sekaquaptewa, Helen. *Me and Mine: The Life Story of Helen Sekaquaptewa as Told to Louise Udall,* ed. Louise Udall. Tucson: University of Arizona Press, 1985.

Sellers, Charles Grier. *The Market Revolution: Jacksonian America, 1815–1846.* New York: Oxford University Press, 1991.

Shahar, Shulamith. *The Fourth Estate: A History of Women in the Middle Ages.* Trans. Chaya Galai. New York: Methuen, 1983.

Shea, Daniel. *Spiritual Autobiography in Early America.* Princeton: Princeton University Press, 1968. Reprint, Madison: University of Wisconsin Press, 1988.

Shoenberg Rozen, Frieda. "The Permanent First Floor Tenant." *Mennonite Quarterly Review* 51 (October 1977): 319–28.

Shover, John L. *First Majority — Last Minority: The Transforming of Rural Life in America.* Dekalb: Northern Illinois University Press, 1976.

Siemens, Anna Z. Friesen, ed. *Genealogy and History of the J. R. Friesen Family, 1782–1990.* Meade City, Kans.: Privately published, 1990.

Simmons, Leo W., ed. *Sun Chief, the Autobiography of a Hopi Indian.* New Haven: Yale University Press, 1942.

Simon, Rita James, and Caroline B. Bretell, eds. *International Migration: The Female Experience.* Totowa. N.J.: Rowman and Allanheld, 1986.

Sklar, Kathryn Kish. *Catharine Beecher: A Study in American Domesticity.* New Haven: Yale University Press, 1973.

Smith, Daniel Scott. "Family Limitation, Sexual Control and Domestic Feminism in Victorian America." In *Clio's Consciousness Raised: New Perspectives on the History of Women,* ed. Mary Hartman and Lois W. Banner, 119–36. New York: Harper and Row, 1974.

Smith, Hilda. "A Prize-Winning Book Revisited: Women's Historians and Women's History, a Conflation of Absence." *Journal of Women's History* 4 (spring 1992): 133–41.

Smith, Timothy L. "Religion and Ethnicity in America." *American Historical Review* 83 (1978): 1155–85.

Smith, Willard H. *Mennonites in Illinois.* Scottdale, Pa.: Herald Press, 1983.

Smith-Rosenberg, Carroll. *Disorderly Conduct: Visions of Gender in Victorian America.* Oxford: Oxford University Press, 1985.

Snyder, C. Arnold. "Agnes Linck from Biel." In *Profiles of Anabaptist Women: Sixteenth-Century Reforming Pioneers,* ed. C. Arnold Snyder and Linda A. Huebert Hecht, 32–37. Waterloo, Ont.: Wilfrid Laurier University Press, 1996.

———. *Anabaptist History and Theology: An Introduction.* Kitchener, Ont.: Pandora Press, 1995.

Snyder, C. Arnold, and Linda A. Huebert Hecht, eds. *Profiles of Anabaptist Women: Sixteenth-Century Reforming Pioneers.* Waterloo, Ont.: Wilfrid Laurier University Press, 1996.

Sprunger, Keith L. "God's Powerful Army of the Weak: Anabaptist Women of the Radical Reformation." In *Triumph over Silence: Women in Protestant History,* ed. Richard L. Greaves, 45–74. Westport, Conn.: Greenwood Press, 1985.

Statement of Christian Doctrine and Rules and Discipline of the Eastern Pennsylva-

nia Mennonite Church and Related Areas, Sixth Statement. Ephrata, Pa.: Publication Board of the Eastern Pennsylvania Mennonite Church, 1993.

Stayer, James M. *The German Peasants' War and Anabaptist Community of Goods.* Montreal: McGill-Queens University Press, 1991.

———. "Was Dr. Kuehler's Conception of Early Dutch Anabaptism Historically Sound? The Historical Discussion of Anabaptist Münster 450 Years Later." *Mennonite Quarterly Review* 60 (July 1986): 261–88.

Stayer, James M., Werner Packull, and Klaus Deppermann. "From Monogenesis to Polygenesis: The Historical Discussion of Anabaptist Origins." *Mennonite Quarterly Review* 49 (April 1975): 83–121.

Stoesz, Edgar, and Muriel T. Stackley. *Garden in the Wilderness: Mennonite Communities in the Paraguayan Chaco, 1927–1997.* Winnipeg, Man.: CMBC, 1999.

Strong-Boag, Veronica. "'Pulling in Double Harness or Hauling a Double Load': Women, Work and Feminism." *Journal of Canadian Studies* 21 (fall 1986): 32–52.

Thomas, Jim. *Doing Critical Ethnography.* Newbury Park, Calif.: Sage, 1993.

Tiessen, Hildi Froese. Introduction to "Mennonite(s) Writing in Canada." *New Quarterly* 10 (spring–summer 1990): 9–12.

———. Introduction to "Mennonite Writing." *Prairie Fire* 2 (summer 1990): 8–11.

Tilly, Louise, and Joan Scott. *Women, Work and Family.* New York: Holt, Rinehart, and Winston, 1978.

Titiev, Mischa. *The Hopi Indians of Old Oraibi: Change and Continuity.* Ann Arbor: University of Michigan Press, 1972.

Toews, John B. *Czars, Soviets and Mennonites.* Newton, Kans.: Faith and Life Press, 1982.

Trotta, Cathy Ann. "Crossing Cultural Boundaries: Heinrich and Martha Moser Voth in the Hopi Pueblos, 1893–1906." Ph.D. diss., Northern Arizona University, 1997.

Turnbull, Colin M. *The Human Cycle.* New York: Simon and Schuster, 1983.

Turner, Victor. *The Ritual Process.* Ithaca: Cornell University Press, 1977.

Ulrich, Laurel Thatcher. *A Midwife's Tale: The Life of Martha Ballard Based on Her Diary, 1785–1812.* New York: Knopf, 1990.

Umble, Diane Zimmerman. *Holding the Line: The Telephone in Old Order Mennonite and Amish Life.* Baltimore: Johns Hopkins University Press, 1996.

Umble, Jeni Hiett. "Mutual Aid among the Augsburg Anabaptists, 1526–1528." In *Building Communities of Compassion: Mennonite Mutual Aid in Theory and Practice,* ed. Willard M. Swartley and Donald B. Kraybill, 103–18 (Scottdale, Pa.: Herald Press, 1998).

Umble, John S. "Catalog of an Amish Bishop's Library." *Mennonite Quarterly Review* 20 (July 1946): 230–41.

Unrau, Ruth. *Encircled: Stories of Mennonite Women.* Newton, Kans.: Faith and Life Press, 1986.

Unruh, John C. *In the Name of Christ: The Story of the MCC from 1920 to 1951.* Scottdale, Pa.: Herald Press, 1952.

Valerio, Adriana. "Women in Church History." In *Women, Invisible in Church and Theology,* ed. Elizabeth Schüssler Fiorenza and Mary Collins, 63–71. Concilium, 182. Edinburgh: T. and T. Clark, 1985.

Van Braght, Thieleman J. *The Bloody Theater, or Martyrs' Mirror of the Defenseless Christians Who Baptized Only upon Confession of Faith, and Who Suffered and Died for the Testimony of Jesus, Their Savior, from the Time of Christ to the Year A.D. 1660.* Trans. Joseph F. Sohm. Scottdale, Pa.: Herald Press, 1950.

Van Gennep, Arthur. *The Rites of Passage.* Chicago: University of Chicago Press, 1960.

Voth, Heinrich. *Historical Notes of the First Decade of the Mennonite Mission Work among the Hopi of Arizona, 1893–1902.* North Newton, Kans.: General Conference Mennonite Church, 1920.

———. *Traditions of the Hopi.* Publication 96, Anthropological Series 8. Chicago: Chicago Field Colombian Museum, 1905.

Walker, Alice. "In Search of Our Mothers' Gardens." In *In Search of Our Mothers' Gardens: Womanist Prose.* New York: Harcourt Brace, 1983.

Walkowitz, Judith, Myra Jehlen, and Bell Chevigny. "Patrolling the Borders: Feminist Historiography and the New Historicism." *Radical History Review* 43 (1989): 23–43.

Wall, Helena M. *Fierce Communion: Family and Community in Early America.* Cambridge: Harvard University Press, 1990.

Warkentin, John W. "Carving a Home out of Primeval Forest." *Proceedings of the Fourth Mennonite World Conference,* 1948, 196–99.

———. "New Settlers Receive Much Help from Older Colonies in Paraguay." *MCC Services Bulletin* 1 (January 1948): 2.

Watkins, Marilyn P. *Rural Democracy: Family Farmers and Politics in Western Washington, 1890–1925.* Ithaca: Cornell University Press, 1995.

Weaver, Carol Ann. "Quietly Landed." Score and drama performed at "The Quiet in the Land? Women of Anabaptist Traditions in Historical Perspective," Millersville, Pa., June 1995.

Weaver, Laura H. "Beyond Cap and No Cap: Reentry into Life and Scholarship." In *The Road Retaken: Women Reenter the Academy,* ed. Irene Thompson and Audrey Roberts, 48–54. New York: Modern Language Association, 1985.

———. "Independence and Community in Mennonite Women's Work." Paper presented at "The Quiet in the Land? Women of Anabaptist Traditions in Historical Perspective," Millersville, Pa., June 1995.

Weber, Max. *The Sociology of Religion.* Trans. Ephraim Fischoff. Boston: Beacon Press, 1922.

Weinberg, Sydney Stahl. "The Treatment of Women in Immigration History: A Call for Change." With comments by Donna Gabaccia, Hasia R. Diner, and Maxine

Schwartz Seller. *Journal of American Ethnic History* 11 (summer 1992): 25–69.

———. *The World of Our Mothers: The Lives of Jewish Immigrant Women.* Chapel Hill: University of North Carolina Press, 1988.

Welter, Barbara. "The Cult of True Womanhood: 1820–1860." *American Quarterly* 18 (summer 1966): 151–74.

Wessinger, Catherine, ed. *Women's Leadership in Marginal Religions: Explorations outside the Mainstream.* Urbana: University of Illinois Press, 1993.

Whiteley, Peter M. *Deliberate Acts: Changing Hopi Culture through the Oraibi Split.* Tucson: University of Arizona Press, 1988.

Widmoser, Eduard. "Das Täufertum im Tiroler Unterland." Ph.D. diss., Leopold Franzens Universität, Innsbruck, 1948.

Wiesner, Merry E. "Beyond Women and the Family: Towards a Gender Analysis of the Reformation." *Sixteenth Century Journal* 18 (fall 1987): 311–21.

———. *Women and Gender in Early Modern Europe.* New York: Cambridge University Press, 1993.

Willauer, George J., Jr. "Editorial Practices in Eighteenth-Century Philadelphia: The Manuscript Journal of Thomas Chalkley in Manuscript and Print." *Pennsylvania Magazine of History and Biography* 107 (April 1983): 218–34.

Williams, George Huntston. *The Radical Reformation.* 3d ed., Kirksville, Mo.: Sixteenth Century Journal Publishers, 1992.

Wolf, Naomi. *The Beauty Myth: How Images of Beauty Are Used against Women.* New York: Morrow, 1991.

Yoder, Donna. "Mennonite Refugees Leave for New Homeland." *MCC Services Bulletin* 1 (March 1947): 1.

Yoder, Paton. *Tradition and Transition: Amish Mennonites and Old Order Amish, 1800–1900.* Scottdale, Pa.: Herald Press, 1991.

Yoder, Paton, and Steven R. Estes, eds. *Proceedings of the Amish Ministers' Meetings, 1862–1878.* Goshen, Ind.: Mennonite Historical Society, 1999.

Yousey, Arlene. *Strangers and Pilgrims: History of Lewis Country Mennonites.* Croghan: N.Y.: Privately published, 1987.

Zehr, Kathleen. "First Mennonite Church, New Bremen, New York: A Brief History." Unpublished paper. Lowville, N.Y., n.d.

———. "History of the First Mennonite Church, New Bremen, New York." Unpublished paper. Lowville, N.Y., n.d.

Contributors

BARBARA BOLZ, PH.D., received her doctoral degree in 1997 from the English Department at Indiana University. Her chapter in this book was based on her dissertation, which examined autobiographies of American Quaker women from the eighteenth century to the present. She currently teaches in the English Department at Indiana University.

HASIA R. DINER is the Paul S. and Sylvia Steinberg Professor of American Jewish History at New York University. She holds a joint appointment in the Skirball Department of Hebrew and Judaic Studies and the Department of History. Formerly she was professor and chair of American studies at the University of Maryland at College Park. She received her doctorate from the University of Illinois at Chicago in 1975. Her numerous publications focus on the history of American immigration and ethnicity, women's history, American Jewish history, and the history of American religion. Her most recent book, *Hungering for America: Italian, Irish, and Jewish Foodways in the Age of Migration*, was published in 2001.

MARLENE EPP is an assistant professor of history and peace and conflict studies at Conrad Grebel College, University of Waterloo, Waterloo, Ontario. She received her Ph.D. from the University of Toronto in 1996. She has published a number of articles on the history of Mennonite women and also *Women without Men: Mennonite Refugees of the Second World War*.

BETH E. GRAYBILL is pursuing a Ph.D. in American studies at the University of Maryland at College Park. She holds a graduate certificate in women's studies from UMCP and is adjunct professor of women's studies at Franklin and Marshall College in Pennsylvania. She is also the women's concerns director for Mennonite Central Committee, United States. Her dissertation research concerns Amish women who own small businesses.

LINDA A. HUEBERT HECHT received her master's degree in history in 1990 from the University of Waterloo, Ontario. She is an independent scholar whose work focuses on research and writing projects related to sixteenth-century Anabaptist women. Her publications include *Profiles of Anabaptist Women: Sixteenth-Century Reforming Pioneers* (coedited with C. Arnold Snyder) and several articles on related subjects.

KATHERINE JELLISON is an associate professor of history at Ohio University. She received her Ph.D. from the University of Iowa in 1991. Her publications include *Entitled to Power: Farm Women and Technology, 1913–1963*. Her current work includes a manuscript on the commercialization of American weddings.

JULIA KASDORF is an associate professor of English at Pennsylvania State University. She received her Ph.D. from New York University in 1997. Her poetry has received numerous awards, including the Agnes Lynch Starrett Poetry Prize awarded to *Sleeping Preacher,* which was published in 1992. Her most recent book of poems, *Eve's Striptease,* was published in 1998. *The Body and the Book: Writing from a Mennonite Life* was published by Johns Hopkins University Press in 2001.

ROYDEN K. LOEWEN is an associate professor of history and chair in Mennonite studies at the University of Winnipeg. He received his Ph.D. from the University of Manitoba in 1990. His numerous publications include *Family, Church and Market: A Mennonite Community in the Old and New Worlds, 1850–1930*. His current work focuses on gender theory and Mennonite history.

JANE MARIE PEDERSON is a professor of history at the University of Wisconsin at Eau Claire and graduate coordinator for the Department of History. She received her Ph.D. from Columbia University in 1987. Her publications include *Between Memory and Reality: Family and Community in Rural Wisconsin, 1870–1970* and several articles on rural women. Her current work focuses on gender and the justice system in the rural Midwest.

STEVEN D. RESCHLY is an associate professor of history at Truman State University in Kirksville, Missouri. He received his Ph.D. from the University of Iowa in 1994. His book *The Amish on the Iowa Prairie, 1840–1910,* was published in 2000. He continues to do research in Amish history.

MARGARET C. REYNOLDS received her Ph.D. in American studies in 1996 from Pennsylvania State University. Her dissertation on the Old Order River Brethren is currently on review for publication by the Pennsylvania State University Press in connection with the Pennsylvania German Society. She died of primary pulmonary hypertension in early 1999.

KIMBERLY D. SCHMIDT is an assistant professor of history and director of the Washington Community Scholars' Center of Eastern Mennonite University. She received her Ph.D. in American history from Binghamton University in 1995. Her publications have focused on Mennonite women' history and on Conservative Mennonite and Amish women's dress and work-related choices.

CATHY ANN TROTTA received her Ph.D. in history and political science from Northern Arizona University in 1997. She is an independent consultant and researcher. Her current work focuses on women's history, ethnographic studies of the American Southwest and historical interpretations as they relate to indigenous people, Mennonite history 1820–1920, Southwest indigenous land issues, and cross-cultural studies of photographic and artistic representations of the Southwest landscape and sacred places.

JENI HIETT UMBLE, M.A., M.DIV. is an ordained Mennonite pastor in Elkhart, Indiana. Her continuing interest in Anabaptist history, particularly the sixteenth century, has most recently led to the publication of "Mutual Aid among the Augsburg Anabaptists, 1526–1528," in *Building Communities of Compassion: Mennonite Mutual Aid in Theory and Practice,* edited by Willard M. Swartley and Donald B. Kraybill.

DIANE ZIMMERMAN UMBLE is a professor of communication and chair of the Department of Communication and Theatre at Millersville University. She received her Ph.D. from the Annenberg School for Communication at the University of Pennsylvania in 1991. Her book *Holding the Line: The Telephone in Old Order Mennonite and Amish Life* was published in 1996. Her current work focuses on media constructions of Amish culture.

Index

Page numbers in *italics* denote illustrations.

Center Books in Anabaptist Studies

Carl F. Bowman, *Brethren Society: The Cultural Transformation of a "Peculiar People"*

Perry Bush, *Two Kingdoms, Two Loyalties: Mennonite Pacifism in Modern America*

John A. Hostetler, ed., *Amish Roots: A Treasury of History, Wisdom, and Lore*

Julia Kasdorf, *The Body and the Book: Writing from a Mennonite Life*

Donald B. Kraybill, ed., *The Amish and the State*

Donald B. Kraybill, *The Riddle of Amish Culture*, rev. ed.

Donald B. Kraybill and Carl F. Bowman, *On the Backroad to Heaven: Old Order Hutterites, Mennonites, Amish, and Brethren*

Donald B. Kraybill and Steven M. Nolt, *Amish Enterprise: From Plows to Profits*

Lucian Niemeyer and Donald B. Kraybill, *Old Order Amish: Their Enduring Way of Life*

Werner O. Packull, *Hutterite Beginnings: Communitarian Experiments during the Reformation*

Benjamin W. Redekop and Calvin Redekop, eds., *Religion, Power, Authority, and the Anabaptist Tradition*

Calvin Redekop, ed., *Creation and the Environment: An Anabaptist Perspective on a Sustainable World*

Calvin Redekop, Stephen C. Ainlay, and Robert Siemens, *Mennonite Entrepreneurs*

Steven D. Reschly, *The Amish on the Iowa Prairie, 1840 to 1910*

Kimberly D. Schmidt, Steven D. Reschly, and Diane Zimmerman Umble, *Amish and Mennonite Women in History*

Diane Zimmerman Umble, *Holding the Line: The Telephone in the Old Order Mennonite and Amish Life*

David Weaver-Zercher, *The Amish in the American Imagination*